News From No Man's Land

Also by John Simpson

Strange Places, Questionable People

A Mad World, My Masters

JOHN SIMPSON

News From No Man's Land

Reporting the World

MACMILLAN

First published 2002 by Macmillan
an imprint of Pan Macmillan Ltd
Pan Macmillan, 20 New Wharf Road, London N1 9RR
Basingstoke and Oxford
Associated companies throughout the world
www.panmacmillan.com

ISBN 0 333 90574 1 (HB)
ISBN 1 405 00637 4 (TPB)

1 3 5 7 9 8 6 4 2

A CIP catalogue record for this book is available from
the British Library.

Typeset by SetSystems Ltd, Saffron Walden, Essex
Printed and bound in Great Britain by
Mackays of Chatham plc, Chatham, Kent

*To the good friends and colleagues whose company
I was fortunate enough to share during our time in Afghanistan;
and to my dearest wife and fellow-traveller Dee, who would
have been there too, but couldn't be*

Acknowledgements

Extracts from *Scoop* by Evelyn Waugh (Copyright © Evelyn Waugh 1938) are reproduced by permission of PFD on behalf of the Evelyn Waugh Trust.

Couplet by Humbert Wolfe is reproduced by kind permission of E. A. Wolfe.

Extract from John Masefield's 'Epilogue' is reproduced by kind permission of The Society of Authors as the Literary Representative of the Estate of John Masefield.

Thanks to the BBC and the *Sunday Telegraph* for permission to use extracts from my work for them.

Every effort has been made to contact copyright holders of material reproduced in this book. If any have been inadvertently overlooked, the publishers will be pleased to make restitution at the earliest opportunity.

Contents

List of Illustrations

Photos not credited are from John Simpson's own collection.

SECTION ONE

A short walk to Kabul *(Filmed by Joe Phua © BBC)*
Taliban soldier
Women in Kabul *(Filmed by Peter Jouvenal © BBC)*
Aziz
Setting fire to President Bush *(Filmed by Peter Jouvenal © BBC)*
Wearing burka
Peter Jouvenal in burka
Jeep being repaired
Group picture on Anjuman Pass
Tony Rippon
Joe Phua
Khalil
Peter Emmerson, Ian Pannel and Peter Jouvenal
Lunch with Hajji
Dinner
With soldier *(Filmed by Peter Jouvenal © BBC)*

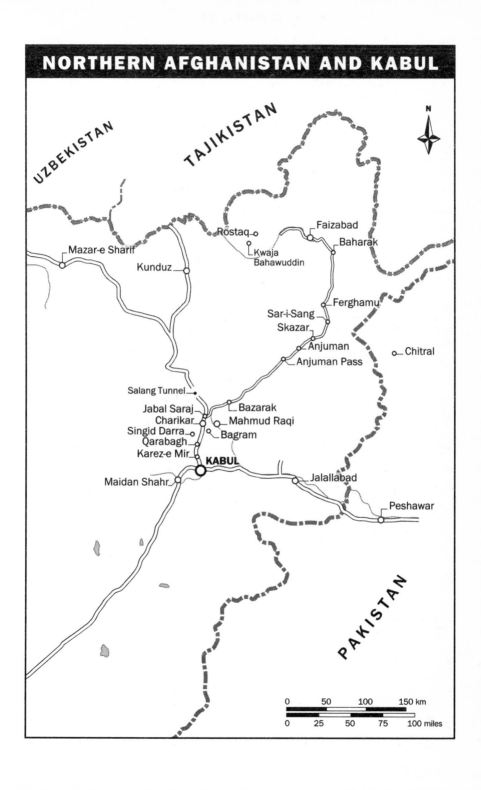

NORTHERN AFGHANISTAN AND KABUL

UZBEKISTAN

TAJIKISTAN

N

Mazar-e Sharif

Kunduz

Rostaq

Faizabad

Baharak

Kwaja
Bahawuddin

Ferghamu

Sar-i-Sang
Skazar

Anjuman

Anjuman Pass

Chitral

Salang Tunnel

Jabal Saraj
Charikar
Singid Darra
Qarabagh
Karez-e Mir

Bazarak

Mahmud Raqi

Bagram

KABUL

Maidan Shahr

Jalallabad

Peshawar

PAKISTAN

| 0 | 50 | 100 | 150 km |
| 0 | 25 | 50 | 75 | 100 miles |

CENTRAL ASIA AND THE GULF

Tabriz

Caspian Sea

TURKMENISTAN

ASHQABAD

TEHRAN

Mashhad

Esfahan

IRAQ

IRAN

Basra

KUWAIT CITY

KUWAIT

The Gulf

BAHRAIN

QATAR

RIADH

DOHA

DUBAI

Abu Dhabi

Gulf of Oman

SAUDI ARABIA

U.A.E.

MUSCAT

OMAN

News From No Man's Land

Introduction

In the ears of a long-serving BBC lifer allowed out into the community on parole, the pronoun 'I' always has a mildly indecent feeling to it. 'That is the one word that never appears in the BBC reporter's dictionary,' said one of my stuffier editors to me in 1969; it faintly crossed my mind to use one or two other words to him which weren't in the dictionary either, but I decided not to. Instead, I nodded ingratiatingly. And the older I get, the more I find I agree with him.

A certain calm, impersonal tone is still, after all these years, characteristic of the Corporation; just as much as when, in the late 1960s, a veteran BBC correspondent emerged from the jail cell in Salisbury (now, of course, Harare) where he had been thrown by the particularly unpleasant Rhodesian Special Branch and got to a telephone. He put across an understandably enraged dispatch describing his treatment.

'Now, now,' came the reproving voice of the foreign duty editor across the line. 'Remember: this is the BBC.'

The correspondent re-recorded his report in calmer and less personal terms, and it had far more force that way.

There have been various times over the last three decades when I have had occasion to hear that voice in my head, and changed what I had been intending to write. In a world where everyone seems to be shouting at you and trying to manipulate your emotions and thoughts, the quieter, calmer, less egocentric tone seems to come across better.

That, at any rate, is what I tell myself; yet I don't think I have ever written the word 'I' so often in my entire life as I have in the series of three autobiographical books which I have clumped together under the title 'Out To The Undiscovered Ends'. The first (*Strange Places, Questionable People*) was an account of my life; the second (*A Mad World, My Masters*) was a book about my travels; and this, the third, is a look at the business I have been in for virtually my entire adult life: the broadcasting of international news. It still feels faintly immoral, somehow. I first started planning this book in the early summer of 2001, when it would have focused partly on the fall of Slobodan Milosevic and the revolution the year before. Soon afterwards, though, the attack on the Twin Towers in New York and the Pentagon in Washington took place, and I found myself deeply involved in the BBC's coverage of the war in Afghanistan which followed.

As a way of illustrating the way in which we cover news events for television nowadays, I have gone into some detail about the three months of travelling and struggle which led up to our reporting of the fall of Kabul in November 2001: one of the more exciting events which I have been fortunate enough to witness. As with my previous books, this one is mostly based on stories and anecdotes. I didn't want to write a 'how to be a television correspondent' book, though you could probably work out how to do it simply by doing the opposite of everything I have done. This isn't a handbook, then; it's simply intended to explain, as honestly as I am able, what really happens behind the scenes in television news.

In order to do that, I have traced the history of television journalism back to its origins in newspaper reporting and cinema newsreels. It has not always been a particularly noble inheritance, but it has left its mark clearly on our ways of doing things. The more we realize that, the better we can understand ourselves and our craft.

The fall of Kabul marked the point at which the BBC emerged finally as the dominant force in international television broadcasting. I have sought to provide a rather different picture of the BBC and its achievements from the one you might have gathered from the British press. It's my firm belief that the BBC, far from being in decline and depressing its standards to satisfy the demands of the lowest common denominator, has in fact entered a new golden age of achievement; and I have done what I can to point out why you shouldn't necessarily believe it when you are told from all quarters how debased the BBC has become.

But I have tried to be honest, both about the BBC and about myself; if not, what reason would there be for anyone to think that I would be honest in my reporting? I have looked at the political pressures on the BBC, and the way it has coped with them over the years; and I have addressed the question to which so many people think they know the answer: does the BBC take an editorial line on the big questions of the day? It's the kind of book that won't make me any friends, but which I felt ought to be written.

The Afghan theme runs right through it, from beginning to end. The months which led up to the capture of Kabul were a hard but deeply satisfying time for me. I worked with some of the best colleagues and companions anyone could have, under conditions of great difficulty and occasional privation. Unfortunately the companion I would most have wanted with me couldn't be there. My wife Dee, who works as the producer of the News 24/BBC World programme *Simpson's World*, had obtained all the necessary visas to come to Pakistan and on to Afghanistan with me, and had even assembled the entire wardrobe: headscarves, long sleeves, shapeless dresses. Then we had a call from South Africa to say that there was serious illness in the family, and we felt she had to go there instead. It was hard for both of us.

So Dee, whose professional life is as closely involved with mine as our personal lives are, was an absentee for much of the action of this book. There may well be other absentees, whom I have left out through stupidity or absent-mindedness: for that I apologize sincerely. In writing about my colleagues – always a dangerous proceeding – I have had to omit all sorts of people, especially in the section where I talk about good writing and good on-screen reporting. I know how hurtful it can be to find you have been left out of such lists, and I would particularly ask my colleagues not to regard this as any kind of criticism: my examples were chosen with the instinct of a magpie, not with the intention of compiling a definitive account. I would dearly have liked to include excellent reporting material from the many people I admire in television companies other than the BBC, but found this impossible.

Other people have been left out of my previous books with less excuse. In *Strange Places, Questionable People* I foolishly made no mention of the distinguished journalist and academic Ian Hargreaves, who played an essential part in rebuilding BBC television-and-radio journalism in 1988. That failure I have addressed in this book. I haven't been able to do anything about an inexcusable mistake of mine in *A Mad World, My Masters*, when I wrote about a trip I made to Latin America and got one cameraman mixed up with another. It should have been my good friend Nick Walker, and I humbly apologize to him. It always seems to be the best and nicest people one makes mistakes about.

I started writing this book in December 2001, in the room in the cottage on the Natal coast where Alan Paton wrote Cry, *the Beloved Country*, in the forlorn hope that some of the magic might rub off on me. But although that hasn't happened, there are plenty of people other than the shade of Paton who do deserve my thanks: my PA and sister-in-law, Gina Nelthorpe-Cowne, for making my complex professional life run smoothly at last, and doing it so pleasantly; her husband Mark, who stayed up almost all night working on the cover to this book; Katie Pearson, who did a great deal of the research; Louise Coletta, who chased up all sorts of facts and pictures for me; Phil Goodwin, who took several of the photographs; Mark Starowicz, whose research on the history of newsreels I relied on heavily; Vin Ray and Tira Shubart, whose advice and help I am most grateful for; Richard Sambrook, who was as relaxed and rational about this book as about my others; Adrian Van Klaveren, who has always been patient, kind and understanding; Malcolm Downing and Jonathan Baker, good and supportive friends throughout the incidents I describe in this book; Dominic Lawson and Robin Gedye of the *Sunday Telegraph*, who let me have time off from writing my column to write it. Georgina Morley remained impressively calm despite the lateness of the manuscript, and my agent Julian Alexander, to whose advice I owe a great deal, was a splendidly diplomatic go-between. As ever, I owe great thanks to Philippa McEwan and the rest of the Macmillan people for being so supportive. As I told them at a recent conference, I bless the day that Julian and I decided to switch to their publishing house. And, finally, I should like to express my affection for the Corporation, Auntie herself, who has been remarkably tolerant of her wayward nephew for so many years.

My delightful and resourceful wife Dee was of course unfailing throughout the whole enterprise, and came up with some excellent ideas, many of which took shape in this finished version.

Fortunately, at long last, she has been able to come here with me. I take her to the nicest places.

Kabul, June 2002

1

A Short Walk to Kabul

Kabul: Tuesday 13 November 2001

The city lay below us, as vulnerable as an oyster on the half-shell.

Kabul, at last. Standing there in the chilly November dawn, with my flak jacket weighing heavily on me, I couldn't take my eyes off it. For the past three months I had been directing almost every thought, every effort, to getting back there.

I had last been in the city three months earlier, in September 2001, just before the attacks on the World Trade Center in New York and the Pentagon in Washington. Then, on 9 September, the Taliban ordered me out and I left, even though they were so disorganized that I could probably have stayed on for a while. It wasn't the finest decision I have ever made. Having been in the right place and left it unnecessarily, I felt that I had something to prove to myself.

Now, after all this waiting, Kabul was only a short walk away.

But there was a problem: the Northern Alliance army with which we had travelled had been ordered to stop there on the outskirts of the city, rather than enter it. It was clear to me that we would have to disobey these orders and head down into Kabul, even though it was still occupied by the Taliban and their foreign allies, Al Qaida. Would my BBC companions come with me? After living alongside them for so many weeks, I felt pretty certain they would. But it might be risky.

A tough-looking Northern Alliance soldier stood in the roadway, with a red scarf tied round his head and an RPG-7 rocket grenade-launcher cradled in his arms. His back was to Kabul, his face towards us. He had orders not to let anyone pass. And yet he wasn't the main obstacle; that was the man in charge of the Northern Alliance advance on Kabul, General Gul Haidar. He had been told by his political bosses that after smashing through the Taliban front line he must halt his men at the gates of Kabul and allow a trained force of policemen to enter the city to restore law and order there. The Northern Alliance didn't want a repeat of the street-by-street fighting which went on in Kabul when the mujaheddin were in charge of it last time. No one else – us included – would be allowed in.

Gul Haidar was a pleasant, noisy, ebullient man in his early forties, short and bulky, with a rolling walk like a sailor going down a village high street. He probably had the walk even before he lost his leg to a landmine. When the mad dash of the Northern Alliance to the gates of Kabul was halted, a few minutes earlier, we filmed him haranguing his men, shouting at them and warning that if any of them disobeyed him and headed into Kabul he would kill them. Sulkily, they agreed.

But we weren't Gul Haidar's men. We were free agents, and all we had to do was persuade him to let us pass. After that, we would see if the Taliban would fire on us as we entered the city. I thought probably not, as long as they could see we were journalists and unarmed: but there was no way of finding out, except to try it.

I looked round. In the glorious reds and oranges of dawn, arching over us, the vehicles of the Northern Alliance were halted awkwardly all round. We were standing in an open, desert area, where the road went down between some low hills and revealed Kabul below us. It was chilly, and we needed our flak jackets for warmth rather than protection against enemy fire. There was no enemy fire anyway; and we hadn't heard any since the battles of the previous day. Up here, the Taliban had vanished altogether, except for those who were lying dead in the road. The rest were presumably down there in Kabul.

There were eight of us from the BBC altogether, and apart from Anthony Loyd from *The Times* and a freelance photographer, Seamus Murphy, who had been living alongside us for the previous month, I could only see three other journalists: Tony Davis, a wise and wiry Australian who knew the country well and had been a useful source of ideas and advice for me over the past few weeks; and the attractive and dashing Barbara Jones from the *Mail on Sunday*, plus her large, bearded American photographer. Seven Brits, an Irishman, an Australian, an Afghan, a Singapore Chinese and two Americans. Maybe, in the tailback of Northern Alliance vehicles, there were other journalists; there were stories about a French photographer – though in my experience there always are stories like that. The world's media had gathered in Afghanistan for the culmination of the entire campaign, but we were the only ones on hand now that the key moment had arrived.

It wasn't just chance. All of us had shared a determination to be there first, rather than to keep with the herd, and we had each in our way sacrificed everything to that determination. In the case of the BBC people, plus Loyd and Murphy, we had lived rough for an entire month in a dirty, cold, shattered building close to the front line which had been used for years as a public latrine. To be here now represented our reward for all that.

A small red car came screaming up the hill in low gear from the direction of Kabul. It had taken several bullets – in the doors, through the roof. It stopped close to us, and a familiar dark hairy head poked through the window on the driver's side: Hajji Bari, the Northern Alliance commander who had been our landlord throughout the previous month. He had been trying to negotiate the surrender of the Taliban in Kabul, and it didn't look as though he'd had much luck.

Hajji was the BBC's secret weapon in this whole enterprise. It was an extraordinary piece of good fortune to have linked up with him. Even the fact of paying him so much money for the privilege of living in his disgusting building counted in our favour now. We had nicknamed him Hajji Dollar, but he had consistently looked after us, and made absolutely sure we were with him and the rest of the Northern Alliance's spearhead force on this morning's mad dash to Kabul. He even gave us his official jeep to make sure no one would stop us.

Instead of his jeep, therefore, he had been driving the little red car; and as Gul Haidar's second-in-command, he had driven it down the hill into Kabul about twenty minutes earlier, alone except for a single guard, to see if he could ensure a peaceful entry into the city for the Northern Alliance. The bullet holes were the Taliban's response. Hajji was lucky to have escaped with his life, and his eyes were as red as the bodywork with fatigue and fury.

So now we knew what to expect. I turned to the rest of the BBC team: would they, even so, take a walk with me into the city?

I had been fortunate enough to have the services of two camera-men on this trip. One was Peter Jouvenal, the doyen of Afghan combat journalists: an impressive-looking ex-army man constructed along the general lines of a Victorian explorer-adventurer. I knew what his response would be, because I had been with him on so many other visits to Afghanistan. It was Jouvenal who, against all common sense, accompanied me to Kabul in 1989 when the Communists were in power and the people who smuggled us into the city claimed to have infiltrated the secret police there. They had, but it was a close call. Jouvenal was a careful man, and didn't take silly risks; but I couldn't imagine him waving me goodbye as I headed off down the hill alone.

'No point in getting killed,' he said as he thought it through.

'Absolutely not. But if we walk down there they'll see we aren't Northern Alliance, and they might not fire at us.'

I could see he was tempted. He had often told me about being in the lead helicopter into Kabul in 1992 when the mujaheddin captured the city from the pro-Communist forces. If he comes with me now, I thought, he can make it a set.

I cast around for a way of clinching it, and realized that Joe Phua was standing near us: he was the other cameraman working with me. I had come to like and admire Phua immensely. He belonged to a famous clan of Singapore Chinese television news cameramen: his uncles, cousins and father were all in the business. He had come close to death a couple of weeks ago, when a Taliban missile landed right beside his car; but characteristically he kept on filming. I knew what he was going to say, even before I asked him.

'Sure, no problem.'

Yet there was a problem: a serious one. A week or so before, while clambering through a window, Joe had fallen and injured his ankle. It got so bad that we had to call in the local Afghan bone-setter several times to sort it out. Joe had been hobbling around ever since, filming away; nothing could stop him. I had been feeding him with the ferocious painkillers my doctor had given me, and he insisted he was feeling fine. But there was no way of knowing with Joe; was he really up to a long, fast walk carrying his gear, with Taliban gunmen prepared to open fire on him?

I looked at him as he stood there, tall and rangy, a scarf tied round his head like a pirate from the South China Sea. I honestly didn't think his ankle could take it; but I knew he'd be devastated if I ordered him to stay behind. And he'd probably follow us down the road anyway, which wouldn't do anyone any good.

Then there was Kate Clark, the BBC Kabul correspondent who had been thrown out by the Taliban the previous March because of her reporting. That, of course, was a badge of honour, and yet Kate had something to prove too. Kabul was her patch, and she was determined to get back there with or without the approval of the Taliban. The reason I had been in Kabul at the beginning of September was to try to persuade them to accept her back. They refused point-blank. So the only way she would be able to return to her office was with the help of the Northern Alliance army. She had endured the hardships of Hajji Bari's boarding house near the front line for an entire month, and she certainly wasn't planning to go back there tonight. She, I knew, would come with us.

Peter Emmerson, standing close to her, checking his recording equipment, was a BBC radio engineer whose skills – diplomatic and journalistic as well as technical – had brought him considerable seniority in the BBC. A quiet, peaceable man in his early forties, with a neatly trimmed beard which reminded me slightly of Napoleon III's, he nevertheless hinted at another side of his personality by driving a sky blue Morgan when he was in London. Not that he was in London much. He was always travelling for the BBC to the big international news stories and he didn't just choose the easy ones that involved staying in five-star hotels. Peter was here in Afghanistan because he wanted to be; and beneath the greying beard and the gentle, slightly nerdish engineer's appearance there was real grit. No doubt about him.

Nearby, recording the sounds of the occasion on his tape recorder, microphone held high above his head, was the correspondent for domestic radio, Ian Pannell. Thirtyish, pleasant and well read, he typified the new BBC. In the distant past we used to appoint tough, assertive people to the job of reporter, but gradually we found that those who stayed the course better were not the big, swaggering egos but thoughtful, reflective, intelligent people with a touch of irony and a good sense of humour. Pannell was just such a one. He was a good quarter-century younger than me, but I had enjoyed his companionship greatly over the previous month; even at the worst and most uncomfortable of times he had been cheerful and amusing. He had a young family back in London, and I felt I must ask him to think carefully before he agreed to come down into the city. No shame would attach to anyone who felt on reflection that it wasn't a good idea, I told him. I was wasting my breath. Before I had half finished the sentence he was nodding vigorously.

No doubts, either, about the last-but-one member of the team. John Jennings was a completely different character from the rest of us, with a completely different background. He wasn't even employed by the BBC. He was an American freelance writer, a former member of the US Marine Corps, who nowadays worked in an ER unit at a New York hospital. I knew him through Jouvenal: he used to live in Peshawar, on the North-West Frontier of Pakistan, and was an expert on Afghan politics. He spoke good Dari, and had been our translator when we hunted down an Afghan warlord who was responsible for many crimes and had come to settle in, of all places, Mitcham in south-west London. Jennings was an ideal member of the team. He could translate for us, and if we got hurt he could patch us up.

The final member of the group was our Afghan translator, Khalil. Kate Clark had bumped into him in the street in a little town we passed through on our way southwards from the Tajikistan border a month ago. Khalil was a medical student whose studies had been brought to an end by the arrival in power of the Taliban. His English was pretty good, and he had a relaxed and easy way about him which meant he never grumbled about the privations and dangers of working on the front line. He would certainly come with us now. I looked at him: he nodded.

Eight of us, and we were all in agreement. Having come so far, and stuck together so long, no one felt like dropping out. But there was the slight problem of the armoured personnel carrier parked across the road, and the man with the RPG-7 who had orders not to let anyone pass. There had been, it was true, a certain leakage from the Northern Alliance forces gathered there at the entrance to the city. Every now and then you could see individual soldiers wrapping their long *patous*, their dun-coloured blankets, around themselves and slipping past the sentry down the road into the city. Perhaps they were Kabulis who were planning to lose themselves in the crowds and quietly rejoin their families. But there weren't many of them.

This was the critical moment. If we were stopped here now, it could be hours before we got down to Kabul. The vast army of journalists, based well behind the lines, would have a chance of catching up with us, and our month-long effort to be in the vanguard would have been squandered.

And then Gul Haidar's car drove slowly past us, and he made the mistake of winding down the window.

'Hello, Peter,' he said.

For him, Jouvenal was always the chief among us.

'Go on, Peter,' I hissed. 'Tell him we want to go into Kabul.'

Peter was crucial as far as our relations with Gul Haidar were concerned. The two men knew each other extremely well. When they first met, in the early 1980s, Jouvenal was merely a young and inexperienced photographer, but Gul Haidar was already a first-class guerrilla leader in the mujaheddin resistance. Before the Russians invaded Afghanistan in December 1978, he had been a butcher in Kabul. Afterwards he turned himself into a butcher of Russians. It was his habit to creep into Soviet bases during the night, slit the throats of the unfortunate sentries, and bring out their weapons. On one occasion he trod on a landmine on his way in and lost his leg. Jouvenal, even though he had very little money in those days, paid for him to be brought to London and fitted with a prosthetic leg. Possession of this leg gave Gul Haidar greater prestige than ever among the Afghan mujaheddin. He rose quickly in the estimation of the leaders, and now he was the general in charge of the assault on Kabul. Being an Afghan, he could never forget a debt of honour.

Sitting in the passenger seat of his car, he pursed his lips. I could tell what he was thinking.

'He says it's too dangerous.'

'But will he stop us if we go on foot?'

Jouvenal put the question to him. Gul Haidar puffed out his cheeks and spread his thick, butcher's hands, the hands that had slit so many Russian throats.

'Well, if you're going to go on foot . . .'

He couldn't refuse Jouvenal. Leaning farther out of the window, he shouted an order: a soldier would go with us, to give us a bit of protection.

Maybe I should have invited the other newspaper journalists

to go too, but I didn't. Although I liked them a lot, I didn't intend to share our good luck – Gul Haidar's debt of honour to Jouvenal, for instance, or our links with Hajji Dollar – with anyone else. My job was to make sure we were the unquestioned leaders. The BBC would be in Kabul first.

As it happened, the BBC was there already. One of Kate Clark's predecessors as Kabul correspondent, William Reeve, had managed to use his contacts with the Taliban to get them to allow him back a few days earlier. Willy, a polo player and a definite eccentric, had done two difficult tours of duty in Kabul and knew the Taliban well. In the meantime Rageh Omaar, a correspondent who had previously worked in the outfit of which I am the nominal head, the BBC's World Affairs Unit, had persuaded a group of Muslims to take him to Kabul as well. Rageh was brought up and educated in Britain, but his family came from Somalia. Now he is a highly successful correspondent in South Africa, charming, witty and well read, but with an underlying toughness, like the rest of the new breed of correspondent. He had taken a big risk by mobilizing his Muslim links to get him to Kabul, and it had paid off handsomely. With these two was another cameraman I enjoy working with, Fred Scott, a quiet, extremely witty Californian who lived in London.

The three of them had had a difficult time once they got to Kabul; a nearby house was hit by an American bomb just as Willy Reeve was in the middle of an on-camera broadcast from the BBC office. The pictures were spectacular: the wall and ceiling seemed to be coming in, and Willy shouted, 'Jesus Christ!'; quite restrained under the circumstances, people felt. The enterprise and drive that had got two correspondents and a cameraman into Kabul had been the BBC's best single achievement in the entire series of events which began on 11 September.

You must bear in mind that I'm paid to sing the BBC's praises, like an ancient harpist in the halls of a sixteenth-century Irish chieftain. But you shouldn't discount what I say merely for that reason. If I thought it had done badly, or behaved in a feeble or stupid way, I should certainly say so; I am too old and tired and bad-tempered nowadays to be polite about things, and there is no point in writing all this if I can't be honest. All of us who worked for the organization abroad knew by this stage, 13 November 2001, that the crisis which had begun two months before had pitchforked the BBC into a position of clear dominance in the business of international television news. The audience for BBC World, the poorly funded yet most-admired jewel in our broadcasting crown, had swelled to a third of a billion people worldwide. What was required now, I felt, was some sort of capstone on the entire achievement; and here it was. We would go ahead of the Northern Alliance into Kabul, and join our colleagues there.

It wasn't the moment for making a Shakespearean speech. I set off down the hill, confident that the others would follow me and that no one would stop us. I grinned at the man with the RPG-7, and he stood aside to let us pass. The road ran steeply downwards between two bald, dusty hillocks. There was Kabul lying before us, a colour- less sprawl of mud brick innocent of suburbs or high-rise buildings, looking like a monochrome steel engraving in an early Victorian travel book. This must have been Kabul precisely as Alexander Burnes saw it when he reached this point in 1839. 'Bokhara' Burnes was a famous Central Asia explorer, who was destined to die in the Afghan uprising of 1841 when the British Army of India was wiped out. *Absit omen*, I told myself.

But I had no sense of foreboding. Instead, I felt as though the burdens of the past two months had been lifted off me. My heavy flak jacket scarcely weighed on me at all now; I had shed twenty-five years, and was a young man again with everything to play for.

This first part of the road was pretty steep, and we headed down it at quite a rate. It was obvious to me that the others weren't tamely going to let me go first: it was turning into a kind of race. There were a few local people around, standing and watching us, cheering and shouting as they realized who we were and what organization we represented. Seventy-five per cent of the population of Afghanistan listened to the Farsi and Pashtu services of the BBC, and when they understood how we came to be walking down this road, they started going crazy, shouting and waving their arms and trying to shake our hands. I turned to look at Ian Pannell, who was striding alongside me, holding up his radio mike to record the noise of greeting.

'Get a shot of him,' I shouted to Joe Phua, who was hobbling down the hill as fast as he could, keeping up with Ian and filming him. I was determined that this should be a BBC achievement – no point in all our travails together if it was turned into something personal, and something exclusively about television. The script started forming in my head: 'Television and radio, side by side.' It's a line I used later, for our *One O'Clock* and *Six O'Clock News*.

The crowds were getting bigger and noisier, and I could hear them shouting 'BBC London', both greeting us and explaining this strange regiment of people to each other. They knew from the fact that we were there that the Northern Alliance must be close behind us, and that they had been liberated from the rule of the Taliban. Hands reached out to grab me, shake my hand, touch my flak jacket.

After all the waiting, all the fear, all the anxiety about failure and being beaten by our opposition, a superb sense of elation built up inside me, and I raised my arms to greet the crowds, forcing my way through them. A bus was stuck in the throng, and everyone inside it who could get an arm through the windows tried to touch me. I grabbed as many hands as I could, laughing with the relief and pleasure of it all. To be the first journalists out of so many to enter the most closed and difficult city on earth: it was a superb moment.

Ahead, I could see the sign in the middle of the road which marked the boundary of the city. Peter Emmerson was a little ahead of me, as he had been for much of our walk. I sped up, wanting to be the first to pass it. Childish, of course: after all, what did it matter which of us got past the marker first? But I was still in the grip of the fierce will to win we had all experienced, and which had brought us all here, far ahead of our competitors.

My legs were becoming painful with the effort of walking down-hill so fast, so laden with body armour and the rest of my gear. A small piece of jagged blue lapis lazuli, which I had bought in the Charikar market a few days ago and brought with me partly for good luck and partly so the Afghans wouldn't steal it back at our base, was making a painful bruise where it rubbed on my thigh. No matter: these small pains merged into the wider sense of freedom and achievement. I looked at my watch: 7.53 a.m. Kabul was no longer a Taliban city, and no one had fired a shot at us.

By now the crowds were huge, and I needed all the momentum of my walk downhill and the weight of my body armour to get through. I had been so caught up in the extraordinary excitement of the moment that I hadn't once thought to look back: I suppose I wanted the others to keep up with me, rather than slow down myself. Now, though, I could see that we still had a long way to go to the centre of the city, and we would need some form of transport. A taxi crept forward through the crowd, full of sightseers who'd hired it to take them to see what was happening to the Northern Alliance.

I looked round to suggest to the others that we should take it. Only John Jennings and the soldier Gul Haidar had sent with us were still with me.

'What about the rest?'

Jennings shrugged. 'I've been keeping up with you.'

So now it was just the three of us. Maybe I should have gone back to see what had happened to the others, but I was too anxious to get to the Hotel Inter-Continental and start reporting. They would, I know, expect me to do that. And at least there was no danger that anything bad could have happened to them: not with the crowd in this mood of celebration, not with the Taliban escaping as they had.

The morning wore on. The rest of the team arrived at the hotel soon after me, and Peter Emmerson and Ian Pannell actually got there before I did. The real achievement was only now beginning: the satellite dish, which had been brought all the way from the north of the country, an extremely perilous journey which had taken many days through the mountain passes and the snow, had now been brought through the front line and was just arriving at the hotel. We had done well to get here first, but to get our satellite dish in before anyone else was a logistical triumph.

I remembered Evelyn Waugh's *Scoop*, which I had been rereading in the days before the battle:

> What the British public wants first, last and all the time is News. Remember that the Patriots are in the right and are going to win. *The Beast* stands by them four square. But they must win quickly. The British public has no interest in a war which drags on indecisively. A few sharp victories, some conspicuous acts of personal bravery on the Patriot side and a colourful entry into the capital. That is *The Beast* Policy for the war.

I sat in the thin sunshine on the roof of the hotel, sheltering from the wind behind a convenient parapet, waiting to go live into the *Today* programme on BBC Radio 4. We had had, I reflected, our colourful entry into the capital, and things had gone extraordinarily well for us. I felt immensely proud to have been part of this group of ours, and even prouder that the BBC should have done so remarkably well in the entire crisis since 11 September. It's not often in our business that you have such a clear view of a broadcasting triumph. And we had all got through the hardest assignment I had ever been through, and, apart from Joe's ankle, were unscathed. There was a great deal to feel proud about. And of course I still felt pretty charged up by the rapturous reception the crowds in the street had given us. Too charged up, perhaps.

Down the line I heard the attractive voice of Sue McGregor, one of the *Today* presenters:

'I don't quite understand. If the Northern Alliance troops didn't enter Kabul but the Taliban have gone, then who liberated it?'

Sitting there in the sunshine, savouring the pleasure of it all, I made a mistake: quite a bad one, as it turned out. I cracked a joke.

'I suppose it was the BBC,' I said.

2

The Journalistic Imperative

Kabul: Tuesday 13 November

Never make a joke; the British tabloid press has no discernible sense of humour. In my case they went to town. It was partly because the Home Secretary, David Blunkett, was sitting in the *Today* studio waiting to be interviewed while Sue McGregor was talking to me live.

'What do we need the armed forces for, if we've got John Simpson?' he said.

Of course there was a whiff of acid about it: have you ever met a politician who doesn't make barbed remarks? But this one was mild enough; perhaps it was even meant to be slightly affectionate. Yet the story went around the tabloid offices that morning that David Blunkett had launched an attack on me, and newspapers – even those which are hostile to the Labour Party – like to range themselves on the side of the powers that be.

British newspapers in general, and the tabloids in particular, have little affection for the BBC. Sure, they report its doings endlessly; they would be lost without the celebrity-babble it generates. But for most British newspapers, even the serious ones, the BBC is a valuable source of stories about erring stars, waste, ludicrous mistakes and loony management decisions. The BBC's successes get much less attention; and the successes of BBC News least of all.

It is, after all, the one section of the BBC which is in direct competition with newspapers. In the 1920s and 1930s the newspaper industry successfully put pressure on the government to restrict the length and quality of BBC news broadcasts. By the 1960s they firmly expected television news to undermine the sale of newspapers; and even when it became gradually clear that this wasn't going to happen, some of the old animosity remained.

As a result of the events of 11 September 2001, the BBC became the most praised, and the most relied-on, source of information around the world. Yet few British people knew anything about this. BBC World wasn't seen in Britain, so they had little idea of its quality, or the nature of its appeal. They could, of course, have watched BBC News 24, whose standards are equally high, but cable television stations were still lagging behind the terrestrial ones. News-papers almost everywhere, and especially in the United States, carried articles praising the BBC. This scarcely got a mention in Britain; praise for the BBC isn't something most British newspapers feel is worth reporting.

What some of them did think was worth reporting instead was my part in the events surrounding the fall of Kabul. Some, the *Guardian* in particular, were wryly generous in their comments. Others reported that I had claimed to have liberated Kabul person-ally. The *Mirror* (which had recently announced that it was becoming more serious) was breathtakingly unpleasant: 'What A Burka!', said its headline about me. I knew about it because a friend went to the trouble to let me know; it always is a friend, I've noticed. Soon afterwards someone in London who knows about these things explained to me that because the *Sun* had praised me, the *Mirror* naturally had to take the opposite view. Oh, of course.

Then the columnists joined in. Against all reason, since they are newspaper journalists themselves, they seem to believe what they read in the press; so they started from the premise that I had indeed said I had personally liberated Kabul. Then they pronounced judgement: I had trampled all over my colleagues; I had actually diminished the BBC's main achievement, which was to get a cameraman and a couple of correspondents into Kabul. One columnist said I would be better at my job if I would only give a little credit occasionally to the people I worked with. Soon it seemed to become a question of whether I had invented the entire episode. 'I don't have any opinion on the controversy over whether you really did get to Kabul first or not,' someone wrote to me, 'I just wanted to say . . .' and he went on, very kindly, to praise something I had written.

To be honest, I didn't read any of the press coverage (with the exception of the *Guardian* article, which someone sent me) either at the time or later. Life is too short for that kind of thing, and would probably have been even shorter if I'd read the text of, say, 'What A Burka!' Newspapers that believe that the actions of a middle-aged and rather short-tempered television reporter are of any interest at all at a time when important events are happening are newspapers that aren't worth reading; even if they think they've become more serious.

Even so, I should have known. After I had reported for television from Baghdad during the Gulf War, my ex-wife (this was seven years after we had parted) was besieged in her house for four days and nights by journalists from the *Sunday Mirror*, the *Daily Mail* and other tabloids, who tried all sorts of tricks and aggression to get her to say something derogatory about me. They taped her doorbell down so it rang incessantly for hours. The police would do nothing to help – not their job to interfere with the press, they said. What the journalists wanted, one of them said afterwards, was a story along the lines of 'He may be a hero to some, but to me he's just a rat.' Not having been a hero in the first place, it seemed to me like a world gone mad.

A few years ago my new wife, Dee, and I flew back to Gatwick Airport from an assignment somewhere difficult and dangerous. We were observed together by some delator who rang, I think, the *Mirror*. Many of the tabloids invite their readers to spy on celebrities and tip them off; the readers often have the impression that they will be paid handsomely, but this very rarely happens. Dee had recently changed her hair colour, which presumably made her look different from whatever picture the *Mirror* had of her; the immediate assumption was that this was someone else. Excited by the prospect of a major story – Elderly Television Person Travels on Plane with Woman of Different Hair Colour – the *Mirror* sent a reporter and a photographer round to the flat where we were staying in London.

'Excuse me,' said the *Mirror* reporter when Dee opened the door, 'we've been told you and your husband have split up.'

'You scumbag!' she shouted, chasing him off the doorstep. It is always unwise to stir up Afrikaners; their blood is easily heated.

'I'm not a scumbag,' the reporter bleated as he went. 'My editor told me to come here.'

If the tabloids behave like this to people who are of no public interest whatever, you can imagine how they behave with celebrities. Best, as I say, to avoid them as much as possible. Even the serious newspapers have to be treated with some care. When the famous and much-feared newspaper writer Lynn Barber came out to South Africa to interview me for the *Observer* in my post-Kabul holiday retreat on the Natal coast, I took considerable pleasure in her company. She was, apart from anything else, the perfect guest, bringing us carefully researched presents and writing us a charming note afterwards. But however much I liked her, I knew I had to be careful. When you are in the hands of newspaper interviewers, you have absolutely no idea how they will use your words. It's not like television or radio, where at least some of what you say will make it to air for the viewers and listeners to make up their minds about. In a newspaper, everything – your words, your appearance, your manner, your mood – is filtered to the reader through the prejudices of the interviewer. A friend of mine who was the subject of a big magazine profile asked the interviewer quietly not to raise a particular subject because it might upset the family: the interviewer quoted this in the final article.

Lynn Barber had actually read one of my books of autobiography, to find out what I say about myself; she is one of the few journalists who have bothered to do so before interviewing me for a newspaper. Most interviewers, I find, do little more research beyond reading 'the cuttings' – that is, other people's interviews with you in the past, which naturally contain all the accumulated mistakes and misunderstandings which have accrued over the years, handed down as it were from generation to generation of interviewers. I enjoyed being interviewed by Lynn Barber over the couple of days she spent with us, but as I dropped her off in Durban for her flight home I promised myself I wouldn't give another newspaper interview for a very long time. Why bother? Most interviewers, Lynn excepted, don't listen particularly carefully to what you say and often don't get the basic facts right. And when they quote you, they make you sound like a moron.

The British press is like a force of nature: it strikes more or less at random. The people who are most surprised if you take their work seriously are journalists themselves; they know better than anyone else how hurried and unprepared their work is. 'Never complain, and never explain,' said Disraeli, according to the great biographer John Morley. Excellent advice; and if I were not writing a book about journalists and journalism I promise you I wouldn't even have mentioned the subject of the way my actions in Afghanistan were reported. As for Lynn Barber's interview with me, it was a model of accuracy and was pleasantly written and generous. Or so I am told. I didn't read it myself.

The British press in full cry is an unattractive sight; think of the *News of the World*'s campaign a year or so ago against paedophiles, during which the house of at least one doctor was attacked by a group of angry parents who had heard she was a paediatrician and thought that meant the same thing. But like all forms of mob activity, press attention very quickly turns to some other subject. The only thing to do is to wait till the heat dies down; it always does, and then you realize that the vast majority of people took no serious notice of it all, anyway.

In 2002 the Reith Lectures, a grand BBC tradition, were given by Onora O'Neill, a leading academic from Cambridge University. The title of her lecture series was *A Question of Trust*, and in it she looked at the public reputation and standing of our public services and professions. For journalists, her lecture entitled 'Licence to Deceive' made painful listening. Most institutions and professions, she said, were now subject to rigorous audit and regulation. Not so journalism. Reporters, she said, wrote a great deal about the untrustworthiness of others, yet were themselves largely unchecked and uncheckable. How do we know whether we are being told the truth? Broadcasters were subject to considerable legislation and regulation. Not so the press:

> Newspaper editors and journalists are not held accountable in these ways. Outstanding reporting and accurate writing mingle with editing and reporting that smears, sneers and jeers, names, shames and blames. Some reporting 'covers' (or should I say 'uncovers'?) dementing amounts of trivia, some misrepresents, some denigrates, some teeters on the brink of defamation. In this curious world, commitments to trustworthy reporting are erratic: there is no shame in writing on matters beyond a reporter's competence, in coining misleading headlines, in omitting matters

of public interest or importance, or in recirculating others' spec-
ulations as supposed 'news'. Above all, there is no requirement
to make evidence accessible to readers.

Well, of course, anyone who has suffered at the hands of the
British press will agree. Yet Onora O'Neill's proposals to make
newspaper journalism more accountable seem to me to be almost
as bad as the evils she wants to remedy. Of course it would be
wonderful if the newspapers could be obliged to be fair or truthful or
open. But the only way that can work is if their readers demand it.
Unless that happens, newspapers will find ways of getting round the
accountability rules, just like they find ways round the stuttering
and pathetic efforts of the Press Council to stop them intruding on
people's private lives; and the journalist in me will somehow cheer
them on. If the choice is between an honest but dull press and a lively
but untrustworthy press, then I would rather have liveliness and
untrustworthiness.

Journalism is a strange business in all sorts of ways. It isn't at all
like being a banker or a solicitor. It encourages apparently normal
people to do some very strange things. Why, after all, should Rageh
Omaar and William Reeve have gone to such lengths to infiltrate a
city that every sane person wanted to get out of? Why should Kate
and Ian and I, together with the rest of our team, have directed all
our efforts at joining them there? And if, as the tabloids suggested in
my case, every performer on television and radio is just in the business to thrust themselves forward, what about the cameramen and
engineers who came with us? What was in it for them?

Joe Phua disobeyed specific orders from London in order to stay
with the team in Afghanistan long after he was supposed to have
handed over to another cameraman. He went beyond the call of
duty, day by day, and marched into Kabul on a broken ankle; yet
when the television industry handed out some of its most prestigious
prizes for the affair, and Joe's pictures (together with Peter Jouvenal's)
were shown again and again, Joe wasn't even invited to the ceremony;
and he certainly didn't do what he did for the speeches and applause
and the graven images of brass and perspex which we carried away,
and certainly not for the standard chicken dinner.

If not personal glory, then money? Not, let's face it, with the

BBC. The licence fee is chopped up very finely indeed when it comes to paying the staffers in News, and this is as it should be. News organizations which pay their on-camera staff over the odds often get pretty inferior results. The BBC is in the extraordinary and enviable situation of paying its people comparatively little, while being able to rely on their wholehearted loyalty and enthusiasm.

The fact is, no matter how bumbling and uncaring the BBC can sometimes seem, it still embodies an ideal: the ideal of public service, of honesty, of impartiality. This transcends money, just as it transcends one's personal comfort. It's why we joined in the first place. It means we can look at ourselves in the mirror in the mornings, and not feel too bad about our work. No one who works on the news side of the BBC can honestly say, hand on heart, that they joined it believing they were going to get high pay or even particularly good treatment: the Corporation's way with staff and salaries was established right at the start of the reign of King Reith, and it has stayed like that ever since.

But it was more than the ideal which brought us to Kabul. The ideal, you could say, kept us going and dictated how we should broadcast, but it didn't oblige us to risk our necks. An altogether different set of instincts did that. There was something in us which wanted to see things for ourselves, rather than hear about it from other people's reports. This feeling, of course, isn't restricted in any sense to the people who work for the BBC, or for television in general. It is something which a great many journalists feel. It makes them journalists in the first place, and it sustains them in the job over the years.

If we were involved in some other business – selling insurance, for instance, or building cars – you might think that we were forced to go beyond the normal boundaries of our job because we were afraid of losing it. I can't answer for the hundreds of other journalists involved in reporting the fall of Kabul; but I doubt if that was the case for any of them.

To take just a single example, the *Guardian* correspondent Maggie O'Kane: one of the best and bravest journalists around, who never seems to me to be afraid of anything. In October 2001 she made her way across the Pakistan border into Afghanistan on foot and in disguise, sleeping rough in the wintry mountains for four nights. She didn't make a big fuss about it, as I and others did; for her, it was just a small part of a much bigger job – the job of finding out what was really going on. I like and respect Maggie a great deal, but she worries me too, because I feel she is the real opposition.

Sure, the other television organizations are our immediate competitors, but in terms of getting through to the actual story and reporting it, Maggie O'Kane is the one to worry about. She is always there, at every big event; she will always produce some of the most memorable reporting. Her accounts of the siege of Sarajevo and the Serbian camps in Bosnia were among the best things that modern journalism has produced: the real Martha Gellhorn tradition.

So it is a little hard to believe that someone who isn't afraid of gangs of armed smugglers capable of carrying out any crime would be shaking in her shoes at the thought of what the *Guardian* foreign editor might do to her if she failed to find the story. No; the compulsion comes from within her, and from within the rest of us. Why that should be, and the root causes of this need to find things out and be the first to tell people about them, would probably require the services of a team of psychiatrists working round the clock on all of us.

Maybe one day the BBC will hire some. As an organization it always seems to me to be self-defeatingly tolerant of failure, rarely carrying out post mortems to see what went wrong on some major news story, nor even what went right. Perhaps it is too nervous about what it might uncover; perhaps it is just too busy covering the next big event. On the other hand, the BBC is obsessively concerned with the safety and comfort of its staff; and this is not merely because it is worried about being sued for neglect. The Corporation has not been nicknamed 'Auntie' for nothing (though the staff never call it that among themselves, sometimes preferring 'the Broken Biscuit Company'), and there are times when you feel almost stifled by its fussing. The day will no doubt come when the foreign editor will send out emails checking whether everybody is wearing their long winter underwear and eating enough roughage.

No; there are all sorts of reasons why all of us should have gathered for the fall of Kabul, and not many of them have much to do with comfort or self-preservation. There is a militant curiosity about the typical foreign correspondent, an instinct to see things for ourselves no matter who tries to stop us.

Journalism is a refined version of the instinct that makes people slow down and crane their necks at the scene of a road accident: the difference is that we are employed to stare. I have seen an elderly and distinguished journalistic knight, deep into some complaint about the way the world was going, perk up and stick his head out of the window of the Garrick Club merely because a police siren was sounding in the street outside. There have been famous cases of leader-writers and diplomatic or economics editors writing a hundred and fifty unwanted words about some ludicrously unimportant event that they witnessed on their way to or from work, simply because that is what journalists do.

The desire to see things and write about them doesn't evaporate with age, as the desire to draft a conveyancing document or tot up a page of figures tends to vanish the moment a solicitor or an accountant retires. Retired journalists seem to me to be unhappier than members of just about any other profession; except perhaps for retired politicians, whose anxiety to tell you what they said in the House in 1978, or exactly what advice they gave to Margaret Thatcher at the time of her first election victory, is such a depressing spectacle.

The point of being a reporter, then, is to see things. When the starter's gun goes off and a news story opens up, journalists become surprisingly careless of themselves, their comfort, their families, their lives. In the 1974 version of *The Front Page*, directed by Billy Wilder and starring Jack Lemmon and Walter Matthau, Lemmon plays the star reporter working on his last big story before marrying his fiancée and giving up journalism altogether. The fiancée, whose name is Peggy, taps on the door of the room where Jack Lemmon is hammering away on his typewriter.

'Who's there?'

'Peggy.'

'Peggy who?' asks the man who is about to give up journalism for her sake.

Being a reporter is one of the few genuinely all-consuming professions. When you are deeply involved in a story, nothing else matters.

A little of that gets over to other people. At dinner parties, on board aircraft, in dentists' waiting rooms, strangers will usually tell you that being a journalist sounds a really interesting kind of job. Yet the strangers know, and you know yourself, that this does not mean it is particularly respectable. Surveys have shown time and again that journalists languish in the lower reaches of public esteem, together with other riff-raff such as lawyers, politicians and estate agents. People may read and listen to the words of journalists with interest, and sometimes even a certain modicum of respect, but they know perfectly well that there is something dubious, untrustworthy, and faintly grubby about them. Journalists are inclined to borrow money off you for a taxi fare or a dinner, and never quite get round to paying you back. They are statistically more likely to run off with your married daughter, drink too much, smoke when everyone else has given it up and (though I haven't seen the figures to prove this) fail to clean their fingernails.

'Has it ever occurred to you,' a friend of mine once said as we walked through the BBC newsroom, 'that "journalistic" is only a term of praise among journalists?'

He was quite right. Everyone else – academics, say, or publishers, or even book reviewers who are themselves journalists of a kind – routinely uses the word as a mild form of abuse. If there were a journalists' dictionary, the entry would read:

> **journal'istic**, adj. (from 'journal', qv): Possessing the qualities journalists most profess to like. Bright and readable. Racy, yet reliable. Altogether admirable.

In everyone else's dictionary, of course, it means 'flashy, inclined to cut corners both in terms of work and of strict accuracy. Lacking in substance. Totally unreliable.'

It is certainly true that if you have ever been present at an incident which has got into the newspapers or onto radio or television, you will find that its presentation always seems skewed or inaccurate in some way. Even if all the facts are correct, the interpretation or sometimes merely the implications will be subtly wrong. This may well be more to do with the frailties of human perception than with the inadequacy of individual journalists; but there are sizeable numbers of people who have been asked a loaded question or two at some time in their lives by some scruffy character in a mackintosh, then found a simplified, stilted and somehow uncharacteristically expressed version of what they said in inverted commas in the next day's tabloids.

It is like listening in court to something the accused is alleged to have said. Whenever I am quoted in one of the tabloids, they make me sound like an I-Speak-Your-Weight machine; except that I-Speak-Your-Weight machines have long since gone the way of bullseyes, Tizer, and signs saying 'Commit No Nuisance'. And of course it is tabloid journalists who have driven down our profession farthest and fastest in public esteem; most people seem to regard radio and television reporters as belonging to a different and much more respectable business altogether.

They aren't right, though. Journalists are essentially one profession, whether we work for the *Sun* or the *Guardian* or the BBC; just as authors are one profession, whether they are writing advertisements (think of Salman Rushdie) or *Cymbeline*. And just as you can tell an actor immediately, so you can tell a journalist. There is usually a complete absence of any kind of snobbery, and an irreverence which pervades even the grandest newspapers and magazines. The famous, much-respected and long-serving foreign editor of *The Times*, Louis Heren, once famously said that writing a column was 'like having a good shit'. There tends to be a certain unkempt quality about all journalists, good or bad, grand or obscure, a hint of vagueness strangely allied to a driving force which can at times be obsessional, the otherness of a confirmed outsider.

The clear and often ferocious ability which is present in any newsroom is nevertheless shot through with other, more vitiating characteristics. The intelligence, the worldliness, the all-too-evident ambition are often intermixed with something else, as dealers cut high-grade cocaine with talcum powder. Sometimes this something else is a surprising lack of confidence; sometimes it is a disastrous way with personal relationships; sometimes it is merely drinking and smoking too much.

Senior journalists are more inclined than people from other professions to walk down the corridor with one shoulder rubbing against the wall: C. P. Scott of the (then) *Manchester Guardian*, perhaps the greatest editor in British newspaper history, the man who wrote, 'Comment is free, but facts are sacred', was one such. Journalists of all kinds are more likely than other professional people to live on their own in a single room, to eat their dinner out of a tin, to have lost contact with their children, to have nicotine-stained fingers or chewed nails or grog-blossomed cheeks. Without the slightest statistical evidence, I would guess there were more only children in journalism than in any other profession. The writer Julie Burchill, much more fiercely, once wrote, 'Journalism is show business for ugly people.'

Above all, most journalists seem to share an abiding feeling that what they do lacks any serious value. Every sane person laughs at his or her job, of course, yet you feel the journalist sometimes does it to excess. Perhaps it is because, even though writing is essentially creative, writing for newspapers or for radio and television is one of the most ephemeral things a person can do. Only advertising copy-writers, in my experience, place a lower value on what they write.

If journalists leave their trade and find another, they are usually amazed to find how absurdly seriously journalism is taken by everyone else. Graham Greene may well have been thinking of his old profession when he created Holly Martins, the anti-hero (played by Joseph Cotton) of the film *The Third Man*. At a British Council gathering in Vienna, Martins seems quite upset to find that the audience has mistaken him for a serious author, when in fact he writes mediocre Westerns.

§

The most primitive people I have ever come across (apart, of course, from the crowd at a Millwall match) were members of the Ashaninca tribe living in the farthest and densest part of Brazilian Amazonia. They had never had anything but the faintest contact with the world outside their immediate section of the rainforest. Yet each of them had characteristics we would all recognize at once: there was the eternal optimist, the incessant whinger, the bullied wife, the hen-pecked husband, the sharp-tongued, disappointed man in late middle age. You could take any one of them at random, scrub off his face paint, teach him a bit of English, set him down at the saloon bar of the Chelsea Potter with a fiver in his hand, and no one would ever know the difference. Human beings are human beings, and if all you knew of doctors came from watching Molière's *Le Malade Imaginaire*, you would spot a specialist in Harley Street the instant you met one.

In something of the same way, the profession of foreign correspondent has remained virtually unchanged since it was thought up by some unknown executive on the staff of the *London Morning Post* in 1835. He decided that the paper's readers would like to know what happened to a group of British volunteers who were recruited to fight on the side of the Queen of Spain in a civil war which had just started there. So he asked one of these volunteers, a man called G. L. Gruneison, to send letters to the paper, describing what was going on. Gruneison wasn't much of a writer, nor much of a journalist, and he wasn't much of a fighter either; but he did send a few letters to the *Morning Post*, which attracted a certain limited interest. The war, which ended in 1837, has been virtually forgotten ever since.

So Gruneison was technically the first foreign correspondent; but no one thought of repeating the experiment for a while, and the disastrous Afghan campaign of 1838–42, which saw the British Army of India wiped out almost in its entirety, went unreported except for the rather self-serving dispatches of the military men involved. The same was true of the two Punjab wars, during the course of which the humane and liberal-minded General Charles Napier captured the province of Sind: a pity, since Napier would undoubtedly have liked the company of journalists.

It was only nineteen years after the *Morning Post*'s bright idea that the art of the war correspondent precisely as we know it today was invented. As with so many other significant elements in British national life, the inventor was an Anglo-Irishman. William Howard Russell, like many another practitioner of the correspondent's art, felt uncomfortable with the job description. He wrote later:

When the year of grace 1854 opened on me I had no more idea of being what is now – absurdly, I think – called a 'War Correspondent' than I had of being Lord Chancellor.

But the events of 1854, and the outbreak of the Crimean War, didn't simply make Russell an ordinary war correspondent; they made him the greatest exponent of the trade. And he remains that to this day, although there have been many contenders for the title. One of them is Max Hastings, who reported memorably on the Falklands War for the *Daily Telegraph*, became the paper's editor, and left that to edit the *Evening Standard*. Hastings caught the vague and completely adventitious nature of the war correspondent's job when he wrote, in an introduction to an edition of the collected dispatches of William Howard Russell:

> Many reporters merely cover one war successfully, and thus find themselves despatched to another, without any design on the part of the journalist or his editor. So it was with Russell, and so it has been with many of his professional successors. A reporter discovers, often to his own surprise, that he possesses hardiness, determination, and some literary talent allied to the most important characteristic of all: the ability to get on with soldiers. Thus, he becomes a 'war correspondent'.

Exactly. And each of us who has been sent off to do the job will recognize with a familiar and perhaps slightly painful clarity Russell's description of the moment his entire life changed:

> As I was sitting at my desk in the Times office one evening, I was informed that the editor, Mr Delane, wished to see me, and on entering his sanctum I was taken aback by the announcement that he had arranged a very agreeable excursion for me to go to Malta with the Guards. . . . [E]verything was painted couleur de rose.

That should have warned him. In my experience, editors often seem to have a mysterious instinct which tells them when some particularly difficult assignment is coming up, and they know precisely how to lure you into taking it on. In this case it really did seem quite agreeable: the British government was sending a contingent of Guards to the Mediterranean as a warning to the Russians not to threaten Turkey. Neither John Thaddeus Delane nor anyone else could know that this gesture would fail, and that there would soon be a full-scale invasion of the Crimea by Britain and France. Yet somehow you get the feeling Delane could sense that something worth the serious attention of *The Times* was about to happen. And Russell was the perfect choice of correspondent to send.

He had, as Hastings suggests, considerable toughness and determination, bags of literary talent, and a proven ability to get on with soldiers. Russell possessed the cardinal Irish virtues: he was excellent company, full of jokes and cheerfulness under the worst conditions, he enjoyed a drink, and there was never the slightest snobbery or sense of superiority about him. The officers liked having him around, and continued plying him with information and whisky even when their commanders tried to drive him out by cold-shouldering him. He was also perfectly at home with the NCOs and private soldiers. He particularly admired them, and they loved him.

What is noticeable about Russell's dispatches from the Crimea is that although he is often ferocious in his criticism of the completely inadequate leadership which the British generals provided, nothing he says is personally spiteful or unfair. He often praised the courage and hard work of Lord Raglan, the commander-in-chief, while piling on example after example of his inability to manage and command a large army. In the end, when Raglan's career was wrecked as a result of Russell's dispatches, and the British government itself fell through bad management of the war, Raglan himself scarcely disagreed with Russell's verdict on him.

The infantry commander Sir George Brown deliberately made life a misery for Russell from the very start of the campaign, and hated the fact that the War Office in London had accredited him to cover the war. Russell makes this abundantly clear in his dispatches, yet he also makes a point of praising Sir George's bravery under fire. It would of course have been easy to gloss over incidents which showed Sir George in a good light, or to slip in some caustic reference which would have undermined him. Russell never did that; instead, he allowed his readers to make up their own minds about him. In his description of the Battle of the Alma, for instance, he tells us how Brown behaved when he received orders that the 23rd Regiment of Foot should capture the Russian guns. He

> seemed to have but one idea – to lead them slap at the battery, into the very teeth of its hot and fiery jaws. As he rode in front, cheering on his men, his horse fell, and down he went in a cloud of dust. He was soon up, and called out, 'I'm all right. Twenty-third, be sure I'll remember this day.' When Sir George Brown went down, a rifleman assisted him on his horse again, and with

the greatest coolness, as they stood under a murderous fire,
saluted the general as he got once more into his seat, and said,
'Are your stirrups the right length, sir?'

That is typical of Russell's style. He expresses himself in the plainest
English, and is often slangy ('down he went') in a way few other
Times correspondents then or later would have dared or even wanted
to be. His descriptions of the set-piece battles are full of personal
incident like this, and he is just as interested in the way the ordinary
soldiers behave as he is in the actions of the big names.

He spares his readers very little. He thinks they should know
how bad the latrines smell, what people look like when they have
been murdered and mutilated by Russian looters, what effect the
cold has on men who have been obliged to campaign throughout
the winter without the right equipment and with completely inadequate medical facilities. And he wasn't just concerned with his own
side, as most war correspondents are. He is just as sympathetic to
the Russians who have been wounded, and just as frank about the
conditions they, too, have to endure. Here, for instance, is his report
on the Russian hospital at Sebastopol when he managed to enter it.
The soldiers

> were left to die in their extreme agony, untended, uncared for,
> packed as close as they could be stowed, some on the floor,
> others on wretched trestles and bedsteads or pallets of straw,
> sopped and saturated with blood which oozed and trickled
> through upon the floor, mingled with the droppings of corrup-
> tion. With the roar of exploding fortresses in their ears – with
> shells and shot pouring through the roof and sides of the rooms
> in which they lay – with the crackling and hissing of fire around
> them, these poor fellows, who had served their loving friend and
> master the Czar but too well, were consigned to their terrible
> fate. Many might have been saved by ordinary care. Many lay,
> yet alive, with maggots crawling about in their wounds. Many,
> nearly mad with the scene around them, or seeking to escape
> from it in their extremest agony, had rolled away under their
> beds and glared out at the heart-stricken spectator.

No matter how strong Russell's descriptions were, *The Times* printed
them for the entire nation to read over the breakfast table. I couldn't

get the BBC to broadcast that kind of thing today, and I doubt if it would appear in the British press either. Too much reality is unacceptable nowadays.

You can feel the anger and horror welling up in Russell as he, 'the heart-stricken spectator', writes. And since he had to put together his dispatches with great speed – sometimes he would write sixteen thousand words in a single day and night, the equivalent of this chapter and the previous one put together – it is almost as though he is talking to himself and not to us, the readers, so far removed from the scenes of battle and carnage that we can have little appreciation of the things Russell himself has experienced. He is a superbly graphic writer, and his greatest strength is his mastery of precise, telling detail.

Yet he also has a firm grasp of the overall strategic situation, way beyond the immediate misery and danger of the soldiers' experience. It is much easier to concentrate on the immediate, the emotional, the pitiful circumstances right in front of you, but this doesn't really tell your viewers or readers anything they can't guess themselves. You also have an obligation to give them some idea of the wider context of all this suffering and pain: why it's happening, what it's for. In writing this book I have reread all of Russell's Crimea dispatches, and it is almost impossible to find any faults in them. They are as exciting, as compelling, as affecting as they were influential.

Russell fits precisely the profile of the typical journalist. He was born in 1820 into a mildly disorganized, perpetually hard-up middle-class Protestant family, living just outside Dublin. He was given his start when his cousin, who worked as a political correspondent for *The Times*, came to Ireland to report on the 1842 election and hired him as a temporary freelance or 'stringer' – the term was in use even then. Russell, scarcely out of Trinity College, Dublin, got the kind of scoop any journalist today would appreciate: he hung out at the main hospital in Dublin and interviewed the casualties from the day's political rallies. *The Times* was impressed, and gave him a job at Westminster, reporting on the debates in the House of Commons. Then it sent him back to Ireland to report on the series of mass meetings which Daniel O'Connell, the campaigner for Home Rule, was holding throughout Ireland. Russell, as a Protestant, was an

instinctive Unionist before the term was invented; but he was a man
of wide and ready sympathies, and he took to O'Connell and liked
the kind of people who turned out to hear him speak.

He was also careless, absent-minded, and a little naïve. When
O'Connell was arrested and tried on essentially political charges,
Russell reported on the case. He organized an elaborate set of travel
plans, of a kind any television journalist would appreciate today,
in order to achieve a scoop for *The Times*. This was before correspondents could send their dispatches by telegraph, so he had to get
his copy back physically to London. He had horses ready outside the
courthouse to speed him to Kingstown, now Dun Laoghaire. A
chartered steamer took him across the Irish Sea to Holyhead, where
a hired train (known as a 'special') was waiting for him. At the
terminus in London a cab whisked him to the office of *The Times* in
Printing House Square, just opposite Blackfriars Station.

As he ran towards the main entrance, a man who was lounging
by the doorway asked him what the verdict on O'Connell and his
associates had been. 'All guilty, but on different counts,' Russell
shouted. The lounger was working for the *Morning Herald*, which
duly splashed the result of the trial first. Russell's far longer, far more
detailed dispatch was only published in the following day's *Times*.
His editor, the great if sometimes wrongheaded Delane, was so
furious he almost sacked him on the spot. It was the start of a long
series of rows and disagreements Russell had with his bosses; they
blazed up furiously yet always seemed to be settled amicably in the
end. Russell might have made a great many mistakes, but no one ever
doubted his commitment to his job and his loyalty to his newspaper.

And so, even before the outbreak of the Crimean War, which
made him one of the most respected men on earth, William Howard
Russell understood the tradecraft and practice of modern journalism.
Basically, it's the same job: the need to get the news accurately and
fast, the technical challenge of filing, the intense competition. Russell
was as mobile as any television foreign correspondent today. Only
ten days after returning in triumph from the Crimean War he was off
to Moscow to report on the coronation of the new Tsar. Later he
covered the American Civil War, but his dispatches about the coward-
ice and poor organization of the Union armies in the early stages of
the war (completely accurate and justified though they were) soon got

him ostracized. Americans didn't enjoy criticism from foreigners any more then than they do now, and the military commanders weren't obliged to put up with him as the British generals had been in the Crimea. It became clear he wouldn't be allowed back to the front lines, so he returned to London in a state of some depression.

But by now newer, hungrier correspondents were starting to join the profession which Russell had almost single-handedly invented. His report on the Battle of Sedan on 1 September 1870, when the Prussians smashed the French army and captured Emperor Napoleon III, was as good as anything he had ever written; but since he insisted on hand-carrying it to London it wasn't printed in *The Times* until 6 September; whereas a story written by a British correspondent working for the *New York Tribune* reached London much faster and was published on 4 September. Yet again *The Times* was furious with Russell, and ordered him to file by telegraph in future.

But Russell disliked the tight schedules and need for brevity which the telegraph imposed on him, and he much preferred mailing the immensely long, magisterial dispatches which had made him famous. You had to pay per word when you telegraphed your material, and a big story could cost *The Times* a third of Russell's annual salary. So a new style was starting to emerge in the British and American press: the new foreign journalism was brief, terse, far less considered and well expressed than anything Russell could write, yet it arrived on the breakfast table the next morning, rather than at some more leisurely time in the future.

If Russell represented one lasting tradition in journalism, another major nineteenth-century war correspondent, Russell's great rival Archibald Forbes of the *Daily News*, represented another. I admire Russell greatly both as a man and as a writer, and I have great respect for his independence of mind. Forbes was in many ways Russell's opposite: tough, ambitious and determined, certainly, but also devious, spiteful, snobbish, self-laudatory, pompous, and with a creaking, turgid style of writing. Worse, he was a toady, who admired authority and willingly kowtowed to it. He early on identified Russell as the man to beat, and concentrated his attack on Russell's many weak spots.

During their years of competition Russell had every advantage over Forbes except one. His political judgement was usually highly

accurate, while Forbes often got things badly wrong. Russell forecast
the victory of the Northern states over the South in the American
Civil War, and of Prussia over France in 1870, when most people
expected the opposite. By comparison with Russell's clear, short,
perceptive sentences, filled with an instinctive humanity, Forbes was
ponderous and bland, and usually opted for the passive voice where
Russell characteristically uses active verbs. But Forbes was the master
of a single art, and in many ways it was the most important of all: he
got his copy back first. While Russell was still checking his facts and
polishing his phrases, Forbes's much more second-rate copy was
already being set up ready for print. Knowing Russell's weakness,
Forbes sacrificed everything – accuracy, clarity, his paper's money –
to being first with the news.

It worked. Time and again Russell was scooped by Forbes, until
in 1871, when the Prussians entered Paris as conquerors, Forbes got
his story back to London earlier. Russell's account makes infinitely
better reading today, and it is instinct with the horror and sadness of
the occasion, while Forbes rather sympathized with the Prussians (he
was, after all, a kind of journalistic Prussian himself). But this was a
contest where the first, rather than the best, won the prizes. Effectively, his defeat of Russell brought Russell's career as chief foreign
correspondent of *The Times* to an end at the age of only fifty. He
went on travelling and writing for other newspapers and magazines,
but *The Times* no longer wanted him to compete head-to-head with
the younger, sharper men who were coming to the fore in Fleet Street.
Like many journalists, Russell thought he would try his hand at
novel-writing; and, like many journalists, he based his main character
on himself – an Irishman, who wanders among the great and achieves
some surprising successes; and, like many journalists, found that his
novel (called *The Adventures of Dr Brady*) was an utter flop.

In his memoirs, *Memories and Studies of War and Peace*, published in 1895, Forbes claimed to admire Russell. But he gives us, in
the most self-laudatory way imaginable, the secret of his victory over
him:

> At a casual glance it might seem that the chief qualification
> requisite in the modern war correspondent is that he should be a
> brilliant writer, able so to describe a battle that the reader may

glow with the enthusiasm of the victory, and weep for the anguish of the groaning wounded. The capacity to do this is questionless a useful faculty enough; but it is not everything – nay, it is not even among the leading qualifications. For the world of today lives so fast, and is so voracious for what has come to be called 'the earliest intelligence', that the man whose main gift is that he can paint pictures with his pen is beaten and pushed aside by the swift, alert man of action, who can get his budget of dry, concise, comprehensive facts into print twenty-four hours in advance of the most graphic description that ever stirred the blood.

There is no question who he's talking about: the brilliant writer ('a useful faculty enough', Forbes says patronizingly) is Russell, the 'swift, alert man of action' is Forbes; how full of himself he is! Yet we needn't feel too sorry for Russell. If Forbes failed to understand why he was so great, others did not. Russell died, surrounded by affection and respect, at the age of eighty-seven; and a couple of years earlier, in 1905, he had hobbled on his bad legs up the steps of the throne at Buckingham Palace to be knighted by his good friend Edward VII, who had a soft spot for raffish Irishmen. And Edward VII had whispered to him, 'You mustn't trouble to kneel, Billy. Stoop!'

Far more valuable than any honours, though, Russell remained true all his life to his outsider's vision, clear-sighted, sympathetic, unclouded by nationalism and imperialism. He loathed slavery in the Southern American states so much that he was unwilling to report on their side in the American Civil War. Later, he refused to stay with the Prussians when they besieged and bombarded Paris, because he thought they were barbarians. He was an instinctive Tory and even stood for Parliament once, though characteristically he failed to get in; yet he never lost that essential radicalism that has nothing to do with party politics, and everything to do with understanding people and respecting them.

Just as he sympathized with the ordinary British and Russian soldiers in the Crimea, so he sympathized with the ordinary Egyptians when the British and French descended on them in 1882; he had come to know and love Egypt over the years. When the overbearing

Sir Garnet Wolseley crushed an Egyptian force at Tel el Kebir – the equivalent of the Western powers' defeat of Saddam Hussein in 1991, though the Khedive was certainly no Saddam and gave the British very little pretext for war – Russell wrote about it all with a despair which echoes through his unusually disjointed sentences.

> What will history say of all this? I doubt present voices. Why are we encouraged to occupy and annexe? . . . The correspondents are almost as bad, with two exceptions – three, perhaps. It is sickening to read columns of description of such an affair as that of Chalouf, where the gunboats in the canal could sweep the Egyptians with their Gatlings like flies, and cover the advance of the infantry without the least danger; where we had no casualty at all, and where 168 Egyptians were killed by mitraille and musketry; but it must be very gratifying to the Telegraph Company.

It was of course the telegraph company that carried (at great profit to itself) the bombastic, irreflective dispatches of the correspondents who reported on the Egyptian campaign; and it was the telegraph company that had assisted Russell's downfall as a foreign correspondent. He is really writing about his dislike of the entire way in which the profession he had himself founded had elected to go.

Russell was an absurd figure in many ways. He drank too much, and was much too fond of being recognized and praised. He was a show-off, who wore the uniform of a deputy lieutenant of the Tower of London (one of his minor honours) when he attended the ceremony to mark the proclamation of the German Empire in conquered Versailles in 1871. It caused a lot of sniggering. Yet even people who thought he was ludicrous liked him; it seems to have been impossible not to. And his essential humanity far outdistanced his minor follies: that sympathy for ordinary people caught in terrible circumstances, that ability to remain the outsider, the onlooker, the radical. These are qualities which the best journalists of the following century demonstrated – George Orwell, Richard Dimbleby, Ed Murrow, Martha Gellhorn, Bill Deedes. And they are qualities to which, it seems to me, every decent journalist should aspire.

§

Russell's greatest achievement was to force the government of the day to understand that the conduct of war and foreign affairs wasn't simply the perquisite of generals and diplomats and statesmen – that the people who had to bear the cost of these things, and whose sons and daughters were caught up in them, also counted. The British government's overriding attitude, then as now, was to say in effect, 'Leave these weighty matters to us, little man. We know far more about them than you could possible know. When the time comes to applaud us, we'll tell you. And we'll also tell you when to pay the price.' Russell demonstrated that this grandeur and superiority often covered up for foolishness and bad organization; and his dispatches from the Crimean War empowered British public opinion in a way that had never happened before. The family at the breakfast table now knew almost as much as the men making the decisions in Whitehall, and sometimes more. Suddenly, Whitehall had to start taking account of public opinion.

Archibald Forbes took precisely the opposite view. He did not believe that his readers had a right to know what was being done in their name; on the contrary, he thought it perfectly acceptable for governments to keep journalists in the dark and stop them from going to places and seeing things, if the circumstances seemed to warrant it. In his memoirs he accurately forecasts the stifling, damaging censorship of the First World War, twenty years later.

> In all future European wars, by an international agreement the hand of the censor will lie heavy on the war-correspondent. He will be a mere transmitter by strictly defined channels of carefully revised intelligence, liable to be altered, falsified, cancelled or detained at the discretion of the official set in authority over him.

But just when you assume that Forbes must disapprove of this future state of affairs, he shows his true colours.

> I am far from objecting to the changed conditions, in the capacity of a citizen of a nation which may have the wisdom to prefer victories to news.

In other words, the truth doesn't matter as long as the generals fighting a war are successful. That can be acceptable at certain moments, and questions of security must always be considered in any war. But the problem is, this approach on the part of the journalists encourages the politicians and the generals to hide the truth as a matter of course, merely for their own convenience. And what happens if they are not successful? What if they are as incompetent as poor old Lord Raglan in the Crimean War, and the national interest is put at risk?

William Howard Russell would never have revealed the amateurishness and inadequacy of the British military command if he had sat tamely by, watching the unnecessary slaughter and deciding not to write about it on the grounds that it wouldn't be patriotic. There is always something painful about watching journalists, people who should regard themselves as free men and women, hugging their chains and thanking their jailers. It happens in every country, every time there is a war. And the more amateur and ineffectual the conduct of the war, the more the generals and government ministers need to silence the journalists.

If William Howard Russell had been a war correspondent at the Battle of the Somme in 1916, when the British army suffered 60,000 casualties on the first day alone, it is hard to think he would have wanted to keep quiet about it. It is true that the generals of the day were nothing like as stupid or callous as fashion has regarded them ever since; and maybe, given the technology of the time, the First World War was unwinnable by any other tactics. But the people who were making the sacrifices had a right to know what was going on. And it is impossible to think that Russell would have tried to pretend to those people, and their families and friends back home, that everything was going well. The war correspondents from the *Daily Mail*, in particular, found their very lives were at risk from British soldiers in the front line; such was the hatred which the fighting officers and men felt towards those who consistently told propagandistic lies about the way the war was being fought. The *Daily Mail* correspondents didn't report that, either.

But, as Russell realized in the Crimean War, the journalist has a duty which goes wider than simply trying to give the impression that our boys have won another victory. If our dispatches are merely obedient and unquestioning, then we have crossed that completely invisible yet somehow always clear-cut line which divides the observer from the participant.

Archibald Forbes was desperate to participate. He longed for British victories in all those sad little wars he covered, in which Gatling guns wiped out entire Afghan tribes, entire Zulu impis, entire armies of Egyptian fellahin. It didn't matter to him how the victories were won, just so long as the final scoreline was right. William Howard Russell, by contrast, understood that by observing correctly and reporting back what he saw, rather than what his patriotism or the generals in command wanted him to see, he was doing his country a much greater favour. When he reported from India in the aftermath of the Mutiny he revealed that some British and Indian troops were carrying out savage acts of vengeance on captured and defeated mutineers. For Russell, honesty came before comfort.

It isn't pleasant for a normally gregarious kind of person with no great longings for martyrdom to be shunned by his fellows and attacked by the powers that be; but if Russell had kept his mouth shut and reported the Crimean War or the Indian Mutiny in the way the *Daily Mail* reported the First World War, the British army would have continued to be led by incompetents, and even more people would have lost their lives. To keep quiet when you know things are not right is the reverse of patriotism: it is to cover up for those interests that stand to gain from silence. It is to be a partisan of inefficiency and stupidity and mindless cruelty.

Nowadays our wars are like Archibald Forbes's wars, in that the Great Powers take on the inferior forces of some obscure Third World country. If you criticize the conduct of these wars – and I for one have serious doubts about the ethics and effectiveness of bombing a country from 15,000 feet – then you will probably get a drubbing from the British or American governments, who demand Forbes-style obedience from the media. When politicians are worried that things may go wrong, they usually like to have a crack at any dissenting voice, claiming that they are somehow speaking for the nation. Journalists, it seems to me, have a duty to resist being simply corralled into obedient silence: it isn't good for journalism, and it isn't good for government.

§

> You cannot hope
>   to bribe or twist,
> thank God! the
>   British journalist.
>
> But, seeing what
>   the man will do
> Unbribed, there's
>   no occasion to.

Humbert Wolfe died in 1940 at the age of eighty-five, but his words were based on bitter personal experience and remain precisely accurate today. Perhaps because journalists so often have a low opinion of themselves and their craft, they respond with painful enthusiasm to any sign that they are respected and wanted. One reason why Robin Cook was such a poorly regarded Foreign Secretary between 1997 and 2001 was that he ignored most of the diplomatic writers, feeling no doubt that they and their opinions didn't matter much. If he had cosseted them, as many of his predecessors had, it might have altered the way the newspapers, in particular, wrote about him; and he might not have been downgraded to Leader of the House of Commons.

Sir Geoffrey Howe, who served Margaret Thatcher long and faithfully as Foreign Secretary until he went to the back benches and duly knifed her, was unremarkable though very bright. If he hadn't been assiduous in courting the diplomatic journalists (of whom I was one throughout his time in office), he might well have had a much harder time of it. He used to hold tedious off-the-record briefings over breakfast at his official residence in Carlton House Gardens, at which he would often tell us less than he would say in public at the dispatch box later the same day.

The only reason I used to turn up was that his spokesman, the witty and personable Christopher Meyer (later British ambassador in Washington), would brief us amusingly and with great clarity afterwards. As we walked away we would often agree that fifteen minutes with Meyer were worth hours of Sir Geoffrey; journalists are not good at understanding or respecting dullness. And yet we rarely gave Sir Geoffrey a hard time, because he noticed us. These are not particularly honourable reflections, but they do, I think, illumine the delicate relationship between government ministers and the journalists whose job it is to report on their doings.

The smile of a journalist means little, and when you are in the presence of a group of journalists you must never make the mistake of thinking you are among friends. The things you say may be taken down and used in evidence against you: out of context, if necessary. The Queen Mother, when in her nineties, went to a dinner party where a well-known journalist friend of mine was a guest. Her table talk, which included all sorts of unreconstructed comments about Germany and the Labour Party, duly found its way into print. You might think that the incautious ramblings of an elderly lady should have been allowed to remain private; they were not. The *Spectator* published them. The phrase 'public interest' was used, as it so often is when journalists and their readers are showing an intrusive curiosity. And yet I think it was right to have done so.

Of course the whole episode showed deplorable bad manners; but journalists are the kind of people who tread mud onto your best Isfahan carpets and pick their teeth absent-mindedly at the dinner table. Well-behaved, safe, house-broken journalists are usually bad journalists. And as in the case of the Queen Mother, who was after all in the position of a public servant, a free press has to be prepared to print everything, no matter how embarrassing or awkward, otherwise it is not free. She would have had every right to be angry, as everyone who has been given a thorough going-over by the press usually is; me included. But on balance, if you want the benefits of a free press, you have to be prepared to pay the price.

Above all, good journalists should never allow you to feel comfortable in their presence. I am not in favour, personally, of betraying confidences and letting down friends, but I do not wish to be taken for granted. There ought always to be a sense of underlying menace about the presence of a journalist; it should be like hanging out with gangsters. Do not trust us too much, because we can turn and rend you. And our ways of doing that are spiteful and vicious.

Back in 1966, when I was a sub-editor in the Colditz which we called the BBC Radio Newsroom, they still talked about the revenge of one of our number who had been sacked a few years earlier for some offence. On the last evening of his final shift, he was asked to write a story about the ending of a strike in the steel industry. He put it into skilfully camouflaged anapaests, which went unnoticed by the quick-scanning chief sub-editor's eye:

> There were scenes of delight in Port Talbot tonight, as news of the settlement spread. The unions were pleased that the crisis had eased, and the firm was delighted, it said.

> You must say it out loud to get the best effect. Some unfortunate newsreader had to.

3

The Archaeology of Television News

London, Islamabad, Peshawar and Kabul:
Thursday 31 August to Tuesday 11 September

It was Thursday 31 August 2001, and I was packing a small suitcase to take with me to Pakistan and, I hoped, to Afghanistan. It never occurred to me that I might be away for three months. Why should it? The world seemed quiet enough – as quiet, that is, as it ever gets. Only the situation in the Middle East seemed to give any great cause for anxiety. But then, like the Balkans a century ago, it always does.

As I lugged my bag to the waiting car, I congratulated myself for having kept my gear to a minimum. I don't usually pack light, because the cameraman I'll be with will be carrying a reasonably large amount of gear, and a few more kilos in my suitcase won't make the slightest difference. In Afghanistan, though, you can end up carrying your own bags for miles; there, lighter is definitely better.

I was alone. Usually my wife, Dee Krüger, a freelance television producer who worked for the BBC in her native South Africa, comes with me to direct the programme I do for BBC News 24 and BBC World; it's called, I'm afraid, *Simpson's World*. We have worked together in all sorts of difficult places, from Iran and Colombia to Belgrade during the NATO bombing campaign of 1999, so Taliban-controlled Afghanistan presented no great anxiety for her. The trouble was, her mother was ill in South Africa, and we felt she had to be with her. Given the length of time this Afghan trip would last, that was probably a wise decision; but I missed her very greatly over the next three months.

The car headed out into the traffic, and I sat back into the leather cushions. A comfortable car, a driver too tactful to talk unnecessarily or play his radio, a pleasant sunny day, plenty of time. I learned long ago not to worry about the places I travel to: time enough for that when you actually get there, I feel. It never turns out as you expect, anyway; the places you think will be death sentences prove to be charming and delightful, the ones you expect to be relaxed and easy are suddenly terrifying. And so, when you find yourself a cushy number, you should devote all your energies to enjoying yourself. Who knows how long it will last?

Certainly, this did not seem like a difficult trip. Physically hard, perhaps, but not dangerous. I always liked going to Afghanistan, and (although it has become heresy to admit it since the 11 September attacks) going there had become a lot easier and safer as a result of the Taliban's five years in power. They had stamped out the brigandage and murder of the days when the mujaheddin (the West's favourites, of course) were in control.

So I anticipated a brief but pleasant stay in Peshawar, on Pakistan's North-West Frontier, then a hard drive to Kabul, and a week or so under difficult but not really harsh conditions there while I tried to persuade the Taliban government to allow Kate Clark, the BBC Kabul correspondent, to return to her job. After that, I hoped I might persuade the Taliban Foreign Minister, a man I rather liked, to let me roam around Afghanistan for a while, reporting on the famine and on the drugs trade. Not, maybe, a memorable trip, but as good a way of passing three weeks as I could imagine.

We went first to Paddington, where I met Peter Jouvenal at the office of Frontline, the agency he works with and helped to found, and we headed on to Terminal 4 at Heathrow. There we checked in the gear – it's always a pleasure to get rid of the stuff – and headed for the duty-free shops. We needed quite a lot of things: a couple of bottles of Laphroaig, since booze was illegal in Afghanistan and one had to make a stand somewhere; a box of twenty-five good Cuban H. Upmanns at the cigar shop, because both Peter and I like to end the day in a cloud of choking blue smoke; books and magazines in some numbers; and, finally, a present for Mutawakil, the Foreign Minister.

That, however, posed a problem. What do you give the man to whom almost everything is forbidden? Not, certainly, a bottle of good single malt whisky, the present of choice for government ministers throughout the Islamic world. Ties were expressly banned. Nothing with pictures of living creatures was remotely acceptable, especially if they showed women with naked hair. In the end I settled for a large and hideously expensive diary, bound in what looked rather like human skin, with tags and toggles hanging off it and a golden pencil of sorts tucked in at the side; just the kind of gift, I felt, that a Taliban government minister might think was classy.

Peter and I sat drinking champagne and eating oysters and smoked salmon at the bar in the departures lounge. If I had only known it, this was the last day either of us would get champagne, oysters or smoked salmon for months to come. We climbed on board the British Airways flight to Islamabad. (After many decades of travelling, the BBC agreed some years ago to let me turn left instead of right as I get on a plane, but it is always distinctly awkward if I am travelling with someone else. Especially my wife.) Someone came and put a white tablecloth on my table, fed me lobster, and gave me more and better champagne. Life seemed, on the whole, pretty good. After all, what could go wrong?

In Islamabad the next day, at the Marriott Hotel, we met Abdul. I spotted him right across the marble football pitch which is the hotel lobby. He was unmistakable: the beard, the deep-set light green eyes, the long, loping stride, the stringy turban. Abdul is the eternal Afghan: cleverer than everyone else around, always living on his wits, always proposing some plan whose outlines you can barely discern in the surrounding uncertainty. He has been many things: among them the manager of a Chinese restaurant in Brooklyn, and a minder for the Taliban's superbly named Ministry for the Suppression of Vice and the Promotion of Virtue.

Abdul is the only Talib I have ever met with a profound Brooklyn accent. You don't expect 'KnowwaddImean, ferGadssakes?' to come from a long, flowing grey beard and a green turban. Abdul and I did not get along at first. We had a violent argument in Kabul once, when I felt he was trying to prevent us from working and he thought I was putting his life in danger by quoting on camera something he had said to us in private.

Slowly, though, Peter Jouvenal persuaded me that I was wrong about him. Peter has always liked him. And once I realized that, whether he was in Kabul or Brooklyn, Abdul was basically just working for Abdul, my whole approach to him changed completely. I began to understand something of the deep complexities of his character. Abdul was a man who could operate anywhere; and not just operate, but absorb remarkably different types of influence. Which other Taliban official (or New York Chinese restaurant manager, for that matter) was an expert on antique Mont Blanc fountain pens? Abdul could talk for long periods about the suction mechanisms of the 1939 Mont Blanc, and sometimes, on our travels through Afghanistan together, he did.

Now we embraced, and he called me 'Mister John'. His beard was longer, greyer and more impressive, his strangely light eyes deeper set than ever. The problems of getting out of Afghanistan had clearly weighed on him. So had the problems of getting me back into Afghanistan. The BBC had hired Abdul in order to get this done, and like any Afghan he was utterly loyal to the terms of his contract. He would fight for the BBC's interests with the utmost ferocity regardless of any damage it might do him in future – but only as long as the money lasted. Once the clockwork had wound down, he would find someone else to work for and be loyal to. Now he had a scheme, but it was too deeply convoluted – too Abdul-like – for me to be able to grasp it entirely.

'See, the Taliban won't have you 'cos you from the BBC. Know what I mean? So I say you on Mr Peter's staff from Frontline.'

'But they'll know who I am. They'll know I'm from the BBC.'

'Sure they will. But you going as Frontline. That way they don't have to let the BBC in. Right or wrong?'

'But—'

I gave it up. Abdul was always right about these things, I had found. If he said he could get me in, it would happen. It's just that I would have liked to understand the mechanism a little. With Abdul, the mechanism was the one thing you could never understand. You just had to take it on trust.

The date was Friday 31 August. The ambassador at the Afghan embassy had promised to be at his desk, even though it was the day of rest.

'Who are you?' said the loutish Talib who was in charge of the embassy in the ambassador's absence.

I bristled, unwisely. 'I'm the world affairs editor of the BBC.' It's a title that generates a certain amount of amusement in London, but elsewhere sounds moderately impressive.

The lout was impressed. Abdul, however, wasn't. He pulled the lout aside and murmured to him in Pashtu. I heard the word 'Frontline', and guessed what was going on.

'So you lied to me,' the lout shouted. 'You aren't from the BBC at all.'

I felt the red mist rising, but fought it down; this was no time to make a stand. Abdul's strange eyes were on me, passing me warning messages. I shrugged, and everyone relaxed.

Nothing, however, could be done today. Worse, since Pakistan works to the Western week, the ambassador wouldn't be back until Monday. We could use the time fruitfully in other ways, but we wouldn't get visas for some time.

If, indeed, we got visas at all. The prohibition on the BBC's entry into Afghanistan had so far been entirely watertight. After the Taliban had blown up the giant figures of the Buddha at Bamian some months before, the BBC Pashtu- and Persian-language services had fully reported the worldwide revulsion. In the course of the BBC's coverage, an Afghan exile living in the United States had used a Pashtu word during a recorded interview which implied that the Taliban were crude savages. And since three-quarters of the population of Afghanistan listened daily to the BBC, this had a certain effect in the country itself.

Like most revolutionary movements, the Taliban contained both extremists and moderates. The Foreign Minister, Mutawakil, was unquestionably a moderate. He did not believe that allowing his image to be captured on video was tantamount to creating a graven image, and he seemed to like both me and the BBC. He also had influence with his strange, reclusive leader, the one-eyed Mullah Mohammed Omar; he had formerly been his close aide, and the Mullah (not a particularly bright man) listened carefully to what he had to say. But there were other, far more extreme voices competing for Mullah Omar's ear, and they argued that allowing the BBC to return to Kabul in any form was a dangerous mockery of everything the Taliban stood for. And so Mullah Omar had settled on a strange, rather hallucinatory compromise: the BBC would only be allowed to return to Kabul if someone senior from the BBC first went there to negotiate the terms of the deal; and until that happened, no one from the BBC would be given a visa to visit Kabul. It was very Taliban.

Hence Abdul's methods. What was extraordinary was that they worked. On 4 September we received our visas – among the last that the Taliban ever handed out. They were nothing but an oblong, fuzzy black stamp with room for a few squiggles of writing, but they represented something of a victory for patience and determination. That evening we drove to Peshawar, close to the Afghan border, and stayed the night in one of my favourite hotels anywhere, the Pearl Continental.

Sitting in my room, I read the official list of items which were forbidden in Taliban-controlled Afghanistan:

> Alcohol
> Pork products
> Lipstick
> Nail varnish
> Audio recorders, compact disc players,
>   cassettes and discs
> Video recorders and video cassettes
> Any item made from human hair
> Chess sets
> Musical instruments of any kind, including
>   pianos, grand or upright
> Billiard tables
> Statues
> Christmas cards
> Neckties or bow ties
> Books, newspapers, postcards containing
>   any image of any animate object,
>   human or otherwise.

In Peshawar I repacked, this time with Afghanistan in mind. Into the bag I was taking with me I put my only tie, plenty of compact discs, a travel chess set which I had bought in the bazaar especially for the journey, and a variety of pictures of people, especially women. And in lieu of billiard tables or grand pianos I put in a litre of superb cask-strength Laphroaig single malt whisky. Not in its own distinctive bottle, though; my sister-in-law Gina had provided me with an empty and thoroughly deflavoured bottle of disinfectant for trips such as this. It wasn't in any sense a gesture against Islam, a religion for which I have a profound liking and respect; it sprang purely from a dislike of being told what to do.

It took the three of us – Peter, Abdul and me – some time to get clear of the Pearl Continental the following morning. The service there is the best I know anywhere, and a certain amount of tipping is required. In this hotel the staff are so polite that, on an occasion back in the 1980s when I was planning to cross the border in Afghan dress and had to walk through the lobby on my way out, the under-manager and the head porter both greeted me in Pashtu in order to pretend they had been taken in by the deception.

The road from Peshawar up through the Khyber Pass to Torkham, the main crossing point into Afghanistan, is as romantic as any on earth: the magnificent views as the road winds up the mountains, the forts which date from the period of the British Raj and where the old insignia of the British regiments once billeted here are still kept brightly painted. The road, now as then, is guarded by men of the Khyber Rifles, smartly turned out in their black uniforms, their old .303 rifles over their shoulders. A sign propped up at a strange angle by the roadside announced that tourists couldn't go any farther, and a bus full of Germans was parked in a lay-by overlooking the superb valley where Afghanistan begins. It seemed a badge of honour to drive past them, and the sign.

Pakistan only seems as though it belongs to the Third World when you are approaching Afghanistan. When you leave it and come back into Pakistan again it feels like returning to the First World: the roads are well maintained, the houses are neat, the police and army disciplined and well turned out. As the tourists in their air-conditioned bus stared down into the valley, they were looking at a very different society indeed, one of the most backward anywhere in the world. This was one of the world's most obvious frontiers. On the one side an established judicial system and an effective civil society flourished. On the other, as you passed through the gate at Torkham, you were entering Looking Glass territory.

The gate itself is a slightly absurd affair, two miniature castles scarcely eight feet high support a two-leaved metal gate; they are faintly reminiscent of the kind of garden ornaments you might see at an Ideal Home Exhibition. It's perfectly easy to get round it, as I found myself a few years ago when I arrived from Kabul to find the gate closed and was faced with the prospect of postponing a bath and a decent bed for another twenty-four hours. On another occasion, lacking an Afghan visa, I lost myself in the noisy crowd which was going through from the Pakistan side, and was swept across the frontier unchecked and unnoticed in a torrent of excited people. There is something about Afghanistan that suspends the normal, dull procedures of life, a touch of lawlessness that is part of its attraction.

This time there were no problems. Our visas were in order, and the officials on the Pakistani side, being loyal viewers of the BBC, gave us cups of very sweet, very milky tea while Abdul, the best of fixers, managed to arrange for a couple of Afghan taxis to pass between the little garden-ornament towers so that they could pick us up when we had finished our tea. Of the many crossings I had made into Afghanistan, this was the easiest.

A huge crowd had built up on the other side, desperate to get into Pakistan. They pressed their faces against the windows of our taxi as we crossed the frontier, begging for money, demanding help. A great movement of population was going on here, on a par with the migrations of the Dark Ages. The basics of normal life were collapsing inside Afghanistan. There was a serious drought, and the Taliban's heavy-handed control was becoming fiercer and harder to bear. The United Nations, urged on by the Americans, had imposed an international quarantine on Afghanistan, and government was in the hands of the most rebarbative and restrictive political movement anywhere in the world.

To remind us that we had now left all rationality behind, a large sign on the Afghan side of the gateway read:

ISLAMIC EMARAT OF AFGHANISTAN
Faithful People With Strong Decision Entry Afghanistan!
The Sacrifice People Heartly Welcomes You With Pieases.

Yet if reason and the English language had evaporated under the Taliban, the rule of law had not. There was a time when the 140 miles of road from Torkham to Kabul was frightening and dangerous

– when bandits could poke their AK-47s in your face and demand money. The town of Sarobi, two-thirds of the way to Kabul, was a particularly nasty place, where a famous robber called Zardad, assisted by a terrifying being called the Human Dog, would stop travellers and steal their money if they were lucky and torture and kill them if they weren't. (Zardad, inexplicably, found shelter in south London after the Taliban cleaned out his robbers' nest, even though the British Home Office had rejected so many decent and deserving cases from Afghanistan. Later in this book I shall describe how we went to pay him a visit at his home in Mitcham.)

The Taliban had succeeded in sweeping away bandits like Zardad. It was their first real achievement as a movement when they captured the city of Kandahar, and it proved to be of major psychological importance in the campaign they waged against the mujaheddin government. The Taliban presented themselves as a purifying force, cleansing the old, corrupt, evil ways, and they were surprisingly successful at persuading the armed groups that controlled the country to come over to their side. The Taliban were never good fighters themselves; they relied heavily on the military skills and sheer numbers of the forces which joined them. And when they said they could capture Kabul, with God's help, thousands of commanders, great and small, believed them. It was a major public relations campaign, and in 1996 they won it.

The Taliban realized they had to make good their promise to sweep away disorder, and they did it very well. As we drove through the town of Sarobi it seemed remarkably peaceful in the late afternoon sun; and when we passed Zardad's lair, a Talib soldier standing in front of the kennel where the Human Dog had lived gave us a friendly wave. No one stopped us on the entire journey, and no one asked us for money – no one, that is, except the kids who went through an exaggerated show of sweeping the worst places along the dusty track directly they heard us approaching.

It took us seven hours to complete the 140 miles: a fast journey, given the dreadful conditions. The road from Torkham to Kabul was terrible; and yet, thanks to the years of neglect and violence, it was one of the best in the entire country. For most of its length it was composed simply of rocks and deep potholes. Dust flew up like a fog and covered the lumbering trucks, the buses and the battered taxis we passed, and the unfortunate passengers perched on the roof pulled their scarves round their faces and shut their eyes against it. Sometimes the road would vanish altogether, and the trucks and buses and taxis would have to lurch down into the adjoining desert and make their way through dust as thick and deep as water in a ford before getting back onto it again. The temperature must have been well above one hundred degrees Fahrenheit, but a young man who had lost his right leg in a landmine explosion stood for hours beside this detour, hoping someone would stop and give him money or water, and occasionally they did. But only occasionally.

This shattered road was Kabul's lifeline, bringing food and other supplies from Pakistan. Only one section of it was remotely good – the first few kilometres out of Jalalabad. The surface had been tarred, probably at the expense of Osama bin Laden, who operated from a set of caves in the White Mountains here. In 1998 Peter Jouvenal filmed a CNN interview with him somewhere round there. As we passed, Peter pointed out a rough track leading to the mountains. This, he thought, was where their guides had turned off the main road on the way to bin Laden's headquarters; though he and the others in the CNN group were blindfolded for the journey.

Peter reached into his pocket and pulled out a photograph. It was a happy snap of Peter and two others sitting with bin Laden in a cave. They were smiling, he looked as though he had swallowed something unpleasant. Peter carried it around with him as a kind of amulet against arrest and ill-treatment in Afghanistan, and it was always interesting to see how much respect he received from the Taliban as a result.

'How did bin Laden treat you? What was he like?' I asked, as our car jerked and shook its way past the mountains where bin Laden was still probably hiding.

'I thought he was a bit like a bank manager,' Peter answered; 'formal and cold.'

I stared hard at the White Mountains. It seemed so tempting just to branch off the road and drive along the track for a mile or so, to see what we could see. Abdul didn't like it when I mentioned what I was thinking.

'They'd be watching us,' Peter said in his laconic way. 'And they'd wonder what we'd come for.'

A billionaire fanatic with twenty-five million American dollars on his head was likely to have a certain amount of protection, I reflected. I didn't suggest to the driver that he should turn back and take the side track, after all.

We arrived in Kabul shortly before six o'clock that evening, shaken and tired, just as it was closing down for the night. It scarcely seemed like a modern city at all; thanks to the UN sanctions there was no electricity and little petrol, so our car was one of the few that navigated a river of homeward-going bicycles through the growing darkness. Dogs dashed into the road, barking at our wheels, as though we were passing through some remote country village. Dust everywhere, confusion, noise, people staring at the strange European faces: nothing had changed. We turned into the private road up to the Hotel Inter-Continental, and our headlights showed me that there were fewer trees in the park than I remembered. Kabul was a city fuelled by firewood.

The hotel lobby was dark and desolate, and only two other guests were actually staying there. The staff were much the same as ever. From 1980 to 1992 they shaved occasionally, wore ties, and reported on the guests to the Communists. From 1992 to 1996 they gave up shaving, wore *peran tomban*, the long, loose Afghan pyjamas, and reported on the guests to the mujaheddin government. Now they had let their beards grow long, their *peran tomban* were grubbier than ever, and they reported on the guests to the Taliban. They weren't bad or treacherous men. They had just been trapped by circumstances: the country's, the hotel's and their own.

I was given room 208, as usual. Maybe they put me there because it was bugged, though it was impossible to believe that the Taliban would have the equipment, the electricity, the English or the wit to listen in to my conversations. Whatever the reason – and I suppose it was most probably just habit – room 208 was a slum. The thin carpet bore some nasty stains, the bed was grossly uncomfortable, and the bathroom smelled of previous occupants. In other words, nothing had changed.

Downstairs in the hotel's gloomy restaurant an hour later the choice lay between rice with rubberized meat on skewers and rice with rubberized meat coated in breadcrumbs. Jouvenal had one, I had the other, and they proved to be virtually indistinguishable.

Afterwards we sipped Laphroaig from cups, in an attempt to make the waiters believe we were drinking tea, and smoked our cigars. Life didn't seem altogether too bad in Taliban-controlled Kabul, as long as you had one or two things to make it worth living.

The following day, though, I paid for my hubris. As I sat in my room writing, I heard the sound of excited voices outside in the corridor. Half a dozen bearded, shawled figures with Kalashnikovs over their shoulders had gathered there. They were going from room to room, searching everyone's belongings. They looked like extras from *The Planet of the Apes*, but in fact they were religious police from the Ministry for the Suppression of Vice and the Promotion of Virtue. I assumed immediately that, looking for vice to suppress, they had heard about our teacups from the previous night. After a quick consultation with Peter I decided to sacrifice the Laphroaig.

But we weren't the real targets. There were teams from CNN and German television in town, covering the trial of some German and American aid workers for supposedly trying to convert people to Christianity. The cameramen did what cameramen do and got some shots outside the courthouse, in the process contravening the rule about no images of any living being. Quite why the Taliban should have allowed television teams into the country at all, given that they had this rule, was baffling. So much about them was.

Peter and I had naturally wanted to be there at the courthouse with them, but Abdul had been insistent; if we tried to film, he said, there would be no chance of meeting the Foreign Minister, no opportunity for Kate Clark to return to Kabul, no possibility whatever of being allowed to go and film outside Kabul afterwards. Sometimes you have to trade an immediate interest for a longer-term one, and I could see that Abdul was probably right; but it pained me to leave our competitors, CNN, a clear run in this case.

Then we heard they and the Germans had been rounded up and threatened, and the Vice-and-Virtue men descended on the hotel to search everyone's rooms. Ours would almost certainly be searched as well. The possession of a bottle of Laphroaig, even one disguised as disinfectant, wouldn't be a good career move.

And so I found myself kneeling on the bathroom floor in room 208, staring down into the lavatory bowl in the unwell position. It was full of darkish yellow liquid. I yanked on the handle, the lavatory flushed, and the yellow faded. The best part of a litre of the finest alcohol known to man had just passed round the S-bend.

By the time the Vice and Virtue got down to my end of the second floor, though, they were losing interest fast; and although I flushed the lavatory three or four times to get rid of the evidence, they didn't beat on my door. The sacrifice had been in vain. I didn't altogether blame myself; if I had been caught, a public whipping would have been the least of my punishments. I still wish I had waited a little longer, though.

CNN and the BBC are in fierce competition around the world, of course. Yet when we all met up in the hotel restaurant in the evenings there was no question of any animosity between us. I had considerable respect for Nic Robertson, who (though British) was the CNN correspondent. I knew and liked the German correspondent as well, and Peter Jouvenal had worked for both organizations in the past. But though we were friendly, we didn't socialize too much. The others stayed at their tables, and Peter and I stayed at ours, smoking our cigars and, depressingly enough, accompanying them with tins of warm, unnaturally coloured, sticky-sweet Fanta. From memory, I quoted for Peter's benefit the line from one of W. C. Fields' films – *My Little Chickadee*: 'Once . . . in the wilds of Afghanistan, I lost my corkscrew, and we were forced to live on nothing but food and water for days.'

If we had been working for newspapers, even newspapers which were in direct competition with each other, we would quickly have gathered at the same table and started pooling information. Perhaps because newspaper reporters work alone, they tend to collect together in groups in the field. To that extent, newspaper journalism is a collaborative business, and most writers tend to hunt in packs.

Not so television journalism. We travel round in small groups of two or three anyway, so we have no great need of company. We also have an ingrained prejudice against coming up with the same material as every other television organization, and treating it similarly. Newspaper reporters often huddle together to work out what 'the story' is – that is, what line they should take on it; it is, of course, a particular comfort to the weaker brethren and the latecomers. To television journalists, there is something faintly indecent about this. We are not paid to cooperate, we are paid to compete; and if we get things wrong, and offer up a 'story' which is inferior to the others', we must take the consequences.

It probably sounds selfish and cut-throat, and the newspaper approach is certainly much more congenial. Still, few television journalists I know would want to change it. To us, being fully competitive seems much more straightforward, and much more what our audiences expect from us. Those huddled groups of newspaper journalists, agreeing 'the story' and fixing the exact wording of the quotations from a news conference from their collected notebooks, are not, I think, the way in which the readers of newspapers would really want to receive their news.

§

Kabul was a city of the saints, like Geneva under Calvin or Florence under Savonarola. The Taliban, for their part, reminded me of those crazed medieval flagellants who would occasionally announce the imminent coming of the Emperor of the Last Days and order everyone to obey the instructions of the Elect. They ran the place by the rulebook; and the rules were written in the seventh century.

And so a few women scurried round the streets in their shiny, pleated burkas of sky blue, bottle green or dark, metallic yellow, terrified that the soldiers and secret policemen who seemed to hang around at every street corner would arrest them for accidentally showing a wrist or an ankle. Men who had trimmed their beards were in perpetual danger of a beating. After some discussion the Taliban finally decided not to force the few Sikhs and Christians who remained in Kabul to wear coloured armbands when they went out in public; Mullah Omar, not being a man of any education, may not have heard of Hitler and the SS, but someone – possibly Mutawakil – had, and clearly whispered something about it in his good ear. Every week there were public beatings at the football ground, and sometimes executions: crazy affairs, in which the guards would hand AK-47s to the relatives (male and female) of someone who had been murdered, so they could shoot the kneeling murderer in the presence of everyone. There was a proposal in several states of the US during 2001 to do something similar there.

Booksellers naturally had to cover up the pictures on the covers of their books, but so did the small shopkeepers working out of re-used containers by the roadside: it was as serious to show a picture of a cow on a packet of powdered milk as it was to show the face of an American housewife with uncovered hair and cleavage on a bottle of disinfectant. Fortunately the Taliban were lazy and became increasingly corrupt, so it was often possible to escape the penalties for crimes committed against this obsessive fundamentalism. Even so, life was extremely difficult and you had to be on your guard the whole time.

The only horror the Afghans were spared was the Stalinist, Maoist, or Iraqi threat of betrayal by their children. The rule of the Taliban was certainly brutal, but it was patchy. They had neither the means nor really the intention to create a totalitarian system where everyone was watched and the schools could educate children to inform on adults. For one thing, half the schools were closed, after the education of girls came effectively to an end; for another, the Taliban were never organized enough to establish real thought-control. Their régime was nasty and brutish, but completely disorganized and inconsistent. If you kept your head down and obeyed the freakish, contradictory rules, you could survive.

It wasn't much of a life, though. The shops and stalls were half empty, food was hard to get, the number of beggars had greatly increased since I had been there the year before. Having seen sanctions applied by the United Nations in various countries over the years, I cannot say I warm to them. The notion of making an entire nation suffer for the actions of its unelected leaders is an unattractive one at best. In Afghanistan, which was already dirt-poor before the sanctions were imposed, the effect was devastating.

All this should have made an excellent story for television; instead, it was deeply frustrating. In Taliban-controlled Kandahar in 1996, Peter Jouvenal and I, together with a *Newsnight* team, filmed the scurrying women, the empty streets, the broken television sets hanging from the lamp posts as a warning to everyone, because we were able to distract the attention of our minders (not Abdul, at that stage) and lull them with carefully phrased assurances that a television camera is only running when its small red light is on. At that stage they were unaware that you could switch the red light off.

We found, too, that the ban on showing the human form was

only as watertight as individual Talibs wanted it to be. One leading figure agreed to let us film him raising a teacup to his lips; but no lips, and no fingers. His aide checked in the viewfinder and realized, as we had, that this was an impossibility; so the interview was cancelled. Another leading Talib, Mullah Balouch, interpreted the rules much more liberally. As long as we didn't show his legs, he said, this would not constitute a graven image. He sat behind his desk and justified the legal penalties which the Taliban had introduced of cutting off the hands and feet of thieves – something which, if no one else was around, he was prepared to do himself. He was, after all, the Minister of Health.

Now, five years later, the Taliban were far more savvy. It was very difficult to go out of the hotel without a minder, and if a Talib saw you filming without permission you were in serious trouble. No one wanted to be interviewed – the Taliban because the rules had been tightened up, ordinary people because it could mean prison or even execution. It was deeply frustrating, and now Peter Jouvenal and I lacked even the solace of a cup of whisky in the restaurant at night. We would walk up the back stairs to our rooms in the dark: no lift, no lights. Kabul under the Taliban had ceased to be a city in the modern sense of the term. There was no telephone service, no television of course, no entertainment of any kind whatever, and no electricity. The inhabitants went to bed when it got dark and rose with the sun.

It was the evening of 8 September: our last night in Kabul. I leant over my balcony and stared into the darkness. It was 8.30, and the only sound I could hear was the barking of dogs, and the only light came from an occasional oil lamp. We had seen Mutawakil that day, and although he had been pleasant and polite to me personally, it was obvious that he had been overruled within the Taliban leadership. The BBC would not be allowed to return to Kabul, nor would it be possible for us to travel round the country and film the effects of the drought. We would have to leave. There was no possibility of an appeal.

It never occurred to me, as I looked out at the dark city, that we were only three days away from the greatest act of terrorism in recent times, and that soon American and British missiles and bombs would be hitting Kabul, bombing it back to the Middle Ages. It wouldn't be at all easy for the target-selectors; since the Middle Ages was precisely where two decades of incessant warfare and five years of Taliban lunacy had already placed it.

§

Everywhere you go in the world, you find a certain level of suspicion about television news. Less nowadays than at any previous time, but it's still there: a feeling that maybe the pictures are being manipulated, that things aren't quite as they are being portrayed. There are, I believe, historical reasons for this, which I shall explain; but – I hope you will take my word for it – this kind of thing doesn't happen much nowadays, unless of course you live in Iraq or North Korea, or Robert Mugabe's Zimbabwe. Even the People's Republic of China is getting better in this respect. In democratic societies, the deliberate misuse of pictures, in which a set of images purports to show one thing while in fact it shows another, is so rare that it is virtually unknown.

During the writing of this book I took the time off to have lunch with a man who, three years earlier, almost gave the order to have me killed. He was a charming chap, who had recently left the US Air Force after a distinguished career. After piloting a plane in the Gulf War, he had been promoted by the time of the NATO bombing of Serbia and Kosovo in 1999 to the task of sending other pilots to attack specific targets. I told him that on 28 March 1999, early on in the bombing campaign, I was taken by the Serbs to examine the wreckage of a Stealth fighter which had crashed during the night near Belgrade.

He laughed over his monkfish and explained that he had been awaiting orders that morning to bomb the wreckage and prevent the Stealth technology from falling into the hands of another power: China, to be specific. Finally someone decided that the death of a group of journalists would cause the United States even more problems than the loss of its technology, so my friend didn't have to kill me after all. Which was good, since it was an enjoyable lunch.

It was clear he understood the value of having journalists reporting from the enemy side in time of war: a concept which the less reflective British politicians rarely seem able to grasp. But although he was too polite to say so, he plainly had his doubts about television reporting.

'Surely you can always play around with the pictures if necessary?' he asked. 'You know, juice them up a bit?'

It's a common enough belief, and – as I shall show – there are good historical reasons for it; yet it happens not to be true. In British television news, I cannot think of an example in the last decade. There was a current-affairs documentary about drug-smuggling which an ITV channel broadcast in good faith, and which turned out to have been fraudulent. It came to light partly because someone involved in making the film had a bad conscience about it. In organizations like Sky News, CNN, ITV News and the BBC there are too many people you would have to involve if you wanted to commit some kind of fraud; and since the self-image of all these organizations is one of straight dealing, someone would blow the whistle.

As for the deliberate intention to deceive for political or other purposes, I don't believe it exists. This is not necessarily true, alas, in written journalism. There, it is all too easy to invent quotations or even entire incidents, without adducing the slightest evidence. Television pictures can be a great nuisance; if they are particularly powerful they can take over a report and lug it off in a completely different direction from the one the correspondent intends. During the Bosnian War of 1992–6 I used to insist on spending a month or two at a time in besieged Sarajevo, in order to be able to give what I grandly called a 'strategic overview'. Yet, despite my best efforts, each day's incidents – five women killed as they stood waiting for water at a standpipe, the murder of aid workers, the grotesque shortages of fuel and food – would always intrude, and hijack my reports. Television is unrivalled at telling you about the here-and-now; it is much less good at providing the wider context.

Yet the demanding nature of television pictures is one of television's best guarantees of honesty. You can't simply make assertions as you can in a newspaper article: you have to produce the evidence on video, and that gives viewers an opportunity to make up their own mind about what you are saying. I am a newspaper journalist myself, and have a great affection for the medium; but although it is far better than television news at dealing with abstract issues and broad subjects, I have learned to trust the television reporting of specific events.

We take these things seriously, in part because television news has always had this question mark hanging over its honesty and transparency, ever since the day it began.

The history of television news hasn't always been a particularly noble one, and the industry in Britain and every other major country has had to shake off the memory of a highly questionable past. The BBC was the first organization to broadcast a television news report, but it was essentially radio news for television, with the newsreader sitting in a studio, out of vision, reading from sheets of paper. There was a strong belief in the BBC that you shouldn't see the newsreader's face, since his or her facial expression might give you a particular sense about the news item which would influence your response to it. It wasn't until after the Second World War, when television started up again, that the BBC began to consider broadcasting film clips to illustrate the news stories. The American networks had already started doing so in the late 1940s, with varying results.

The main problem was that the business of sending pictures was so much slower than wiring news stories. That could be done almost instantaneously; the pictures had to be shipped back by aircraft. As late as the early 1980s, whenever I went abroad for a story, one of my first tasks would be to establish good relations with the captain of a British Airways plane and ask him to take my film back to London with him. In the age of the terrorist bomb it became understandably hard to persuade ordinary passengers to agree to accept cans of film which must under no circumstances be opened, and if possible not to mention the fact to the airport security officers.

The journey times meant that it was only in Western Europe that you could get the pictures back in time for that evening's news. From every other location we showed yesterday's pictures, dressed up by a clever script so that they seemed to illustrate today's news: another completely phoney practice, which television news only gave up with the arrival on the scene of good television news agencies – the predecessors of Reuters and APTN, called Visnews and UPITN – and the technology which made it easier and cheaper to satellite material back to London. (London is and has always been the centre of the international news business. In the 1990s, when the New York-based

Associated Press decided to go into television to compete with Reuters, it naturally tried to establish its television arm in New York; but this proved impossibly difficult and expensive, so AP Television News is in London too.)

It was only in the early 1980s that television news gradually became a more honest medium. Ever since, those of us who work in it have had the uncomfortable feeling that it is necessary to be purer than pure, simply because our audience suspected us and our ways of operating. That battle is finally won, I think; but with luck our guilt about our past will keep us sensitive to phoniness of all kinds.

Modern television news is like the university-educated, sensitive, socially-aware son of some vicious old self-made industrial baron who ground the faces of the poor. There is a perpetual embarrassment about the past, especially among those of us who are old enough to remember some of it. The fact is, television news grew out of the crudest and most dishonest form of journalism, which would make Fox News today look like *Newsnight* by comparison. A decade or so ago, I became involved with a project planned by a distinguished producer from the Canadian Broadcasting Corporation called Mark Starowicz, to examine the dubious origins of television news. In the end, the BBC wanted something slightly different and my connection with the idea came to nothing. But the research was fascinating, and led us right back to the very first day when a true visual recording of an event was publicly shown.

It happened on 28 December 1895, in the Salon Indien, a small cabaret theatre just off the Champs-Elysées. The superbly named Lumière family, father and two sons, had developed a small portable camera which they thought might be used in medical photography, to help train surgeons. It could take moving pictures, and the Lumières also developed a projector – the first – to show them. Their idea was to market the cameras, and they hired the Salon Indien, which was the largest hall available that day, to show what their invention could do. They had made a number of short films as illustrations of their camera's potential.

At this time no one on earth had seen genuine moving pictures of real life. Photography had existed for sixty years or so, perhaps longer, and Eadweard Muybridge and others had experimented with photographs of people and animals which could be made to move.

But the Lumières recorded moving pictures in something of the same way we do today, and showed them as feature films are shown in cinemas today.

At first the audience was amused and diverted. On the screen, people walked around jerkily in the Bois de Boulogne, men doffing their top hats to ladies. There were one or two sudden close-ups. It was all in black and white, naturally. And then something happened in the film which terrified the audience rigid. In the distance a train appeared. It came closer and closer to the buffers, where the camera had been set up, looming huge – and before it could stop half the audience in the Salon Indien were on their feet, trying to get out of the train's way. Women screamed. Angry men were soon demanding apologies and their money back for the outrageous and dangerous trick which had been pulled on them.

Nowadays, if you see this short clip, it seems absurd to think that anyone might be fooled into thinking this awkward, black-and-white object approaching the camera posed any possible danger. But that is because we now understand the principle that moving pictures can be recorded. The audience had never seen anything like it – except for the real thing. And the real thing might well be dangerous, if you were to stand in the way of it.

Lumière *père* was the one person who grasped the meaning of what had happened. They shouldn't market the cameras, he told his sons, they should market the films. In fact they should lock the cameras and the projectors away so no one could imitate them, and they should use them to start making films which could be shown to audiences for a huge profit.

The Lumières found a young factory worker, François Doublier, and trained him to use the camera. They instructed him to keep it with him at all times, even when he went to sleep, and to explain its workings and purpose to no one. He travelled the world, filming short sequences of everyday life, and then increasingly important news events. Eventually, cutting his ties with the Lumières, he went to the United States where the newsreel business was just beginning. These were the days before anyone realized that California had the requisite climate for filming all the year round; America's first movie capital was in East Orange, New Jersey.

By that stage, Thomas Edison had followed the Lumières, and in the United States, Britain and France the first newsreel companies were soon starting up: American Biograph, Vectorscope, Pathé, Fox, Movietone, Gaumont, Vitagraph, Metrotone, Paramount. Several of them are still involved in films and television more than a century later. The competition was ferocious. At one battle in the Boer War, it was said only half jokingly that more shots were exchanged between the competing British and German newsreel crews (who were following the rival armies) than between the British soldiers and the Boers.

There were, as you might expect with such a lively young industry, no ethical controls at all. On 3 January 1914 the Mutual Film Corporation of New York signed an exclusive $25,000 contract with the Mexican rebel leader Pancho Villa to cover his campaign against the United States army. Villa had attacked American territory, and General Pershing was dispatched to invade Mexico and carry out a punitive expedition. The modern parallel would, I suppose, be CNN signing an agreement with Al Qaida to attack American troops in Afghanistan, and paying Osama bin Laden millions of dollars for the privilege. Mutual's contract even specified that Villa should fight his battles between 11 a.m. and 2 p.m., because film emulsions were still too primitive to cope with lower levels of light; though the contract stipulated that if the Mutual cameramen felt the light was acceptable at other times, Villa could fight then too. The lack of scruple was total. 'It was rumoured,' according to one account, 'that prisoners of Villa were used as human targets in telephoto scenes showing the artillery scoring direct hits on enemy emplacements.' Only rumoured, but by no means unthinkable.

Mutual were not ashamed of their coup. On the contrary, they boasted about it, as their advertisement to the distribution trade shows:

MUTUAL MOVIES OF THE
MEXICAN WAR
Made by Exclusive Contract with
Gen. Villa
of the REBEL Army

First reels just in – and being rushed to our branch offices.

These are the first moving pictures ever made at the front under special contract with the commanding general of the fighting forces.

Newspapers throughout the world are printing pages of matter about this war – and the amazing contract of the Mutual Film Corporation with Gen. Villa.

The public is clamouring for a sight of the pictures – which are far more exciting and sensational than any pictures of actual happenings that have ever been shown before.

Wire our nearest branch office for terms and reservations.

Newsreels had started to exert their extraordinary power, stirring up audiences to great heights of patriotic fervour during the Boer War, the Spanish-American War, and other international crises. A showman like Theodore Roosevelt owed his status as an American hero partly to the newsreels, because he realized the secret of success: he cooperated with them, to the point where he agreed to falsify entire scenes for the cameras.

The industry was completely unregulated, and its main purpose was unashamedly to entertain. The twentieth century opened as infotainment. The French cinematographer Georges Méliès faked the entire coronation of Edward VII for the Warwick Trading Company in Birmingham, using actors and cardboard props, in a Warwick-shire barn. Most of the footage of the San Francisco earthquake and fire was faked in a warehouse, where the studio staff set fire to a scale model; a photograph exists of a smiling figure standing over the burned-out model, holding a watering can. Yet the mayor of San Francisco, who watched the resulting film, was convinced it was true.

The sinking of the USS *Maine* was recreated in a large water tub, and audiences became so angry that the United States declared war on Spain as a result. The newsreels faked the battle of Santiago Bay with a canvas backdrop and (like my cameraman in Germany) with cigar smoke. A film of Theodore Roosevelt's much-reported hunting trip to Africa was shot in Chicago with a studio jungle and porters played by actors. An unfortunate mangy old lion was shot on camera for extra realism. François Doublier, the world's first newsreel cameraman, faked reportage of the Dreyfus affair in Egypt with a French army captain pretending to be Dreyfus. Biograph filmed an eruption of Mount Vesuvius with a model volcano, cream for lava, and more smoke. Albert Smith, an American cameraman working for Vitagraph, covered a battle in the Boer War but failed to get any real footage of combat. He wrote in his memoirs:

> When I got back to camp at Estcourt I sat down to figure out just what I had obtained with the camera and I saw that I had little of actual warfare . . . I asked a few of the British soldiers if they would put on Boer clothes and go through a few mock skirmishes, which they did. They fired a few volleys from behind boulders and went screaming past the camera in fine 'forward charge' technique.

British Gaumont staged the signing of the Vereeniging Peace Treaty which ended the first phase of the Boer War. Someone from the company later wrote:

> Our little picture, which was ludicrously imaginative, showed actors posing as Lord Kitchener, Lord Milner and the British staff with the Boer leaders . . . discussing dramatically, and finally signing, the Peace conditions. We included Lord Roberts and only found out afterwards he had not been there.

In the United States, executions were often re-enacted. Biograph released two versions of a film called *The Hanging of Mary Rogers*, in case she was reprieved at the last moment of murdering her husband by drowning him. She wasn't, and the correct version was rushed to cinemas all over America.

Through their combination of realism and fakery, the newsreels created an expectation among audiences that they could and would see some of the critical moments of their own time: that it was perfectly reasonable to expect the cameras to be on hand and rolling at the moment of the San Francisco earthquake; that the French authorities would allow them to visit Captain Dreyfus on Devil's Island; that the violence and uncertainty of battle could be captured easily and conveniently on film; that the great events in the world were really happening for their interest and benefit. A century later, we have these same expectations, and the advancing technology of television has made it possible to satisfy them. We have watched the great disasters of our time; we have watched Nelson Mandela walk free from his jail; we have been able to watch wars and the destruction they bring in close-up. It may have taken a hundred years, but reality has caught up with the Lumières' great leap of imagination in December 1895.

Slowly, the fiction was either weeded out or was more clearly acknowledged. Not at first, though. The newsreel coverage of the First World War was often compiled from filmed sequences showing soldiers in training for the front line. The awful reality of the trenches was sometimes filmed, but was often deemed to be much too depressing for public opinion at home to stomach. The cameramen, like the photographers and journalists, were rarely allowed too close to the action.

To this day you can find books about the Bolshevik Revolution of 1917 which are illustrated with stills from Sergei Eisenstein's film *Oktyabr*, made ten years later. The film was much more convincing than the real thing, which was a bit of a damp squib. In reality a column of Bolshevik volunteers queued up to get into the Winter Palace through a kitchen door which someone had left unlocked, and forced a garrison composed almost entirely of cadets and women soldiers to surrender. In the film, it's much more exciting, with a wild bayonet charge across the square and all sorts of heroics before the capitalist system finally falls. There was no one on hand to take photographs when it actually happened; but the stills *look* so impressive that you assume this is how a genuine revolution must be.

Many of the conventions and attitudes of American television were created in the 1930s by a remarkably influential series created by the team which founded and built up *Time* magazine. Each month, more than one-third of the population of the entire United States – 50 million people out of 140 million – would watch each new episode. It was opinionated, strongly left wing, and beautifully crafted by some of the best directors, scriptwriters and cameramen working in America, and it installed many of the basic conventions that exist in television news today: the use of the sound bite, the notion that each item was a short but fully rounded film in its own right. Many of the camera angles we still use were introduced then.

Yet the creators of the series never sought to hide that they mixed genuine footage with recreations staged by actors. *The March Of Time*, announced its advertisements: 'Dramatization of World's

Greatest News Events.' In the same film, it showed actuality of Hitler, and hired an actor to portray him, while a hostile commentary tells us what he is thinking as he stares into the fire. Stills from this sequence, too, were much used afterwards, as though they were of Hitler himself.

During the Second World War, reality provided all the action that had previously needed to be staged. The cameramen and reporters were given such good access that many of them were killed. This was not a war that needed to be fought for propaganda's sake, it was a citizens' war. No need to hide the conditions for the people back home; often, as with the liberation of prison camps like Belsen and the revelation of the conditions for Allied prisoners in Japan, the horrors simply strengthened public opinion in its support for the war. The technology of cameras and sound recordings made it better, quicker and easier to get actuality from the front line.

Afterwards, the rise of television news attracted many of the newsreel cameramen and journalists who had gained their experience in the War. I worked with several of them in my early days with the BBC, when they were coming to the end of their careers, and was enthralled by their stories of combat reporting, and of the fierce competition between the different newsreel companies. To some extent, though, the competition prevented the newsreels from faking too much: it provided the possibility of cross-checking their versions of the facts.

The commentaries were often empty of sense or understanding, and talked down embarrassingly to the mass audiences who watched them. George Orwell detested them. But the pictures gave people a growing sense of the world outside their immediate experience, and television news took on that quality from the newsreels, without adopting the tone of the commentaries. The news on BBC television was written by the same people who had written the much-praised bulletins for radio during the War and afterwards.

After the end of the Vietnam War – another conflict where the journalists and cameramen were free to go wherever they wanted to report – and the fall of Richard Nixon, a new puritanism swept through the American networks. For a time, nothing could be faked at all. There could be no cutaways, no false footage, no file pictures that were not clearly labelled as such. One unfortunate producer of a report about the ease with which Americans could buy handguns was sacked because he chose to do some filming in the shop of a relative of his, without stating the relationship. Slowly, the mood faded. Viewers didn't appreciate the ugly jump-cuts in the pictures, and got tired of too many disclaimers. But this too left its mark. A standard had been created, and it wasn't possible to sink below it again.

During my time in broadcasting, from 1966 to the present day, I have watched this slow progression of television news from its old, questionable roots to a settled honesty. Partly it's because we in the television news industry were no longer willing to put up with the older habits of fakery, and partly because the technological advances in television have made it possible to capture reality on a regular basis – not only great political moments, but crimes and wars. Television news, in Britain as elsewhere in the world, depends heavily on the news footage provided by the two news agencies, APTN and Reuters; and their bitter competition, even more than that of the post-War newsreels, keeps them on the straight and narrow. Neither side could afford to be dishonest in its coverage, any more than they could afford to be tardy or careless.

Now, as I reach my late fifties, there is a new and highly effective competition, between the BBC and CNN. Although I am paid to compete with Atlanta's finest, I have great respect for it. The better CNN is, the better the BBC will be, and vice versa. CNN's big advantage is still its speed of response; the BBC's, the unmatched quality of its correspondents. Yet nothing remains for long, and there are clear signs that CNN is under heavy pressure from another American channel, Fox News: noisy, hugely patriotic, almost embarrassingly American, largely dismissive of the outside world which fascinated CNN's founder, Ted Turner. Turner was bought out, and eased out, by Time Warner (descendants, of course, of the company that once made *The March of Time*) and is greatly missed within the organization. Nowadays Fox (one of the early newsreel companies) gets the ratings; by comparison, many Americans find CNN too careful, too undemonstrative, too European.

The other networks have faded depressingly from the scene. Once they dominated international news by being everywhere and covering everything; even though scarcely any of it reached American television screens. After the hostage crisis in Iran in 1980–81, and the assassination of President Sadat of Egypt, foreign news became extremely important to the networks. Jobs could be lost because of it; and they were, when ABC was the only network to cover the parade at which Anwar Sadat was murdered. One network hadn't bothered to cover it at all, and the other left early; easy choices to make, when there were so many parades which the foreign desk back home in New York never showed any interest in.

After that, for almost a decade, the Americans were everywhere; and small, under-funded European organizations like the BBC were very much the poor relations. Then John Birt became director-general in 1988, and the money was suddenly made available. Nowadays the BBC dominates every news story in terms of numbers and equipment, and the Americans are usually nowhere. In Kabul, some days after it fell to the Northern Alliance, I met the correspondent whom one of the major American networks had sent to cover this not unimportant event. He had only just arrived, having missed all of the excitement. He was about twenty-three, and was usually the correspondent in a medium-sized town in Southern California. He had found himself an Afghan cameraman, and had supplied him with a little DVD camera which looked as though he had bought it at the airport on his way from America. He was very nice, and completely lost.

Throughout the months which followed the 11 September attacks, the networks covered the unfolding events largely with their correspondents at the Department of Defense and the State Department; that is to say, news about the war and the diplomatic moves which followed was derived very largely from the official spokesmen and -women of the United States government. Good and upright people, no doubt; but I don't think I would want them as virtually my only sources of information about what was going on in the big outside world.

Nowadays Fox News, with its loud, combative, ultra-patriotic stance, is what the American viewers are coming to prefer. Sometimes there are distinct similarities with the tub-thumping nationalism of the newsreels Fox and others put out a century earlier, at the time of the Spanish-American War. All the big networks, plus CNN, are seeing their share of the market fall, and all have been taken over by big corporations whose only real interest in them is financial. The promises the networks made at the time of 11 September, when people accused them of not keeping them informed about the dangers from the outside world, seem to have been forgotten. It's hard to detect any serious increase in the amount of international news, except news from Israel.

When ABC, in recent years the best of the networks as far as international news is concerned, was taken over by the Disney Corporation, it required a good deal of internal lobbying to prevent the Corporation from imposing its logo on the News division. In particular the Corporation wanted to put the logo on the door handles at its London headquarters. The logo is, of course, Mickey Mouse. It's extremely painful to see old friends and colleagues being put through the wringer like this; but it's also extremely difficult to envisage that in a relatively unregulated environment like mainstream American television, news reporting has much of a future. Except, of course, when accompanied by the American flag and American patriotic tunes. The way Fox, the great survivor, does it.

§

The ancestry of television news gives it a raffish, slightly unreliable feeling, like someone who comes from a long line of jilters and bigamists and bankrupts. In many ways the medium's history is the record of its efforts to break with the past and go straight. Nowadays those of us who work in television news feel we have achieved that; yet somehow a folk memory of the past and its ways always seems to remain. Audiences who believe implicitly what they read in newspapers (where, after all, you only have the writer's word for what is said) still occasionally seem to feel that they are being spun a line on television, even when they can see for themselves what happened. It is far harder to manipulate television images than it is to manipulate the written word.

But of course the pictures are carefully chosen and carefully edited, and that can indeed be highly misleading. And we still employ lots of tricks of the trade which we inherited from our newsreel and movie past. They are there to make the wheels run more smoothly, but they are, in themselves, manipulations. Slowly, painfully, we are weaning ourselves off them; but I for one would like to see an end to all these things.

The clearest such example is the 'cutaway'. When you record an interview with someone, it is almost invariably far too long and rambling to be used in its entirety. A two- or three-minute news report requires a short, sharp extract from an interview, in which the speaker puts the case as strongly and concisely as possible. The trouble is, people do not always manage to talk like this; they ramble, they refer to things they have already said, they drop impenetrable bits of jargon or acronyms into what they say. You could always, if you were that kind of journalist, coach them into saying a coherent couple of sentences which you know you will use; but most of us would shrink from that degree of manipulation. Instead, we edit their words when we get back to the cutting room.

The most difficult thing about editing a television report is usually cutting the interview material – what some of us still anachronistically call 'synch', which is a term dating back to the ancient days of film when the picture and the sound came on different rolls and had to be synchronized on the edit table. Others almost as old as I am call it 'sof', which stands for 'sound on film'. Sticklers for accuracy some-times use 'sot' nowadays, which stands for 'sound on tape' but that sounds distinctly odd. The best thing to do with synch is to use a single coherent chunk of it. Yet this isn't always possible. When you are editing what someone has said, you have an obligation to let them speak as effectively as possible; and they can't always make their point well enough in a single short passage.

And so you have to edit two or more chunks of synch together, which causes an ugly jump in the image, jarring to the viewer. There are various ways of smoothing this over, and historically television news – all television news, the world over – has chosen what I regard as the most dishonest option: the cutaway. The cutaway is a device which pretends that, instead of having only one camera at the interview, you have two; one pointing at the interviewer and the other at the interviewee. For most of the time the camera has been behind the interviewer's head, pointing at the interviewee, but when the interview is finished, the cameraman shifts around to where the second cameraman would have been, and gets some pictures of the interviewer pretending to listen, and nodding, interjecting and some-times asking one of the questions from the interview a second time – all for the purposes of making the editing process smoother. If the interviewee is still sitting there, it isn't quite so bad: there is still some interaction between the two of them, and if the interviewer asks one or two of the questions from the interview again you feel that the interviewee can leap up and say, 'Hang on – that's not at all what you asked me.' But real life doesn't always work as smoothly as that. The interviewee is in a hurry, and you are left with an empty chair to nod at, and look interested in, and ask your questions of. There is, to my mind, something mildly distasteful about all this: it's getting a little too close to acting, and a little too far from real life. It reminds me uncomfortably of the worst film-making experience of my life, when I was working somewhere extremely difficult and was asked to make a short documentary about an aspect of life: a young man going into the army to defend his community. A producer was sent out from London, and since I had a lot of daily commitments to report the news I left most of the work to her. That was a mistake. It got so bad that by the end she was coaching everyone about the minutest details of what they should do and say.

'John, if you walk in through the door here and put your hand out, then you, sir, can stand up and take John's hand and shake it. Then maybe you could say something like, "Welcome to my house." Is that OK?'

It wasn't, of course; it was dreadful, and we ended up screaming at each other. Even some of the television critics – not normally the most aware of people – noticed the stilted nature of it all. One said it seemed odd that when the army rookie we were filming arrived at the barracks for the first time to become a soldier, he wasn't carrying a kitbag of any kind. It wasn't odd at all, since the rookie had arrived the previous day, with all his gear, and we were making him re-enact his arrival. By that stage I had abandoned all interest in the film. There were reasons why I couldn't just walk out of it; but I swore I would never let myself in for such manipulation again, and I haven't.

The acted-out cutaway shot is, in the broader scale of things, pretty harmless. The plot of the Hollywood film *Broadcast News* turned on a cutaway, in that the rising young television news star, a handsome phoney with no regard for the great and noble traditions of journalism (you can tell this was made in Hollywood), goes out and interviews a young woman who has recently been raped. The interview proceeds as normal, and then the moment comes for the cutaway. The star sits there, reacting into space; and as part of this reaction he squeezes out a tear, which rolls picturesquely down his cheek.

The cutaway, when edited into the interview, causes a sensation – until someone remembers that the star had only gone out with one cameraman. In other words, the cutaway cannot have been genuine. No shit, Sherlock, as they say in California. To me, the great mystery is why anyone would think that there was any possibility of getting two cameras for a routine interview. The American networks, like the British ones, usually only send a second camera on big political interviews. But without the tearful cutaway there would have been no *Broadcast News*; this wouldn't, in my opinion, have made much dent in civilization, though it was successful enough at the time.

So if cutaways are phoney, what should replace them? That's easy enough; all you need is some visual device to represent the series of dots which show that words have been left out of a printed account. A fade down and fade up is the most elegant, but until recently it required three editing machines instead of two, and rarely seemed to be worth it. You could fade very quickly to black and then back to the picture; you could put half a second's worth of black frames in, just enough to register on the minds of the audience that something is missing here.

The trouble is, it requires a cultural change to introduce these things. They happen in documentaries, they happen in current affairs: but they don't happen in news. News, in the television services of most Western countries, is always more conservative than current affairs; partly because the news people have far less time to put their programmes together. Fades and other devices take time. Still, what is needed is an acceptance by the broadcasters that any kinds of falsity, even the harmless, purely cosmetic type, are best avoided. Perhaps, too, we need an acceptance by the audience that although they are seeing something which is different and perhaps more awkward than they are used to on the news, it does tell them frankly that something has been done to the words they are hearing. That way, perhaps, we can ditch one of the last vestiges of the undeniably dodgy past of television news.

4

Hidden Agendas

Peter Jouvenal, Abdul and I had returned from Kabul to the Marriott Hotel in Islamabad. The events of 11 September had brought in fresh supplies of journalists, camera crews, and mountainous equipment by every plane that landed. People I had known for decades were hanging around in large groups at the tables in the coffee shop, since there was no bar and nowhere else to go. It was almost impossible to do anything in secret. If you spoke to some local contact, everyone would see it and guess what you were talking about. The large television screen in the lobby blared out the BBC, so you couldn't propose a theory on air without having it quoted back to you later. Peter and I went backwards and forwards to the studios of Pakistan Television, close by, and it became an embarrassment to have so much praise heaped on us.

In one respect, praise is like criticism: after a while you find yourself instinctively countering it, thinking up the reasons why it might not be right. I almost preferred the days when people complained to me about the bias of the BBC against whatever it might be that they believed in: for a lifelong inhabitant of no man's land, there is something unnatural, unnerving, about finding that you and your organization have suddenly become popular.

Still, I liked Pakistan Television, and going round there to do our live broadcasts reminded me of the old days, when every news event involved navigating the complexities of a new television station and a new set of restrictions and difficulties. You couldn't take anything for granted in those days, least of all the likelihood that your live broadcasts would go through as planned. At Pakistan Television, though, they did; it helped that BBC World was being broadcast live and continuously on one of PTV's channels: part of the global audience of 300 million plus that watched the BBC during the early days of the crisis.

We soon set up our own broadcasting station on the roof of the Marriott, alongside all the other international television organizations. It was like a small branch of the BBC here, with a newsroom, edit suites, crew rooms, a recreation room where people could hang around and watch television. The danger of this kind of thing, of course, is that it makes your operation distinctly insular; it's a little reminiscent of all those stories about the US networks having hamburgers and American coffee flown in every day from the other side of the world, in order to keep their camera teams happy. But it's hard to run a big 24-hour operation during an international crisis any other way.

In the distant past, when dinosaurs walked the corridors of Television Centre, big international events like this would have resounded to the clash of egos. One star broadcaster would have refused to take second place or work alongside another, and the unfortunate producers and camera crews would have kept their heads down until the titanic battle was over. In the meantime, of course, the opposition would have walked all over us and we would have missed the big story we had all come to cover.

Believe me, I do not wish those days back. I think the greatest improvement that has been made during my years in the BBC is that the right people are now in charge: not the big egos, but the producers who don't have any personal axe to grind and can look at the interests of our reporting as a whole. Nowadays, on these big events, there is a clear-cut chain of command, of the kind that ITN and the American networks established years ago. It took us a long time to catch up. At last, though, we have a single producer who is in charge. He or she makes all the dispositions, from the question of who does which report for which news programme to who gets the floor and who gets the bed in an over-booked hotel room.

Correspondents have become precisely what we should be: names on a board, to be shifted around as and when it seems sensible, not hotel-corridor gladiators who fight each other and everyone else for the best programme slots. Only a few years ago, on a major story, the foreign duty editor in London told me she had received forty-two calls in a single day from two correspondents, vying with one another to get on the main news. They were spending so much time ringing her, she said, that they couldn't possibly have been doing what they were paid to do: reporting out in the streets. It is a genuine relief to see that a proper balance has finally been struck, and like the movie stars of the 1920s and 1930s we performers have been forced into line.

Face-guys, as the old-fashioned but rather pleasant American television argot used to call us, are all very well in our way and probably necessary, but it was never a good idea to have allowed us to have so much say in what we did. There was a genuine problem, of course: we face-guys are paid to shout and bully our way into places where we aren't wanted, in order to do our job and get the necessary television coverage; no one pays us to keep quiet and sit at the back and help other people to go first. So it's only natural that we will also shout and bully our way onto our own airwaves, unless a calmer and more rational system is imposed. Now, thank God, it has been.

In American and French television the face-guys and face-gals often climb to vertiginous positions of power. They can overrule the judgement of the correspondents on the ground, and they can even veto their appearance on television altogether. This isn't a good idea either. It involves much too much politicking and toadying, as up-and-coming people grease their way into the favour of the big stars. It creates a vicious atmosphere within the organization. And ultimately it means that no one will pluck up the courage to speak openly to the topmost people and tell them when their work has become too mannered, or isn't up to scratch. The more American television news becomes like Hollywood, the closer it gets to the old Hollywood system where the Goldwyns and the Meyers controlled the performers like lion-tamers, cutting them down to size when they felt it was necessary; though nowadays it's the best of the lions who are holding the chairs and the whips, and wearing the top hats.

Still, real power in American television lies nowadays with the dull, unimaginative characters on the top floors of dull, unimaginative buildings, who can step in at will and replace even the most senior and respected of television journalists with vapid chat-show hosts. These dull, unimaginative characters aren't interested in quality broadcasting, whatever else they are interested in.

The BBC, thank God, operates in a completely different atmosphere. For us, power lies, not with the men and women in suits so much as with the programme makers: in other words, where it *should* lie. Public service broadcasting may need occasional defending, but in Britain at least the principle is clear, and it works – at any rate, for the moment. But it's something that needs to be watched and protected all the time.

And in my own small corner of the television world, rationality has finally been restored. Editors edit, producers produce, reporters report. If you're going to run a big outfit – the biggest in the world, as the BBC likes to boast – then you have to operate in a sane, calm manner with a clear decision-making hierarchy.

And yet, in the Marriott Hotel in Islamabad, I didn't feel at ease. I admired the sheer size of the organization we had created there, was impressed by the quality of its decision making, its reporting, its engineering, and took full advantage of the praise it was getting from everyone around me, but I felt I was in the wrong place. The wide open spaces beckoned; it was time to cut my ties with all this rational behaviour and do a little first-hand reporting – preferably inside Afghanistan. But how to get back in? The first thing that each of the journalists who were still arriving in Islamabad by every flight did after they had checked in at the Marriott was to go round to the Afghan embassy to apply for a visa. You had to queue just to get in through the gates. By now the conversation in the hotel coffee shop turned on nothing else but how to get into Afghanistan.

The Taliban, though, had raised the stakes. They announced that no journalists would be allowed there, and that any who tried to enter the country illegally would be arrested. This didn't stop people applying; journalists characteristically have enormous faith in their ability to convince others to let them do what they want, and the fact that the Afghans were continuing to hand out visa application forms encouraged the feeling that things might change. Personally, I felt that the forty-dollar application fee might have something to do with the embassy's willingness to hand out the forms.

Peter and I tried other ways of getting back to Afghanistan. The

UN was still flying in, but refused to take anyone who didn't have a valid Taliban visa. It so happened that Peter's and my visas had not been stamped or cancelled on our previous trip and still had some weeks to run, so we tried hard to persuade the UN to take us. Once we seemed to be getting close; then, somehow, the moment passed. By now, anyway, we had been joined by a producer, Paul Danahar, who didn't have a visa. We couldn't easily enter Afghanistan without him because he was an expert in communications; if we managed to get in, we would have to broadcast several times a day.

So we would have to slip across the border without permission. Once upon a time, when the Russians and their stooges were in charge there, you could always rely on Pakistani military intelligence, the ISI, for help in getting into Afghanistan. Not any longer: the ISI were the Taliban's main supporters, and it seemed unwise to trust them. Peter Jouvenal suggested getting away from Islamabad and Peshawar, where there were so many foreign journalists, and trying somewhere like Chitral, close to the border with northern Afghanistan. I agreed: we had passed through Chitral from Afghanistan before, and had some good friends and contacts there. But there was a problem: that part of Afghanistan was controlled by the Northern Alliance, who were fighting the Taliban and regarded Pakistan, the Taliban's main supporters, as their enemy. Getting across wouldn't be easy there either.

Still, it seemed worth a try.

We drove up to Chitral; it took fourteen hours through the mountains by road, compared with only an hour and a half by plane, but the ISI kept a close watch on the airports and our journey would quickly be known to them.

It was 7.30 in the evening when we arrived, and we headed straight for the pleasant garden of the old-fashioned hotel to meet our contact there. He seemed eager to help, but something was clearly troubling him. It was hard to say what it might be – until we heard that the Pakistani army had reinforced its presence all the way along the border, and had orders to shoot anyone who crossed illegally from either side. There might be another way, said our contact, but it would cost us money. We demurred, but agreed to have another meeting with him.

The next morning we gathered in the garden over breakfast. It was clearly no use: even our contact admitted we couldn't get across the border at the moment. Peter Jouvenal wanted to stay in Chitral and try some patient negotiation: always the best method in Pakistan. I agreed in principle, but felt that since it was unlikely to happen quickly we had better get back and do some more broadcasting; that, after all, was our reason for being here at all. The drive back was harder, and our driver, a faithful Muslim, felt obliged to stop and pray at regular intervals. The road seemed worse than I remembered, and the precipices deeper and closer to our wheels. I did some praying myself.

We didn't go back to Islamabad, though. That was too far away from the Afghan border, too full of journalists, too comfortable. Islamabad is a new city, a pleasant, green, wooded place constructed along the lines of New Delhi, which in turn was constructed along the lines of Hampstead Garden Suburb. It felt all wrong that we should ride out a major international crisis in an Asian Hampstead Garden Suburb. Instead, we headed for Peshawar, which at least had the merit of being only thirty miles away from Afghanistan, and where trouble was expected. I was certain of it myself, and went round telling everyone to be very careful once it started. It wouldn't do to have Western cameramen on the streets when the demonstrators were angry, I said.

I was wrong. There was indeed a certain level of genuinely violent passion: the terrible, pointless murder of the American journalist Daniel Pearl in Karachi a few months later showed that. But the demonstrations in the streets of Pakistan's cities always looked a great deal worse than they actually were. The morning after we arrived from Chitral there was to be a big demonstration in the old centre of Peshawar, starting at one of the mosques – it was a Friday – and parading through the city.

It reminded me of all the other demonstrations I had reported on at times of trouble, from Belfast in the early 1970s to Soweto in the 80s, Baghdad in the 90s and the West Bank in 2000–2001. At times like these, journalists may sometimes be seen as the enemy, but they are always regarded as the necessary conduit through which the crowd can express its anger. For that reason, and sometimes only for that reason, you have a certain limited degree of immunity: the crowd wants to show you its feelings more than it wants to attack you.

Accordingly, the journalists who were waiting to cover the demonstration gathered in an awkward group near the entrance to the
mosque. There is a kind of safety in numbers – or maybe it just feels
that way. Even at a time like this, one or two passers-by quietly
acknowledged me and said they watched BBC World; but there was
a resentful, angry look about the crowd of young activists who came
pouring out of the mosques when prayers were finished, and they
started chanting and shouting immediately.

It was hot in the September sun. Peter Jouvenal stood there sizing
up the demonstration, his camera on his shoulder, looking more
like a Victorian army officer than ever. Even his *shalwar kameez* was
khaki, which was suitable since Peshawar was the place in British
India where khaki, the predominant colour of the buildings, the
ground and the mountains beyond, was first introduced for the British
soldier. There were about fifteen of us, journalists and cameramen,
and the large crowd broke around us like angry waves against a rock,
shouting and chanting.

Peter's driver, Aziz, had given himself the task of protecting me
that day. I had first met him at Peshawar airport in 1989, when I
arrived to cover the Soviet withdrawal from Afghanistan, and had
been struck right away by his combination of gentleness and extraordinary knowledge of everyone and everything. Independently of
me, Jouvenal met him, and hired him every time he was in town.
They had a very pleasant working relationship which amounted by
now to a real friendship. When Peter went searching for particular
military objects in the bazaars of Peshawar, Aziz would go with him
and drive the bargains. The two of them had developed a vocabulary
of their own about the places and items they searched for: 'the dusty
shop', for instance, which sold old army uniforms.

I once went to visit Aziz at his farm on the outskirts of Peshawar:
a smallholding with a house hidden behind high mud-brick walls in
the old-fashioned way, with a large carved wooden gate to protect it.
Inside the gate it was a little familial paradise: children running
around the open courtyard, a bullock and a couple of goats cropping
the grass, women covering their faces in attractive dismay at the
entrance of a foreigner, and Aziz's two brothers and his father
busying themselves with small tasks. On a charpoy lay a very old
man, reading a newspaper with the thickest imaginable glasses.

'My grandfather, sir,' said Aziz.

I asked how old he was.

'Very old, sir. Now ninety-eight.'

I found it hard to believe, as I went to shake the old gentleman's hand. The old gentleman murmured something.

'Says, sir, it was a bad thing for this country when the British left.'

It could, of course, merely have been politeness on the old gentleman's part – or on Aziz's.

He and his family were not rich, but they were clearly satisfied with each other and with their lives. There was a real sense of peace in their compound, and afterwards I often found myself thinking about them rather wistfully, as though I had had a glimpse of an older and more contented world.

Now Aziz walked along parallel to the demonstration, keeping me in view the whole time, making his way politely through the crowds of onlookers: a slight figure in his late thirties with a wispy moustache, slightly thinning hair, and a permanent, gentle smile on his features. It would be a serious mistake to confuse any of this with weakness. Aziz is about as weak as steel cable, especially when he is on a mission. Today his mission, self-appointed, was to make sure nothing happened to me.

Yet even as we walked along at the head of the procession, with Peter walking backwards filming it, guided by Paul Danahar, it was starting to become clear to me that the menace which the demonstrators were showing was primarily intended for the camera lens, not for us. This is not to say that everything was completely safe. Crowds anywhere are potentially dangerous, and the sudden appearance of some lunatic could have changed the entire atmosphere within seconds; I have described elsewhere how, during the Iranian revolution, a perfectly friendly crowd turned on us when a man standing at the back accused us of working for the Shah, and we were lucky to escape being torn to pieces.

Now the crowd was howling and shouting, and the temperature seemed to be rising; but when I looked at the policemen walking stolidly along, they seemed completely relaxed. No one hit us, or spat at us, or insulted us in any way. We reached an open market area, and the crowd halted. Phase two of the ritual was about to start.

Someone pulled out an American flag, and a lumpy, stuffed shirt and trousers with a hat on and a badly written sign round its neck saying 'George W. Bush' was produced. Someone else doused it in petrol and produced matches, and George W. Bush caught fire so fast the man carrying him had to drop him, and his clothes were set alight.

It would have seemed completely uncontrolled and frightening, except for the laughter on the faces of the demonstrators. Yet when the pictures were shown around the world, they were used to illustrate the extent of the violent hatred towards the United States. Not, I have to say, in my report that night; I made it clear that the whole event had been deliberately staged for the cameras, and that it was part of a ritual of anger and abuse which did not necessarily involve violence at any level except the purely verbal one. It didn't matter. These pictures were used on television channels around the world for weeks afterwards, because they seemed to be emblematic of public anger in the Islamic world. They reinforced Western notions of Muslim savagery and brute ferocity.

In fact, of course, it was probably more dangerous to be an Arab, or anyone whom an ignorant passer-by might mistake for an Arab, in New York or London or even Sydney, than it was to be an American or an Englishman in Peshawar or Kabul. Sikhs were regularly beaten up in America, merely because they wore turbans; there were even some deaths. Perfectly innocent refugees from Afghanistan, who had fled the religious extremism of the Taliban, were attacked and insulted. So were Muslim girls and women who, thanks to the religious freedoms we are so proud of in the West, wore the veil in the streets of Western cities. A despicable and cowardly form of mob rule occasionally comes over Americans and Europeans at times when we feel our societies are under threat; and at the very moment when you might hope that we would most demonstrate the qualities we profess, we often behave the worst.

This is less often the case in Islamic countries. I have noticed many times how Westerners are treated as individuals, rather than as representatives of and potential scapegoats for their governments' policies. Perhaps Muslims tend to be less tribal than Westerners; perhaps it has something to with having been colonized, so that they feel that no ordinary person has any say in government or any control over the policies of the officials who run their lives, and that it would be unreasonable therefore to attack an individual for what is done in his or her name. Perhaps it is simply because Muslims still regard foreigners as guests, and guests as people to be looked after and respected. Whatever the cause, in September 2001 it was better to be a Westerner in a Muslim country than a Muslim in a Western country.

I stood apart from Peter Jouvenal and the rest of the cameramen and photographers, partly because I thought I would be in the way, and partly because I wanted Peter to get some shots of me in the middle of the crowd so that I could make some of these points about feeling safe despite the noise and the burning effigies. The crowd I was with pushed and shoved, as crowds will; but at six feet two inches I towered over the people around me, and those closest to me tried not to barge into me too much.

Then I heard Aziz making his way through the crowd, using his fists and feet freely, hissing his disapproval of the way I was being treated. He carried a plastic bag, which turned out to be full of ice-cold drinks from a nearby shop. It was like having a sub-continental Jeeves to look after me. Then, while I downed a Pepsi or two, he marched around me in a little circle, forcing the crowd back on all sides. In the end I was standing in a clear area of about three feet in diameter. He patrolled this circle continually, pushing people back here and rebuking them there; and although there was so much anger and resentment being expressed by speakers and demonstrators against the evil aggression of the West, no one objected to the efforts Aziz was making to give one particular Westerner a little unfair advantage.

By now the demonstration was drawing to an end. A dreadful windbag who screamed into the microphone and deafened everybody was persuaded at last to hand over to a master of ceremonies, who handed out a few more pro forma insults against President Bush and American policy, and suggested that the attacks on the World Trade Center had been planned and perhaps even carried out by Israel to discredit Muslims. After that he said it was necessary at times to carry out attacks like this to demonstrate the determination of Islamic resistance. Altogether it wasn't a particularly impressive performance, except in terms of decibels, but it finally came to an end, and our ears stopped ringing. Within ten minutes the entire area was empty of demonstrators, the police were back on patrol, and the stall-keepers were selling their wares again. Only a fresh scorched and blackened mark on the ground, where a shirt, some trousers and a hat had made the ultimate sacrifice, showed that anything unusual had happened here.

As for us, we were on our way back to the Pearl Continental Hotel. A smaller version of the international television operation in Islamabad had been established there. It too was up on the roof, where the black-headed crows hopped around, their harsh cries clearly audible over the microphones. (British soldiers based in Peshawar used to call them 'shite-hawks', from their habit of diving down and stealing the food off the plates.) Already the pictures of the demonstration were on their way round the world, and everyone was happy: the editors of television news programmes, because the demonstration seemed so ferocious, the demonstrators themselves, because that had been their intention, and the journalists, because they had the kind of graphic material that would lift their reports higher up the running order.

No one else seemed to think it was worth reporting that no violence of any kind, verbal or physical, had been offered to the Western journalists who had witnessed all this.

§

Television is an intensive medium: it heightens the significance of everything it looks at, merely by paying attention to it. The viewers get the feeling that they are being shown something of particular importance. And there is an unconscious corollary: anything which television news doesn't pay attention to can't be that important.

It comes down partly to a matter of space. Newspapers usually have somewhere in the recesses of the home or foreign pages where they can slip in paragraphs about events of lesser importance. Television rarely does this. Even its brief round-ups of domestic and foreign news are given a special kind of significance, thanks to the medium. It is true that a newspaper is just as heavily edited and its news just as selective as a television news bulletin; why, otherwise, would the *New York Times* claim in its fatuous masthead motto that it provides 'All The News That's Fit To Print'? But there is a big difference, and that is space.

Yet this can be exaggerated, both by people who work in journalism and those who are simply consumers of it. Every week I churn out a column of foreign affairs for the *Sunday Telegraph* – a newspaper which, under my friend Dominic Lawson, is always provocative and interesting, and does not simply wish to give its readers information to back up what they already believe. This column of mine is 800 words long. No one, I assume, suggests that the columns in a serious Sunday newspaper are too short. If I wrote for the *Sun* or one of its imitators, I would be lucky to get 350 words; and even that seems long enough to get over some basic ideas.

In television news, the rule of thumb is that speech is broadcast at a rate of around three words per second. The average length of a foreign report on the *Ten O'Clock News* is probably around two minutes, fifteen seconds. That, if my arithmetic is correct, makes 405 words: some way longer than a column for one of the tabloids. When, however, we cover something of greater importance we are likely to be allocated quite a lot more time. My report for the *Ten O'Clock News* on the fall of Kabul, for instance, was six minutes long: the equivalent of 1,080 words. Neither the *Guardian* nor *The Times* devoted much more than that to the city's fall.

And of course what neither the *Sun*, the *Guardian* nor the *Sunday Telegraph* can offer is moving pictures of the event to accompany their words. If every picture really is worth a thousand words, then a six-minute television report would be longer than any newspaper: including the *Sunday Times*, which weighs so much that when you stoop to pick it up from the doorstep you have to pray to avoid a hernia.

So the notion that television news is just a once-over-lightly affair, which screams a few headlines at you and then tells you nothing serious, is not necessarily an accurate one. It all depends, of course, on who does the telling, and how much time they are allowed. These are questions I will come back to later in this book, but for now I want to look at a more fundamental question: are television pictures by their very nature misleading? Does the viewer receive a false sense of the world as a result of them?

I have made my opinion clear, in writing about the anti-American demonstration in Peshawar, that the television pictures gave the impression of a violent, angry, seething crowd venting its opinions;

while the reality was a group of people whose feelings were no doubt passionately anti-American, but who restricted themselves to burning the American President in effigy rather than venting their frustration on the Westerners who stood by and watched them. This led to a significant failure of understanding. The world in general expected a violent explosion of feeling in Pakistan, which would cause great difficulties for its President, General Pervez Musharraf, and perhaps for the leaders of all the other countries which supported the Americans in their campaign against Afghanistan. Musharraf loved it, of course; every time the West asked him to do something difficult, he could refer to the television pictures, which everyone had seen, and explain that there could be an explosion of violence if he went too far.

What actually happened was that the destruction of the Taliban resulted in a sullen, gloomy acquiescence by the very people who had been so angry and so noisy in demonstrations like the one in Peshawar. In other words, the images of their anger had fooled us, and led us to make a mistaken judgement of the likely outcome.

Yet how much was this the fault of the images themselves, and how much the fault of the people who edited and broadcast them? As viewers, we expect the correspondents and editors to guide us through the mazes and tell us what the pictures mean. In this case, many of the correspondents and editors thought they knew what the pictures meant, yet got it wrong; and so they misled us.

Our expectations, prejudices and cultural values show up heavily at such times. There is a clear belief in the West that Islam represents a threat to our values, and that confrontation with the Muslim world may well be the next conflict after the end of the Cold War with Marxism–Leninism. For what it's worth, I think that is a wrong-headed and shallow paranoia, based on watching the pictures from too many demonstrations of precisely this kind; but it is certainly the filter through which most Westerners see events like the Peshawar demonstration.

So it was the presentation of the television pictures which was misleading. That shifts the blame a little, but leaves it with television still. Yet every newspaper and magazine in which I saw a report on the Peshawar demo either took the same line, or allowed its readers to assume that big trouble was indeed on the way. After all, big crowds don't gather to burn people in effigy if they just feel a little riled about something.

In other words, the fault lay not with television alone, but with just about every medium which dealt with the subject. There wasn't any problem with the facts: how many people took part, what they did, how many arrests there were, and so on. That was all fine. The problem was one of interpretation: what does a demonstration like this mean? How strongly do these people really respond to the likelihood of an American attack on Afghanistan? What is the link between their present actions and their likely intentions? And how much is all this a generalized reaction to a sense of vulnerability to the power of the United States, which most Third World people (and some First World ones) feel has no interest in their concerns?

If the world's media had paid a little more attention to the actual behaviour of the crowd, and a little less to the expectations they habitually bring to bear on something like this, they might have got it right. It's a little like Sherlock Holmes reproving Dr Watson: 'You see, my dear Watson, but you do not observe.' The mote – or maybe it's a beam – lies not so much in the eye of one particular medium; it lies in the generalized cultural make-up of people who half expect alien religions and alien cultures to be hostile to them. When we watched the pictures of the Peshawar demonstrators, we saw what we expected to see, rather than what the pictures actually showed us.

There are, of course, very real problems about the use of television pictures. They are indeed worth a thousand words apiece, in that they give a far more intense feeling about what is going on than any newspaper article could possibly achieve. Which of us has not seen television pictures of violence from some city where we know a relative or friend of ours to be, and has not felt anxious about them? And, conversely, who has not been in some city where some act of violence has taken place, often miles away, which we scarcely noticed, and has not been irritated to get anxious inquiries about our safety from relatives and friends?

An extreme form of this is the frequent response of Americans (but it can perfectly well be that of Europeans too) when something bad happens in a particular region. I was once staying on a game reserve in the South African bush, and got talking to a couple of fellow-guests who ran a guest house in Cape Town. Wasn't this, I asked, a difficult time for them to get away? They explained that as a result of the recent bombings of US embassies in Kenya and Tanzania, all their American guests had cancelled their bookings. Dar es Salaam is 2,298 miles from Cape Town, Nairobi is 2,549 miles away, and there are seven or eight countries in between. No matter: someone is planting bombs in Africa, and Cape Town is in Africa; ergo Cape Town is dangerous.

Even worse is another response, natural to all of us. Television news pictures are specific and precise, yet we somehow manage to interpret them as being general. That's to say, we assume because a particular incident took place somewhere that it is typical of the entire town, city or country where it has happened – even though in our own particular lives we know this is not true. People in Belfast are justifiably annoyed when it is assumed their lives are lived out to the constant accompaniment of IRA bombs and bullets; Chicago has taken on a reputation as a gangster's paradise ('It was just like a scene from Chicago') because of a massacre that happened in the 1920s.

When you watch television news, you have to tell yourself con-stantly that you are watching a few quick images selected from one particular event – not a typical incident in a daily process. The trouble is, journalists from all the different media inevitably concentrate on the biggest or worst or most alarming facts, because that is what draws attention; and journalists want attention. The famous compe-tition on the sub-editors' desk at *The Times* to write the dullest headline (won by Claud Cockburn with 'Small Earthquake in Chile: Not Many Dead') is an illustration by negative means of the way in which journalism – all journalism – operates. News is exceptional, surprising, alarming, contrary to every expectation; it may be some-thing of a distortion, but who would want to find their newspapers or their television bulletins filled with items such as 'Nothing much has happened in Switzerland', 'Lack of any political crisis in Vene-zuela', 'No famous person got married, divorced, had a heart attack, or died in Hollywood today'?

Years ago now, a friend and former colleague of mine, Martyn Lewis, declared that there was too much concentration on bad news, and that the BBC should be reporting more positive items of news. The then Prime Minister, John Major, whose government and party were in the process of collapsing around him, said much the same thing: maybe he hoped that a bit of good news reporting would rub off on his fortunes. There was a fitful debate about it, carried on in terms of growing irritability by people like me; then, as with all such suggestions, it died away. The idea could never have worked, because it was much too manipulative. The only question that people who run news programmes should have in their minds is, 'How important is this piece of information?' – not 'Will this go down well?' or 'Will this make people feel better or worse?' Television news is not a kind of electronic upper, to be popped every time society feels bad about itself and is in need of a little cheerfulness.

What is genuinely both depressing and wrong, and this may be what Martyn Lewis really meant, is an unrestricted diet of doom and gloom. Apart from anything else, it feeds all those dreary old stereotypes: Muslims are violent, Africans are poor and hungry, Latin Americans can never get it together. But that is a criticism of the imagination and intelligence of the reporters and editors of a television news programme. It doesn't affect the principle that events have to be reported, whether they are positive and uplifting, or make you feel sick to death of the world you live in.

§

Here are some extracts from letters I have received in the last year or so from unsatisfied viewers:

> I know it is the BBC's policy to endorse the Euro and the Common Market, but must we have so much of it? I pay my licence fee like anyone else, and I do not want to have these things forced down my throat.

> Who decides in BBC that you always should attack Serbian people and our President, Mr Slobodan Milosevic? You nothing do but tell lies against him. You should be shamed.

> I was happy to read that you and your bosses were bombed by IRA. Now you know what it is like for Israelis day after day, year after year. The BBC encourages terrorism in Israel by supporting the Palestinians. Serves you right when it happens to you.

When I was a young reporter, I always wondered if there really was someone who decided what line the BBC should take on the big issues of the day; and when I was appointed political editor in 1980, at the tender age of thirty-six, I thought with a faint flutter of trepidation that I would at last find out. Someone would quietly take me aside and induct me into the mysteries. Over a pink gin at the Travellers' Club some shadowy figure I had never seen before, with leather patches on the sleeves of his tweed jacket, would puff meaningfully on his pipe for a minute or so. Then he would take out the pipe and begin.

'As head of policy, thought I'd just pass on one or two things for your consideration. Felt you ought to know we've decided to back the present government for a while, but if things get a bit tricky we'll probably want to shift over and give the other side a bit of help. Nothing too much, just enough to twitch the reins so they all know who's really in charge. Oh yes, and Europe: we're completely in favour of course, and want to push on as fast as possible with turning it into a superstate. Just keep in touch from time to time, and I'll let you know how policy develops. Good luck: you're going to need it.'

What actually happened was that one of my predecessors took me out to lunch and suggested that I should watch out for old So-and-so, who worked in the department and was a nasty piece of work who really ought to be booted out. That was all. No guidelines, no long-term goals, no views on Europe or Serbia or the future of Jerusalem.

Somewhere in the upper echelons of the Corporation, along one of those windowless corridors at Broadcasting House where, in the bad old days, the topmost management had keys to locked lavatories which lowly workers from the word-mines weren't allowed to sully, there does indeed exist a Head of Policy. As far as I know I have never met him or her, and have no idea who actually does the job. What I do know, though, is that he or she spends his or her days working out how much violence the BBC should show, how many 'fucks' we are allowed to use per square minute, and whether some leading television cook or sports personality is doing too much advertising and will not have his or her contract renewed. That, for the BBC, constitutes policy.

From time to time, the ambassador of Israel or some leading Arab country, or the head of some major lobbying group, or an EU commissioner will take people like me out to lunch, rather like the tweed-jacketed figure of my earlier imaginings, and will pour their complaints into our ears. We will be extremely polite, and occasionally privately appalled, and will promise to pass on the views of the ambassador or the commissioner to our colleagues. We will leave them with assurances that we are neither against them nor in favour of them, but are doing our level best to be objective. And they will go off down the street, still not believing us; but they will at least be able to tell their colleagues, or their minister, or whoever, that they left us in no doubt about their fury. And, no doubt, they will say that the BBC promised humbly that it would try to do better in future.

I never really know whether people at that level believe it when we assure them that we genuinely don't have an editorial line. I am absolutely certain that the writers of letters like the ones I quoted above don't. I have spent large sections of my entire career trying to persuade people that the BBC is as neutral as it can possibly be, and I don't suppose I have managed to convince any of them. In fact, as you read these words, I don't suppose you believe them either. 'Of course he's got to say that, or else they'd sack him,' you're saying to yourself.

The whole argument simply goes round in circles. All I can say is that with thirty-six years' knowledge of the outfit I can promise you that there is no policy. There is no line. There are only thousands of BBC journalists all labouring away in their different mediums, trying to make sense of what is going on; and not a single one of them is instructed, even in the most oblique way imaginable, to be in favour of the euro, or against Slobodan Milosevic, or the state of Israel. It may be, as its Chairman Gavyn Davies has suggested (though he regretted it immediately the words were out of his mouth), that the BBC is largely staffed by white, middle-class, university-educated people from the South of England; and it is perfectly possible that most white, middle-class, university-educated southerners are privately in favour of the EU, dislike Milosevic and Israeli tactics against the Palestinians, and take a broadly liberal view of the world. Nothing wrong with that, any more than if they hate the EU and support Milosevic or Israel to the hilt – as long as they leave their private views out of their broadcasting.

But do they? The evidence of listeners and viewers with strong views on subjects like these is often suspect, because they tend to be such supporters of one particular cause that the concept of balance and lack of bias is something they would find it hard to recognize. Yet they know whether or not they feel they're being fairly dealt with; and if they feel they haven't been, then it is the BBC which has a problem. Personally, I never mind if people dislike what I broadcast, because you are never going to please everyone if you are reporting on deeply contentious problems. What does seriously worry me is if they can demonstrate to me that I have been unfair to them and their point of view; and then I don't rest until I make good my failure.

Even here, though, I do not believe that good reporting consists merely of a bland recitation of contrasting positions: 'The Bosnian government claims that thousands of Muslim men and boys have been murdered at the town of Srbrenica; the Bosnian Serbs say the men have simply been taken away for their own safety.' Such reporting tells the viewer or listener nothing – it merely leaves them in a state of complete uncertainty. People like us are paid to stick our heads over the parapet, and to say what we believe to be the truth.

We are not expected to be moral eunuchs. As long ago as 1969, the director-general of the day, Sir Hugh Greene, said he did not believe the BBC had a duty to be even-handed between right and wrong; and he specifically mentioned the issue of apartheid in South Africa. At the time, of course, there were plenty of people in Britain who supported the South African government and its policies, and the BBC was always coming under attack for its 'bias' against the apartheid régime. The National Party in South Africa, which introduced apartheid, has long since ditched it and apologized publicly to the non-white population of the country for the wrongs the policy did them, so this scarcely seems like a live issue. But there are equivalent subjects today, and the Greene doctrine still applies: if something is clearly wrong – racism, for instance – we shouldn't behave as though it deserves equal time and equal respect.

Yet this is not the same thing as taking an editorial line, which is what most of the BBC's critics assume we do. The assumption is not altogether surprising. Newspapers have clear policies, and their readership knows what they are. Most newspapers are owned by someone, and that someone will usually tell his editors the line he wants them to take – on the euro, on the question of bombing Iraq, on Israel and the Palestinians. And even if he (it always seems to be a he) doesn't tell his editors in so many words, they know more or less what he thinks on the main issues of the day, and have to decide whether they want to contradict the views of their ultimate boss.

I am fortunate in writing for the *Sunday Telegraph*. Its editorial stance may be right of centre, but there is never any pressure on me as a columnist to follow the paper's line. In fact, I have the strong impression that the editor, Dominic Lawson, rather enjoys it when I take an independent approach. And although the proprietor, Lord Black, is inclined to tease me about my views when we meet, he prides himself on owning a newspaper chain which lets its writers say what they believe.

There is no Conrad Black at the BBC: no proprietor, no ultimate boss with a set of views. Of course the director-general is appointed by the board of governors, who are themselves appointed by the government of the day; and the government of the day always, it seems, has its battles with the BBC. But as far as those of us who work at the coalface are concerned, we simply do not get instructions to be favourable to one side or another in a particular issue or dispute. If we did, you can imagine how quickly the memo would reach the gossip columns of the newspapers.

It doesn't matter what I say, though: people who believe that the BBC takes an editorial line will always continue to do so. It would probably be too unsettling for them otherwise. Every time I look at a copy of the *Sunday Telegraph* to check how my column has been used, my eyes will stray to another column, by Christopher Booker. He believes, with utter certainty, that the BBC is a propagandist for the euro and greater European integration, and merely to disagree with him brings down bucket-loads of vituperation on one's head.

'For God's sake, don't take issue with Booker,' someone on the paper told me. 'You'll never hear the last of it.'

Christopher Booker is by no means alone. During the Iranian presidential election of 2001 I was interviewed for a programme on Iran's 24-hour news service.

'Are you prepared to talk about anything?' my questioner asked me politely beforehand.

'Anything,' I said, and the contest began.

I am very fond of Iran and Iranians, and was flattered that a television programme should spend thirty minutes talking to me. The interviewer proved to be well informed, and his English was excellent. Better than that, he had a real understanding of the way the world outside Iran worked. But he couldn't accept the idea that the BBC was a free agent where its reporting was concerned.

It isn't altogether surprising. The BBC Persian-language service was set up in 1941 to persuade Iranians to turn against their Shah, who was publicly pro-Nazi, and to accept his son in his place. I tried, of course, to persuade my interviewer and the audience that things had changed a little in Britain and the BBC since 1941, but I could see I wasn't getting anywhere. Even for the most cosmopolitan and intelligent Iranian, the BBC is the voice of the British government. Finally, the interviewer slipped the knife in.

'But the British government pays for the BBC Persian service. You aren't going to tell me that they just spend their money without getting anything back for it?'

It was a good point. I countered it as best I could.

'The British government isn't like the government of Iran. It spends its money because it wants to support British values; and those values include independence and honesty.'

I could see I had made absolutely no impact at all on my questioner, and I assume I had made even less on the audience. I wished, above all, that it were true – though I knew from my own experience how often the British government had tried to get the BBC to take a particular line in its reporting at times of difficulty: during the revolution of 1978–9 in Iran itself, for example. The bosses of the Persian service fought back hard, and did not give way; but the pressure was there, all the same.

Personally, I would be in favour of scrapping the government grant-in-aid which pays for the external radio services of the BBC; as long as it is there, it lays us open to the charge of being a tool of the British government. The fact is, of course, it couldn't be done without increasing the licence fee to impossible levels. We're stuck with it. But it doesn't feel good.

§

I talk a great deal about the BBC as though it exists entirely in isolation from the rest of the television industry. Partly, no doubt, this is because I have never worked for any other television or radio organization, and have contracted the terrible BBC disease of thinking that the BBC *is* television and radio; much as New Yorkers think their city is the world. The BBC isn't broadcasting, of course, but it is *sui generis*. It operates the largest broadcast-news organization in the world, and it maintains that, plus all its other activities, on the basis of the licence fee. If, as some of the more irreflective British politicians often advocate, the licence fee were to be taken away, the BBC would never be able to find anything like the same amount of money from advertising. There simply isn't enough to go round the commercial TV companies and supply the BBC as well. Why is it that the commercial companies are among the strongest defenders of the BBC licence fee? Because they know they would have a far harder time if they had to compete head-to-head with it for advertising.

As for the BBC, it would shrink alarmingly, and would have to concentrate solely on getting mass audiences. The licence fee is a nuisance and an anomaly, an expensive poll tax which has to be paid whether or not you want the services of the organization which benefits from it. Revolutions have sprung from such causes. Yet without it, the BBC would be a sad and decaying shadow of its present self. I never care when people who openly want the BBC to be abolished call for an end to the licence fee: they are merely being honest, since this is the best way to kill it off. What annoys me is when people who profess to support the BBC suggest that it is somehow in the BBC's interest to move to some other system of financing. That is dishonest and disingenuous.

But if it gets its money in a different manner from every other broadcaster in Britain, this doesn't mean that in the field of television news it is necessarily all that different: it is just bigger, that's all. When I talk about the independence of the BBC, and its concept of balance and neutrality, I don't mean that ITN and Sky and the rest somehow have lower standards, or are more manipulated by the government. On the contrary, I think all the British television news organizations share very much the same problems, and aspire to precisely the same standards of objectivity and balance. If the BBC seems to have the problems more acutely, that is because of its size and range, and because – in the past, anyway – governments thought it was more open to pressure.

Interestingly, the natural history of television news indicates that there is something in the medium which seems to enhance its independence. Earlier, I wrote about the pressures on newspapers from having proprietors with views that they insist on seeing in print. Sky has a proprietor; in fact, in Rupert Murdoch it has one of the most opinionated and interventionist proprietors of all. And yet I have never seen any real sign that Sky News is obliged to take account of Rupert Murdoch's opinions. There are all sorts of differences between the various television news organizations, but they are differences of style and tone. I have never seen anything remotely like the loaded reporting you often find in Rupert Murdoch's newspapers. You don't even get those plugs for other parts of the Murdoch empire: no equivalent of those little paragraphs which appear from time to time in the *Sun* or the *News of the World* about how good Sky is, without troubling to remind you that the same proprietor also makes his money from it.

This is partly because British television is carefully monitored, and all sorts of things that seem to be tolerated in newspapers are unacceptable on television; but I believe there are also things about the medium which make it harder for anyone to control – including, as we shall see, the people who edit and administer the programmes.

§

It always used to irritate me to hear journalists referring to real incidents in the lives of real people as 'stories', with all the connotations which the word brings with it: dramatic incident, neatly rounded narrative, a satisfying ending. Gradually, though, I came to realize that the most important function people like me could perform was indeed to tell stories: not in the sense of making up comfortable lies to keep the viewers happy, but of providing an accurate digestible way to make sense of the confusion and apparent chaos of everyday life.

But what constitutes a 'good' story – that's to say, a worthwhile and interesting one, which will justify spending the kind of money which a television news operation requires, and will make the viewers feel they have seen a satisfying and understandable account of a particular incident or situation? This, of course, is one of the key questions involved in the business of television news, and answering it correctly is critical to running any successful programme. Like the elephant in the old poem, a good story is something which is hard to describe in the abstract, but immediately recognizable the moment it hoves into sight.

Here, for the sake of it, is the abstract definition: a good story should be well filmed, with pictures that please and intrigue the eye; it should contain all the necessary elements to convince the viewer that it is true and accurate; it should interest or shock or stir or please or inform; and it should remain in the memory afterwards, feeding the mind and the emotions. All fine, and all utterly meaningless without concrete examples. It was to provide the concrete examples that I began to write this book. I wanted to explain to you what it is my colleagues and I are in search of when we head out into the world with a camera and a notebook; and what it is we hope to come back with when we are finished. No doubt my account will be deeply self-serving, and will provide me with plenty of opportunities to praise my own work and get my revenge for any slights and injuries incurred along the way; but if you have read any of my autobiographical books, you will be expecting that.

Let me start off with an example which I hope will demonstrate some of the qualities of 'a good story' in negative terms, by showing how I turned a superb and important event into something extremely dull. Back in 1979 I reported on Ayatollah Khomeini's triumphant return to Iran from his exile in Paris. It was a remarkable occasion in every way, made all the sweeter because the cameraman and I were instructed by the BBC in London not to board the Ayatollah's plane and did so anyway. (Why is it, by the way, that when these things happen, as they do from time to time, the people who tried to stop you doing what you knew was the right thing scarcely ever come up to you quietly later and thank you for having taken no notice of them? After all, we all make mistakes; with some of us it is the most consistent thing we do. Yet over a career of thirty-six years I can only think of one occasion when this happened, and I admire the man involved for doing it. In the usual way an embarrassing silence hangs over the entire incident for evermore.)

The Ayatollah's flight home was a frightening affair, made all the worse because our fellow-passengers were convinced that we would be shot down. Many of them claimed to welcome the opportunity to become martyrs for Islam. Having no desire to become a martyr myself, I found this profoundly annoying. We filmed a little on the plane during the journey, and interviewed Khomeini briefly. He wasn't what you might call a bubbly, communicative man at the best of times, and in fact turned and looked out of the window when I asked him a question. Then, since we weren't shot down, we filmed his arrival down the steps of the aircraft. 'Filmed' is the correct technical word here, since it was in the days before electronic cameras and videotape. While we waited for him to appear at the aircraft door we did that awkward thing known as a piece to camera, and recorded a commentary without having had the benefit of seeing the pictures. We handed our material over to someone else to be edited and transmitted to London. Some months later our report received a prestigious award of some kind.

That, I suppose, convinced me that what we had done was of pretty high quality, and when anyone congratulated me on the award I would reply modestly:

'Oh well, we only did part of it, you know. The other team who were in Tehran did the real work.'

I knew that was likely to be true, but I knew also how extraordinary and dangerous and frightening our side of things had been, and I was proud of what we had done.

And then, as part of the research I did later for a book on Iran, I got our filmed report out of the BBC library and looked at it for the first time. I was appalled. The word 'amateur' scarcely begins to describe my performance, and it can only have been because there were so few other television crews on board Khomeini's plane that our report was included in the entry for the award; there was a rarity value about our pictures, nothing more.

It consisted of the following. No proper beginning, just a few dull shots captured during the flight. A glimpse of Khomeini's profile by a porthole, and a grumpy word or two from him, entirely unintelligible. More shots of someone else looking out of a window. Then, suddenly, we were on the ground and I appeared, wearing a sports jacket that should never have been seen on television. I talked to camera for an absurdly long time, as we waited for the Ayatollah to come down the steps of the aircraft. Finally the old gentleman made it down to the ground and bowed to someone, and that was it. I pressed the 'off' switch when the report was finished, and sat back, embarrassed and angry with myself. How could I have turned in a report of such thundering dullness after one of the most vivid events of my entire life?

There are various explanations, but first among them is the fact that I was still new to television and knew very little about the best ways of translating experience to the screen. It certainly wasn't the cameraman's fault; Bill Handford was one of the best we had. But I failed to direct him properly. There were, admittedly, other problems: film required far better lighting than video, and we had no proper lights with us; the Ayatollah's officials had no great love for the BBC, and weren't prepared to put themselves out for us; and there was the general, vitiating feeling that we were probably going to be killed anyway, so there wasn't much point in making an effort. And of course I hadn't seen the pictures when I wrote the script, so I couldn't use words to underline whatever qualities they might have possessed.

Altogether, it was a screw-up. Worse, it actually detracted from the superb pictures of Khomeini driving in triumph through the streets of Tehran. It didn't exactly make me feel good to realize that the BBC had only won the award because the judges had been kind enough to overlook my part of the show.

What was really wrong with our report was that it failed utterly to give the viewers any real sense of what everyone on the plane had gone through: the anxiety, the sense of destiny, the fanaticism, the strange, inhuman calm of Khomeini himself, who said he felt nothing as he returned to his native country for the first time in sixteen years, the unpleasantness of circling for an hour or more over Tehran while the Shah's air force debated whether to shoot us down; then the tension of the long wait while Khomeini put off the moment when he appeared in the aircraft doorway and made his way shakily down the steps. It had everything that a good, even a great, story should have; and yet our account of it was wretchedly poverty-stricken.

It's the dullest of truisms, and seems to have originated with that unutterable bore Aristotle, but it's accurate all the same: a good story requires a beginning, a middle and an end. One powerful action sequence alone will rarely make a good story. Bill Handford, the cameraman who flew on the Ayatollah's plane with me, filmed some remarkable fighting when the revolution proper broke out a fortnight later. His sound recordist, David Johnson, had joined us, and the three of us were peering round a corner at the battle which was going on fifty yards away from us.

'This is going to win us an award,' David shouted above the noise of the automatic weapons.

'Don't think so,' Bill shouted back. 'Not enough other things to back it up.'

It was several years before I started to understand properly what he meant. A good story is just that – a story, a narrative that has to be told. It isn't enough to say, 'We were walking down the street when we heard the sound of gunfire and poked the camera round the corner to show you – this.' The viewers need to know who is involved. They need to have it explained to them why they should care about it. They need to see where the event fits into the wider scheme of things. They need to follow the event through. I don't think a story can genuinely be good if it doesn't have a sense of completeness, so that the audience can see the event you are describing as something separate, an episode in its own right.

When you achieve that, you have something worth more than rubies. Sometimes it can be a small and not necessarily important incident – but it must have a significance of some kind, which sheds light on a wider subject. After thirty-odd years of doing these things, a few random examples come swimming to the surface of the memory: some of them light, some of them terrible. But they all had the quality of completeness, which made them incontrovertible proofs of a much larger proposition.

For instance, during the Tiananmen Square crisis of 1989, which ended a couple of weeks later in massacre and horror, I felt I had to get out of Beijing and take a look at what was happening in the countryside. Although the Chinese Communist authorities seemed paralysed, they were putting a certain amount of effort into propaganda for the peasants. Perhaps they realized they had lost the cities – they had unquestionably lost the greatest of them – and wanted to reinforce their position with their basic supporters.

Somehow I got it into my head that we must visit a village which had never had any contact whatever with the outside world. I asked my translator for help. He was a middle-aged poet called Mr Tang who was widely suspected by our younger Chinese support staff of being a spy. I suppose he probably was: he certainly wrote everything we said down in his notebooks, but since he maintained it was because he was going to turn his experiences with us into a short story I refused to sack him. I saw him as a kind of Chinese Somerset Maugham, I suppose. Anyway, Mr Tang found a village some way beyond the Great Wall for us to go to, and we drove out to it one brilliant morning, with the May sunshine gleaming on the wet road.

Even as we approached, I could see this was the perfect place, surrounded by the craggy rocks and lone trees which feature so strongly in Chinese paintings. The buildings in the village itself probably only dated back to the start of Communist rule, but China manages to lay a wash of antiquity over everything and the place looked as though it had been there since the Han dynasty – except, that is, for the loudspeakers on every corner, which were pumping out hysterical-sounding speeches about the disastrous and treacherous behaviour of the students in Beijing: all part of the story, of course.

The headman of the village appeared. He was an elderly man with a small collection of dark brown teeth which stuck out at strange angles, and he seemed extraordinarily shifty. He looked mistrustfully at the camera.

'Ask him,' I said to Mr Tang, 'if they have ever seen foreigners here before.'

'Oh yes,' Mr Tang said in his precise, British Council-course English, after a few explosive, toothy sentences from the headman. 'He says many foreigners have been through this village.'

I wanted to yell at Mr Tang. Not only was he a spy whom I tolerated against all my better instincts, but he had failed to find us a village of the kind I had demanded. Still, I didn't yell at him because the camera was running – and because we had nowhere else to go now. Then a thought occurred to me.

'Ask him when these foreigners came here.'

'It was apparently in the thirteenth century,' Mr Tang translated, with his unexcited, even precision. 'When the Mongols passed through this part of China. They destroyed the village and killed fifty-seven of its inhabitants.'

Perfect. I didn't have to assert in my script that time moves with extraordinary slowness in rural China, that the past is a real presence; the headman had emphatically done it for me. He made it sound as though foreigners like us were always turning up here, disturbing the peace of the village.

He went on to say all the right things about the students too: how life had been improving in the countryside, and might now be wrecked by what was happening in Tiananmen Square. He even asked Mr Tang for his work number – the equivalent of his identity card – in the most menacing way. Altogether it was a perfect report: the pictures were stunning, and the impression remained in the mind long afterwards. You can't cut out a television report and pin it on your notice-board; you can't reread it and jot down the points it makes; you can't refer to it when you've half forgotten what it said. That's the great weakness of the medium. But there is no better way of conveying an atmosphere than a good and effective television report; and the atmosphere is what stays with you long after you have forgotten the precise detail of what you have seen.

Memories of other 'good stories' come to mind: the time in March 1991, for instance, when my BBC colleagues and I went to the ruins of the Assyrian city of Nimrud in Iraq immediately after the Gulf War to check the truth or otherwise of Saddam Hussein's accusation that the American bombing had damaged the superb monuments there. Normally Nimrud was out of bounds (we dis-covered that a chemical warfare factory had been built opposite, in the hope that the archaeological site would give it some protection from attack) but in the immediate wake of Saddam's defeat the authorities seemed prepared to let us go anywhere we wanted. They assumed he wouldn't last long. I assumed that, too; which shows how wrong you can be.

I asked the cameraman to keep rolling at all times when we reached the ruins of the vast ziggurat at Nimrud; you never knew what might happen. We were shown an ancient mud-brick wall which had collapsed from the vibration of an American helicopter which had hovered over the site, firing rockets at the chemical weapons factory. Fortunately the wall had been of no great artistic value.

'Can we see inside the shed?' I asked. The shed was enormous, and seemed likely to contain some of Nimrud's main treasures.

'Why not?' replied our minder, wearily. It was the minders' habitual answer at that time.

An ancient, ancient man in a dark grey dishdasha which may once have been white came hobbling out when the minder banged on the door. It didn't seem to be his job to show things to visitors; on the contrary, he seemed to want to tell us that we couldn't see anything. The minder spoke to him quietly, and money changed hands.

Reluctantly, the ancient man switched on the lights. Vast objects fifteen or twenty feet high stood under polythene wrappers, looking like icebergs. Some instinct made the cameraman switch on and start filming; which was fortunate since, with a surprisingly fluent motion of his arm, the ancient grabbed a corner of polythene and pulled it away.

You could hear our gasps on the soundtrack. There, in the light of the hurricane lamps, stood the most superb Assyrian figure I had ever seen: a gigantic eagle-headed creature grasping a kind of handbag and sculpted in the act of striding forward angrily to fulfil some dreadful curse. It was far better, far more real and menacing, than anything I had seen in any museum anywhere in the world. And it was coloured. I hadn't realized, though I might have, that the Assyrians painted their colossal figures. We saw others which were just the colour of their greyish marble, like the ones you see in the books; but this one was covered with reds and blues and purples, a ferocious and wonderful thing. And then the guardian of the place chased us out, taking the light with him. I don't suppose any Westerner will see it again until Iraq's leadership changes.

But that movement of the old man's on camera, pulling aside the plastic sheeting, stayed with me, and with many others who saw it, forever. If the cameraman hadn't been filming I wouldn't have asked the ancient keeper to wrap it up and reveal it again: I hate staging things, and he was the kind of old man who would never have done it again properly. He was too irritable. It was the clearest demon-stration you could imagine of the purpose of the story: to show that, here at least, the American attack had spared objects of sublime artistic value.

Neither these nor many, many other 'good stories' I have had the fortune to cover were particularly important in the scale of things.

So often when big events do take place, the cameras aren't there, or aren't running: the assassination of Yitzhak Rabin, the Israeli Prime Minister; the massacre at Srbrenica, when thousands of Muslims were murdered on the orders of the Bosnian Serb commander, Ratko Mladic; or the hijacking of the four passenger aircraft involved in the attacks of 11 September. What you see on television is usually the immediate aftermath, and we have to deduce what, exactly, happened at these key moments.

Many of us were close by on the night of the Tiananmen Square massacre in Beijing, watching from the balconies of a nearby hotel; but no Western journalists were in the Square itself, and even the video made there by one brave demonstrator didn't make it absolutely clear what happened. As a result the Chinese authorities have always been able to maintain that no one died in the Square itself, though we witnessed dozens of killings in the avenue leading up to it, and the final evidence does not quite exist to disprove their claim.

One of the biggest (it can scarcely be called best) stories I have covered was the massacre at Sabra and Chatila in Beirut, in September 1982, when Elie Hobeika's Christian Phalangists murdered hundreds of defenceless Palestinian women, children and old men. We had all the evidence we needed that a massacre had taken place, but some of the killings had taken place several hours before my team and I arrived.

Even in time of war it is quite hard to get pictures of the precise moment when something happens; that is why Robert Capa's famous, and famously questionable, photograph of a volunteer being shot during the Spanish Civil War has exerted such a fascination, as has the murder of Lee Harvey Oswald by Jack Ruby immediately after the assassination of President Kennedy, and the execution of a Vietcong suspect by a South Vietnamese officer. In the century when more people died violently than at any other time in human history, death became something we almost never saw. Nowadays the BBC's rules against showing violence are so strict that we would think long and hard about showing Oswald's murder on the news; and I am certain the Vietcong execution would be banned.

There are great television moments, of course. No one who watched President Nicolae Ceauşescu of Romania being interrupted during his speech from the balcony of the Communist Party head-quarters in December 1989 will ever forget it. The moment led directly to his overthrow. Five years later I went back to Bucharest and found the man who had started everything off. He was a thoroughgoing dissident who had been greatly stirred up by the brutal suppression of anti-Ceauşescu demonstrations in the city of Timisoara. When it was announced that there would be a big rally of support for Ceauşescu in the capital he went along, determined to make his mark.

As Ceauşescu was busy orating, he worked his way into the crowd of faithful Party hacks and started shouting, 'Timisoara! Timisoara!' The crowd around him assumed that this must be one of the official slogans designated by the Party for chanting at the rally, so they obediently took it up. That infuriated my friend, who threw every pretence aside and yelled out, 'Death to Ceauşescu! Death to Ceauşescu!' Even the Party hacks, not the swiftest of people, realized that something wasn't quite right about that, and they started pushing away from him in fear, certain that the Securitate would come in and start arresting everyone.

The resultant crush, with its screaming and shouting and breaking of banner-poles, was what attracted Ceauşescu's irritable attention from the balcony; he wasn't used to being interrupted, and he was a bad-tempered old swine. And since the occasion was being broad-cast live everyone in the country quickly knew that Ceauşescu was in trouble. It helped that Ceauşescu's head of security walked over to him and whispered audibly into the microphone, 'Time to go, Mr President, the crowd's breaking in.' In fact, it was all part of a much wider plot against Ceauşescu, orchestrated by (relative) liberals in the Securitate – but that's another story. Soon, the first television revolution was in full swing.

Yet, as the succeeding years have shown, the example didn't really catch on. Because television news is an unwieldy medium, needing time to organize itself and its equipment, the planners and organizers inevitably have to operate according to advance schedules and future diaries. Plots, massacres and assassinations do not appear on advance schedules and future diaries, and it takes a little time to get the cameras into place. Not too much time, admittedly; our reaction times can be impressively short nowadays. But enough so that the critical first incidents are often lost.

Sometimes, of course, luck and a little forethought can lead to spectacular results; and that makes 'a good story' in its own right. After the Russians shot down a Korean Air jumbo jet which had strayed over Soviet territory in 1985, the Politburo in Moscow stayed silent for an extraordinarily long period of time. Day after day followed, with no statement of any substance. Finally, Andrei Gromyko, the long-serving Foreign Minister of the USSR (known to the Foreign Office as 'Old Ice Bottom' in the days of Stalin because he would sit for so long at international meetings, saying nothing whatever), decided to go to Madrid for an East–West conference on European security. The camera crew and I felt that we must get close to Gromyko at all costs, and throw a question to him about the Korean airliner.

As we were driving to the conference centre we heard a loud braying of sirens behind us, and a column of cars overtook us at speed. The sound recordist suggested that we should follow in the line, and get into the conference centre that way. The picture editor put his foot on the accelerator and swung into the wake of the police car at the end of the convoy, and I leant the upper half of my body out of the window on the passenger side, like the cop in the car in front, and waved my police badge (actually, as far as I remember, it was my reader's card for the London Library). That got us all the way into the bowels of the conference centre, unchecked.

Then we queued up at the door to the hall itself. There were one or two other cameramen there with the proper credentials, but they were just there to get the requisite shots of the start of the conference. No one took any notice of us: as so often happens, a television camera was all the credentials we needed and everyone assumed we had a right to be there. The doors opened. The organizers had allowed ten minutes for the kind of filming the agency cameramen were there to do. I spotted Gromyko coming in at the back, and sitting down at his desk with 'USSR' on the sign in front of him. We walked up the steps towards him, not too fast because we didn't want to attract unwelcome attention.

'Good morning, sir,' I said, in my most ingratiating fashion.

Gromyko grunted.

'I wonder if I could ask you . . .' and I was off.

The extraordinary thing was that, after the days of utter silence, Gromyko immediately opened up about the Korean airliner disaster.

It was, he said, the Americans' fault, because they had used the aircraft to spy on Soviet installations (a suspicion that many people in the West harboured too). But, he said, there would be a thorough inquiry into the way the Soviet air force had handled the matter. He went on about it all for quite a long time; so long, in fact, that I wondered afterwards if the old fox hadn't been planning to speak to someone in Madrid about it, and we happened along at just the right moment.

Afterwards, I was stunned by what had happened. 'Moscow Breaks Its Silence' was the banner headline in the afternoon papers in Madrid, London, and most other capitals around the world. Most of it was luck, of course, but part of it was our determination to ensure that, if Gromyko did have something to say, we were the ones he would say it to. And although it wasn't 'a good story' in the sense of being a rounded narrative, it broke new ground.

It was a lesson to me in the practice of journalism, too. After that, I never thought of news as something that simply happened, and of which we were simply the passive observers. I started to think in terms of the end result we would ideally like to achieve, and then work backwards from there to see how we might obtain it. Of course, in the years since then fifty or more of my best-laid plans have gone wrong for every one that has worked; but those which do work can be quite satisfying.

'A good story': the phrase has an irritating touch of the nursery about it, as though real life exists merely to interest or amuse or shock the readers of newspapers and the viewers of television news. The fierce, unreconciled Marxists I used to know accused those of us who worked in the capitalist media of ensuring that the proletariat was lulled into its ignorant slumber. I don't suppose there are very many fierce, unreconciled Marxists around nowadays, and those I used to know are often employed by the very media organizations they used to despise. And thus the whirligig of time brings in his revenges.

Even so, I'm not sure their analysis was completely wrong, just blinkered and bigoted. If you give people an unrestricted mental diet of the private doings of footballers and actors in *EastEnders*, you are scarcely providing them with the information they need to understand their world and the things that are happening to them. And it certainly helps to keep a shadowy collection of international capital-ists in money, and therefore in power. But the Marxists weren't right to suggest that serious journalism was just another form of capitalist bubblegum. I would say, though I am an unreconstructed old Reithian, that those of us who have the job of providing people with information have a duty – the very word sounds embarrassing and outmoded in most ears nowadays – to tell them as much, as widely, as deeply, and as honestly as possible about what is going on in the world around them.

But this doesn't mean we have to bore them. Nor that we must keep them at arm's length, as though understanding the real world is only for people with university degrees, or a certain level of income. That's why, despite my occasional twinges of anxiety about 'good stories', I have spent my professional career looking for them. Because 'good' doesn't have to mean sentimental or phoney or stupid; a good story can be something which illumines the real world, so that it stays illumined permanently.

5

The Use of Words

Peshawar: Thursday 20 September

By now, the Marriott in Islamabad and the Pearl Continental in Peshawar had been turned into sizeable television stations, with guests arriving all the time to be interviewed on the large number of broadcasting positions on the roof, and the lobby filled with the comings and goings of camera crews. Hundreds of thousands of words were being pumped out in dozens of languages about the same very few basic facts. People who had previously been uncertain exactly where the 'h' went in 'Afghanistan' now passed as experts in its internal affairs.

I suppose it is only human nature to want to operate in clearly recognizable grooves according to set timetables, and television news, with all its logistical problems, runs more smoothly when it is well organized. And of course television journalists know how to seem believable, even when they have only just arrived on the scene. I do all these things myself. I still didn't like it, and I knew that Peter Jouvenal didn't either.

Watching him as he came into the lobby of a hotel filled with journalists reminded me of introducing a free-range chicken into a battery farm. As for me, I was acutely aware of how far we were from Afghanistan, and how close I had been for a while. True, CNN and the German crew which had been allowed into Kabul to report on the trial of the aid workers had long since been thrown out, which was something of a relief to my conscience. I made myself a promise: if ever I am remotely in the same sort of position again, I said, I will never leave while there is another television crew there – not unless I am physically carried to my vehicle and driven to the border.

I was more and more reminded of the situation twelve years

before, when large numbers of journalists had crowded into the hotels of Islamabad and Peshawar at the time when the Russians were staging their final withdrawal from Afghanistan, leaving behind them the puppet régime of President Najibullah.

In circumstances which I have often found myself repeating over the years, Jouvenal and I linked up with a mujaheddin group called Harakat-e Islami, which claimed to have infiltrated President Najibullah's much-feared secret police, Khad, and offered to smuggle us into Kabul to see this for ourselves. With great misgivings we accepted – and found that Harakat kept its promise. We had a tricky time of it, but we survived.

Now, in September 2001, I kept thinking how we might join up with Harakat-e Islami again. And, as though it was part of some master plan, I was awakened at seven o'clock one Sunday morning in the Pearl Continental in Peshawar by a phone call. The man at the other end had a heavy accent, but he told me that Harakat-e Islami's leader, General Sayyed Hussein Anwari, had heard I was in town and wanted to pass on his greetings. I mumbled something appropriate, and then thought the man at the other end asked me if I was interested in being smuggled back to Kabul as in the good old days of a dozen years before. At this point I started to wake up.

'Come to see us in our office in the city,' said the voice, and gave me an address. 'We can talk about it.'

I must have written the address down slightly wrongly, because Aziz had trouble finding it. Finally we ended up in a dusty side street filled with modern houses: expensive ones, by Peshawar standards, since they were four storeys high, and had a front garden guarded by a high wall. Car horns blared, boys shouted at heavily laden donkeys, flies buzzed around us.

'Must be this one, sir.'

Aziz pulled the loop of thick wire which did service as a bell-rope.

There was a pause. Then a small postern, four feet high, opened in the main gate, and a face peered out at us. I knew we had come to the right place.

Not that I'd ever seen the old man who was standing in the open postern. I just knew the people, the ethnic group, he came from. He was short, tough-looking and bandy legged, with a seamed wide face the colour of an apricot. His eyes were slanting and shrewd, and he was laughing pleasantly at us. I laughed back, and greeted him like a long-lost relative. Once, long before, Peter Jouvenal and I had trusted our lives to people like him, and had not regretted it.

In the entrance hall stood a dusty showcase full of photographs. The old man peered at them and showed his gappy teeth in a cackle: a younger Peter Jouvenal and a younger John Simpson appeared in several of them. Alongside us in the pictures stood a group of armed men, each of whom looked like younger versions of the gap-toothed ancient with us now. From their features, you might think they were Mongolians. Their distant ancestors had been, eight hundred years earlier; but these people came from deepest Afghanistan.

They were Hazaras, and I have always found them remarkably interesting. Most Afghans don't. They regard them as thieves and rogues, and their Shi'ite faith divides them from other Afghans, as well. They differ utterly in appearance from other Afghans, too – the tall, rangy, hawk-featured Pashtuns, say, or the dark, striking Daris who speak Persian. According to their own legends, the Hazaras are descended from the Mongols who invaded Afghanistan between 1229 and 1447. 'Hazara' (literally a thousand) is the word the Mongols used for a battalion.

Under Genghis Khan, the first Mongol leader to invade Afghanistan, they were the most ferocious army in the world. The Mongols didn't hold with cities, and enjoyed razing them to the ground. It was said you could smell their army a mile away. But over the centuries the Hazaras lost their ferocity and even their own language, Mogholi. Nowadays they speak a dialect of Persian, which Afghans call Hazaragi and they themselves refer to as 'Azra', and ten per cent of which is made up of Mogholi words.

One of the earliest Western travellers to write about them was Sir Alexander Burnes, who wrote in his book *Cabool*, published in 1841:

> The Huzaras state themselves to be descended from two brothers, Sadik Kumr and Sadik Soika, Sadik being a title among them. They are particularly mentioned in the annals of Jinghis Khan's wars; and 3,000 families are said to have been left by that conqueror, and 1,000 by Timourlane.

For most of the twentieth century, this sort of thing was looked down on by ethnologists as absurdly romantic. A Soviet ethnographer, N. Temirkhanov, insisted that they were simply a mixed-race group:

> [T]he Huzaras are the descendants of Moghol soldiers and Tajiks, the Turks, and to some extent the Pashtuns or Afghans (and possibly Indo-Iranians) . . .

Slowly, though, the older view began to come back into fashion. Scientists who had once dismissed the notion that they could have had anything to do with Genghis Khan began to listen to the Hazaras' own theories and folklore, just as Alexander Burnes had. They found that the Hazaras used the word *moghol* to mean well-behaved, decent; when they teach their children good manners they say: 'O *bachah, moghol beshi*', or '*Moghol bokhor*' ('Sit up properly, child', or 'Eat politely'). No other Afghans use this expression – understandably enough, given what they had to go through with the Mongols. They didn't find them that polite.

Some older Hazaras still address each other as O *couch-e Changhiz* ('O son of Genghis'). Many of their tribal names are connected to thirteenth-century Mongol commanders. The Behsudis, a big Hazara clan, seem to be named after one of Genghis's cousins, Bisud. Another clan is called Day Choupan; Amir Choupan was a Mongol general who, on Genghis's orders, settled his men in central Afghanistan.

But Hazara history has never been properly studied; Afghanistan's rulers have discouraged it right down to the present day. Many of their important documents and writings are held secretly. Nowadays what was once called the 'Hazarajat', the Hazaras' region of central Afghanistan, is no longer marked on the map. The Taliban were among their worst oppressors, massacring them and destroying their villages because they believed that, as Shi'ites, they were heretics. Although they came as conquerors, the ancestors of the Hazaras were much more primitive than the people they had defeated, and over the centuries the descendants sank to the level of an underclass: servants for the people they once terrorized.

Alexander Burnes, who clearly liked them, writes:

The Huzaras are a race of good disposition: but are oppressed by all the neighbouring nations, whom they serve as hewers of wood and drawers of water. Many of them are sold into slavery; and there is little doubt that they barter their children for cloth and necessaries to the Uzbeks. All the drudgery and work in Cabool is done by Huzaras, some of whom are slaves and some free: in winter there are not less than ten thousand who reside in the city, and gain a livelihood by clearing the roofs of snow and acting as porters. They make good servants, but in their native hills their simplicity is great.

During the Soviet occupation the Russians made great use of the Hazaras, on the Marxist assumption that they represented the true proletariat and would welcome the benefits of greater education and better jobs. They did – but that didn't make them love the invaders any more than most Afghans did. Many of them joined the underground Hazara resistance, Harakat-e Islami, and when the Russians pulled out in 1989 they continued the fight against President Najibullah.

An envoy from Harakat, hearing that we wanted to get into Afghanistan, approached us and offered to smuggle us into Kabul. They would, he promised, show us how deeply they had infiltrated Khad. He even undertook to have us driven round Kabul in the jeep that belonged to Khad's commanding officer.

It all seemed highly unlikely. Treachery traditionally plays a big part in Afghan politics, and it sounded as though they might want to ingratiate themselves with President Najibullah and with Khad by handing us over to them, in order to demonstrate their loyalty. And yet there was something about these tough little men which inspired trust and respect. Jouvenal and I talked it over, and eventually decided to put ourselves in their hands.

I have told this story more than once elsewhere, so I shall simply give a brief précis of it here. Our long and difficult journey to Kabul ended just before dawn one March morning as we crept between two government watchtowers while the soldiers in them fired off their guns occasionally to discourage infiltrators. The next few hours were as extraordinary as any I have ever spent. The Hazaras made good their promise, and the jeep belonging to the chief of Khad was indeed waiting for us.

A superb character called Abu Faisal, big and burly, with only faint signs of his Hazara ancestry, drove us round Kabul in it, with the radio squawking. We went past the presidential palace, the Defence Ministry, Khad headquarters. Abu Faisal even insisted that we should get out and walk near the long-abandoned British embassy, while Peter filmed us. Over the next three days and nights we changed houses frequently. We interviewed senior officers from Khad, who were moles for the Hazara opposition. On camera they wore scarves round their faces, of course. We even filmed the firing of a home-made missile at Khad headquarters, from close range. (It still missed.)

In the end, though, we were betrayed and were lucky to escape with our lives. Seven Hazaras died in the manhunt that followed, together with a Khad colonel. Abu Faisal himself was later shot several times in the chest, and only just survived. But we saw none of this. The Hazaras bundled us into a taxi driven (like most taxis in Kabul) by one of their supporters. Yet Khad even knew how we would be travelling, and all round us we could see soldiers stopping other taxis at gunpoint.

Somehow they didn't stop us. We slipped out between the watch-towers again, and just after we had passed there was a mighty outburst of firing, which went on for almost half an hour: the Communist authorities wanted to trap us inside the city boundaries, but they were just too late. Once again the Hazaras had been too quick for them, and had protected us at the risk of their own lives.

In the run-up to the battle for Kabul in 2001 Peter Jouvenal and I came across Abu Faisal himself. Despite his injuries he was still a giant of a man, and he threw his arms around me in a Hazara welcome which drove all the air out of my lungs.

'We did what we promised, didn't we?'

I nodded, unable to speak. Our instincts had been absolutely right. Genghis Khan's descendants were people you could trust.

And now, twelve years later, we were back with the Harakat-e Islami people again, looking at the photographs of that time. One of them showed a ferocious-looking Moghol figure glowering out at us and holding an AK-47 in one hand and a familiar-looking blue and green plastic bag in the other. I knew it well; in the darkness on our way into Kabul I had snatched it up to put my things in, not knowing what it was. It said 'Heffers Bookshop, Cambridge' on it in large letters. The picture had been taken after our escape from the city; fortunately Khad hadn't been big readers.

Still, times had changed. The Hazaras were now the victims of the Taliban, discriminated against and hunted. After the call I had received at the Pearl Continental in Peshawar that morning I had worked out all sorts of possibilities. Maybe Harakat-e Islami could smuggle me back into Kabul on my own, and I could do some broadcasting from a safe house with the videophone. It was a frightening prospect, but I knew the Hazaras would protect me if they could.

A senior figure from the movement was summoned from upstairs by the aged doorkeeper. We sat down in a room with pictures of Harakat martyrs on the walls. There was no shortage of them.

The moment he began speaking I realized I had misjudged the entire thing. Harakat had merely heard we were in town and had invited us round for a social call. It was nothing more than that. By the time the old man came hobbling in with a tray of tea and sweets it was obvious to me that there was no going back to the glory days of 1989. We made polite conversation for the rest of the time, waiting till the tea was finished.

'Sorry,' said the official simply. He knew what I had been hoping for, and how little he was able to provide.

We walked past the photographs in the hall, but I scarcely glanced at them this time. No one spoke for a while, as we left the building and got into Aziz's car.

'Where to, sir?'

Not to Kabul, I thought. Not yet, anyway.

§

In the early 1960s the BBC broadcast a famously disrespectful programme – what we used to call 'satire' but was really mostly knockabout comedy at the expense of the great and the good, and the not so good – called *That Was The Week That Was*. It's hard for me sometimes, when I see David Frost on television interviewing the great and the good nowadays, to think of how he would have dealt with them in those days. Nothing was beyond the programme's reach; and of course it was always getting into trouble as a result. It had a profound effect on the way many of us saw our world. I even fell in love with a girl because she looked like one of the stars of the show. And for years one quick, passing joke the programme made was remembered in a cautionary kind of way in television news. Even now, among the older British inhabitants of the electronic village, you sometimes hear references to it.

The joke was at the expense of the literalism of television news: the way in which, directly something was mentioned, you would see a picture of it. Mention the Palestinians, or France, or world hunger, and up come shots of demonstrating crowds wearing *k'firs* and waving pictures of Yasser Arafat, or the Eiffel Tower, or emaciated skeletal children, regardless of the coherence of the film, or the unities of time and place. It's the dullest, least imaginative way of giving people the news on television, because it is so formulaic; and it happens when there is a shortage of people and imagination, and an overworked and uninventive news reporter writes and records a script without thinking about the pictures which will accompany it, and an equally overworked and uninventive picture editor gets the recording and simply matches pictures to the words, regardless of coherence, quality, sense, or anything else.

The fact that you don't see this sort of thing too much on the BBC is partly due to a sketch on *That Was The Week That Was* in 1962. It was a spoof news item about the Conservative politician Edward Heath, who at that time had the ludicrous and outmoded title 'Lord Privy Seal'. The newsreader introduces an item about Heath, in which every single word is illustrated with a picture. So when his title comes up, there is first of all a picture of an old man in an ermine gown and a coronet for 'Lord'. Then a lavatory for 'Privy'. And for 'Seal' there is, of course, a large shiny black animal balancing a ball on its nose.

Nothing affects us quite as strongly as mockery, and the sketch drove that kind of literalism out of television news in Britain forever: or at any rate up to the present day, forty years later. Now only people in their late fifties (and there aren't many of us left at the BBC) even remember it; yet a few years ago I heard a young editor and a youngish reporter discussing whether a picture sequence was 'too Lord Privy Seal': that is, too literal and obvious.

The essence of television news is the interplay between words and pictures. But it's interesting how many television journalists think it's the words which really count, while the pictures are simply the background illustration: unavoidable, but a complete nuisance. The writers of song lyrics must sometimes share the feeling. Good quality television reporting, and there is quite a lot of it nowadays, cannot be done by writing an excellent script alone. The pictures have to be accentuated, their full meaning brought out and enhanced, if the report is to be effective. Sometimes you hear a reporter launching out into the purplest of prose, paying no attention to the pictures which will accompany it, and you know that he or she is off on some private planet which has little to do with communicating with the audience.

Not that writing to pictures means telling the viewer what they can see already. On the contrary: that's a wasted effort. If the American President comes bouncing out of the aircraft door with a smile on his face, you don't have to say 'He had a smile on his face,' any more than you need to say 'Then he walked down the aircraft steps.' But you can perhaps say he seemed full of optimism or was glad to be back or anxious to get going, or whatever the reality was, because that explains the fact that he's grinning.

The words should run parallel to the pictures, enhancing their meaning, and then intersecting with them at the key moments when something needs to be explained: 'There was a certain irony in all this, because the last time the President was here, the man whose hand he's shaking so enthusiastically now told the press that Mr Bush was an ignoramus who knew nothing about the real world.'

Personally, I found it very hard to learn how to write for television news. As a radio journalist who did a good deal of work for newspapers, it seemed strange not to be describing in words exactly what had happened. By comparison, writing a television news script felt like playing chess in several dimensions. But then television news is more complicated than any other type of journalism. That's its attraction. It requires far more effort, both intellectual and some-times physical, in logistical terms as much as in terms of investigating the event you are reporting on.

But the results can stay in the mind for years. When the Americans pulled out of South Vietnam in 1975, a few brave journalists decided to stay on in Saigon. They had no idea what might happen to them: in neighbouring Cambodia the Khmer Rouge would have put them to death in agonizing fashion. Might the victorious North Vietnamese army do the same? Among those who stayed were Brian Barron of the BBC and his cameraman, Eric Thirer. Thirer's pictures showed a tank barging its way towards the presidential palace. Barron's words, allied to the pictures, were just as unforgettable; and I, watching from the comfort of my sitting room, was on the edge of my seat.

> With the panache of a General Patton, the first North Vietnamese
> tank swept into Saigon. The men from the jungle had arrived.

The line about General Patton was simply good writing to pictures: the tank was bursting its way through the obstacles at speed. But 'the men from the jungle' was a superb touch. In five words it told you everything you needed to know about them.

But you have to be careful. Too much description, too many purple adjectives, and the words no longer complement the pictures; they swamp them. Understatement always seems to work better. Here is another famous television moment: Martin Bell at the scene of one of the worst massacres of the Bosnian war, in a burned house with corpses around him:

> What happened here can frankly not be shown in any detail, but
> the room is full of the charred remains of bodies and they died
> in the greatest agony. It's hard to imagine, in our continent and
> in our time, what kind of people could do this.

Sometimes it takes a few words to point up the significance of a particular detail. In 1999, for instance, Fergal Keane – one of the best writers the BBC has employed in my thirty-six years there – went to a hospital in northern Albania, where a huge flood of refugees from Kosovo had passed through. The pictures showed that in one ward, which was filled to overflowing, a single bed stood empty.

> It is overcrowded, and there is little dignity for the old. Last
> night an old man died, the empty bed a testament to a life that
> ended far from home in an anonymous room.

Sometimes what is needed is a sense of the big moment, and of the tension which surrounds it. Kate Adie has, I've noticed, a particular ability to sum up this kind of occasion. This, for instance, is the start of the NATO attack on Serbia in 1999:

> Earlier than expected. Bigger than expected. The attack was
> prepared at sunset from the ships of the US 6th Fleet in the

Adriatic. We could just make out the Yugoslav coast as the
unseen electronic countdown began.

Good writing for television, then, is a matter of enhancing the
detail, of hinting at the atmosphere. It always treats the pictures with
respect. Brian Hanrahan, who has put this quiet skill onto the level
of an art form, reported from Belgrade before the final downward
spiral of Serbian politics at a time when the political parties in the
former Yugoslavia were trying to reach a new accommodation with
each other. He was filming in the restaurant of the national parliament:

> Most politics in Yugoslavia goes on behind closed doors. It takes
> crises to force them ajar and give the public a glimpse of what
> the politicians are doing. And with more parties in parliament
> than tables in the dining room, it's an opportunity for endless
> intrigue.

Good television writing is also a matter of entering into the lives
of the people you are reporting on, and giving your audience a
glimpse of what it must be like to go through what those people have
gone through. All you need to do as a reporter is to show the pictures
and add a little context. Here, for instance, is David Shukman in
Sierra Leone:

> If the arms trade has a face, this is it. These people are victims of
> the civil war in Sierra Leone. Rebels attacked them with weapons
> that are sold in their millions every year, usually legally, but
> often not.

> Kanu is six. He was maimed by the same gunshot that killed his
> mother. There are so many guns here that, at times, you can buy
> a rifle for the price of a chicken. Every year around the world,
> guns kill more people than the atom bombs did in Japan. And,
> as ever, it's the civilians who are caught in the middle, while the
> dealers profit.

> [*Interview with Mohammed Sessie, a refugee*]: We will never
> forgive them really. We are really down on our knees, begging
> them to think twice, that we are the same human beings like

them. Let them think twice by not sending this sort of thing to destroy our lives here.

No need for Fleet Street adjectives like 'tragic', as empty of real meaning as a piece of orange peel is devoid of juice; the pictures give you the extent of the real tragedy, with children whose lives have been wrecked by the gun trade. Too many words dull the impact. What Shukman supplies is the sense, the context, and he leaves it to his interviewee to add the emotion. Frankly, it comes better from someone who knows from personal experience what suffering is, rather than from an outsider.

Sometimes what is necessary is to give a full sense of the drama and violence of an occasion. Ben Brown won an award for this graphic piece of reporting on rioting in Jerusalem in October 2000:

Friday prayers in Jerusalem. At first they looked peaceful enough, but there were fears they could spark off more fighting, and they did. Palestinians emerged from their worship, many clutching rocks. They were about to start a riot. They began by tearing down security cameras within the walls of the Old City: to them, hated symbols of Israeli authority.

Then they set about attacking an Israeli police station. Several officers were trapped inside, besieged by the rioters. With increasing desperation the policemen fired tear gas, trying to drive back the protestors. It didn't work. The protestors kept inching closer. They even managed to break the lock, so the policemen couldn't escape. A fire was burning inside, and I could hear them screaming for help.

Israeli reinforcements arrived and tried to shoot open the police station door. Still they couldn't get in. Colleagues provided covering fire, while Palestinians kept up their onslaught. Eventually the trapped Israeli policemen staggered out, spluttering from the smoke. They'd been lucky to escape with their lives.

The Palestinians had promised that this would be a day of rage, and they've been true to their word.

Allan Little is a distinguished radio correspondent who made the change to television. He has a fine, highly developed style of his own, full of passion and meaning, but I sometimes wondered how it would transfer to the terser medium of television. The answer was, it transferred remarkably well because his concern is never to try to show us how clever he is; the complexity of his writing reflects an awareness of the complexities of the things he is reporting on. Here he is, for instance, at the funeral of the corrupt former President of Congo:

> Laurent Kabila bequeaths this continent a legacy of chaos and fear. Fury, not grief, is the public sentiment here: the pent-up rage of years of state brutality. The sins of the father are suddenly, and in a literal sense, visited upon the son. At thirty-one, Joseph Kabila inherits his father's civil war. He finds himself at the heart of a conflict involving at least seven African nations.

Matt Frei is another excellent writer, with an enviable ability to come up with phrases which stay in the mind for a long time afterwards:

> While East Timor has abandoned all hope, the UN has decided to abandon East Timor.

> Listen to the sound of hunger.

> Another reminder that it was Indonesia that coined the phrase 'to run amok'. And Ambon is just one of a score of places where they are doing just that.

He made a memorable report in 2001 about a fourteen-year-old Afghan refugee who was working in a coal mine in Pakistan:

> Sultan's shift above ground has ended. That was the easy part. It's time for him to get below, with only this to protect him: a page from the Koran.

> The pulley plunges a thousand feet into the earth. The descent into hell takes fifteen minutes. No helmet, no harness and not much air. The bottom of the mine is an oven. The mine is worked from 7 a.m. to 4 p.m. every day, for a dollar a day.

> Sultan thinks he's lucky to be working here. That's the saddest part of this story.

The man who filmed this, Darren Conway, wrote a brief note about this assignment when it was put in for an award. It's worth reading, in case you think that the camera crews who work on these things don't really care much about the people involved, and are just interested in powerful pictures. On the contrary: Conway was evangelical about what he had seen.

> I probably broke every health and safety rule in the book, but the only way to witness what Sultan had to do to survive was to see it through my own eyes. To tell the story in any other way would have been unfair to him. In many ways Sultan represents all refugees in this crisis, he no longer has a home and lives a harsh life without much of a future to look forward to. I hope that this is portrayed through the pictures, but I also hope that the story will portray the strength and the hope that people who have been forgotten about for many years manage to grasp onto. That hope alone deserves our continued efforts.

Sometimes it is tempting to think that the best television reporting is all about these extreme cases: wars, disasters, child labour, gross misery. Not so. The best television reporting is the reporting which touches your understanding, which makes its mark on your mind. The BBC's political editor, Andrew Marr, showed right from the moment he joined (he had been, among other things, editor of the *Independent* newspaper) that he had a vividness of phrase and an ability to put over a genuine interest and enthusiasm about British politics.

I find them dull and parochial for the most part, but whenever I see that Andrew Marr is going to tell me about them I sit up, waiting to be enlightened and entertained. This was how he reported on the re-election of the Labour government in June 2001. Marr writes for the rhythms of everyday speech, which makes his delivery a pleasure to listen to:

> *Marr*: Still in his forties, here is the History Man: the first
> Labour Prime Minister ever to win a second full term.
> The size of his majority historic, the low vote that made it,
> historic. The scale of the job waiting in his in-tray,
> enormous. On days like these, you scrabble for fresh words.
> *Blair*: It has been a remarkable and historic victory for my

party. It is a mandate for reform, and for investment in the
future, and it is also very clearly an instruction to deliver.
Marr: Yes, an instruction, not just the gift of power.
Throughout the month-long campaign Tony Blair, family
man, has been heckled by a public angry at the sluggish
pace of change in schools, hospitals and the transport
system.

Marr has brought a sense of ease and freedom to the stiff
conventions of television news, and it is a real pleasure to hear him
using the kind of language he would use if he were talking to you in
the street or the corridor or the bar. After a session at one Conservative Party conference was over, he went up onto the podium to record
a piece to camera about the bravura performance of the then rising
star, Michael Portillo:

It takes quite a bit of guts to come and stand on a stage like this
and speak without any notes or autocue for the best part of an
hour.

Finally, one of the best television reports of recent times. In
1999, when he was reporting on the NATO campaign in Kosovo,
Jeremy Bowen went to the flat of an old Serbian woman, which had
been trashed by Kosovo Albanians. He gives you the details the
camera can't, rounds out the old woman's life so that she isn't just
another faceless statistic, and then makes a series of unforgettable,
unanswerable moral hammer-blows. It is, like much of the best
journalism, deeply disturbing:

The flat stank of urine and decay. Something was very badly
wrong. She said her name; she is seventy years old, and a Serb in
a place where Serbs are no longer welcome. She was weak and
confused. Her front door had been kicked in, the neighbours
said, by Albanian fighters from the KLA.

Her photo album was open: the family in better times. A young
Serb paramilitary, perhaps a grandson with a machine gun, and
her husband in the Yugoslav army in the Second World War.

She kept looking back. Then we realized the decomposing body
of her husband was in there with her. He'd been dead for six
days.

In normal countries you'd call the police. But in Kosovo there are no police. NATO smashed their buildings and forced the policemen, all Serbs, to leave. NATO's armoured columns provide overall security, not social services. Twenty-four hours later, she was still there.

This is reporting of the highest order, it seems to me: something William Howard Russell would have understood perfectly. It moves from the life of a single disregarded individual to the level of international politics in a few terse, underwritten sentences. And it is deeply discomfiting. As you watch the pictures and listen to the words, you are forced to consider what happened to the old woman and why; and about our own involvement in this entire campaign. And yet Bowen doesn't tell you what to think: he just presents you with the painful facts, then leaves it up to you to decide.

All the examples I have used here – and I could of course have used plenty more from my own colleagues, people of the calibre of Bridget Kendall, Orla Guerin, Adam Mynott, Adam Brooks, and a dozen or more others, and from first-class journalists at ITN, CNN or Sky – have one thing in common. Not one of them was formulaic, and the emotional undertone was never that of the routine, cynical tear-jerking you so often find in some other forms of journalism. During my thirty-six years in the job, the quality of reporting on the BBC has never been higher than it is now.

But there is a great deal too much dull, routine journalism on television, of course. Directly I hear a report which starts with an expression like 'They came in their thousands . . .' I know I am going to be offered tired, unimaginative goods. By contrast, when Dennis Murray began a report on a confrontation in Northern Ireland by showing pictures of riot police in helmets and body armour pouring out of helicopters into a field, he used these words:

A quiet, rural corner of the United Kingdom, at the end of the twentieth century.

Who wouldn't watch the rest of a report that began so thought-provokingly?

If a reporter's commentary begins 'Elsie Kennedy' (or it might be 'Ismail Khan' or some other name) 'suffers from . . .' some disease or 'is getting ready for work' or whatever else he or she is going to do, you know exactly what is going to follow. A shot-list of the report will go like this:

Elsie Kennedy does something around the house

Shots of something in the house, e.g. medical equipment, to explain the problem this story is about

An expert (doctor/scientist/lawyer) tells us what is wrong

More pictures to show how widespread the problem is

A junior government minister says that unfortunately nothing whatever can be done to help

An opposition spokesman says this is outrageous

The correspondent appears in vision and says it's all very difficult, and probably on the increase [see below]

Mrs Kennedy sits in the house looking at photographs of her 'loved ones' [see below]/makes a cup of tea with great difficulty/ pushes a child on a swing and looks off into the distance. This final section will start with the words 'But for Mrs Kennedy . . .'

['On the increase': Bob Friend, the presenter of Sky's *Nine O'Clock News* and a famous humorist, once jokingly listed the four all-purpose questions for an television interview. The fourth was, 'Is it on the increase?']

['Loved ones': an expression used exclusively by television reporters to mean close family members. Never known to have been said by a real person.]

There was a time when almost every television report about British politics would introduce an interview with a politician by showing him or her walking awkwardly and rapidly past the camera, clearly trying to remember (a) not to look into the lens and (b) to put the left arm forward with the right leg, and vice versa. Then, the instant the politician's figure cleared the frame there would be a cut so fast that no human being could possibly have stopped naturally in the time, to reveal the politician in full, animated flow of conversation.

Fortunately that particular cliché seems to have been laughed off the screen now. There are plenty of others; I know, because I have used them myself. But when you are watching television news, and one of these dreadful conventional reports comes along, you start to lose interest in the report the instant you recognize the signs; after all, if so little thought has gone into the construction of the news report, what are the chances that the journalism is going to be much more imaginative?

In one of his letters Anton Chekhov says of the dull, predictable dramas of late nineteenth-century Russia, 'If you see a gun in Act Two, be sure that by Act Four it will be fired.' William Goldman, writing about contemporary Hollywood, points out that when someone in a film pulls their wallet out to pay for something, they always have exactly the right amount of money in it; that when they drive to the office or the shops or the bank, there is always a parking space right outside; and that whenever a television set is switched on in the background, it will invariably start broadcasting a news item which is directly related to the subject of the film you are watching.

Those of us who work for television news also have our boring, predictable conventions. It is time to stamp them out. How can news be new if you know in advance what you are going to hear and see?

§

Here is the deconstruction of the script of a report I made in Jerusalem in February 2001, on the night of the Israeli election which brought Ariel Sharon to power by a landslide. It's a pretty run-of-the-mill account, and certainly nothing that would win any awards for good writing or exciting pictures. I have chosen it merely because the subject is a minefield, and because it raises particular issues of reporting and the use of material. I've tried to explain, as frankly and honestly as possible, why I said the things I did, and why we included the elements we did.

Pictures	Script
Ehud Barak, the out-going Labour Prime Minister, casts his vote	This is the election which will show that the old peace process is finally dead – and with it the hopes of Ehud Barak, the Prime Minister.

[*These were dull, predictable pictures to use for the opening of a report, which should be the moment at which you grab the viewers' attention and tell them that something worth watching is coming up. On the other hand, it is an election, and that means voting shots are pretty much unavoidable – and we hadn't yet got the result, though it looked (and indeed was) a foregone conclusion. So I went for the obvious start; the more especially since poor, doomed Mr Barak said the following three words here, which were certainly worth using, if only because of their indomitable chutzpah:*]

| Ehud Barak speaks | I'm not worried. |

[*Like most British television reporters, I much dislike three-word sound bites; they smack too much of American television, and are much too easy to miss. These three, however, were said very clearly, they were the only words he spoke, and they were full of irony.*]

| Crowd of onlookers and supporters | If not, he's the only Labour supporter who isn't. Mr Barak came in by a landslide only twenty-one months ago, promising peace. He's failed utterly to deliver it. |

[*These pictures were, frankly, little more than wallpaper; not something which I like to use, because you should always have pictures which mean something and are worth pointing up in the script. In this case, though, I had to explain – in seven seconds! – why Barak was going to lose. At least we didn't use one of those cutaways of cameramen supposedly focusing on the*] *action, which are invariably shot before the action has actually started and are completely phoney.*]

Ariel Sharon campaigning

By contrast his opponent, the old warhorse Ariel Sharon, has a ferocious reputation but has been promising in this campaign to bring peace – peace, that is, on Israel's terms. It's an unbeatable offer; if it can be done.

[*These pictures were several days old, but we felt we had to avoid using more pictures of people voting: that would be just too much.*]

Library pictures of Sharon

Last September he went for a walk on the Temple Mount in Jerusalem – sacred to Muslims as Al Haram al Sharif – and the current Palestinian uprising began. The resulting violence is likely to sweep Mr Barak away, and Mr Sharon into power.

[*I also dislike using library (i.e., old) pictures, because it breaks into the clear sense that you are writing about today's events; but in this case I felt we needed to remind the audience of Mr Sharon's involvement in the outbreak of violence in 2000. Not wanting them to misunderstand the pictures – some of our viewers might have thought that Mr Sharon had gone back to the Temple Mount – I both put in a date reference ('Last September') and we put up a caption saying when they were filmed. This section lasts for about fifteen seconds, which is probably too long for library pictures, but it was absolutely necessary to give both names for the area where Mr Sharon went. Jews would have been offended if I had simply called it 'Al Haram al Sharif', and Muslims would have been offended if I hadn't used the name.*]

Israeli settlers at a roadblock

In what are probably Mr Barak's last hours in government, settlers on the West Bank block a road, and the police move in to stop them. The settlers expect that under Mr Sharon this will all be different.

[*These pictures were our opportunity to bring the focus of the report back to what was likely to happen if and when Sharon was victorious; and the settler, though deeply hostile to Western television, makes the point neatly and in English that was reasonably understandable, if a little contorted. I disliked having to introduce him ('The settlers expect . . .') but felt that this was so important that I had to make it absolutely clear who was speaking; and by setting up his meaning, it would enable the viewers to grasp immediately what he was trying to say. If I had simply used another Aston ('So-and-so, Israeli Settler') the viewers' attention would be momentarily distracted from trying to make out his heavily accented words:*]

Interview with settler

Do you see all these soldiers? Sharon, instead of making them fight against Jews and settlers, will bring them to fight the Arabs.

Shots of the Old City of Jerusalem

Whether that'll happen or not, Mr Sharon does enjoy confrontation. In the Old City of Jerusalem, he owns a house right in the middle of the Muslim Quarter.

[*This was a change of gear, and a change of place. We allowed a second or two of street noise to intervene after the settler's last words, and my first words ('Whether that'll happen or not') were intended to do two things: they showed that all this was part of a discussion, an argument, which was ongoing – and yet they were undemanding enough for the viewer to be able to continue*]

*digesting the settler's meaning as I spoke them. He was the
witness we had called to give evidence for the proposition that
Israelis were expecting Ariel Sharon to be tougher and more
confrontational. What follows is one small piece of further
evidence for the proposition, which the viewers (with the settler's
words in mind) can then make up their own mind about.]*

House with huge Israeli flag

He doesn't really live here, but
there's a guard on the place
day and night. His Muslim
neighbours regard it as an
affront. But they're so
frustrated by Mr Barak's
failure to bring peace, they
insist there's no difference
between the two Israeli
leaders.

*[In producing the next three witnesses, I wanted to explain this
apparent lack of common sense. I had assumed that the people
we spoke to would express anxiety or anger about Mr Sharon's
likely election; it was a surprise for me that they should take this
line.]*

Palestinian interviews

1st man: 'For me, it doesn't
matter. I prefer Sharon.'

2nd man: 'Maybe it will mean
an end to the occupation.'

3rd man: 'I don't believe in
peace in this country.'

*[A fourth man told us baldly, 'Sharon is Hitler.' I agonized a
long time about using this when we started editing our report. It
was clearly the view of most Palestinians, given Ariel Sharon's
part in the run-up to the massacre of Palestinians at Sabra and
Chatila, on the outskirts of Beirut, two decades before; but this
remark seemed in the end to be far too strong, far too personally
offensive, and ultimately grotesque. It would take over the entire
report, and nobody would remember anything else about it. In
the end I decided to edit it out.]*

| More street scenes | That's a reaction born of utter despair. Nearby at the Muna tea house . . . |

[Another, milder gear change; having been seen speaking to the three Palestinians, I then had to get myself to the tea house, a little way away. So I didn't appear in the first shot.]

| Interior of tea house | . . . the regulars would probably have supported Mr Barak's efforts in the past. |

[I knew they did because I had been there and talked to them at various times in the past. But I didn't want to interview another group of Palestinians, because it would use up too much of our time and duplicate what the others had told us. I also had the feeling they were taking a harder line because they were speaking direct to camera, and were recognizable. I decided we needed to get that sense of anxiety about the future under Sharon, and here, because I didn't interview them and simply showed a wider shot of the group as a whole talking, they felt freer to talk about their fears; which they duly did.]

| I talk to a group of regulars | Now they too think Mr Sharon will bring violence and bloodshed. |

[Finally, a piece to camera; not because I particularly like to end a report on one, but for a couple of small but pressing reasons. Firstly, it was starting to get dark by now, and that would show in the picture. It would be too obvious if we inserted the piece to camera earlier on in the report, between sequences that were much brighter. There would be a subconscious sense in the viewer's mind that something wasn't quite right. Secondly, this piece of camera was intended to sum things up – and until we had spoken to everyone I genuinely couldn't be certain how to make sure the report was correctly balanced. As it turned out, what I had to balance was the sense that Mr Sharon would inevitably 'bring more violence and bloodshed'.]

More street scenes

The optimists on both the Israeli and Palestinian sides don't necessarily accept the idea that Mr Sharon's election means an automatic Armageddon. On the contrary, some of them even think it might be easier for him to bring about a negotiated peace. But it's hard to think that's altogether realistic. John Simpson, BBC News, Jerusalem.

As it turned out, my piece to camera was too meek and mild, and indeed the entire report was pretty undistinguished. But although I had to sum up the situation and the changes that Ariel Sharon would introduce, I didn't want to put myself in the position of making a judgement on Israeli politics – of suggesting that Ariel Sharon's election would prove a disaster, and that Israel's interests would have been better served by voting Labour. It wasn't my place to say such things, and it wasn't the BBC's. Palestinian and Israeli friends of mine who were involved in politics believed that if a deal were eventually to be done it would be easier for someone from the Israeli right to do it than someone from the Israeli left. Yet that seemed a little too optimistic to me: hence my final sentence. Given the car bombings of 2002 and the Israeli invasion of Palestinian towns and cities which followed, I'm glad I put it in.

§

Live broadcasting demands entirely different qualities from the kind of formal, carefully constructed reporting which I have been describing. You may not have much time to produce a two-and-a-half minute film, but at least there is a chance for second thoughts. Although picture editors don't like it if you demand to re-cut or re-voice the early part of the report, if it has to be done, it has to be done. There is no going back over a live broadcast. Every word you say commits you; you are judged for every moment you speak.

Hesitation, faulty pronunciation, vagueness, uncertainty: these are the enemy of the live broadcaster. Some people can do it easily, others can't.

There are some wonderfully fluent live broadcasters, including the Dimbleby brothers, Brian Hanrahan, Jeremy Thompson of Sky (whose walk into Kosovo with NATO in 1999 was a high point of television news in recent times), Adam Boulton of Sky, and the doyen of BBC World, Nik Gowing. I have particular respect for Nik's intellectual range and grasp of international politics. One of the most impressive live broadcasters I have ever come across is Lyse Doucet, the presenter of various programmes on BBC World and the World Service: virtually unknown in Britain itself, yet one of the most famous broadcasters everywhere else in the world.

Lyse is ebullient, great fun, hugely sympathetic, and full of a passionate energy that never lets her rest. She dominates every major occasion she reports on, through sheer knowledge and hard work. If you need to know the background of the ministers of finance or agriculture, Lyse will have met them and know everything about them, from the names of their children to their weaknesses for drink. As for the President, he or she will greet Lyse like a long-lost friend; to the embarrassment of other journalists, who will be left standing in the hallway.

She has a strange accent, which sounds part-Canadian and part-Irish, but she comes from an Accadian family in New Brunswick. The Accadians, early settlers in Canada from France, were chased out in a form of ethnic cleansing by the British in the eighteenth century, and drifted southwards. Most ended up in Louisiana, where they became known as the Cajuns. There are still apparently lots of Doucets in New Orleans, but Lyse's family returned home to Canada at some point, and now they speak English rather than French. Once, when she met Prince Charles in Beirut alongside all sorts of Palestinians who had been chased from their homes, she explained to him about the Accadians and half hoped to get an apology from him on behalf of the British nation; but he merely said something about history being so cruel, and wandered away.

Lyse is utterly fearless in her interviewing, yet she has a charm which makes it hard for people to resent her questions. Instead, they seem to try harder to explain themselves to her; I find it highly entertaining. Now she is a superstar to rival Christiane Amanpour – someone any politician has to take seriously.

She is at her best, though, at live presentation. I often wondered how, with the miniscule budget which BBC World possesses, she managed to persuade her bosses to get her the kind of researchers she needed, plus the autocue which none of the rest of us are allowed. Now that I have worked alongside her, I understand entirely: she does her own research, much better than anyone else could, and she has the ability to speak without verbal tics or verbal static, and has a simply phenomenal memory for names. There is no autocue.

In 2002, Zimbabwe held a presidential election. There was never any doubt that Robert Mugabe, who was becoming ever more dictatorial and corrupt, would win it, and he had the services of a particularly distasteful press adviser called Dr Jonathan Moyo. Moyo had once been an opposition intellectual, always good for a thoughtful analysis of Mugabe's descent into brutality; then he saw where his interests lay, and joined Mugabe's side. By 2002 Moyo, a cynical but still articulate figure, was in full control of the Zimbabwean government's information policy; which included deciding who should and who should not be allowed to cover the presidential election.

Moyo, of course, banned the BBC. It would always be impossible for a big organization like the Corporation, with a strong and active African service, to keep on the good side of a government like Mugabe's. Turning the knife in the wound, as he thought, Moyo invited ITN and CNN into Zimbabwe. We, by contrast, had to cover the election from South Africa. This might have been a disaster – except for Lyse Doucet.

She knew Zimbabwe, as she knew so many other countries, well. With her producer, and no one else, she established herself in the BBC bureau in Johannesburg, introducing special programme after special programme on the Zimbabwean election. The fact that we weren't officially allowed into the country didn't matter, because we had full access to all the pictures of the two big television news agencies, and we also had several teams working away under cover. Lyse dominated the airwaves with her interviews and her information; so much so that several Zimbabwean government ministers rang the BBC in Johannesburg and asked if they, too, could appear on her programme. And when the government decided to allow the polling stations to stay open much later than expected, it was Lyse who announced the news first: before the agencies, before any of the television organizations that were actually inside Zimbabwe. A government minister had of course told her.

At one stage I sat next to her in her small, overheated studio, being interviewed about the Mugabe I knew; and when the interview was over and the camera was switched off we sat and talked about our plans to go back to Afghanistan. And then she put her hand up and said there was someone in another studio she had to interview down the line. She turned immediately to the camera and without any preparation or forethought launched into a complicated introduction. She reeled off the complex, quadrisyllabic name of a leading academic from Harare from memory, announced him, and began to interview him. All this without having taken five seconds to get her thoughts into shape. If there is a better live broadcaster, I haven't seen one.

I quite enjoy broadcasting live myself, because danger is always so close. The slightest of slips, the least misunderstanding or misstatement, and you know you could be one of the most humiliated people in the world. Once, years ago, I answered a question on air by saying I thought Mrs Thatcher was trying to put some lead in President Reagan's pencil; it was only when I came out of the studio that someone explained to me this metaphor had strong sexual connotations.

In 2001 Britain decided to celebrate Holocaust Memorial Day for the first time, with a service and concert in Central Hall, Westminster, attended by the Prince of Wales, the Prime Minister, and a host of other people. The BBC asked me to present it. The night before, I suffered the severe pains of a stone in the kidney; a problem I have had at various times in my life. I crawled to Central Hall the next morning, and the poor long-suffering producer in charge was appalled. But it was too late to replace me, and anyway he was a resourceful man. He got a doctor in, who gave me a powerful painkilling injection, and the producer found me a bed where I got over the worst effects. By the late afternoon I was feeling fine, but the producer thought we should have a doctor on hand when we went on air, just in case.

He turned out to be a charming Middle Easterner, so elderly that he actually wore a wing collar. He examined me and declared me fit to run, and we went into the final stages of preparation for the big occasion. Then, ten minutes or so before the start, there was a brief pause.

'Do you have any pain?' the doctor asked.

When I told him I didn't, he looked so disappointed I thought I'd better give him something to do, so I said I had a headache. It was true, but only just.

'No problem; roll up your sleeve.'

By this stage I was checking through my final scripts and timings, so I absent-mindedly undid my cuff button and rolled the sleeve up. As I was reading, I felt a needle in my vein: the old boy had given me a pain-killing injection.

'Three minutes to air,' announced the charming and able production assistant sitting beside me. There was an air of heightened tension.

'This injection – there won't be any side effects, will there?'

'No, no,' said the doctor, 'only you will feel sleepy, that's all.'

'Sleepy? But we're just at the beginning of an hour and a half's live broadcast.'

'No problem,' said the doctor. But I thought he looked troubled, and he soon drifted away.

It was fine when we started, because the adrenalin coursed through my veins so fast it held the doctor's injection at bay. But this was an evening of cultural events as well as speeches and ceremonies, and during the first poetry reading I found my eyelids drooping. The production assistant kept looking anxiously at me. Then she came up with the solution.

'If you just keep going for another twenty minutes, there's a long recitation by the Israeli choir that'll last three quarters of an hour. You could take a nap then.'

I did. The solemn, gorgeous cadences of the choir faded quickly for me, and I lay on my broadcasting desk fast asleep; until the production assistant tapped my arm gently and gave me a cup of tea, five minutes before I had to make the next introduction. It all passed off well in the end; but the beauty and the danger of live broadcasting is that you never know until it ends whether it is a success, or the most embarrassing, dreadful failure.

§

The kind of interviewing you do for news is altogether different from the kind of interview a current-affairs programme wants. *Newsnight* or *Today* aren't usually looking for a brief, quotable, informative line from someone; they want gladiatorial combat. People with a strong view on something – politicians, spokesmen and -women, heads of big companies, union leaders and many others – come into the studio knowing that there will be single combat. They prepare themselves for this at some length and expense. Now, fortunately, there is a ban in most broadcasting organizations on allowing television and radio presenters to train politicians and industrialists in the art of being a successful interviewee; though a decade or so ago it was often possible to hire someone you might meet later across a studio table and get them to teach you how to say as little as possible graciously.

You can often see the signs that a politician, in particular, has been professionally trained in interview-technique.

There is the retort jovial: 'Oh, come now, Jeremy,' they say, full of false bonhomie, 'don't tell me you've fallen for that old chestnut.'

Or there's the retort democratic: 'I don't think the people of this country would appreciate it, John, if I announced government policy on the *Today* programme before I explain it to the House of Commons.'

Or there's the retort threatening: 'This is just typical of the negative, hostile approach you people at the BBC take.'

Nowadays politicians are taught not to accuse their interviewers of being biased against them; it never works, and it grates on the more objective, uncommitted people in the audience. But I suspect they would still like to do it. It was only about seven weeks from the last complaint of political bias against the BBC from the outgoing Conservative government in 1997 to the first complaint about it under the new Labour government, and both parties seemed to believe the accusation implicitly.

The fact is, the aggressive, no-holds-barred political interview is one of the great glories of British life: a way in which a check can be maintained on the pompous, the inept, the crooked, and the plain self-contradictory. It is quite hard for the traditional structure of British politics to put ministers and opposition figures on the spot in a way that gets over to the public. Parliamentary committees are often superb instruments for this, but not enough people watch the televised coverage of them or read about them in the newspapers. Sometimes leading politicians have found their careers going downhill as a result of a poor performance on radio or television, and virtually every single one of them deserved it.

The studied languor of Jeremy Paxman, the terrier-like determination of John Humphrys, the calm ferocity of Jon Snow, the sledgehammer blows of Tim Sebastian: these can, at times, be as publicly valuable as they are informative and entertaining. Michael Cockerill, who specializes in interviewing present and former politicians, once told me he thought his most effective weapon was simply not to answer a follow-up question at all, but just to sit there in silence.

'A lot of politicians can't stand it,' he said. 'So they start talking again, and quite often they say exactly the things they came there meaning not to say.'

Jeremy Paxman has a verbal technique which has something of the same effect: the non-question.

'How can you possibly sit there and say that?'

It works exceedingly well.

In the run-up to the election of 1979, one local Conservative constituency party started putting out some fairly dubious, near-racist literature. Lord Carrington, a splendid Tory grandee, who resigned as Mrs Thatcher's Foreign Secretary three years later because he had failed to foresee the Argentine invasion of the Falklands – the last time, alas, a British minister has done the honourable thing after a major failure – was chairman of the party at the time. He was interviewed by ITN's then political editor, Julian Havilland: himself a grand, charming and distinctly patrician character.

Lord Carrington took the line that this incident was of no importance whatever, and was nothing to worry about or even take notice of. Havilland was never rude, never accusatory, but equally he never gave up. Did Lord Carrington himself, did the Conservative Party, think that this kind of thing was acceptable in any way? If he didn't, why was no action taken against the local party? Lord Carrington, who had started the interview wondering wearily why so much fuss was being made about trivia, ended it by apologizing for the local party's actions and promising to root this kind of thing out of the party. It was one of the best and most polite interviews I have ever heard, and it made me think even better of Lord Carrington than I had before.

Maybe those days are past now. We live in tougher times, and tougher times need tougher interviewing techniques. It rarely worries me if Humphrys or Paxman or Snow interrupt the minister they are interviewing; after all, British politicians have all won their spurs in the noisiest and most aggressive parliamentary system in the developed world, where sometimes even maiden speeches can now be interrupted by heckling and points of order and information.

The era when a British government minister felt aggrieved if a journalist or a member of the public tried to question him or her about a matter of policy has, thank God, finally closed. In the first volume of my memoirs I described how Harold Wilson, then Prime Minister, punched me in the stomach in public on the morning of my first day as a news reporter because I dared to ask him if he were thinking of calling a general election. That was in 1970: not an unthinkably long time ago. Nowadays even the most deferential member of a political party would wince a little to hear the famous recording from the front door of 10 Downing Street in 1956:

> *BBC reporter*: Have you anything you wish to say to the
> nation, Prime Minister?
> *Sir Anthony Eden*: No, not at the present, thank you very
> much.

Nowadays we regard our politicians as working on our behalf, not as our masters telling us what we should do.

Some of them respond in kind. Margaret Thatcher, as I have noted elsewhere in these memoirs, was the first British Prime Minister whom you could approach in the street or in the corridor and ask questions of. She might ignore you, if she didn't like the way you spoke to her; but if she answered, she would do it at some length. I can't pretend I liked her much as a politician, though like everyone else I can see the benefits of her rule as well as the disadvantages. But I admired her. Apart from anything else, she didn't care what people thought of her.

Once, during a visit to India, she went with her press secretary Bernard Ingham, various detectives, her husband, and a group of travelling journalists to see an old British graveyard. It was badly overgrown, not being under the care of the Commonwealth Graves Commission, and it was gutsy of her to walk round it at all, given that her detectives were so worried about the possibility of snakes. I decided to ask her a question or two about some issue of the day, and she was giving her usual intense response, moving through the graveyard, head poking even further forward than her handbag. And at some key moment as she was talking she put her foot into a rat-hole and went down a real purler.

There was an immediate rush to help her up, and she stood up slowly, brushing off her knees.

'That piece of film never sees the air,' said Bernard Ingham to me menacingly. It has long been a familiar characteristic of Downing Street press officials to get the language and technology of television wrong.

And then came words for which I forgave the old girl a great deal.

'Oh Bernard, don't make such a fuss. I just tripped over, that was all. It doesn't matter one way or the other.'

Knowing her own strengths, her own support, she cared so little for the way she was seen that she had no problems at all about being seen falling over. Not many politicians would have said that; they are usually mortified by anything that shows them as awkward or clumsy. Of course we didn't broadcast the sequence of her falling down: what did it signify, anyway? But as we made our way out of the graveyard I went on asking her some tough questions, and she went on answering them.

The robust British attitude to political interviewing is not always appreciated in other countries. This creates occasional problems for people like me, in that our audience expects a firm interview while the interviewee – usually a person of some power or influence, and sometimes downright dangerous – is used to much milder treatment.

Grovelling to the great names of the world may ensure that they come back as guests on your programme, but what is the point of merely collecting well-known names if you don't ask them anything interesting? Sometimes, perhaps, the interviewers are star-struck.

Henry Kissinger, for instance, whose trial for war-crimes and for gross interference in the affairs of other countries may possibly take place at some future date (this, I take it, is one reason why successive US governments have been so resistant to the idea of an international court), is a beguilingly clever man who usually manages to ensure that he gets the softest of interviews.

Watching him appear on Ted Koppel's *Nightline* was one of the most depressing television experiences of recent times. A journalist with the background and intellectual capacity to take Kissinger on was content to let him state, largely unchallenged, his sanitized view of the dreadful things which had happened in the world during his time as the chief foreign policy authority of the United States: the bombing and subsequent collapse of Cambodia, the tolerance of Pakistan's brutal repression in Bangladesh, the encouragement of the coup in Chile and the disappearances in Argentina, the Turkish invasion of Cyprus, the Indonesian takeover of East Timor. This is quite a record, and Kissinger was involved in some way before each one of these things happened. When the opportunity arises to ask him about them, it seems a little sad not to take it.

Still, I know the attraction Kissinger can (or at least could) exert. In 1976 I went to a press conference he gave in Brussels, and was bowled over by him. Here, I felt, was a man with the range and scope and brilliance of a Bismarck. I laughed aloud at the things he said, and wrote down his clever aphorisms with delight. Almost every one of us at the press conference did. It made us feel as though we could feel the cloak of history touching us as it passed.

I was sitting next to one of the very few exceptions to this general adoration, a much older American correspondent called Mort. I'd learned a lot from him, and enjoyed his company. He had taught me that there were two types of journalists in the world, 'Gee whizz' ones and 'Aw shucks' ones. The 'Gee whizz' ones were habitually excited about everything and understood very little about what they saw; the 'Aw shucks' ones had seen it all before and weren't particularly impressed by any of it. On this occasion, despite my determination to be an 'Aw shucks' journalist, I reacted to Kissinger with full 'Gee whizz' enthusiasm. But I felt Mort getting restless beside me.

'Ask him about the bombing of Cambodia,' he whispered. 'That'll wipe the self-satisfied smile off his stupid face.'

A short walk to Kabul

A Taliban soldier. He has the eyeshadow, but not the nail polish or the high-heeled gold sandals. He didn't seem to think that by taking his photograph I was making a graven image of him.

Kabul under the Taliban. Most of the destruction was caused by infighting between the mujaheddin leaders from 1992–6. At least the Taliban brought that to an end.

The assiduous, thoughtful, deceptively tough Aziz in Peshawar

Peshawar, September 2001: President Bush is burned in effigy; yet the crowd's mood was nothing like as ferocious as the pictures suggest.

The author in drag. I am hunched down in the approved meek fashion.

Peter Jouvenal at a more relaxed moment on our trip across the border. I took this picture of him through the face-panel of my burka; hence the dark blurs.

One of our drivers in characteristic position under his Russian jeep during the long drive southwards to Charikar

A moment of victory: we have just reached the top of the Anjuman Pass. From left: Mohammed Shah, driver; 'Noel', driver; Kate Clark; Peter Emmerson; Peter Jouvenal; Joe Phua

Tony Rippon, our first security adviser, at Sar-i-Sang while Joe Phua takes the happy-snaps

Joe: one of the best cameramen I have ever worked with

Khalil, the translator we were lucky enough to find on the way

At Bin Laden Mansions. From left, Peter Emmerson, Ian Pannell and
Peter Jouvenal

Lunch with Hajji Bari. From left, Kate Clark, Hajji, me, Mardan from the BBC
Persian Service

Dinner chez nous. Andy Faulkner, our second security adviser,
is on the left.

Piece to camera with friend

I did ask him – but my question was much too soft. Had the bombing really been necessary, and why? Kissinger, of course, twisted a question like this around in his podgy white hands and tied knots in it. I simply couldn't follow what he was saying: I didn't know enough about the subject. So I didn't challenge what he was saying. I didn't even ask him another question.

'Too easy. You let him get away with it,' whispered Mort. 'Asshole.'

I realized Mort didn't mean me. But I also realized I had fallen under the Kissinger spell. That is how some journalists are; they are so desperate for recognition and acknowledgement, like ladies at a Jane Austen ball, that they are prepared to suspend whatever judgement they have in order to receive it. Journalists like Jeremy Paxman, who said once that his formula for a good interview was to ask himself, 'Why is this lying bastard lying to me?', find it much harder to get invitations to see the great man; which is much in Paxman's favour.

I am not, by instinct, a ferocious interviewer myself, but I appreciate it in others. A friend of mine in Jerusalem – an Israeli, as it happens, though I am certain that many Palestinians would have reacted in precisely the same fashion – told me what joy it gave him to watch a couple of interviews by the presenter of *Hard Talk*, Tim Sebastian, over a period of two days.

'I watched him lay into this government spokesman, asking him these terrible questions, and I thought, "This is like watching a Nazi interrogation – this is awful. How can this man be allowed to get away with being so vicious to an Israeli?" And then I watched him the next day, and he was doing the exact self-same thing to some Palestinian spokesman – just ripping him up into shreds and throwing the pieces away. And I think I started to see what you guys mean about the way you do things.

'This Tim Sebastian – he didn't take any sides, he just went for the jugular. And you know, I think it did these guys good to have done to them. They're gonna be more careful the next time they step in the ring. Not so smug, you know what I mean? They're going to think about things a little more carefully.'

If you have a journalistic culture which is quiet and peaceful and unobtrusive, where the interviewers are really part of the same system as the politicians, then you get one of two things: a political culture which is arrogant and doesn't have to explain itself, or a political culture which is dull and boring, and which ceases to be properly representative. I don't know which of these is worse; but I do know that it cannot easily happen if a John Humphrys or a Jeremy Paxman is around.

It is one of the pleasures of the morning in Britain to wake up and listen to John Humphrys interviewing someone. Knowing him as well as I do, I can spot the causes of his growing irritation. Sometimes it is just a word, a phrase, some initials used in a way that indicates that the interviewee and a few members of his or her inner circle know what it means, and the rest of us don't count. Sometimes it is a question of the interviewee's general attitude.

Then, whatever I am doing, I stop in order to give Humphrys my full attention, because he is going to go for them. And he does. It's a delight. And as someone who has come across a good few of the people who provoke his morning explosions, I know he is usually right. These are not innocents who deserve kinder treatment; they are pompous, or else they are trying to put one over on those of us who are listening. They are asking for a bit of a shake-up.

The Netherlands is a country I have come to love very much over the years. I like the neatness and politeness, the genius for compromise which makes it possible for sixteen million people to crowd into a relatively small area, much of it reclaimed over the centuries from the sea, the sense of modesty and calm. But time and again I have found the political structure intolerably cosy. The different parties are almost indistinguishable in their policies, and the journalistic culture is such that the newspapers, radio and television seem to think of themselves as being part of the same system. If any country needs a dose of the Humphrys-Paxman-Sebastian medicine, it's the Netherlands.

I first read about Pim Fortuyn in February 2002. He belonged to a relatively mild right-wing party, and was expelled from it for attacking conservative Islam and demanding an end to unregulated immigration. Then he stood in the local elections in Rotterdam, where immigrants from mostly Muslim countries constituted fifty-two per cent of the population according to some estimates, and he won resoundingly. Shortly before the national election in May 2002, when right-wing parties all across Western Europe were getting back into government, I went to Rotterdam to investigate some of the stories I had been hearing about Pim Fortuyn.

It was plain to me that he wasn't just a standard ultra-rightist along the lines of Jörg Haider from Austria, or Jean-Marie Le Pen from France; though neither of them were entirely standard, either. Fortuyn, who was openly gay, was critical of Islam precisely because it was intolerant of homosexuality. An imam in the Netherlands described gays as being lower than pigs, and this properly brought a fierce response from Fortuyn. Nevertheless it was plain that he was part of the general backlash in Western Europe against the comfortable political consensus which supported immigration and condemned anyone who questioned it as a racist.

As it happens, I believe that immigration is the lifeblood of a country, providing it with a constant new flow of diversity and richness. Britain has always benefited from the large influx of people from abroad, and in my own lifetime its cultural and economic life has blossomed as a result of the arrival of West Indians, Hong Kong Chinese, West Africans, East African Asians and Europeans of all kinds. But I understand that people have to be allowed to express their feelings about the changes that take place in their society. It is true that immigration from the Third World to wealthy countries is completely unavoidable; it doesn't happen as a result of some decision taken by politicians, it's part of the iron laws of economics. There is no stopping it, though it can perhaps be managed; but it has got to be discussed openly, for the health of society. In the Netherlands, it never was. The political and journalistic culture closed down any question of a debate on the subject. You had to accept the sudden changes that were taking place, or be regarded as un-Dutch and a likely extremist.

In May 2002 I went to Pim Fortuyn's house in Rotterdam: a pleasant oasis in an area nowadays dominated by large blocks of flats where many immigrants lived. He had some excellent paintings and sculptures, large numbers of books, a butler (like himself, unapologetically gay) and two spaniels. Also a press spokesman with a little moustache who seemed distinctly nervous, both of Pim Fortuyn and of me.

Fortuyn was being interviewed by someone inside the house, so the producer Paul Simpson and I, together with Steve Lammiman, our cameraman, decided to set up the gear outside in the charming garden. There was a small fishpond with no fish in it; a heron had apparently flown in and taken them all, I was told, as if this were some kind of parable for what was happening in the Netherlands. A local journalist was also there, waiting with some enthusiasm to observe and report on my interview with Pim Fortuyn. His Dutch newspaper and television colleagues never gave him a hard time when they saw him, he said.

'Dutch journalists are too polite, I find.'

It seemed to be my task to remedy that. The rougher approaches of British television had not yet come Mr Fortuyn's way.

The cameraman set up his gear. I sat in a delightful little rotunda while the great man's spaniels snuffled at my shoes and the butler poured me a cup of lapsang souchong, and we carried on waiting while the previous interview dragged on. Pim Fortuyn liked being interviewed, and usually took his time over it.

And then, finally, there was a sudden upheaval and he was with us: a tall, slim, elegant, energetic figure in his early fifties, superbly dressed, and entirely, startlingly bald. He looked like an eighteenth-century dandy whose wig had unaccountably fallen off. His head was shaven to a knobbly, mirror-like blue shine. You couldn't take your eyes off the man, and he knew it. He was a magnificent sight, but as menacing as a weapon made of blued steel.

'Yess, Mr Ssimpsson.' He had a marked sibilance in his speech, like Kipling's Kaa, and spoke as if we were continuing some pre-existing conversation.

There was something distinctly, deliberately, amusingly sinister about his conversation. I had met a good deal of right-wing people like him; he exuded a kind of jocular menace, as though he had already decided we were enemies but wanted to amuse himself before we got down to business.

I regard myself as an open-minded interviewer. There are questions that have to be asked, and will be asked, but I reserve the right to decide whether or not I like the person sitting opposite me, and I do not do so on the basis of some form of political correctness. In my time I have taken to some unlikely characters: Ayatollah Khomeini, Colonel Gadhafi, more than one warlord in the former Yugoslavia and in Afghanistan. I even used to enjoy interviewing Margaret Thatcher, though you had to be on your toes with her.

Pim Fortuyn didn't match their standard. Perhaps he hadn't been in politics long enough: the three months since February, when he became a figure of national importance, were scarcely enough to give him much experience. And anyway the Dutch reporters had been remarkably unconfrontational. He did nothing to hide his contempt for the journalists he met. With me, he was mocking, and more sibilant than ever.

'Ah, you are very famous, Mr Simpson. Everyone knows you are the saviour of Kabul. It must be wonderful to be so famous. Yes, Mr Simpson.'

We sat down in his rotunda, with his press secretary self-importantly beside him. Pim Fortuyn took absolutely no notice of him. His political party, the Fortuyn List, named all sorts of candidates, including the press secretary, but everyone knew there was only one name on it that counted, and Pim Fortuyn knew that better than anyone.

The first thing that struck me was his poor command of English. In a country where every educated person spoke good English, Fortuyn, a university lecturer and political commentator, spoke it quite haltingly. Was this, I wondered, why he seemed to have such a chip on his shoulder about the British, so unusual among Dutch people?

'You have not any more your empire, Mr Simpson. The British are thinking they are very important, but just following the United States in everything. They are not any more important. No more than those Dutch.'

He was, I felt, a little hubristic in answering my questions in a language he was not at home in. Yet I admired that in him, just as I admire Jacques Chirac for replying in English on the three or four times I have interviewed him over the years. Chirac's English is, frankly, of the meat-grinder variety, but it is impressive that he has the self-confidence to answer questions in someone else's language, and I admire him for it. The difference is that no one really expects a President of France to speak good English, and we are impressed when he does. The Dutch, by contrast, take good English for granted, and are offended when one of their own speaks it badly.

Pim Fortuyn, utterly unused to having his views challenged, quickly degenerated from his rather menacing charm to outright rudeness. It is the worst thing a politician can do, because it showed he was rattled. This being the case, I decided to head straight to the key section of the interview, a little earlier than I had intended.

JS: What's so bad about having people of different cultures in your country?

PF: Because it gives a lot of problems, because most of them cannot integrate because it is very difficult to integrate if you have not the same culture and cannot speak the language, then you have big difficulties to get a position in economics. So you stay at home, you are a member of the lower classes. You have a class system in England, you have lower classes and middle classes and upper classes. In the Netherlands we want not this system. We try to have one class. But now in the Netherlands we have a lot of guests that are trying to take over the house, and the owner of the house doesn't like it.

Humphrys-like, I was irritated by this idea of trying to 'take over' the house. I moved in fast.

JS: Forgive me, but that sounds very racist to me.

PF: Give me a definition of racism. You don't know what a racist is, because you have Negroes who are Muslims, you have white men who are Muslims, you have yellow men who are Muslims, so how can you connect the Muslim religion and culture with a race? Then you are very stupid, Mr Simpson.

JS: Well, thank you for that. But the last time I interviewed Jean-Marie Le Pen, he said very much the same thing. I know you don't like that.

PF: I want not that comparison with Mr Le Pen, and as you do it another one, then the interview is finished now.

This was just a tactic, clearly. He didn't want to break off the interview, and when I asked him another question about the comparison with Le Pen he answered it. There were two further occasions on which he threatened to walk out, but we completed a twenty-minute interview with him before he shook hands with me and we stopped.

Pim Fortuyn wasn't necessarily a racist at all, but he was certainly as insulting about conservative Islam in general as one or two conservative Muslims had been about him. He resented the comparison with Jean-Marie Le Pen, because Le Pen was a successor to Poujade and an apologist for Marshal Pétain, and clearly didn't believe in the historical reality of the Holocaust. Fortuyn was passionately pro-Israeli and pro-Jewish. Above all, he was a flamboyant character who brought real colour into the greyness of Dutch politics. And unlike the country's journalists, he was prepared to talk openly about a subject it hadn't been politically correct to mention.

None of it really mattered. Our interview with Pim Fortuyn was broadcast on the night of Friday 3 May. On the late afternoon of the following Monday, someone fired six shots into that elegantly shaven head and Pim Fortuyn died almost at once in a car park at Hilversum. The police had never given him the bodyguard he believed he needed when he left his own city of Rotterdam. Fortuyn's murder was deeply shocking to the entire country, and well beyond; and you didn't have to like the man to realize that democracy had been seriously damaged.

His supporters started accusing the conventional left-wing politicians of being responsible for his murder, because they had attacked him. I myself received a number of emails, in an English similar to Fortuyn's, accusing me of sharing in the guilt for his death. And yet in the end it turned out that his murderer was an animal rights activist, who had killed him because of something characteristically sarcastic he had said about mink farms. Tough interviewing didn't kill Pim Fortuyn; on the contrary, it made him and his views famous. And if there had been a little more tough interviewing, and tough reporting of the issue of immigration into the Netherlands, Pim Fortuyn might never have reached such prominence in the first place.

'Don't you think,' an interviewer for a Dutch newspaper asked me after the murder, 'that if there had been less critical reporting like yours, there wouldn't have been a problem?'

I thought for a moment.

'No,' I said, 'I think that the more critical the reporting is, the better everyone and everything becomes.'

And I believe that very strongly.

6

Truth or Consequences

Islamabad and Peshawar:
Thursday 20 September and Friday 21 September

The Afghan embassy had become the most popular stopping-off place in Islamabad for Western journalists. They filled out visa application forms with obsessive care, handed over their passport photographs, paid their fees. I imagine the officials who ran the place simply pocketed the fees, and put the forms and photographs in the waste-bin. Once or twice when I went past the embassy I caught a glimpse of the fat official I had disliked so much before Abdul managed to get us to Kabul. He was in his element, strutting around and giving everyone instructions. From time to time the ambassador gave absurdly badly organized press conferences, which the world's journalists fought to get into and then fought to get out of afterwards.

Back at the Marriott, visas were almost the only topic of conversation.

'I think I've got a pretty good chance,' someone sitting near me at breakfast said. 'They know who I am, and they like the paper. We've always been fair to them, and they know it. So I'm just waiting and hoping, really.'

But of course the Taliban didn't read the Western press at all, and didn't care what was said about them. They were aware of the BBC slightly, but all that counted for them were the Farsi- and Pashtu-language services, with their large audiences throughout Afghanistan. Otherwise the Taliban existed in the seventh-century cocoon they had created for themselves. And it was perfectly plain to me that they had no interest whatever in allowing Western journalists to come stamping all over the country, looking for stories, alerting the Americans to possible targets, reporting on the position of women, and encouraging opposition.

Journalists find it understandably hard to come to terms with the fact that no one else much likes them or thinks they are a good thing. Even advanced Western governments go to considerable lengths to keep journalists away from their officials and their operations, and regard it as a serious failing if the press gets wind of what is going on behind the scenes. Since the Taliban saw no reason whatever for journalism to exist, 'the right to know' was a concept they couldn't understand; why should they? And so the chances that anyone whatever would get a visa were so small that it seemed to me that we, in particular, could forget all about applying.

That meant there was only one thing left to do: enter the country illegally. I still thought it might be possible to smuggle myself into Kabul; someone must be able to help me. Of course I would have to watch out for informers, and I would probably have to keep my head down until the Taliban government was overthrown. But it would be a fascinating story, and I would have recaptured a slightly better feeling about the way I had behaved.

Entering Afghanistan without permission would, of course, be illegal; but we journalists tend to feel that there is a higher law that justifies our going to countries where we are not officially welcome if there might be a decent story to be told. I myself crossed into Poland during martial law, and have entered Russia, China, the former Czechoslovakia, Iraq, Serbia and various other countries without the proper paperwork.

The more repressive governments, as well as plenty that are not repressive but simply rather fussy, usually demand that you travel to their country on some kind of press visa: something which takes time and a great deal of form-filling to obtain. Of course, the correct thing to do is to put in the necessary application well in advance, answer all the questions honestly about what you intend to do and how you intend to do it, and then wait for some jack-in-office to decide whether or not to allow you in. Somehow, though, life often seems too short for this kind of thing Still, if your papers aren't entirely in order, it is a really good idea to do your best not to get caught.

The Taliban were already warning journalists that if they were caught entering the country they would be subject to various unpleasant-sounding penalties; but it seemed pretty unlikely that they would catch us if we were careful. I asked Peter Jouvenal to get onto his contacts and work something out.

My basic aim was to see how far we could get, and whether it might be possible to go all the way to Kabul in relative safety. To me it seemed a distinct possibility, though I knew Peter had his doubts. Paul Danahar, the producer, did too. The best thing would, I thought, be if Peter and I went into Afghanistan on our own; Paul would have to do what he could to get us out if everything went wrong.

A few hours later, Peter had come up with the solution. A group of cross-border smugglers had agreed to take us over the border as far as we wanted to go. Their only stipulation was that we should go in disguise. As women.

I thought it was funny, of course, and almost irresistible. There were definite overtones of the pantomime dame and Charley's Aunt about it, but it would make a good story, in the sense of something you could tell your friends to make them laugh; and I have never been able to resist a good story. I could see the sense in it, too. Afghan women wearing the all-enveloping, face-covering burka (which Persian-speaking Afghans call the *chadoori*) are featureless and indistinguishable. This would not be *Some Like It Hot*: there would be no need for any of the arts of the female impersonator – no pillows down the front, no wigs, no make-up. The burka would do the job all on its own. It might even, I thought, get me to Kabul.

Aziz took us to the old centre of Peshawar. It is hot, dirty, crowded and noisy, and yet there is scarcely anywhere else in the world I would rather wander round. You feel the past as a real presence there. Once, making an edition of my programme *Simpson's World* in the bazaar, I came across a dish of old silver coins and found, among the chunky *dirhams* of Haroun al-Rashid's Baghdad and the bright, wafer-thin coins of Sassanian Persia, a shilling of Queen Elizabeth I. I bought it so I could brandish it on camera, to show how much of a crossroads the bazaar in Peshawar had always been; and ever since I have carried the Elizabethan shilling in my wallet as a kind of token of mysterious journeying. How and when could it possibly have reached the distant mountains of the Hindu Kush?

The surprises here are endless. One evening in late summer Peter Jouvenal and I were wandering through the winding, narrow, malodorous streets in the old part of Peshawar when we passed a tottering example of an old merchant's house of wood and crumbling brick dating from the early-nineteenth century. Nowadays these older houses are disappearing fast. People demolish them for their materials, and they make way for some featureless concrete box; Peshawar is not a sentimental place. As I looked up at the house, I saw it had a wrought-iron balcony running along the entire side of the building. Each wrought-iron panel contained a large portrait of Queen Victoria, copied from the head on the silver rupees you still find in large numbers in the bazaar.

The entire ultra-loyal display was presumably commissioned by some local merchant after what we call the Indian Mutiny, and the Indians themselves, with a lack of understanding of history which equals our own, nowadays call the First War of Independence. Pakistanis tend not to have the same hang-ups as Indians do about the awkward fact that their ancestors mostly accepted British rule and supported it without question; their problem lies with the massacres and wars which followed Independence. As for the house, I suppose it has been knocked down by now.

When we told Aziz we wanted to buy a couple of burkas, he was at his most Jeeves-like: not a hint of surprise or disapproval. And of course he knew a man who sold them – a friend of his, he said. He drove us to an area where Afghans did their clothes buying, and there in the dusty street, with a crowd of beggars and pedlars and sellers of fruit and general onlookers staring at us, he stood tactfully aside to let us do the business: far enough away so we could be private, close enough so that if we needed help with the burkas or the crowd he could be with us.

There was a slight problem: the burka-seller watched my programme on the BBC.

'Ah, *Simpson World*,' he said joyfully.

He started enumerating the recent episodes he'd seen. But he, too, was tactful. If two big Englishmen from the BBC turned up, wanting to buy women's clothes, it wasn't for him to ask why.

Tea came, of course, and gradually the crowd gathered in the street began to drift away. There seemed no point in excluding Aziz, so he had tea with us. Even now neither of them asked us what we were doing; and they never did.

When I explained that we wanted burkas to take home to our wives as presents, the shopkeeper didn't allow a flicker of disbelief to show. And when we told him we wanted to try them on first, he didn't ask us why, if the burkas weren't for us.

We wanted the largest in stock, we said. He hooked one down from a display near the ceiling of the shop. I put it over my head, Aziz whistling his professional disapproval at my clumsiness and adjusting it for me. Much too small – and my size-ten boots stuck out embarrassingly. Another few moments' fishing with the pole, and the shopkeeper found one which looked bigger.

Aziz lowered it over my head this time, and the panel of coarse lace fitted directly in front of my face, as it should. The little integral cap went tightly but not uncomfortably over my head; the shimmering, pleated, metallic blue burka billowed out all around me. I may be a large chap, but they put a lot of material into these things and it covered most of me rather satisfactorily. It didn't, of course, reach down nearly as far as it should, and the lower part of my legs and my boots were completely uncovered; we would have to do something about that. But when Aziz took my shoulders and guided me to the mirror, I thought I looked pretty good. I had vanished into the burka entirely.

Outside, the small group of onlookers who were left hooted and applauded sardonically; I bowed my head in acknowledgement, and they loved that. I felt like Old Mother Riley.

Frankly, though, I thought Peter's choice of colour was poor. Admittedly my metallic blue was the most common colour for women in Afghanistan, but at least it was attractive. Jouvenal wanted a hideously unflattering one in chrome yellow, and I couldn't convince him otherwise. But Aziz approved, so that was that. The shopkeeper folded them up into neat brown-paper parcels, we paid, and Aziz put them in the boot of his car. Our disguises might be ludicrous, the whole enterprise might be foolish, the chances of being caught might be too great for comfort, but at least we were ready for it.

We were very careful not to talk to anyone in the hotel about it, and we didn't let the office in London know what we were thinking of, except in the broadest terms. Paul Danahar took care of all that, anyway. I had spent so much time in Peshawar over the years that I was well aware how much interest Pakistani military intelligence, the ISI, took in the affairs of journalists. It was safe to assume that all our phones were tapped, and that several of the lone characters who sat in the lobby or the coffee shop, lingering over their sweet tea and their newspapers, were listening to our conversations. The sequel showed how right we were. Nor did we want to let any of our fellow-journalists know what was happening. The ISI might find out through them; worse, they might want to do the same thing.

I still had serious doubts about the whole business – its absurdity, as much as anything else. But the smugglers offered the most promising way to get back into Afghanistan, and going in with the smugglers meant dressing up in burkas. It would be distinctly awkward if we were caught: a general air of dodginess would probably hang over me for evermore. I knew how close that could come, and how dangerous it could be.

In 1992, after I had spent five weeks travelling round Peru with a *Newsnight* team, reporting on the army's involvement in the cocaine trade and humans rights violations, the country's Vice-President warned us privately that the security police were planning to plant some cocaine in our luggage when we left the country, in order to discredit us. I was worried: the newspapers in Britain would make a huge and mostly unsympathetic fuss about it, and no matter how much I insisted that it had been a set-up, a whiff of scandal would always linger around me. In the end, knowing that the Peruvians were listening to every phone call we made, I rang the BBC, the Foreign Office, Reuter's local correspondent, and the *Guardian* in London to tell them not to believe the cocaine story if it came up; and although several suspicious characters hung around us rather obviously when we passed through the airport, no packets of white powder or anything else were slipped into our luggage. It was a great relief.

§

If you work in television, you are constantly faced with issues of truthfulness and ethics. It is a difficult medium to work in, not least because it usually requires some form of acceptance and agreement by the people you are reporting on; less nowadays, admittedly, with the increasing use of hidden cameras, though these in themselves raise all sorts of ethical questions which must be clearly addressed.

Most Western countries take the view that journalism is a proper activity, which should be carried out without interference by the government. If that means you will say unpleasant things about the country you are reporting on, so be it: the wider interests of Britain, or the United States, or Australia will be better served by permitting full and proper freedom of speech than by preventing it.

Unfortunately, of course, this is not the majority view in the world. Most governments are nervous about the way they are portrayed abroad, and want to control the entry and movement of foreign journalists as much as they can. All sorts of countries which should know better demand that you obtain some type of press visa, which involves describing in some detail what you want to report on.

This often involves you in some form of deception. If you ask for a press visa for Malaysia or Zimbabwe, and explain that you want to report on the repression of the political opposition, you won't get one. Sometimes, if you are lucky, you can get away with some broad, unspecific expression such as 'Reporting on matters of interest and importance'; but it doesn't often happen. You mustn't, however, leave yourself open to accusations of bad faith, if only because there always seems to be a price to pay for it later. You always find yourself returning to the country you deceived, and meeting the person you double-crossed; and he or she is usually in an even more important and influential position than before.

Much better, therefore, to be honest; especially when it comes to interviewing someone. It is easy enough to grease up to someone and pretend you are planning to do some kind of flattering report on them. Everyone is vulnerable to praise and self-delusion, and these qualities are easy to play on. But the disadvantages are two-fold: it doesn't make you feel better about yourself and your job if you behave like this, and it will be distinctly awkward the next time you bump into your victim.

Within the BBC, there is a distinct difference of approach over this between the news and the current-affairs programmes. The people who work in news have to go back to the same countries again and again, and they have to bear in mind that some kind of ongoing relationship with the governments of those countries is unavoidable. Current-affairs programmes, by contrast, don't have to worry so much. Their reporting of a country's affairs is not a continuum, their budgets are smaller so they are unlikely to return for a long time, and they aim at the definitive statement rather than the latest top-up of news. In other words, current-affairs programmes go for broke, while a news team will be more inclined to tread carefully.

And so the people who are based in a particular country for the news feel distinctly uncomfortable when a current-affairs team is in town. Sometimes it is merely feathers which are ruffled: you may have to make grovelling apologies for a current-affairs reporter who has failed to show up for an interview with the leader of the opposition because someone more important and interesting had presumably come on the scene. On two occasions I have had to leave a country where I was based, after some big BBC current-affairs exposé made it impossible to stay around. Yet it would be wrong to complain about this: if a subject is of public interest, then journalists have a duty to bring it out into the open; and it is often easier for someone from outside to do it, rather than for a resident correspondent.

As a journalist, you must never allow yourself to be regarded as safe, tame, basically friendly, 'on message'. If governments are suspicious of you and uneasy about what you are doing, this is a badge of honour. Their officials must never be allowed to think they are entirely in the company of friends when they are with you. Your fundamental duty is to the facts, not to a government or a country: any country.

At the risk of sounding embarrassingly pious, the truth comes first; and if you are wondering what happens if your own country is up against it, and you have information which may not altogether help its interests at a critical moment, then read the following transcript of a conversation with one of the great newsreaders of the Second World War, Stuart Hibberd.

I remember Stuart from my earliest days as a news sub-editor in 1966–8; he was a friendly white-haired old character who used to prop up the bar in the BBC Club every lunch time, full of stories from the past and generous advice to anyone who wanted to listen. I wish now, of course, that I had spent much more time in his company; as the seventeenth-century biographer and antiquary John Aubrey wrote, 'I love listening to old men, as living histories.' At that age, I didn't love it as much as I should, and I didn't realize what I was missing.

In 1972, not long before his death, the BBC interviewed Stuart Hibberd about the wartime days when he had been the head of news-reading, and the kind of reporting the BBC did:

> It was objective news, not with any frills, just giving the people the actual position; just as in the early days when we gave out at the beginning the news of the war, we had to give out news objectively, good or bad. While we might in the tone of our voice say, 'Two more German submarines sunk', rather with a slight thrill in our voice, when it came to announcing our own casualties we didn't conceal them, but we said, 'Two of our et cetera, et cetera have been sunk too,' you see, that kind of thing. Of course, sometimes there was censorship on certain movements, but, apart from that, objective news, up to the minute, accurate, good or bad, was our aim.

Precisely; and although Stuart was an elderly man when that was recorded, and inclined to ramble a little, it is a statement of intent – a 'mission statement', as the dreadful management jargon has it – which Stuart's colleagues sixty years later would still recognize as their prime duty.

'Objective news, up to the minute, accurate, good or bad': a journalist for whom that is their prime concern, and there are many, is a dangerous person to have around. There are, of course, journalists who are little more than public-relations officers for the people, the causes or the countries they report on, but it's hard to have much respect for them. True journalists are natural members of the awkward squad, difficult, unpredictable, dangerous to be with, untrustworthy in the sense that you can't take them and their work for granted, impossible to buy off with money or honours. It is easy enough when you are in your twenties and thirties; but as you get older and more keen on recognition and a quiet life, there is a growing temptation to resign your awkward squad membership. At such times you have to remember the old Turks who never stop being a nuisance: Charles Wheeler, Robin Day, David Sells, John Humphrys, and half a dozen others who have provoked complaints and outraged letters to the newspapers at an age when other journalists are thinking of accepting some comfortable retirement job. Theirs is the true path of honour.

In some ways an openly hostile environment is easier to work in than one that seems outwardly friendly. Comparing notes with friends and colleagues after the end of the Gulf War, I realized that in some ways I had had it easier in Baghdad than they had, when they were reporting from the side of the Americans and their Coalition partners. The Iraqis always suspected us, and were always trying to catch us out. For them, we were the enemy; so there was no moral pressure they could put on us to keep quiet in the name of patriotism or the lives of our servicemen. (When this happens, incidentally, it is usually a sign that some senior military commander or politician thinks he may have got things wrong and is afraid that other people will start to find out.)

During the run-up to the Gulf War my television reports were censored heavily; it was easy for the Iraqis, because relatively few foreign television organizations were allowed into Baghdad, and individual censors could be attached to them. I came to loathe our censor, and things got so bad that eventually my colleagues used to make me stay behind when they took our finished and edited report to the television station for censoring. Part of the problem was that, although we were of course trying to say things we weren't allowed to, the censor thought his grasp of colloquial English was so good that he could detect all sorts of nuances that weren't there.

'Aha, Mr Simpson,' he once said. 'You see, I have found you up. Here you are saying "the President's palace". I know what you are meaning. You are trying to say that our President has many palaces and is very rich man. But you know well that everything in Iraq is owned by the people, so the palace not belonging to the President himself. You must change this to "the presidential palace".'

'Fine,' I said, not believing for a minute that there really was a recognizable difference between 'the President's palace' and 'the presidential palace', or that any of our viewers might think there was one.

But the censor was right in believing I wanted to get other

messages past him, and he missed a particularly important one during my time there.

> The demonstration was a big one, made larger by the school-children who were let out of class for the day and given flags to wave, and by their teachers who were given the banners they are holding in support of Saddam Hussein. There were plenty of other people who were encouraged to come out too. You could see them going through the motions.

I knew I was right about the general position. Schools, factories, office blocks were selected by rota to provide the crowds for the daily demonstrations, and anyone who failed to turn up, or who looked bored or gloomy, was liable to be punished harshly. But I was nervous about that last sentence of my report. It was the kind of thing that someone who understood colloquial English well would spot in an instant, and I might easily be told to pack my bags and go. Our censor's English wasn't that good, but he knew instinctively there was something wrong with what I had written, even if he couldn't quite put his finger on it. And since he boasted about his good English, that made it harder for him to ask me, or anyone else, to explain phrases he couldn't understand.

'What is this "going through motions" you are saying?'

'Well, look, Abdul' – his name wasn't Abdul at all, but it amused me to get it wrong every time, poor little man – 'you can see what they're doing: they're waving their fists in the air. We call that a motion. They're going through the motion of waving their fists in the air because they're angry at the Americans and the British. That's what I do to you every night.'

'Ha, ha, Mr John, but always you are trying to twist your words to tell lies about our country and our President. I think this is another one of the lies you are always saying.'

'Well, if that's what you think, Abdul, you will have to tell me what to put in its place. And you know how upset I get when you censor me. I will have to report this to the BBC, and tell them your name as well.'

I feel quite bad now when I write all this. Poor old Abdul: he loved the memories of his student days in Scotland, and was a confirmed Anglophile. All he was doing was trying to keep his bosses happy and his head on his shoulders. But frightened though he was of them, he was also frightened of the BBC. He shared the belief which is quite widespread in the Middle East and beyond, that the BBC somehow knew everything and was capable of announcing over the airwaves on its Arabic service that Abdul had censored us.

At the same time, I had a job to do: I had to let the viewers know that these demonstrations, which we filmed every day, were essentially false – choreographed right down to the slogans the demonstrators chanted and the clothes they wore.

'Well, Mr John, I am not very sure that you are being honest to me. I don't know this "going through motions". But let's look at the rest of your report, because you have said many other bad things.'

I relaxed: the sentence was going to get through.

But if the television reporters received special attention from the censors, newspaper reporters had it easier. Not at first; from August 1990, when I was allowed in, until early October, every phone call you made was listened to and would be terminated directly the secret police thought you were trying to say something you shouldn't. Slowly, though, more and more foreign journalists were allowed in, and it became impossible for the secret police to listen to the phones, so they gave up altogether. As a result I was able to dictate a weekly article to the *Spectator*, of which I was an associate editor, without interference. (This was in the days when the *Spectator* was a magazine for good writing, rather than simply a political vehicle for right-wing Conservatism.) And of course as time went on and nothing happened, I became increasingly outspoken.

I was allowed to stay on in Baghdad month after month, for far longer than any other Western journalist, because I had established a friendly relationship with a leading official who was also a strong Anglophile. I liked him; he had an excellent sense of humour. Once, a couple of weeks before the Coalition bombing of Iraq began, I took a colleague of mine to the archaeological site of Babylon; and that evening we went round for a meeting with the official.

'So what have you two been doing today?' the official asked brightly.

'I've been showing Mike the ruins of Babylon, so he can see what the rest of the country will look like in a few weeks' time.'

Christ, I thought – why must I say these things? I was too nervous even to look up. Finally, when I did, I saw that he was rocking with silent laughter.

One day – it must have been in early November 1990 – I had a call to go and see him. When I went into his office he was sitting at his desk with a pile of old *Spectator*s in front of him, each opened at my article.

'Oh, John,' was all he said.

It was an awkward moment, and my future in Baghdad was clearly on the line. I launched into my rationale, my *apologia pro mea vita*: that I was a journalist, and the only possible justification of my existence was to tell the truth as I saw it; and if that meant doing some writing under the counter, then I was sorry but part of being a reporter was that I would report whatever and whenever I had the opportunity.

I paused, slightly out of breath. The moment was tense: not because the Iraqis might haul me off to prison – they wouldn't do that – but because he could well throw me out, and I would have to miss reporting the war from Baghdad.

'But the things you say about our President . . .'

His gaze wandered nervously to the obligatory portrait of Saddam Hussein on the wall. Saddam was smiling; he wasn't.

'Well, you know how it is.'

He flicked listlessly through the magazines, glancing at my articles. There seemed to be a great many of them, and even I felt a bit embarrassed about some of them. I had rather let myself go on the subject of Saddam's bad taste, for instance.

'You write about a pleasant, highly intelligent official who speaks perfect English. Who . . . ?'

It was him, of course. I might be stupid, I might be reckless, but even I knew an insurance policy when I saw one. I told him, and his features relaxed a little.

'Please, John, try not to be so critical of our President in future.'

He pushed the *Spectator*s aside. The crisis was over. And I had nothing but respect for him for realizing that journalists were indeed dangerous people to have around, and accepting us anyway.

§

As it happens, I have myself been the victim of a deliberate misuse of television pictures. It was so obviously fake that you would have had to be a true believer in order to accept it as genuine. It happened in 1989, after the Tiananmen Square massacre. The Chinese government issued a propaganda film about it which, by the use of some pretty blatant editing, seemed to show me handing money to a student who – the commentary said – then went off and bought guns with it. The guns were duly delivered by the truck-load to the students in the Square, and that was shown as well.

In reality these picture-sequences were completely unrelated. What really happened was that some undercover secret policeman had filmed me autographing a book for some student and handing it back. The same student later had a meeting with some other people, and this was also filmed. Finally a couple of secret policemen drove a truck laden with elderly rifles into the Square. It was a clear and rather obvious provocation by the authorities, and directly it happened the students, realizing they had been set up, called in the ordinary police. They took the guns away immediately.

The video was a pretty crude piece of work, yet even so it must have taken quite a long time to put together. In news reporting there is never the time to do this kind of thing, and it would usually be far too obvious; even if you could find colleagues who would be prepared to do it. To be honest, I cannot think of the words I would use to ask a BBC picture editor to make a phoney, illegitimate cut in order to give the viewer a wrong impression.

Of course, I have often seen pictures which showed one thing being presented as though they showed something else: it's a favourite trick of autocratic governments to do that, in order to prove some point. Iranian television before the revolution sometimes used shots of a crowd at a football stadium when a goal was scored and cut them into reports about the public appearances of the Shah, to show how popular he was. Soviet and Czechoslovak television in particular specialized in using shots of gloomy Westerners queuing in the rain to show how awful life was under capitalism. It's a pretty stupid tactic; and directly it's been spotted by the viewers neither that nor anything similar will ever work again.

In the mid-1980s a big American television network offered the

BBC some pictures from the war in Afghanistan which purported to show an attack on a Soviet army position by a group of mujaheddin. The pictures had been the lead on the network's evening news the night before, and were accompanied by a commentary from the chief presenter which claimed they showed the greatest loss of life suffered by the Soviet army since the end of the Second World War.

Before paying the rather large amount of money the network was hoping for, the BBC foreign desk asked me to look at the pictures and say if I thought they were worth broadcasting. I in turn sought out a friend of mine, Dennis Clarke, who was a picture editor working for *Newsnight*. Dennis's judgement on video of any kind of weaponry was legendary. We sat down in his edit suite and he put the cassette into the machine; and within a few seconds he looked at me and pressed the 'Pause' button.

'This is just crap,' he said.

I'm certainly no military expert, but even I knew what he meant. All you saw were pictures of a shadowy group of men firing at a stone building in the half-light. At one stage an air force jet raced overhead, and there was some confused footage which showed mujaheddin soldiers celebrating.

'How long have the Russians been in Afghanistan?' Dennis asked me.

I knew it was a rhetorical question.

'And you mean to say' – he was starting to treat me as though I had brought the pictures in myself – 'that they haven't yet learned that you can't set up positions below where the enemy might be?'

I looked again: the supposed Soviet base was in a valley, and the mujaheddin were firing down at it from a ridge above.

'And when he says it's the greatest loss of life the Russians have had, where are the bodies?'

There wasn't a single body.

'And finally, take a look at this.'

He spooled through, found the shot of the jet passing overhead, and freeze-framed it.

'That,' he said with the air of a detective in a novel solving the mystery, 'isn't a Soviet aircraft at all. It's an F-14, American-made, and supplied to Pakistan. Whoever put this load of nonsense together just spliced in a picture of a plane because they thought no one would recognize it.'

I made the kind of noises you make when you knew all along that something was wrong; and soon afterwards I wrote something for one of the newspapers about the willingness of some senior people in American television news to put out blatant anti-Soviet propaganda.

An entire year later, a New York newspaper got hold of the story and someone interviewed me over the phone about it. I told him what I thought. The next day the newspaper printed the story on its front page, under the headline 'Brit TV Exec Slams Dan' – Dan Rather of CBS being the news presenter who had insisted on running this material. In the way of these things, the BBC's director-general, John Birt, had arranged to pay a visit that very morning to CBS for talks about closer cooperation with the BBC. The talks, not surprisingly, were frosty and came to nothing – though no one in the BBC ever complained to me about the damage I probably did.

And I wouldn't have expected them to. Broadcasting falsehoods in the news is the one crime which no one could ever seek to defend. I still remember the look of utter contempt on Dennis Clarke's face as he pointed out to me the different frauds in the video. I think I would undergo any danger, face any penalty, rather than have someone like Dennis look that way about something I had done. Dan Rather, though, is a remarkable and complex man, and his defence of proper journalism against the flood of infotainment and militainment that flooded over America after 11 September – and his assertion that patriotism isn't necessarily served by blindly following what your government says – commanded real respect. Everyone must be allowed an occasional mistake, or life couldn't continue.

Selective editing of television interviews, to make someone say something they didn't mean, is something you hear about quite often. Politicians and others who have 'mis-spoken themselves' or been criticized for something they have said are often tempted to suggest that the evil manipulators in charge of television news and current affairs have clipped their words to make them say something they never intended; and their party whips or bosses or shareholders are often willing to believe them.

In my experience, deliberately malicious editing of a television interview is so rare that I can't actually think of an example: though that doesn't mean there haven't been any. Most people don't necessarily know this, but politicians do – and, believe me, any politician who claims that hostile editing has made them say something they didn't mean is almost certainly lying.

What in fact tends to happen is that in the course of a longish interview they say something that, when it stands on its own and is given even greater emphasis by a noisy headline, makes a much bigger splash than they intended, or turns out to be uncomfortable for them. In these days of the quick edit and the sound bite there is no time for the careful build-up, the slow burn, which leads into a sharp but carefully disguised comment. The comment will, almost certainly, be extracted and made to stand on its own. So when someone complains about being edited, what they mean is they didn't want their words to be quite as stark as they finally appeared. But they said them all right, and it is deeply disingenuous to suggest they didn't.

It's often done, though, and it's a cheap shot. I know, because I've done something of the same sort myself, and have felt bad about it ever since. A local newspaper, during the course of an interview about my life and hard times, threw in a few questions about a particular local issue of which I was absolutely ignorant. This didn't, however, stop me from sounding off about the things the reporter told me: outrageous, unacceptable, that sort of thing.

The newspaper led its front page on my uninformed reactions, and when there was a fuss about it, I made the sort of noises about being quoted out of context, and not recognizing these things as being my words, which I have heard generations of politicians say. Actually I didn't recognize some of my words, but it wasn't very noble behaviour: I should have stood by the interview. And indeed after the fuss had subsided I decided I would never complain again if I were correctly quoted, no matter how embarrassing and awkward the consequences might be. So far I have kept my resolution.

Back in 1990, when the Soviet Union was beginning to break up, Peter Snow of *Newsnight* interviewed Boris Yeltsin, who was then metamorphosing into what we in the West would call an opposition politician; though at the time the Communist Party was the only legal political grouping in the USSR. He was deeply critical of the President, Mikhail Gorbachev, and of the Party's official line. The interview was broadcast on the *Newsnight* programme and the sound, in its original version, was broadcast back to the Soviet Union in the BBC's Russian language service.

It caused a sensation among the comrades, and Yeltsin was attacked not simply for criticizing the Party leadership, but for doing so on the airwaves of the capitalist enemy. His response was to deny that he had said any such thing; he insisted that the BBC had distorted his words, editing them in order to make him say something he had never meant. It simply wasn't true, and anyway the interview was broadcast in full, in Russian, by the BBC Russian service, so every Russian who heard it knew precisely what he had said.

But the Soviet Communist Party had become so used to accusing Western broadcasters of defamation and distortion over the years that it was easy to do it again; just as British politicians do from time to time, when the going gets rough. I can only think of one British politician in recent times who has stood by his words, no matter how embarrassing the comeback: the former Tory Chancellor of the Exchequer, Kenneth Clarke. And he lost the vote for the Conservative leadership in 2001.

§

Moral issues of all kinds abound in television news. The act of naming someone, or merely showing their face, can be enough to get them into real trouble. And although it can be very hard to persuade people to be interviewed, it is surprising how often they agree with no thought of the possible repercussions. Instinctively, of course, you want them to give their names and show their faces on screen, because this strengthens the value of your report; yet you have to be concerned about the possible consequences of letting their identities become known.

In the nasty little drugs towns of Peru and Colombia I have often had to persuade people that it would be in their interests if we filmed them from behind, or in silhouette, and disguised their voices in some way; and yet they would rarely bother to check for themselves by looking in the eyepiece of the camera to see that we had hidden their identity sufficiently. They had a rather touching trust in us, which we had to be sure we justified. If you know the television medium and the workings of the real world rather better than some poor *campesino* from the forests of Latin America, the onus is on you to point out the potential hazards of taking part in your programme. Fortunately for the making of good television programmes, there always seem to be people who are brave enough and angry enough to want to tell the truth about repression and violence.

And, curiously, the very act of coming out and making a stand, though it strips a person of their anonymity, can be a form of protection. In the old Soviet days, Russian dissidents quickly learned that by giving interviews to people like me they were providing themselves with the kind of prominence which made it harder for the authorities to victimize them, since the act of victimization would attract further international attention. Secret policemen are, after all, only civil servants. When I was followed around in Ceauşescu's Romania, the secret cops used to knock off at five o'clock sharp every afternoon, and leave us unfollowed for the rest of the evening; you could set your watch by them. And every civil servant knows that you must keep your head down and your nose clean, and not attract notice in the media.

The principle worked even in Peru, where we found that the army in some of the main drugs areas was working closely with the left-wing guerrillas they were supposed to be fighting, in order to protect the flow of coca-paste to the cocaine factories of Colombia, Mexico and the United States. After interviewing a particularly courageous local mayor, who decided that he wanted his name and face to be shown on television, we went round to see the commander of the military base who was involved in drugs smuggling and in the disappearance and murder of several hundred local people.

There was an awkward moment when he spotted that our camera, which the cameraman had left on the commander's desk, pointing at him, was actually running. But once that had been sorted out I made it clear to the commander that if anything happened to any of the people we had interviewed in the town, he would quickly become the most famous man in Peru; and although he understood that we were going to expose his activities, he must also have realized that it would make his position within the army much more difficult if he took his revenge on those who had blown the whistle on him. Certainly, nothing happened to any of our interviewees; and the commander was shifted from his lucrative position soon afterwards. That was quite something in Alberto Fujimori's Peru.

The judgements you have to make in such cases are delicate ones. Of course you can simply go for broke, and name your sources: but the consequences for those who have put their lives in your hands can be terrible. During the 1980 Moscow Olympics, which were boycotted by the Americans as a result of the Soviet invasion of Afghanistan a few months earlier, a member of the Afghan weightlifting team came secretly to a Western television reporter and told him that he and several of his friends were planning to defect. The reporter broadcast it, as the Afghan weightlifter had intended he should. The next day the Afghan Olympic team held a news conference to denounce the capitalist press for its accusations, and to deny that any athlete had spoken to the journalist concerned.

The journalist felt he had to defend himself. He stood up and pointed to the man who had come to see him, as he stood on the platform with the other Afghans.

'He's the one who told me,' he said. 'He's standing there.'

There was uproar, and the news conference was hurriedly terminated. The athlete and his seven colleagues disappeared, never to be seen again. In that case, naming the man most involved may well have led to his death.

Sometimes, every aspect of a news report seems to be hedged about with moral difficulty. In the winter of 1990–91 I took my daughter Eleanor with me to Moscow when I went to cover the increasing hardships caused by Mikhail Gorbachev's reformist economic policies. Eleanor was studying Russian at Bristol, and was acting as my (unpaid) translator. Everywhere you went in Moscow at that time a disturbing new phenomenon was appearing on the streets: old people were begging for a few coins. Having spent so much time in the Soviet Union, I was as shocked by this as were ordinary Muscovites.

We decided to find an elderly beggar, film him or her, and follow them later to the place where they lived. We didn't have to go far to find our first candidate: a woman in her seventies who seemed to be suffering from Parkinson's disease. She was standing by the corner of the National Hotel at the foot of Gorky Street, her head deeply bowed, her hand shaking uncontrollably as she extended it to passers-by in the hope of receiving a few kopeks. There were other beggars around, but they were gypsies and clearly belonged to one of the professional gangs which had recently been springing up. The old woman suited our purposes far better.

So we filmed her, at first without her permission. Then Eleanor went up and spoke to her, asking if she would mind if we met her that evening and filmed her some more. The old woman agreed. She lived rough at one of the big railway stations, she said. We fixed a time to meet her there that evening.

'Tell her that of course we'll pay her,' I said.

'How much shall I say?'

'Five dollars.'

I could see that Eleanor thought this was meanness on my part, and disapproved.

'OK, twenty dollars.'

The old woman's seamed face lit up with joy as I gave her the money, and she tried to kiss my hand; twenty dollars was an enormous sum for a poor Russian at that time. I thought it was too much, under the circumstances, but I wanted to impress my daughter with my generosity.

We went to the station that night. It was a vision of hell. Crowds of poor people seethed around in the gloom, taking advantage of the relative warmth of the place (it was a few degrees less cold than the streets outside) and, sometimes, of the opportunity to pick pockets. The floor was awash with the dirty water from melted snow, and the only alternative to standing up all night was to find a seat to sleep on. But there were only a few of them, and if you got up your seat would be taken instantly. The stronger, tougher-looking beggars occupied the seats. The elderly ones had to choose between standing or lying in the freezing water.

Eventually, wandering round in the half-light, we found the group the old woman had told us she was with. No, they hadn't seen her since the morning. It was unusual, they said – she was always here, every night.

The next day we revisited the spot where we had filmed her begging: she wasn't there, and the gypsies had taken over her place. In the evening we went back to the station, but she had never returned. It was then I realized what must have happened: the gypsies had murdered her for the sake of the twenty dollars. By filming her, I had drawn their attention to her; by paying her so much I had brought about her death.

Three years later I found myself in Rwanda at the time of the genocide by Hutus against the Tutsi population. On the outskirts of the capital, Kigali, we visited a large mental hospital. The doctors and nurses had all long fled, leaving the patients to sort themselves out as best they could, and the building had mostly been taken over by squatters. They had driven most of the patients away, but one or two had become violent and had been killed. Now the squatters had the hospital building virtually to themselves. They weren't bad people: they just wanted to protect themselves and their children from the patients, of whom they had an unreasoning fear.

We heard a strange moaning sound, which came from an out-house close to the main hospital. As we came closer, we could hear that it was the singing and cackling of a madman. He was talking of the sun and his thirst, and laughing manically at what had happened to him. The squatters, finding him too strong and too crazy to kill, had tricked him into going into the outhouse and locked the door on him. He had been there for three days. The drugs which had once been used to keep him under control had vanished, together with the doctors and nurses. Now the squatters were allowing him to die of hunger and thirst; and they gathered round as we filmed, laughing and joking at his antics.

I talked to him through the door; his ravings seemed to be in French. He could talk of nothing except food, water and the sun; cackling, pleading, weeping. I looked at the peeling, sun-blistered blue paint of the door and listened to him. It was, I think, the worst thing I have ever heard.

We had met up with a British psychiatrist who had come to Rwanda as part of a medical delegation to see the effects of the genocide. He was with us now, and I asked him what I should do; should I insist that the squatters let the poor man go?

'They'll just murder him,' said the psychiatrist; and, looking round at them, I could see he was right.

'But if he stays here, how long before he dies of hunger and thirst?'

'In this heat, maybe two or three more days.'

By now the man was sticking his hands under the door, gesticulating, beckoning, begging for mercy and for help with his gestures, and cackling and moaning all the more. The squatters had gathered round, and found it all killingly funny.

If we let him out now and left him here, he would be dead in a few minutes. There was absolutely no way of controlling him without the use of heavy drugs, which we didn't have with us and probably couldn't obtain in the whole of Rwanda at this time, so we couldn't take him with us. If we left him here, he would take three days to die in one of the most unpleasant ways imaginable.

I suppose the best thing we could have done for him under the circumstances was to have ensured he had a quick death. That would have meant opening the door of his death cell and setting him free; but he was still a strong man, and might have killed other people before they killed him. So I chose the cowardly option, the option that did nobody any good whatever, but simply saved my colleagues and me from witnessing any more horrors: I went to our vehicle and got all the water and food I could spare, and shoved it under his door.

He groaned and whimpered with pleasure, spilling the water, fouling the food on the disgusting floor of his prison. The squatters laughed louder than ever: it was part of the show for them. We left.

In my report I tried to be honest about the choices that had confronted us, and acknowledged that what I had done was an unsatisfactory palliative. It didn't matter, of course: I still got some pretty rough letters from viewers.

You heartless coward, leaving a sick man like that to die.

I wish to protest in the strongest terms about your irresponsible behaviour. You cared nothing for the suffering of the man you showed. All you wanted was sensationalism. I hope you are proud of yourself.

You had a duty to save that man's life, and you did not. May his ghost haunt you for the rest of your life.

Believe me, it does. I just wish I could be so confident about such things, so certain (on the basis of watching a television report lasting two and a half minutes) of the rights and wrongs, the blame and guilt in a particular situation. But I know what I did wrong: I chose the way that was easier for me and my colleagues to bear.

§

Television pictures may not necessarily distort meaning, but they can be deeply misleading. The fault doesn't lie in the pictures, but in the assumptions the audience makes when it sees them. To take a simple example, on the afternoon of 11 September 2001 an agency camera-man was out in the West Bank when the news came through of the attacks on New York and Washington. Quickly, a small group of Palestinians gathered in the street. There were, perhaps, eight of them. They started to dance and cheer at the news that America had been the target of a terrorist attack, and a particularly stupid-looking woman with oversized spectacles played up for the camera, dancing and waving her arms and saying that it served the Americans right for helping Israel.

The great majority of Palestinians I knew were stunned by the news of the attack, and realized immediately that it would do their cause nothing but harm. Many, especially those who saw the tele-vision pictures, were genuinely upset by what had happened; and even those who felt, privately, that the Americans had it coming to them kept silent about it, realizing this was no time to air such opinions openly.

But the pictures of eight or so Palestinians rejoicing went around the world. I must have seen them repeated a dozen times over the next few days. The human mind has a regrettable tendency to generalize from particular cases, and the assumption grew, especially in the United States, that Palestinian opinion was strongly in favour of the terrorists who had attacked the World Trade Center and the Pentagon. Over the months that followed, the US government some-times sided openly with Israel in its virtual war with the Palestinians, and President George W. Bush was always issuing strong warnings to PLO Chairman Yasser Arafat to control the outbreaks of terrorism against Israel. The woman with the stupid glasses and her small group of friends had plenty to answer for: but what about the television companies which kept on using the pictures?

We all seem to do this business of generalizing from the few wisps of information we glean about another place from news programmes. If we see graphic pictures of the aftermath of a bombing or a shooting, or even of a big demonstration, we assume that the entire country must be in turmoil. How many people know that you can have a superb holiday very cheaply in Sri Lanka, and never hear even the distant sound of gunfire? Who knows that Colombia has some of the best and most beautiful resorts in South America? Who appreciates the sensational qualities of Iran as a country to travel round? Fortunately for those of us who know the reality about these countries, not many.

It isn't really television's fault: television merely gives us a more immediate, a more graphic sense of something that has happened. The fault lies in our interpretation of the pictures – our sense that they are just a brief glimpse of something much more widespread and even more alarming going on. Maybe, you'll say, the commentary should put the incident in perspective; yet that would become impossibly tedious to listen to.

The real problem with journalism of every kind, and television more than any other, is its selectivity. We separate out the interesting from the dull, and the most interesting from the merely averagely interesting, until every item on every news bulletin, every column inch of every newspaper, is filled with exceptional cases. This is inevitable, if you are telling people news – that is, new things. (The word in its present form dates from the thirteenth century, and is merely the Middle English translation of the Norman French *noveles*.)

Yet this selectivity can be a serious distortion. If your only idea of the game of cricket were derived from the minute-long report that television news devotes to a test match, say, you would probably believe that it was a fast, exciting game full of heroic hits to the boundary, athletic catches, and sudden, hotly disputed decisions about whether a batsman was out leg-before-wicket. The reality of cricket, that a test match lasts five days and that nothing happens during much of that time, might rather pass you by; and it is unreasonable to expect that the correspondent who is assembling the news report should waste the short and valuable time at his disposal by throwing in pictures of elderly spectators dozing to remind you of the essentially soporific, long drawn-out nature of the game. We could of course insert regular warnings, along the lines of the 'objects may be closer than they appear' disclaimers on the rear-view mirrors of cars; but the best policy, it seems to me, is to inform people better, more often and at greater length about the world they live in.

Until September 2001 the people who schedule television programmes regarded news as a clear audience-loser, to be elbowed aside from the best times of the evening. Independent Television News's bulletins were shifted to an impossibly early time in 2000, and then half-heartedly allowed back to their old slot after a large amount of protest. The damage which was done to ITN's morale and its effectiveness was incalculable; and it all happened just in time for the events of 11 September, when news was suddenly in great demand again.

There has to be a proper balance between entertainment and serious broadcasting, and the muddle-headed planners of independent television demonstrated that if it goes too far in favour of entertainment there can be real trouble. And yet all the studies of factual programming in British, French, German and Italian television show that the number of documentaries about developing countries has fallen by up to sixty per cent in the past twelve years or so: since, in fact, the end of the Cold War.

Until 1991 you could get people in the West to watch programmes about what we still called the Third World, because there was the underlying message that countries in trouble were countries which were likely to side with the Soviet Union and thereby present some kind of threat to us. Directly there was no Soviet Union to side with, the West lost interest. We preferred to assume that these countries were mostly sinking into a swamp of violence and poverty, and that there wasn't anything we could do about it. They were, we said, 'basket cases'. And because our television planners were increasingly concerned with what the audience said it wanted, rather than with what they as enlightened programme makers should provide, serious programmes about the outside world started to vanish like an endangered species.

Yet the outside world hasn't gone away. And sometimes, as on 11 September 2001, it breaks into our quiet, wilfully ignorant lives and reminds us forcibly of our existence. And the people who had previously told their focus groups that television should provide them with mental chewing gum began complaining that no one had warned them it might happen.

7

Under the Burka

Peshawar, Khyber Pass, Nangarhar Province and Peshawar:
Friday 21 September and Saturday 22 September

That evening Peter Jouvenal and I packed our gear and our burkas into three small, inconspicuous bags, and had a quick meal in the coffee shop of the Pearl Continental Hotel in Peshawar. Nobody took any notice of us. Then we slipped out, and Paul Danahar saw us off. We had already packed our small generator and the rest of the equipment.

I don't intend to say too much about how we met up with the smugglers who were going to take us into Afghanistan, because, even now, it still creates a certain amount of anger in Pakistan and might get the people involved into trouble. In brief, though, we met up with someone who drove us to a quiet house in Peshawar where, with much laughter, we dressed up in our disguises. Both of us decided to abandon the huge plastic slippers we had bought, and kept our boots on. They didn't look all that much more ludicrous and out of place than the slippers. It would have taken only the most cursory of glances to realize we weren't what we pretended to be; but our hope was that no one would look at us at all.

Not far from the western outskirts of Peshawar, the road opens up towards the Khyber Pass. It was always one of the wild places of the earth, and the British acknowledged this in the Durand Agreement of 1893, which settled the border between British India and Afghanistan but allowed the area to be controlled by its tribal chiefs, with British support. After 1947 Pakistan took over the agreement and operated just as the British had. The main road up through the Khyber Pass is controlled by a locally raised militia regiment, the Khyber Rifles, but as a foreigner you need special permission to go up there, and an armed soldier of the Khyber Rifles in your vehicle to escort you. The tribesmen are still pretty ferocious, and more than capable of kidnapping you for ransom, but they rarely show much interest in kidnapping foreigners. Maybe that's because the security system works so well.

When I was eleven, in 1955, my father bought a large house in London which was fully furnished; and as well as the huge, dusty sofas and the uncomfortable high-backed dining chairs there were a lot of books of a kind that weren't easy to find, even in those days. The previous owner of the house had worked in the Colonial Service, finishing up in northern Nigeria, and the books all seemed to be of a certain type: thrillers and romances of the late Victorian Empire. There was Cutcliffe Hyne's *Mr Horrocks, Purser*, and Guy Boothby's *The Beautiful White Devil*, and Bertram Mitford's *The King's Assegai*, and William Le Queux's *Zoraida*: all unutterable crap, of course.

It wasn't the imperial aspect which attracted me, so much as the excitement of reading about such strange places; and the stories I read merged with my father's tales of sailing round the world in passenger liners when he ran away to sea as a boy only a few years older than myself, and my uncle Alan's stories of heroic deeds fighting behind Japanese lines with the Chindits in Burma, and running the Malayan police after the war.

But my favourite book was bound in faded, unobtrusive blue and (unlike the others) had no illustrations of moustachioed men wearing pith helmets and riding boots. It had no illustrations at all; yet even the title ravished my imagination: *King, of the Khyber Rifles* by Talbot Mundy, first published in 1916. When I reread it not long ago, I could see that Mundy, whose real name was William Lancaster Gribbon, and who was an Englishman who lived in California, was simply purveying a mixture of reach-me-down imperialism, two parts Kipling and one part Rider Haggard, plus a large helping of foggy, half-understood Indian mysticism, to an American audience. No matter: I found the phrases still had a certain romantic power, half a century later.

> King sat and smoked and read; and before he had nearly finished one box of cheroots a general at Peshawur [*sic*] wiped a bald red skull and sent him an urgent telegram.

'Come at once!' it said simply.

King was at Lahore, but miles don't matter when the dogs of war are loosed. The right man goes to the right place at the exact right time then, and the fool goes to the wall. In that one respect war is better than some kinds of peace.

Flies buzzed everywhere. Fat merchants vied with lean and timid ones in noisy efforts to secure accommodation on a train already crowded to the limit.

There were din and stink and dust beneath a savage sun, shaken into reverberations by the scream of an engine's safety valve. It was India in essence and awake! – India rising out of lethargy! – India as she is more often nowadays – and it made King, for the time being of the Khyber Rifles, happier than some other men can be in ballrooms.

It's tosh, of course, masquerading as something better. But if my eleven-year-old self had known, as he sat cross-legged in a convenient holm-oak tree in the back garden reading this, that one day he would be disguising himself to travel from Peshawar through the Khyber Pass into Afghanistan, past roadblocks manned by men of the Khyber Rifles, he would have thought himself in very heaven. Instead of which, of course, I am embarrassed about it, as at a piece of absurd and rather childish theatre.

Nevertheless, it worked. Peter and I sat side by side in our vehicle, he in his yellow burka and I in my blue one, and the men from the Khyber Rifles in their impressively neat black uniform *shalwar kameez* with red shoulder-flashes peered into the car at every road-block and scarcely gave us a glance. It was working.

We spent that evening at one of the small mud-brick fortresses which you catch glimpses of throughout the North-West Frontier area. Our driver hooted and got out to beat on the high wooden gates, and at last an ancient retainer with only one functioning eye pulled them open just long enough to let our vehicle in, then slammed them shut and chained them again. You do not altogether trust your neighbours on the Frontier, and with some justification.

We were in a large open courtyard, the size of a tennis court. At the far end was a single-storied building in mud-brick, whose owner came out and shook hands with us. It took some effort, of course, to produce our hands from under the burka, but he showed no sign of surprise or amusement. He was everyone's idea of a hillman: the type you might read about in Kipling or Talbot Mundy, tall, thin, rangy, with a prominently beaked nose and dark, penetrating eyes under his turban.

He took us inside. It was a large, barn-like room with mattresses scattered around the floor and piled-up boxes of goods which it would have been ill-mannered of us to examine too closely. Our host and the guide talked to each other; Peter and I listened to the news on our radio, and after half an hour the ancient one-eyed character appeared with a huge supply of chicken kebabs, *naan* bread and *shin chai* – green tea. We pulled out the Laphroaig and the Upmann Number 2 cigars, and passed the latter (though not the former) to our hosts, who smoked them wonderingly but put them discreetly aside long before they were finished. At the age of fifty-seven, I reflected self-critically, I had merely succeeded in becoming one with a character in a forgotten, third-rate imperialist novel.

> 'Man alive – get a move on!' gasped a wondering senior, accepting a cigar.
> Nobody knows where King gets those long, strong, black cheroots, and nobody ever refuses one.
> 'Thanks – got a book to read,' said King.

It was midnight before we went to sleep, with the strange sounds of a Khyber fortress all around us.

We were awake at 5.30, with the cocks crowing and the servants stirring outside. The only lavatory was a ditch outside the fortress wall, so we took turns to use that. Everything was slow and lethargic, until some undefined moment when the pace suddenly picked up and the lethargy was replaced with an urgent sense of things about to happen; and indeed we had just got our equipment together when there was hooting at the gate, and someone beat on it as our driver had the previous night. A black Toyota pick-up truck, the vehicle of choice for smugglers along the Afghan border, drove in with four armed men aboard. They were our escort.

Since they were the ones who had instructed us to wear burkas, there was no laughter as we put them on. In the early morning heat I found the integral cap that fitted tightly around my head unbearably uncomfortable; yet the rest of the garment was excellent. I could carry everything I wanted underneath its folds, and no one could see. Better still, Jouvenal was able to hide not only his camera but also a bag of batteries and cassettes under his. The business of disguise, smuggling and illicit filming could not have been carried on in more convenient fashion.

It was just like putting on a cloak of invisibility. Even to these men, who knew exactly who we were and how much we were paying, we seemed to vanish in importance. Instead of asking us what to do, they began asking the man who had brought us here. It was no longer, 'Do you want...?' but 'Do they want...?' We fitted too exactly into the pattern by which women had no say, no function other than the most basic ones, and no real interest for men; we had become as unimportant, as dependable, as taken for granted as beasts of burden.

In other ways the burka was a nuisance. The small panel of coarse lace through which I peered was too limited to be able to see anything more than a field of about eighty degrees, and was only the size of the palm of my hand. I had to turn my head and cock it on one side like a parrot if there was something particular I wanted to look at. The entire world took on a bluish tinge from the colour of the lace; and the tightness of the cap was particularly awkward. I felt the blood throbbing through my forehead, and the sweat soaking through the material in a way that was scarcely feminine.

We shook hands with our host and his servants, and climbed into the pick-up. And, because we were paying, Jouvenal and I insisted on sitting in the cab with the driver while the four armed guards sat out in the open at the back. Not surprisingly, we hadn't driven for more than an hour through the dust and the increasing heat of the border when the driver stopped. He held a conference with the four gunmen and with the dragoman who had been assigned to us.

'Says, they want you to sit at back. Says, no women go in front of car.'

Maybe it was true; or maybe it was simply that the gunmen felt they would lose face if they were seen travelling in the back when a couple of ostensible women had the comfortable inside seats. Whatever the reason, we agreed quickly; we didn't want the gunmen to decide they were pulling out of the deal.

It was a long drive, along the bed of a river which came up to the tops of the wheels and through sand dunes where the grim, clinging, self-coloured dust billowed up and forced its way through the lattice-work of our burkas and between our teeth. We were profoundly uncomfortable, sitting over the rear axles – which is why, as women, we had been put there.

We travelled along a dry river bed as wide as a creek and, when no one was around to see, Peter got his camera out and got some shaky pictures of our journey. There was no trouble about the smugglers seeing us: they knew perfectly well who we were and what we were there to do. But it was important not to let the local people who eked out a living here know; word would get swiftly to the Taliban, who had warned that any journalists caught entering Afghanistan would be arrested and imprisoned.

I didn't think they would know we were coming. For one thing, we had been careful not to make our arrangements by phone from the Pearl Continental. There were three later cases where journalists tried to follow our example and were arrested immediately they crossed the border; which indicated that elements within the ISI, Pakistan's military intelligence, were listening to the phone calls and tipping off the Taliban.

When the Taliban arrested Yvonne Ridley of the *Sunday Express*, it was because she accidentally let her disguise fall. But there was another case that looked like clear evidence of the ISI's involvement with the Taliban; it was the ISI, after all, which had helped the Taliban get started, had smoothed their path across the border into Afghanistan, and had given them the necessary logistical support they needed to take over the country and rule it. The Taliban were, to some extent, the creation of the ISI. It was no great surprise that the lines of communication between them should have remained open.

A Western journalist rang her editor and suggested crossing the border in disguise. He, rightly, was against the idea and they com-promised by trying a dummy run, with Afghan women instead of the journalist. The car was stopped as it crossed the Afghan border, and one of the Taliban guards who stopped them pulled everyone out of the car, yelling that they knew one of them was a Western journalist. The mistake quickly became obvious, of course, but there was no doubt the Taliban had known all about the plan. And the only way they could have known was because the ISI was listening to the phones.

I soon lost interest in trying to see things through the blue lace panel of my burka. Instead I lapsed into a kind of stupor in which I thought as little as possible about everything, because that seemed to ease the discomfort and the boredom a little. This must be life as most women in Afghanistan know it: an imprisonment of the mind, in which you become your own jailer. And the sentence is for life.

Occasionally, when we were well out of sight of human habitation, we were reprieved, and I was able to lift the burka off my head for a brief, blessed moment or two as our vehicle jolted and shook its way across the boulders which constituted our road. Sometimes I could see little mud-brick fortresses clinging to the cliff tops against the brilliant blue sky. Each time, though, one of the guards would spot a shepherd with his flock of ragged brown sheep, or a man leading a line of camels ahead of us, and the cloud of blue would have to be lowered round me again: another prison sentence.

I lost all notion of where we were driving, since the burka made it hard for me even to work out where the sun was and the overpowering sense of lethargy blotted out my desire to know where we were and make plans accordingly. The burka seemed to dampen down every aspiration to take control of my life: I left it to someone else.

It was impossible to work out where the Durand Line ran. The local people think of themselves as being members of a tribe, not of a nation, and the tribesmen wander far into Afghanistan on the one side and Pakistan on the other. Even the smugglers seemed not to understand the question when we asked if we had crossed into Afghanistan yet. We were in their area, that was all. Sometimes we saw trucks carrying consignments of strawberries down to Peshawar. A UN anti-drugs programme had been rather successful here at weaning people off the cultivation of opium-poppies and helping them grow soft fruit instead. If it succeeded with the wild tribesmen of the Afghan marches it could work anywhere.

At last, at some point in the early afternoon, the vehicle stopped at a stone farmhouse which was obviously one of the smugglers' main centres of operation. With an enormous sense of pleasure and relief, we were able to take our burkas off altogether; and it was noticeable that although quite a crowd had gathered round us, no one laughed at the spectacle of two large Western men appearing from the modest, submissive folds. Maybe – and I am only speculating here, because it would have been the worst of bad manners to ask about it – the smugglers used the tactic quite often. The enormous value of the burka as a disguise is that it not only covers up every aspect of your identity, it is quite impossible for any man to search you or investigate who you are. Later, when the journalists in Peshawar heard about what we had done and some of them tried to emulate it, the Taliban introduced women searchers at border crossings; but in the usual way you were entirely free from official inquisitiveness as long as you wore it.

Journalism is an odd business, impelled by forces which are entirely foreign to most real people – not to mention the Afghans we now found ourselves among. Their first concern was to welcome us with due politeness and get down to the congenial business of feasting. My first concern was to set up our satellite phone and dictate my column for the next day's *Sunday Telegraph*: the deadline was fast approaching. Nothing much had happened, of course, and I had scarcely seen anything of conditions along the way. No matter – I had to start.

All I could think of to write about (apart from the obvious business of the disguise) was the sheer, extraordinary emptiness of the area. The smugglers were all commenting on it. There had been a mass migration across into Pakistan, and the local tribespeople had mostly moved their livestock out of range of the Taliban. It soon emerged from talking to the people in the farmhouse that the Taliban had greatly reinforced all their positions in this area, because they believed American troops would attack Afghanistan through Pakistani territory. This seemed so unlikely as to be laughable, but there had been big Taliban reinforcements in the area. In fact, said one old man, his beard dyed an absurdly unlikely red with henna, there was a Taliban position quite close to us here.

'How close?'

Everyone was vague, but they all agreed it wasn't far.

I dictated my report down the phone line to the company in Yorkshire which takes in copy for the *Sunday Telegraph*. Normally the copy-takers show a real interest, and enliven the whole lengthy business of dictation with their comments. In these electronic days I rarely have to send my articles this way, but the reactions from the other end are the one pleasant thing about an otherwise lengthy and tedious business. Not, however, this time. The woman who took it down didn't laugh at the jokes, and she didn't seem to think there was anything remarkable about the things we had done. Maybe she was right; maybe she was just shy, or dull, or preoccupied. But it was an unusual let-down, and when I put away the phone and went out to find Peter and our hosts I felt like an actor who had been greeted by the audience with a stolid silence.

'They're insisting on giving us lunch,' Peter said.

I looked at my watch, and at the sun. It was only two in the afternoon, but the hills around us were high and the valley we were in would soon be in darkness. Still, I didn't even bother suggesting that we should postpone the lunch. Peter was just as anxious as I was about the time, and if he thought we had to go through with it, we must. We were very much in the hands of these people, and it wouldn't be clever to offend them. The most we could do was to hurry them up a little.

I had, it seemed, agreed to buy a sheep from the farmer, though I wasn't aware of having done so. The sheep was lunch; and after some painful squealing around the back of the house the farmer came to greet us, his hands as red as Macbeth's. Even so, I was clearly expected to shake one of these hands, and had to look round carefully for some way to clean my own afterwards.

For many years I was a vegetarian. Nowadays, regrettably, I eat meat again – but our lunch was more than enough to turn the most confirmed carnivore against the whole idea. The Afghans, for a start, seem to have no notion that it is better to hang meat for a while before eating it. The sheep may not have fought hard against slaughter, but in death it resisted furiously. The chunks of strongly flavoured, insufficiently cooked meat were as hard to chew as rubber matting, and about as satisfying. Gritty *naan* bread, burned at the edges and wherever it had touched the live coals, could be used to swamp the flavour a little, and if you were careful you could give the impression you were eating the meat heartily while in fact you were merely chewing the bread.

As the guests and the founders of the feast, we were offered the real delicacies. These included the sheep's kidneys and other internal organs, wrapped in its fat. I have endured some pretty distasteful meals in my life (being expected to eat a boiled goat's head in Iraq was pretty bad, not to mention broiled monkey in the Amazon and mopani worms in Zimbabwe) but getting rid of these bits of sheep organs unobtrusively without actually eating them was the hardest thing I have ever had to do in this line. There was only water and green tea to wash it down.

It was a considerable relief when the Afghans stood up unceremoniously at the end of the meal and pointed to the sun. They had finally noticed that it was descending fast to the top of the nearby mountain ridge, which loomed a good mile above us. I am an active sort of fellow as a result of my job, but it was going to be an effort for me to get up there, the more especially since I damaged my left knee badly during the time of the NATO bombing of Belgrade in 1999 (not, it has to be said, in any way glamorously) and though the resulting operation was a complete success the knee remains slightly stiff-set and awkward.

A group of five lively-looking little horses with pricked-up ears and bright scarlet bridles appeared: the kind that are simply a pleasure to ride. They weren't, however, for us, but for the gear. I wanted to broadcast live from the top of the ridge, looking towards Kabul and out at the Taliban positions in the next valley. We would have to walk.

Our guide stayed with me in the most solicitous and kindly way possible, never letting on for an instant that he had the strength to run up to the top and down again while I was still struggling up. Peter, being a good thirteen years younger than me and in better shape, ploughed on ahead. It was, however, hard going for everyone; hence the decision to take the gear up on horseback.

More than once I thought of calling everyone back and insisting that we do our broadcasting from the side of the mountain rather than its topmost ridge. Yet each time I reflected that we wouldn't be able to see anything if we did; and seeing what was on the other side was the only point of coming this way at all. With this thought I would drag myself further up the crumbling mountain path, resisting the urge to look down at the steep drop behind us.

Even the worst physical effort comes to an end eventually. The pain in my calves and the back of my thighs began to ease off, and breathing became less difficult: the last hundred feet were less steep, and I found myself walking along the ridge. Then one of the guides noticed what I was doing, and hissed at me to get down. I peered over the edge in the direction he was pointing, and saw a Taliban post disturbingly close – well within hearing of us. That was a problem, because we had to run our equipment off the generator which some unfortunate horse had lugged up the mountainside; and generators make a terrible racket.

There was nothing for it, though. The light wouldn't last much longer, and we had to record a piece to camera and get some shots for an edited report, and then do several interviews, either live or pre-recorded, with various television and radio programmes. Our plan was to use a newish gadget called the videophone, whose signal could be transmitted by satellite phone to London. The picture from the videophone was never particularly great, and the relatively low quality of the phone line meant that it was jerky and awkward. But we would be putting out live pictures from Afghanistan, and in the mildly absurd world of journalism that counted for something.

We set up the generator as far down the mountainside and away from the Taliban post as its cable would stretch. To my ears it sounded horribly loud and very obvious, proclaiming itself to be an active generator to all who heard it. But when I peered over the ridge at the post, I could see the man on duty still slumped on his chair outside the small stone building they had taken over. He certainly hadn't heard anything to worry him.

While I wrote a radio dispatch in a fever of haste, checking every now and then to see how low the sun was, Peter set up the video-phone. But when I spoke to the comfortingly calm voices in the Traffic department in London, they couldn't see any pictures. We tried again and again, using up valuable time, but the wretched thing refused to work. Somehow the jolting of the flat-bed truck or the lurching of the horses up the steep mountain path must have damaged it.

'We'll have to cut our losses,' I hissed at Peter; I only spoke at full volume when it was broadcasting time.

The Traffic manager in London gave me the OK – 'Go in five,

John,' – and, after a gap of five seconds, I started reading my hastily written dispatch down the line. That way, the other television and radio programmes I would be speaking to would hear what I had to say, and we would avoid too many of those awkward misunderstandings which can crop up about the whereabouts of the correspondent and the essential facts of the story.

> This part of Afghanistan seems utterly deserted; the reports of people fleeing to what they regard as safety seem to be correct. From the mountain top where I'm reporting I can see a Taliban position not far away. Two days ago, the locals tell us, they weren't here. The Taliban must be anticipating a ground attack from across the Pakistan border.

> This province includes the city of Jalalabad, where Osama bin Laden has often based himself, and there are many training camps in the province. Now, though, the assumption is that the camps have long since emptied.

> We ourselves had little trouble getting here. We were brought in by cross-border smugglers, wearing the burkas which Pathan women wear, and which cover both the figure and face completely. It proved a highly successful disguise; under the Taliban, this is a society where women are virtually invisible.

> John Simpson, BBC News, Nangarhar Province, Afghanistan.

It gave me particular pleasure to read out the last word. In spite of everything, I had come back – even though we were really only just across the border. It hadn't been entirely easy, yet it somehow made up for the failures of the recent past. On the other hand, the enterprise hadn't been as much of a success as I had hoped: we hadn't managed to broadcast live pictures from Afghanistan, thanks to the damaged videophone, and it was abundantly clear to me that the smugglers, good and reliable though they had shown themselves to be, wouldn't be able to take us any further than Nangarhar Province itself; and I wasn't sure they would be much help even in Jalalabad. It was an end to my hopes of getting them to take me to Kabul. That part of the experiment had failed entirely.

The best we could do, I felt, was to make a decent report about getting into Afghanistan. But I would have to explain about the burkas and get some pictures of me dressed up in mine. Peter was reluctant.

'It'll create big problems with the Pakistanis.'

'But without it we haven't got a piece' – 'piece' being the word which journalists since the sixteenth century have used to mean a report or an article.

Normally I would take Peter's advice on something like this almost without question. In this case, although I accepted what he said, I knew we didn't have enough of interest for a news report without the burka element. What, after all, had we seen? A few empty valleys, a couple of Taliban positions; without a proper account of how we got there, it was scarcely of any interest whatever. Even then it wouldn't make a piece with any serious interest in it. It was a stunt, and little more than that.

Reluctantly Peter filmed me as, with the help of one of the group, I put my burka back on. He was still talking about it as we drove away in the back of the pick-up: one burka muttering to another. And he was right. We needed the Pakistanis' help to get back into Afghanistan for a more substantial trip, and they would be seriously annoyed by what we had done. We were rubbing their noses in it. All I could say in reply was that we must hope we could get round them in some way. Peter's approach was entirely rational; mine was the throw of the gambler.

Our problems weren't over yet. On the way back a group of bandits stopped us and peered into the back of the vehicle. They weren't, of course, looking for a couple of large journalists dressed as women, but they were looking for things to steal. Fortunately one of the smugglers had checked our feet very thoroughly a short time before, and our boots, which gave us away faster than anything else, were hidden. I hunched down in the submissive manner of Afghan women and made myself seem a good deal smaller; Peter, I noticed through the little square of blue lace, was doing the same.

The bandits took no notice of us as they flashed their torches around in the darkness, but they starting demanding that everyone should get down from the vehicle. The smugglers refused, saying they were in a hurry. The bandits flourished their AK-47s; the smugglers brandished theirs. For an instant or two it looked as though something awkward might happen; then one of the bandits said something

and waved us on. A couple of hours later we were in the Pearl
Continental in Peshawar, and Paul Danahar was starting to edit our
report.

'You've got some nice stuff here,' he said.

By this stage, of course, our phone reports had long been broadcast on BBC World. A friend of ours was in the bar at the Pearl
Continental (to call it a 'bar' when all that's available is Pakistani
beer, Pakistani whisky and Pakistani gin is stretching it a little, but
the barman is a great fellow) at the moment our first report from
Afghanistan was broadcast on BBC World. The television set was on
in the corner of the room, and a large group of journalists had
gathered to watch the news. According to our friend, the report
caused a sensation. People shouted at the television screen, among
them one whom I had heard of a little, but never knowingly met.

'Fucking Simpson,' he yelled, 'I'll get him the next time I see him.'

He didn't, of course.

At the Marriott Hotel in Islamabad the scenes were less violent,
but just as angry. The journalists here were the quieter, more reflective
sort, and didn't feel the need (as the Peshawar ones did) to be close
to the Afghan border. You can define journalists by the places they
habituate, as well as the organizations they work for. A colleague of
mine was standing in one of the Marriott's lifts when one of the chief
stars of international television news got in. Christiane Amanpour of
CNN doesn't, it should be said at once, behave particularly like a
television star; she wears her fame better, almost, than any other
figure of her stature. She is a serious-minded woman, for whom 'the
story' is more important than her own personality, which, in American television news, makes a welcome change.

Christiane, whose fine looks point to her English and Persian
ancestry, was once turned down for a job by the BBC. It was very
much the BBC's loss, and very much her gain. Since the BBC does
not operate a star system, she would never have reached the levels of
success and fame that she has with CNN.

Now she looked crossly at my colleague as the lift shot smoothly
upwards.

'It was completely irresponsible of John, you know.'

He made the kind of non-committal noises you do on these
occasions.

'It makes things so much more difficult for everyone.'

By which, of course, she meant CNN; as though it was the BBC's job to avoid making things difficult for CNN. I'm fond of Christiane and admire her reporting greatly, but there are times when she sounds just like the head girl of an English public school. Which is probably what she was.

Aside from riling a few people and making a bit of a stir, though, what had we achieved? Not, as far as I could see, a great deal.

> 'You've a brother in the Khyber Rifles, haven't you? Was it you or your brother who visited Khinjan once and sent in a report?'
> 'I did, sir.'
> King spoke without pride. Even the brigade of British-Indian cavalry that went to Khinjan on the strength of his report and levelled its defences with the ground, had not been able to find the famous Caves. Yet the Caves themselves are a by-word.
> 'There's talk of a jihad. There's worse than that! When you went to Khinjan, what was your chief object?'
> 'To find the source of the everlasting rumours about the so-called "Heart of the Hills", sir.'
> 'Yes, yes. I remember. I read your report. You didn't find anything, did you?'

§

In 1994 a new expression started to appear in Britain. You could tell it came from America, because it turned an adjective into a verb. 'Dumbing down' described the process which had been taking place in the United States, as intelligent, thoughtful material was increasingly forced off the main television networks there. It implied a shift to an unchallenging populism for the sake of ratings, and it started appearing a great deal in letters to the British press from people who were more educated, middle class and usually older.

Sometimes, when I scan the British television schedules for something to watch, I can see what they mean. Still, as someone who lives outside Britain and sees a great deal of other countries' television, I think I'm in a good position to judge; and it's clear to me that even though the standard of the main terrestrial channels in Britain has become more populist, there are good and imaginative programmes every evening; so many that you are obliged to miss some of them.

What was true forty years ago is still true today: no other country in the world has as good television as Britain, just as no other country in Europe has as good an arts channel as BBC Four. British television is broadening out and blossoming in ways that would have been unthinkable thirty years ago.

Our memory almost invariably glamorizes the past. If you watch the great television dramas of the past – the original BBC version of *The Forsyte Saga* from the 1960s, say, or the dramatized spy thrillers of John le Carré from the 1970s – you are likely to find them distinctly slow, mannered and unsatisfying. Life has speeded up without our being aware of it, and only the best and quickest entertainment of the past can keep pace with the change.

The same is true of television news. It is hard to be entirely precise, but a study of randomly selected news items from 1978, which was the year I started working in television, shows that although the items themselves are roughly the same length nowadays, or possibly a little longer, the average length of the various elements within them – that is, the interview clips and the pieces to camera – are distinctly shorter.

In 1978 an average extract from an interview shown in a news report was thirty-one seconds; nowadays it is about sixteen seconds. Yet the news reports from 1978 are not, I promise you, richer in information. On the contrary, allowing the interviews to last longer actually provides the viewer with less information, given that the overall length of each news report is roughly the same. In 1978 we required fewer pictures and (since the commentary was shorter) fewer facts than we require today.

Our pieces to camera were far longer, too: an average of thirty-three seconds as against eighteen seconds now. The general effect of cutting down on these two areas has been to speed up the overall effect of the reporting. Each shot is probably slightly shorter today, though it is hard to be too exact about this. In 1978 the length was around seven seconds; now it is around six.

In other words, we provide information quicker now in our news reports, and the audience has learned to absorb it faster now than a quarter-century ago. The style of 1978 is slower and more ponderous, and it seems quite patronizing when you watch it now: unwatchably so, I would say. Over the same period of time, American television news has speeded up to a much greater extent: the three-second shots, five-second sound bites, one-sentence pieces to camera, all of it reflecting the influence of music videos. It becomes quite stupefying. British television news has resisted this extreme brevity, which makes it harder for viewers to understand and take in the detail of what is being reported. We have, it seems, speeded up the effect of our reporting without cutting down on the information we provide.

Looking back on my own work from a quarter of a century ago, I am distinctly embarrassed. In 1978, during the run-up to the Iranian revolution, I found myself in a major riot which led to further deaths and more shootings when the funerals took place, and even more when the forty-day period of mourning was completed. As the crowd rampaged behind me, burning flags and being hunted down by the police, I recorded a paralysingly long piece to camera in which for some reason I compared the situation with the student riots of 1968 in Paris. It seems quite absurd now; and I can only think that I did it because in those days we rarely edited our own reports when we were abroad, and mostly sent the unprocessed film back to London where someone else cut it. If I had sat in an edit suite and watched this, even in 1978, I would have understood what a feeble response mine was to the extraordinary, violent scenes I had witnessed.

My accent has changed too. When I listen to the commentary now, I can only wince at the preciousness in my voice. It's like listening to the Queen in 1953, or that famous recording of William Ewart Gladstone in 1890. Over the years I have unconsciously modified the cut-glass vowels and learned to write much more as I speak: which is the proper way to broadcast. As I write these words I am half listening to a television news broadcast in the background, and the newsreader has just read the following small but indigestible slab of newzak:

> Police have stepped up the search for missing schoolgirl Amanda Dowler, known as Millie.

We will leave aside the disappearance of the definite article in modern journalese, the unquestioning acceptance of a bit of official self-promotion (what evidence do we have that the police are doing more today than they did yesterday, and why weren't they doing more then?), and the pronunciation, solely restricted to broad-casting journalists, of 'police' as 'pleece'. I find the newsreader's accent – from somewhere like Macclesfield, as far as I can judge – rather pleasant. Yet she is as hard to understand as the syntax which has been written for her by some butchering sub-editor; not because she comes from Macclesfield, but because she swallows many of the most important words. This is a purely personal problem, and has nothing whatever to do with her place of birth, her background, her education.

We are what we are, and we have a right to be that way. Presenting the news is like writing a letter: it doesn't matter what your writing is like, as long as it is clear and easily legible. The attractive young woman who is filling my television screen at the moment, telling me that pleece are doing their job better today than yesterday, has bad vocal handwriting. It's not her accent I dislike; it's her enunciation.

When, during the Second World War, the BBC turned the broad-caster Wilfred Pickles into a newsreader, there were howls of protest right across the country. Pickles might have had a silly name and a strong North Country accent, but he was a clever and accomplished broadcaster; and nowadays, listening to recordings of his news bul-letins, it is clear he deliberately muted his natural accent so much that it only escapes occasionally, usually in the vowel sounds. But people across the country were outraged. What they wanted was 'standard English', 'BBC English': the English, that is, of the public schools and of Oxford and Cambridge.

Accent snobbery is one of the nastier sides of life in England, and it's a problem unknown in France, Ireland, the United States, Germany, Russia and just about every other country whose television I watch. It's fading out even in England, and with luck it'll be dead and forgotten within twenty years. But it still crops up every now and then. When John Cole took my place as the BBC's political editor in 1981, there were hundreds of complaints after each of his broadcasts about his supposedly impenetrable Ulster accent. It wasn't just the accent they didn't like, it was the fact that John came from the other side of the Irish Sea; and with that sensitivity and awareness that have made the British so loved around the world, they failed to understand that he was as British as they were. 'Why should we have an Irishman telling us about our politics?' was a point which was frequently made. And yet within ten years he was one of the most popular people on television, and within fifteen years British viewers and listeners were identifying Irish accents as being among the most attractive on the air. At long last, some of the pettier unpleasantnesses seem to be leaking out of British life.

The century-long controversy about cóntroversy or contróversy is, thank God, finally dead. Nowadays even the grosser Americanisms ('The Chancellor, Gordon Brown, is expected to meet with business leaders today', 'It looks like the government is going to announce . . .') don't attract as much attention as they did, and 'skedule' seems to have driven out 'schedule' in the way burgers have driven out fish and chips.

I wrote an article for the *Spectator* in 1992 about the way the BBC has modified its pronunciation over the years, matching the changes in society as a whole, and was of course criticized in its letters page as a result. Now I don't think I would bother to write about the subject, and even a pessimistically inclined magazine like the *Spectator* might not think it worth printing. The generation that complained endlessly about northern vowel-sounds has faded away, and taken its discontents with it.

Life changes, and society changes, and television has to change too. I suppose I speak more or less in the way people used to want, rather than what they want now. There isn't much I can do about it, unless I go in for a thoroughgoing, completely false makeover. I am a middle-aged, middle-class white bloke from southern England, who went to a public school and Cambridge. Sixty years ago that would have been just the thing; now it isn't. But I don't want to change, any more than I want everyone else to speak like me: and any changing I have done has been because people in Britain generally have become more natural in their speech, more slangy, more immediate, more inclusive and less exclusive, and I have unconsciously absorbed all that too; we all have. I certainly didn't do it on purpose. Maybe the BBC will decide at some point that my voice is too plummy and old-fashioned for the mass market – it's happened to others, after all – and I will be shunted off to some quiet programme where I can continue speaking as I do to an audience of consenting adults. Personally, I don't think the way a person speaks matters as long as they are clearly intelligible. It's what they have to say that counts.

§

Interestingly, almost everyone seems to have an opinion about the BBC and the way it does its job. In a very real sense, it is their property. The broadcasting licence fee is precisely what its critics maintain: a tax on everyone who has a television set, regardless of whether they watch the BBC or not. As a result, everyone who pays it has a right to expect that the BBC will be sensitive to their concerns. They can't demand that it will support these concerns; but the BBC has a duty to be aware of their views, and not to insult them by treating their ideas with contempt or disapproval.

Whether you like it or hate it, and most of us often do both at the same time, the BBC is the biggest and most important institution in the cultural life of the United Kingdom, and nowadays it's an increasingly important one in the rest of the world as well. It has reached this position because it has money to spend, on hiring good people and making good programmes. The source of that money is the licence fee, and without it the BBC would start sinking fast. There is not the faintest chance that the BBC could maintain itself as it is now through taking advertising, because advertising would only bring in at most about a third of the income the licence fee provides. It would also destroy independent television in the process.

As for a compromise solution, reducing the licence fee and allowing the BBC to take advertising, this is the process which has reduced CBC in Canada and ABC in Australia from the dominant broadcasters in their countries to minority broadcasters. No: anyone who tells you that the BBC would be better off without the licence fee merely wants to see the BBC dismantled, but prefers not to say so openly. Remember that, when you next hear the argument.

The fact is, the BBC has a lot of enemies in British society. During the long years when independent television had much larger audiences than the BBC, these enemies demanded that the licence fee should be abolished because the viewers were effectively voting against the BBC by deciding not to watch its programmes. Now that the BBC has larger audiences than independent television, and more than ninety per cent of the entire population of the United Kingdom tune in to one of its services at least once a week, the argument has swung round: the BBC, its enemies say, has become too populist, too downmarket. Newspapers which have become depressing shadows of what they once were, and which concentrate increasingly nowadays on the doings of actors and actresses from television soap operas and Hollywood films, are particularly given to accusing the BBC of 'dumbing down'.

Sometimes the opposition is ideological, and comes from a rooted dislike of the entire basis of the BBC's existence. Sometimes it is merely commercial, and the newspapers which attack it are owned by companies which compete directly with the BBC; though they don't often remind you of this fact in their reporting. Grandly, the BBC seems to take no notice whatever. Like a duchess at a dinner party when one of her guests inadvertently breaks wind, it carries on as though nothing has happened.

I don't think it's arrogance, though the BBC is capable of the most breathtaking arrogance at times; I think it comes from a deep-seated sense that there's nothing else it can do. Those of us who were once the BBC's Young Turks, and have slowly turned into its elderly janisseries, sometimes wonder at the BBC's mildness under attack. What other organization on earth would trumpet the fact that it had been accused of betraying the British people? The BBC, in its various press reviews on radio and television, actually seemed to enjoy telling this to its audience.

On Saturday 30 March 2002, Queen Elizabeth the Queen Mother died. Someone in the BBC hierarchy, thinking they were reflecting the way British society had changed over the years, had ordained that the news presenter who announced the Queen Mother's death, when it happened, should wear a sombre tie but not a black one; black ties would be reserved for the days of lying in state and the funeral. It caused an uproar in some sections of the British press: those sections where, for reasons which are sometimes commercial and sometimes ideological, it is always open season on the BBC. In the midst of it all, the truth sometimes vanished from sight. This, for instance, was the opening couple of paragraphs from the lead story in *The Times* on Tuesday 2 April 2002:

The Prince of Wales delivered a rebuke to the BBC yesterday over its 'disrespectful' coverage of the death of the Queen Mother when he pointedly filmed a poignant tribute to his grandmother for ITN.

The Prince, in consultation with the Queen, deliberately chose the commercial channel in protest at the continuing failure of the BBC to rise to the historic occasion of his grandmother's death. The Royal Family is unhappy that BBC presenters alone failed to wear black ties and is upset by a decision by the corporation to scale back its coverage.

In fact, immediately after that report appeared, several of the most senior officials at Buckingham Palace assured the BBC, one after another, that the Royal Family had no complaint whatever about its coverage of the Queen Mother's death. The chief spokesman of the Prince of Wales insisted that there had been no accusation of disrespect. The Prince had recorded the tribute with ITN, his spokesman said, because a few weeks earlier he had recorded a tribute to Princess Margaret with the BBC; it was, quite simply, ITN's turn.

It must, I thought, have been an awkward moment for *The Times*, and I looked in the next day's edition to see how it had handled it. The front page headline read 'Presenters revolt over BBC's black tie rule'. It was described as 'a growing crisis'. The Prince of Wales was now quoted directly: he 'has described the BBC's performance so far as "lamentable".' Pretty sensational use of words, you might think; and yet this quotation was buried so deeply in the story that it only appeared in the twelfth paragraph of a fourteen-paragraph story – strange in itself. And this was how *The Times* dealt with the statements from Buckingham Palace and St James's Palace that they had had no complaints about the BBC's coverage:

> Mark Byford [who was deputizing for the director-general, Greg Dyke] . . . attempted to reassure staff that 'the Palace was not at all unhappy' with the coverage.

That 'attempted to' is an inspired touch. Inverted commas are wonderful things, too – the equivalent of the raised eyebrow in a cutaway in a television comedy show.

The *Daily Mail*'s coverage was more excitable: one of its headlines was 'How the BBC betrayed the British people'.

> As a mark of his anger, Prince Charles decided to give an
> interview in which he spoke movingly of his grief to ITN and not
> the BBC.

I have no idea whether Prince Charles was angry or not; perhaps he
was. Presumably someone relatively close to him must have been
angry in private conversations with the press; though whether this
person actually spoke to the *Daily Mail* is unclear. But the only
evidence which was adduced was the decision ('in consultation with
the Queen', according to *The Times*) to give an interview to ITN
rather than the BBC; and in reality this wasn't a mark of the Prince's
or anyone else's anger.

It all seemed like an example of the 'stands to reason' school of
journalism: if the Prince of Wales appears on ITN, it stands to reason
that he must be angry with the BBC; if he did that, it stands to reason
that he must have cleared it with the Queen first; and if he was angry,
it stands to reason that it was because Peter Sissons, the news
presenter, had worn a dark red tie instead of a black one. The cards
were carefully balanced on one another, but it was all pretty insecure
stuff.

Spokespeople for the Royal Family have to be on duty at all times
of the day and night, because so much is written about them. No one
from *The Times* or the *Mail* seems to have been able to call them by
the time the two papers went to bed on Monday night – more than
forty-eight hours after the Great Tie Horror. There is a famous Fleet
Street institution, The Story Which Is Too Good To Check – in case
it turns out not to be true. Not, of course, that I would dream of
suggesting that such a thing happened at *The Times* or the *Daily Mail*
in this particular case; as W. C. Fields puts it in one of his films, 'I
ain't sayin' this steak is tough, I'm just sayin' I ain't seen that old
horse around recently.'

Evelyn Waugh, who worked in Fleet Street for a while, writes in
Scoop:

> That afternoon Corker told William a great deal about the craft
> of journalism . . . [H]e told of the classic scoops and hoaxes; of
> the confessions wrung from hysterical suspects; of the innuendo
> and intricate misrepresentations, the luscious, detailed inventions
> that composed contemporary history; of the positive, daring lies

that got a chap a rise of screw; how Wenlock Jakes, highest paid
journalist of the United States, scooped the world with an eye-
witness story of the sinking of the Lusitania four hours before
she was hit; how Hitchcock, the English Jakes, straddled over his
desk in London, had chronicled day by day the horrors of the
Messina earthquake . . .

Because *The Times* is fundamentally a serious newspaper, it
printed an article a couple of days later (though only in its media
supplement) which accepted that the stories about royal anger over
Peter Sissons' tie-colour were rubbish. It didn't add that *The Times*
had published these stories, but maybe that is asking too much. As
for the *Daily Mail*, it said nothing more about the subject. Newspaper
journalism is a magnificent art form. Long may it flourish – as long,
of course, as we don't believe absolutely everything we read.

Like the Royal Family itself, the BBC simply seems to shrug these
things off. It doesn't hit back. It doesn't even stop giving its bit-
terest opponents the best free publicity they're likely to obtain. Like
the duchess at the dinner table, it simply acts as though it hasn't
heard a thing. I used to think this was unutterable spinelessness, and
reviled my bosses accordingly; now I have come to realize that it
works. No doubt some readers will have shaken their heads in horror
and disgust at the revelations of the dumbed-down, republican,
irresponsible subversives at the BBC, but I don't imagine many of
them will have switched to other channels in order to teach the BBC
a lesson.

On the contrary, in fact; a survey showed that sixty-one per cent
of *Daily Mail* readers disagreed with the newspaper's coverage of the
BBC, and when the editor, Paul Dacre, returned from taking time off
and found out what his deputy had done in his absence, he was
reportedly furious; which put an abrupt end to the 'stands to reason'
theory that the *Mail* was so strongly against the BBC because Dacre's
brother Nigel was the editor of ITN.

There is another gauge of public feeling: the number of angry
calls to the duty-log. A hundred and thirty people rang to complain
that Peter Sissons had announced the news of the Queen Mother's
death while wearing a dark red rather than a black tie. More than
fifteen hundred complained that the programme schedule had been

disrupted. Most British people, it seems, are a good deal less excitable than most British journalists.

§

The BBC has to be responsive to the people who pay its wages: all of them. It can't be just an agreeable middle-class enclave, because statistically almost half the people who watch it and listen to it do not consider themselves middle class. It can't and shouldn't take a lead in encouraging its viewers and listeners to be pro-monarchy or anti-monarchy, pro-European or anti-European, pro-American or anti-American, because that is not what it was created to do.

At the time of the row over the reporting of the Queen Mother's death, and the colour of the tie one of its broadcasters wore (surely only the British press could get in a lather about such a thing), *The Times* quoted one of the BBC governors, who might have been expected to know better, as saying that the BBC 'should be leading by example rather than following the modernizers.'

In fact, the BBC's charter makes it clear that it exists to inform, educate and entertain; anything else would be social engineering of the dodgiest order. A few months before he became director-general in 1960, Sir Hugh Greene told an audience in Frankfurt that he wanted the BBC to mirror the changes in society and culture.

> I don't care whether what is reflected in the mirror is bigotry, injustice and intolerance or accomplishment and inspiring achievement. I only want the mirror to be honest, without any curves, and held with as steady a hand as may be.

A few years later, in 1963, he went further. He told the Commonwealth Broadcasting Conference:

> We think it is an important part of our duty to enquire, to question authority rather than to accept it, to ask in fact whether the Emperor has any clothes.

For the time being, though, the establishment had a few more suits left in its wardrobe. Sir Hugh was shoved out after nine years of saying this kind of thing, forced out by Lord Hill, who was made chairman of the BBC in 1970. Hill looked like the fat little cabinet minister in the P. G. Wodehouse novel who had been poured into his clothes and had forgotten to say 'when'. During the Second World War he was the Radio Doctor, and broadcast to the nation about the dangers of verrucas and adenoids. Now he was given his new job by the Labour government of Harold Wilson specifically in order to control Greene. Wilson had apparently been convinced (though by whom?) that under Greene the BBC was endangering the very fabric of British society.

Those of us who were young employees of the BBC at the end of the Greene years loathed Hill, of course; probably unfairly. Despite the circumstances of his appointment he strove to maintain the BBC's independence against both the Wilson government and the Heath one which replaced it. But the BBC certainly became a more timid and nervous place to work after he took over, and it was more than a decade before it got its nerve back.

Now, of course, Greene seems like the spiritual father of modern broadcasting. He would have revelled in the questions that Jeremy Paxman and John Humphrys put to politicians; and he would feel that the politicians have had to do a better job because people like Paxman and Humphrys are around. Wilson, as I found out on that first day of mine as a news reporter when I tried to ask him a question, liked to take cover behind his authority. Maybe even then he was aware that he was suffering from Alzheimer's disease, and was afraid of being caught out. Anyway, when Wilson punched me in the stomach, his press secretary, Gerald Kaufman, hissed at me that I would hear more of this. Kaufman, who is still in politics at the time of writing, is always good for a comment criticizing the BBC. He also seems to want to abolish the licence fee.

A director-general gives the BBC its tone; yet the BBC gives a director-general his (so far it has only been 'his', though this will soon change) tone as well. Under Greg Dyke, the BBC is more successful than at any time for twenty years, and is much more confident as a result. Dyke knows how to put his employees at ease in a way that John Birt, his predecessor, never did. Yet it was Birt who relaunched the BBC in its present form, turning its news and current-affairs department into the biggest and most effective any-where, creating BBC World, its 24-hour international news service which occasionally reaches audiences of half a billion, and redirecting large amounts of money back into programme making.

Dyke has reaped the rewards of all this. Slowly, all the things the BBC seemed for a moment to be losing began to come back: big sports occasions, big audiences. If you believed the newspapers, and I hope I have managed to convince you that not everything the newspapers say about the BBC should be taken entirely at face value, you would have the impression that Dyke is selling off everything of cultural and intellectual value, and lowering the traditional old standards all the way round. Yet in terms of its audiences, its reputation and its scope, the BBC is probably better off now than at any time since Sir Hugh Greene packed up his things and left in March 1969. And although there is always a great deal of twittering in the serried nests, I have the feeling that the staff feel easier with themselves, their jobs and their bosses than they ever have. The pay may be as tight as ever, but everyone can see how well the Corporation is doing. 'Govern a great empire as you would cook a small fish,' said some Chinese sage, who may or may not have been Confucius. And certainly the BBC is being governed with a light and reasonably employee-friendly hand at present.

It is, of course, a perennially difficult balancing act that the BBC has to accomplish. If it goes all out for the big audiences, it will be accused of dumbing down. If it concentrates purely on high-minded quality, it will lose the big audiences; and then its enemies will question why it should still be funded by the licence fee, since it no longer attracts the majority of viewers.

News plays a strangely pivotal part in all this. The programme makers inside the BBC are rarely great supporters of the news. To them it seems an audience loser, and they are all too aware that it occupies enviably good times of the day in terms of domestic programming. Shifting the main BBC One bulletin from 9.00 p.m. to 10.00 p.m., which happened in the year 2001, helped everybody. The schedulers were able to put on longer programmes in the evening, unbroken by the sacred rock of the news at nine, and being an hour later meant that the *Ten O'Clock News* obtained higher audiences – something else you may not entirely have gathered from the press.

Nevertheless by 2001 it was clear the pressure on the news from within the BBC hadn't gone away. Audiences for news programmes have been in decline ever since the 1980s, and the audience profile wasn't looking good: too many middle-class, middle-aged southern-

ers, too few of the young, the less well-off, and people in the rest of
the country. You started to hear people inside the organization
pointing out that the BBC had a national all-news channel in News
24; why shouldn't people who were interested in news watch that,
and leave the main channels to concentrate on pulling in the big
audiences?

It wouldn't and couldn't happen, of course; the Board of
Governors, as the guardians of the BBC's conscience, exists to prevent
precisely such destruction of the BBC's core activities. But anyway, events stepped in. It became rather difficult to suggest after 11
September that news was a minority interest. Audiences were huge,
and rose once again every time something important happened. In
the United States, where the programme makers and the suited
characters who had taken over the big networks had previously
united to squeeze factual programmes as much as possible, there was
a new mood of outright scorn for American television news, which
had prepared people so little for what was about to happen to them.
And even afterwards they genuinely had no idea why the attack had
taken place. When a New York woman was stopped by a colleague
of mine on 14 September and asked why she thought the attacks on
the World Trade Center and the Pentagon had taken place, she
replied, 'It's because they want to come to our country and we won't
let them in.'

From a poor, faraway place of which Americans knew nothing
and most Europeans knew precious little, a gigantic and terrifying
blow had been struck against the richest city in the richest country in
the world: what clearer example could there be that it was actively
dangerous to turn your back on what was going on outside your
borders? And when the question of bin Laden's fate and whereabouts
absorbed the interest of just about every sentient person in Britain,
who could continue to say that news couldn't deliver audiences?

But if the position of news in general became clearer, so did the
position of my section of it: international reporting. There is always
a debate about the relative attention paid to foreign news in any news
bulletin, and it is part of my job to argue for more foreign news.
British citizens have to be told what is going on in their own country,
otherwise they cannot make proper, rational, democratic decisions.
Yet it is absolutely clear that to hide one's head under the blankets

and pretend that nothing that goes on outside our borders really matters, as happened in the United States, is disastrous. There has to be a balance; it is as simple as that.

For my taste, the balance isn't always correct. We should be telling people more, not less, about the world around them. No doubt this involves looking more carefully at the things we do tell them about, and how we do the telling; but less information can never be the answer to the problem.

There is, however, nothing new about this. Before 1988, when John Birt brought in a quiet but inspiring figure from the *Financial Times*, Ian Hargreaves, to relaunch every aspect of the BBC's reporting, the amount of foreign news in the main BBC television news programmes was dismally small. Almost all the foreign correspondents worked primarily for radio news; television had correspondents in Washington, Jerusalem, Johannesburg, and Hong Kong – and that was all. Hargreaves, with a determination and vision which amounted to crusading, changed all that. In a matter of a couple of years he had turned BBC Television News into a centre for specialization, for individual excellence. A third-rate department, small and underfunded, was well on its way to becoming the largest news broadcaster on earth. Several people deserve credit for what happened, including John Birt. But Ian Hargreaves, who has had the least, deserves a great deal.

The quality of news broadcasting changed too. Previously, domestic news always seemed to take precedence over foreign news; and it wasn't always the most elevated forms of domestic news either. There was far too much about the Royal Family. Once, the *Nine O'Clock News* ran a story (generated originally by the tabloids, of course) which discussed whether a dress worn by the Princess of Wales had revealed one of her nipples. The report included a freeze-frame with the nipple, or whatever it was, circled for greater ease of observation. Maybe this kind of thing brought in bigger audiences, though I doubt it. It was never the only kind of news we purveyed, otherwise I should have resigned in despair; and there was plenty of good solid journalism going on at the same time. But it was not an easy time to be proud of what we were doing, and it was a great relief when all this began to change. The expression 'dumbing down' hadn't been invented at that stage, but that's certainly what it was. The critics who are so concerned about the BBC now it is healthy and prospering don't seem to mention these things. I wonder why not?

Organizations have a natural, innate level of their own, at which they are happiest to operate. We have seen newspapers like *The Times* and the *Mirror* going up- or downmarket, and then slowly floating back towards their natural level. The same is true of *ITV News*, as we must now call ITN, and of the BBC. Sometimes the BBC has gone unnaturally far upmarket, as when the previous head of news and current affairs, Tony Hall, announced that fifty per cent of the main evening news would in future be devoted to foreign reporting; an admirable but quite impossible aim.

It never worries me when there is a big public outcry about 'dumbing down' and falling standards, because this is a valuable corrective within the BBC. Senior figures get worried, and something is done. This is not the case, unfortunately, with Independent Television News. For much of my career, which spanned the years of Sir David Nicholas as its editor, ITN was far swifter and livelier than BBC News, and had a lightness of touch and an easy-going quality which made it a great deal more watchable than the worthy but somehow rather plonking BBC. It was quicker off the mark, so that we expected to find ITN everywhere before us, and it was far cleverer at pushing itself in the press; so that even when we beat ITN, the newspapers would present it differently.

Nowadays this has all vanished. The Independent Television companies have ground ITN into the ratings dust, first forcing it to abandon the ideal news time, 10 p.m., and then, after a national outcry, allowing it back at that time on some nights but not on others. The programme makers and schedulers have far too much influence on who presents the news and how it is done, and even on which subjects should be covered. This, indeed, is dumbing down; and it has ruined ITN accordingly. When commercial interests and the size of the audience are the only criteria which count, quality of reporting and seriousness of purpose invariably suffer.

Fortunately, *Channel Four News* still maintains the standards which ITN established. For me, *Channel Four News* is unmissable. Not just because Jon Snow (for whom I am constantly mistaken – though I don't suppose he is often mistaken for me) is one of the best and most interesting figures on British television, and because it has an intelligent and able group of reporters; there is another reason. Quite simply, *Channel Four News* is longer. That means it has greater scope for reporting and time at its disposal to go into a subject more deeply. A television news report which is a minute and a quarter long is little more than a collection of photograph captions. It is very hard to say anything serious or interesting or new in seventy-five seconds.

Sometimes we seem to assume that our audience is incapable of understanding anything more complicated than rising house prices, crime, and second-rate hospitals. Yet when I'm in Britain, I watch the *Six O'Clock News* and wonder why there has been so much fuss about it. There will often be as much world news as even I could want, and it deals with difficult subjects and tries to make them understandable: as laudable an ambition as you could have. These things are never as cut-and-dried as they seem. But I do feel that foreign reporting is the conscience of BBC's news programmes. The less foreign news we report, the less well we are doing our job.

8

Pressure Points

Our foray across the Afghan border might have annoyed the rest of the Western press corps, but it had enraged some influential people in Pakistan and Afghanistan. We were going to pay a high price for our stunt.

There were two main sources of anger: the tribal leaders along the Durand Line, and the Pakistani officials who were involved in administering the North-West Frontier Province. The tribal leaders were upset about the use of the burka as a disguise, and over the next couple of days they held a *jirga*, or traditional council, to work out how serious our offence had been. The proceedings were interesting, though the account that reached us was distinctly garbled, and I cannot absolutely vouch for it.

The tribal grandees in their robes and turbans gathered, their beards hennaed or white, some leaning on sticks, some surprisingly young and active. They sat down along either side of the mud-brick hall where they had gathered, and discussed the case. There were two conflicting opinions. One said that my offence had been a religious one, and that the Holy Koran forbade the wearing of women's clothes by men. The other, perhaps more liberal, countered that it was purely a civil offence, in that we had slipped across checkpoints into their territory and crossed an international border illegally and in disguise, but that there was nothing irreligious or impious about it.

The argument went on for a surprising amount of time; *jirga*s usually do. One particular tribal leader, known for his fiery support for the Taliban and his angry hostility to the West, opened the case against me. (I was told, however, that in person he was charming and hospitable to Westerners, and always made it clear that his views were general, and not directed against any individual Westerner. Having myself experienced the kindness of Afghans and Pakistanis who disliked my country and my organization, I tended to believe it.)

'This was a deliberate flouting of religious law,' he was quoted afterwards as saying. 'The *firangee* knew he would be committing a grave offence, and yet he persisted in doing so for his own purposes. The religious authorities I have consulted insist that nothing less than a strong and clear *fatwa* should be issued against him. My view is that this should happen.'

At some stage after the tribal leaders had digested that, and listened to other speeches, a very elderly man had to be helped to his feet to speak.

'We must not exaggerate things,' he said, in a quiet voice which everyone present had to strain to listen to. 'I agree that this Englishman should not have broken the law, and should not have disguised himself as a woman; that is a disgraceful and despicable thing for a man to do. But *firangee*s have a different sense of these things from us, and we should not forget that. Secondly, we can only judge this man as being morally reprehensible if his purpose in coming here was an immoral one – if, for instance, he came to steal or kill or rape.

'As I understand it, he did not come for this purpose and he did not commit any acts of immorality. He came to observe the situation; that is what his function in life demanded of him. After he had observed the situation, he left. As far as I have heard, he behaved himself decently.

'So it is only the manner of his travelling through our territory which we must deplore, not his intentions or his manner of behaving. And it is my view that, while he should be criticized for breaking the civil law, he cannot be said to have transgressed any moral law whatever.'

He sat down, and all round the mud-brick hall the beards nodded in serious, reflective agreement. I wasn't able to find out whether or not a vote was taken afterwards; but it didn't matter, because the sense of the meeting was plain. A mild rebuke would be extended from the *jirga*, but not the far more serious and far-reaching religious *fatwa*, which might have seen me captured and punished when I crossed tribal territory again. Even so, I decided I would have to be distinctly careful the next time I entered Afghanistan from Pakistan.

As for the old gentleman who spoke up so ably in my defence, I shall always be grateful to him: it seemed to me to be a judgement of Solomon, and it was delivered with the grace and dignity which you would expect from a man of his years and experience. I was lucky to have got off so lightly.

The local authorities in Pakistan were less forgiving. They had been given a hard time as a result of the incident. The President watched our report on television, and rang one of his ministers, who rang another minister, who rang another; and so on down the line of responsibility, until someone suffered. Islamabad had shouted at Peshawar, and trouble was threatened for all sorts of officials who received the blame for the fact that we had hoodwinked them. Which was unfair, since journalists are notoriously difficult to control, and allowances should be made for anyone who has to deal with them. Governments, however, are not in the habit of making allowances for their officials.

There seemed to be no point whatever in our hanging around in Peshawar; life, it seemed reasonable to assume, would quickly be made difficult for us there. Instead, we decided to get back across the border into northern Afghanistan by a completely different route: via Chitral. Maybe, we reasoned, that would be easier.

And so at 4.45 on the morning of Monday 24 September we found ourselves standing in the warmth of the summer's dawn on the steps of the Pearl Continental, waiting for a taxi to take us to Peshawar airport. We had decided that the less the faithful Aziz had to do with us for the time being, the better for him. There was the scent of syringa in the air, and the mynah birds and hooded crows were already at work restlessly on the well-tended lawns of the hotel.

We had decided to go by air for time's sake. The road journey is a painful twelve hours up and down the mountain passes; by air it takes an hour and a half, and is comfortable. We knew the interior security people would be watching the arrivals at Chitral airport, but we had sent our equipment by road and hoped that the watchers might just possibly take us for ordinary tourists. We would, of course, have been just about the only tourists to go to Chitral for months.

And yet it was a superb place for tourism. The air was light and cold and clean, and made you feel better with every breath. There was something clean about the light, too, which made the seamed faces of the passers-by and the brightness of their clothes seem even sharper and more attractive. After the heat and pollution of Peshawar, it was like taking off a pair of spectacles, cleaning them, and putting them back on your nose.

We had hired a local fixer; call him Ismail. Ismail was an agreeable, vacant-faced character who was relentlessly optimistic about everything. Or perhaps it wasn't optimism; perhaps he never quite understood any question that was put to him. We couldn't entirely decide.

'Do you think,' we would ask Ismail, 'we might get permission to get across the border?'

'Sure, no problem,' he would smile; he had a pleasant smile.

Then things would start to go wrong.

'Sorry, is saying not possible now.'

'But, Ismail, you said earlier there wouldn't be a problem.'

'Sure, no problem.'

There was a big problem now. The army presence had been greatly strengthened all along the border, and the police were in charge of the roadblocks. As far as our contacts knew, no other journalists had yet tried to get across; but it would be so difficult now as to be impossible. The Pakistani authorities said they had closed the border to stop any more Pakistani volunteers from going to Afghanistan to join the Taliban. Perfectly laudable, of course; except for two things. No volunteer who wanted to join the Taliban would dream of crossing the border here, since the Northern Alliance occupied the other side of the border, and would capture or kill any Pakistanis they found. And you would have thought it was moderately clear that we, and dozens of journalists like us, were not planning to fight for the Taliban. Yet we were the ones who were being stopped, while further south the volunteers were still getting across the border in their hundreds to the area which the Taliban controlled.

At first I was inclined to think it was mere habit; officialdom likes to stop people doing things, and journalists are the most obvious people to stop. Later I decided it was more complicated than that. Pakistan had created considerable links with Taliban-held

Afghanistan. The banking system, the taxis, the telephone system were all provided by or through Pakistan. When, for instance, I wanted to pester my friend the Taliban Foreign Minister to let me back in – he never took my calls, of course – I would ring him on a Peshawar number; the Taliban Foreign Ministry in Kabul had been turned into an extension of the Pakistani telephone system.

So in a quiet way, and only up to a certain point, Pakistan was still helping the Taliban. And yet – and this is only a guess on my part – there may have been another reason for letting extreme Islamist volunteers cross into Afghanistan even at this late stage. I suspect the Pakistani authorities knew that the Americans and the Northern Alliance between them would destroy the Taliban and their foreign friends, and wanted to export as many of their own home-grown extremists as possible on the expectation that they wouldn't be coming back; except in coffins. Politics is not a sentimental business.

Paul Danahar, Jouvenal and I sat in a dirty café in the centre of Chitral, eating unutterably unpleasant-looking scrambled egg off greasy plates which no one had properly got round to cleaning in a long time, and talked it over endlessly. With us was Stephane, a thoughtful, witty Franco-Irishman who worked for one of the big news agencies. He must already have been regretting having come with us from Peshawar: a television team is unpleasantly conspicuous in circumstances that call for a low profile, while a solitary agency journalist can move around without attracting any attention at all.

Sometimes we asked Ismail a question or two, but we rarely got anything worthwhile in the way of an answer: he would just sit and smile and look vacant, and tell us there was no problem. There were four or five other Western journalists staying in the town, and we saw them from time to time wandering along the main street. Two or three discreet watchers would always follow them at a distance; and when we went out to buy some clothes to keep us warm in the Hindu Kush mountains and a few dozen chocolate bars to keep up our strength if we had to hike across the border on foot, there were always some watchers wandering along behind us too, showing an earnest interest in the goods for sale in the stalls and shops every time we turned to look at them.

There was a junk shop near the bridge in the main street which sold goods made for and by the Falash people – non-Muslims who still worshipped the old gods. The myth, much embroidered by Rudyard Kipling, had it that they were the ultimate descendants of the troops Alexander the Great left behind him when he passed through this part of the world. It's certainly true that there are some blue-eyed and golden-haired children among the Falash people, though blue eyes and fair hair are not usually regarded as typical signs of Greek or even Macedonian extraction. Kipling, characteristically, went further in his novella *The Man Who Would Be King*, suggesting that these people were descended from the original Freemasons; as though they might be inclined to roll up their trouser legs or put on a sash when you visited them. I bought a Falash headdress decorated with cowrie shells, and a walking stick to help me through the mountains.

With its long, straggling streets of shops selling provisions, Chinese-made tracksuits, *shalwar kameez* in thicker materials to keep the cold out, and local woolly sweaters, Chitral is a charming, congested, not very clean but highly colourful hill town. The sun shines brightly on the snow-covered mountains which surround the town. Children run out to catch a glimpse of you, then dodge quickly round the corner when you smile at them. Carts pulled by scrawny little horses, decked out with green and scarlet and hung with little tinkling bells, struggle up the steep inclines of the town. A few women, heavily veiled, move swiftly and discreetly from shop to shop, looking at the ground. Hawk-faced old men with brown teeth sit in the tea houses looking out on the world as it goes past. Beggars with unimaginable sores and twisted limbs station themselves in key positions by the roadside, calling out insults at anyone who passes by without dropping a coin in their bowl. You can get excellent photographs and wonderful memories in Chitral, and some powerful stomach bugs which will last as long as the memories do.

Jouvenal and I had a friend here, Prince Shujar, who lived in splendid style at the fort which dominates the town and could show you the bullet holes which were made when his ancestors fought for the British in the siege of Chitral at the end of the nineteenth century; but when we rang him we found he was away, working in Peshawar. We were on our own here, and Ismail wasn't going to be of much help. It was obvious, too, that the more we hung out in the centre of town the more attention we were drawing to ourselves. We needed somewhere to regroup.

'How about the Hindu Kush Heights Hotel?' suggested Stephane.

When we reached it, the Hindu Kush Heights turned out to be one of those places where it is a crime to have to work. Perched on a mountainside overlooking the glorious Chitral Valley, it was the perfect eyrie to settle for a couple of weeks, take a little strenuous exercise, and forget the world. An artfully placed photograph, inscribed in big writing and standing on a shelf in the entrance hall, proclaimed that Robert de Niro had done precisely that, not long before. They won't, I suspect, be putting a photograph of John Simpson alongside it; not for a while, anyway. I caused too much trouble during our brief stay.

We were the only guests in the hotel. International crises involving Islam, Pakistan and international terrorism are not good for the tourist trade – though a lifetime of travelling to such places during crises like this have shown me that there is actually no better time to do a little holidaymaking; and one day, if ever I am finally obliged to hang up my flak jacket, I shall search out small jewels like the Hindu Kush Heights and settle down in them at the precise moments when the rest of the world is staying away. The owner, another prince, had retired from commercial flying and built the hotel to match his own ideas of what a mountain retreat should look like. He was off in Karachi; but his wife, darkly beautiful, invited us in to have coffee and a chat.

There was a younger, quieter woman sitting with her; and when I started pouring out the reasons for our being here, and our anxiety to get across the Afghan border, which was only thirty miles away, the two women spoke to each other in an undertone, and the younger one suggested ringing her husband.

'He is the second-in-command of the Chitral Scouts,' explained the owner's wife.

At last, I felt: when you find the people who know each other and run things in Pakistan, life quickly sorts itself out – and very sociably too. The 2-i.-c. of the Chitral Scouts was a major, and he invited us round to headquarters.

The regiment matched the Khyber Rifles for glamour, discipline and the gorgeousness of its uniforms, and at its headquarters, unchanged in almost a century, every conceivable object that could be whitewashed or polished gleamed. The place shone. I'm not a military-minded person in the slightest, and don't hanker after gunfire or the wearing of uniforms; but I do like soldiers to look like soldiers, just as I like cricketers to look like cricketers and policemen to look like policemen. These soldiers looked more like soldiers than almost any I had ever seen. Their moustaches bristled, their backs were ramrod-straight, and their boots were too bright to look at in the late summer sun.

The Major was perfect as well: elegant, debonair and slim, with a more relaxed yet unquestionably military moustache. Evidences of polo-playing were all around his office. He listened quietly to my story, smiling discreetly when I explained about our efforts to get into Afghanistan in burkas. His eyes strayed across to Peter, and I could see him trying to imagine us as two meek little Afghan women. I came to the critical moment: would he give us permission to cross the border?

He didn't say no. He would have to consult, he said – and could we, in the meantime, get a letter of reference from the British High Commission in Islamabad? I saw no reason why not; I had spent a pleasant hour or so with the High Commissioner not long before, and had got along with him very well. We had brought the satellite phone with us, and we were just setting it up in the middle of the regimental compound when the Major came back.

'Don't worry,' he called out. 'We have the permission. You can cross the border.'

I shook hands with him with real gratitude, and we said our goodbyes.

It was when we went back to town that we made our big mistake. We decided to fill in the police forms to register our presence in Chitral – 'just a formality', someone said. This formality had to be completed at the local police headquarters; and directly we got there we collided with that invisible, apparently yielding yet impenetrable wall which is formed in every country on earth by officialdom and bureaucracy. Somehow, something wasn't in order: impossible to say quite what, or to find out how we could sort it out. The policeman was effusive, endlessly patient, and maddeningly imprecise.

'If only your permission from the Major was in writing, sir. Then everything would be *tik-tak*.'

'And no problems if we get it?'

'No problems whatsoever, sir.'

By now the Major would, we knew, be playing polo. He had told me about the afternoon's game, which was between the Chitral Scouts and the local police: apparently up here in the hills they had developed an altogether rougher type of polo than he was used to in the civilized plains. They played the man rather than the ball. When we reached the polo ground, the game was in full swing before a large and enthusiastic crowd. The players from both sides hurtled down the field like a wild cavalry charge towards the Major, who had to face them alone as he dexterously stopped the ball and wheeled his horse round, head-on to the onslaught. His elegant figure, upright in the saddle, braced for the clash. It happened – and I saw what he meant. The other side was indeed playing the man rather than the ball. We sent someone across the field to him after the play had moved on, and asked him if he would mind having another word with us.

The Major rode over, quite slowly, to where we were standing. He was very forgiving, and unfailingly polite, though even the act of talking seemed to hurt him. He made a phone call, and while he wasn't able to give us anything in writing he sent one of his men with us to give the police a message from him. But when we reached the police station, even this wasn't enough. The permission had to be in writing, the policeman said even more apologetically, or we couldn't go.

There are some journalists who don't feel any awkwardness at all about pestering people to help them; I am not one of them. When we went back to the polo ground, the game was finished. It was the time of day when a polo player who has been played in preference to the ball might be thinking of a hot bath and (if that way inclined) a gin-and-tonic or three. Instead, the Major had to deal with us. I took the cowardly way out, and asked Paul Danahar to explain the position to him. Without a regretful look or a word of complaint, the Major said he would come down and see the police with us. The only way you could tell what he had been through were a couple of painful-looking red weals on his arm and a certain grinding way with the gears of his car.

The Major talked to the police captain, and went away. Eventually, after a lot of argument and waiting, we were granted an audience with the captain. He was as different from the Major as it was possible to be. I didn't like the captain, and it was mutual. We were a nuisance to him, and potentially an embarrassment. It was starting to be obvious now what was going on. The military had no problems at all about letting us go through to Afghanistan, and would still be happy to escort us through the roadblocks to the border: the military roadblocks, that is. But we would need special authority to pass through the police roadblocks, and the police came under the provincial government in Peshawar. The provincial government had been severely mauled by the national government over our antics in the burka. Peter Jouvenal was kind enough not to say he'd told me so, that afternoon on the mountain.

Things were starting to look quite bad. Anyway, darkness was starting to fall, and we would have to stay at the Hindu Kush Heights that night. I looked at my watch: I had promised to call the BBC London before the afternoon editorial meeting, to let them know what had happened. There wasn't time now to wait until we reached the hotel, so we stopped and hauled out the trusty satellite phone, and I explained things as best I could to the foreign desk.

At this point there was an explosion of noise and rage in the darkness of the mountain road. Someone had driven up, or maybe emerged from a nearby car, and was screaming at us: a very large man in civilian clothes. He was going on about arresting us, and secret communications, and breaches of security. Presumably he had been following us, and we had unnerved him by taking out the satellite phone. It proved extremely hard to tell him why we should be making a phone call by the side of the road like this. He didn't seem to be open to explanations about editorial meetings.

There is something about secret policemen in any country which gets a journalist's hackles up. To be watched, listened to, spied upon, threatened, always makes the red mist come before my eyes. I suppose I have the feeling that what I am doing is open and of value, while people like him are doing a job which no self-respecting human being should do. This large fellow and I had one of those interchanges where you prod each other's chests with your forefinger, and say things you regret afterwards. He wanted us to go immediately to the Mountain Inn in the centre of Chitral, a nice enough little hotel near the centre of town with a lovely garden, but distinctly police-infested. Thinking of the comforts of the Hindu Kush Heights, I refused; and eventually he caved in and escorted us there up the mountain track.

The charming lady who ran the Heights with her husband was equal to the occasion. I should, she suggested, ring the British High Commissioner. After all, her tone seemed to say, he would surely want to help the BBC when it was in trouble.

Some of my best friends are British ambassadors. I don't, though, suffer from the belief that British diplomats as a whole are particularly well-disposed towards the BBC, or to any other journalists. Like the rest of us, I suppose, they are mostly concerned with their own lives and careers, and (except when they think the BBC can be of some use) they prefer to have as little to do with us as possible. Making calls to angry Pakistani politicians in the late evening on our behalf was not something the British High Commissioner would be likely to want to do.

And so it turned out. I rang some other character from the High Commission, whose home number I had, explained things to him, and asked him to contact the High Commissioner and ask him to call me. Half an hour later the same character rang back.

'Sorry, old boy,' he said; or at least, if he didn't, he was of the kind who might well call you 'old boy'. I'm not sure he didn't call the High Commissioner 'the HC'.

After I'd listened a while, I put the phone down on him. I had had enough pomposity, obstructionism, prat-like behaviour, secret policemen and officialdom to last me for a very long time. Most of all, of course, I cursed myself for the way I had gone about everything. It was all my fault, and I had made a real mess of everything.

Pakistan being a remarkably relaxed country, I rang various local and national government ministers at home that evening and in their offices the next day. Most were very pleasant, especially when I showed a certain genuine contrition. But the key man, the only one who could give us permission to get through the police checkpoints, remained resolutely unobtainable. Sometimes, according to his long-suffering wife, private secretary, major-domo, or whoever else happened to answer his private phones, he was in a meeting. Sometimes he was having a nap. A couple of times he was in his car, and once he was in the lavatory. But wherever he was, he never rang me back.

By late afternoon a mutual friend called him for me. In person, the key minister was apparently relaxed, witty, and privately amused by the whole affair; and – considering the roasting he had had from Islamabad – remarkably non-vindictive towards me. But having got into trouble after one border crossing of mine, he simply wasn't interested in helping me make another. I can't say I blamed him.

Directly we heard that, we packed our bags and got ready to leave. This route into Afghanistan was irrevocably closed to us. It was 5.30 in the afternoon before we finally got under way. Ismail, who had been less than no help the whole time, insisted on coming with us in our flying coach, and took up the space I had been hoping to stretch out in. The driver was dreadful – careless on the terrifying mountain ledges we had to inch down, and inclined to fall asleep as the twelve-hour journey dragged on. I forced myself to stay awake, staring at his protuberant eyes in the mirror and poking him with my Chitrali walking stick every time his lids began to droop. We arrived at the Pearl Continental at 4.15 a.m., having decided that there was no future for us in Pakistan and we should get out of it as quickly as possible. That meant getting up two hours later and leaving for India.

The fact is, an alternative way of getting into Afghanistan did in theory exist. It was just that it was so long, so roundabout, so complicated and so uncertain that until now we had been prepared to do almost anything to avoid it. Now, though, we had no choice; we would have to make our way around the Gulf and across Central Asia to the former Soviet republic of Tajikistan, on Afghanistan's northern border. The Tajiks might or might not let Western journalists into their country, and they might or might not let us through to Afghanistan. It had always seemed to me to be a discouragingly hard and unlikely route. Until now, that is.

In this atmosphere of despair and utter failure there was only one faint consolation: a joke that began circulating on various Pakistani Internet sites. The CIA approaches the Taliban and says, 'If you will hand over Osama bin Laden, we'll send you Julia Roberts in exchange.' (Some variants specified Kate Winslet.) The Taliban, notorious for their homosexual tendencies, reply politely, 'Thank you, but our religious principles wouldn't permit that. We might consider exchanging Osama, though, if you would send us John Simpson. In his burka, naturally.'

§

I hope I haven't shocked you too much by this revelation that people like me are sometimes less than welcome at British embassies around the world. It's by no means invariably true; I have been the guest of various ambassadors in different places, and have the pleasantest of memories of embassies and high commissions in countries from Iran to Cuba, Iraq to China, and the Netherlands to the United States. British ambassadors and members of their staff have at times done me great favours in the way of work.

But the relationship is by no means automatic. I have noticed that the more formal and starchy an ambassador is, the less likely he or she is to help you. They always seem happy to talk to you, and to describe the local situation as they see it. But there are times when you need more help than that; which is where the character of the ambassador comes in. There are those who see that Britain's national interest, of which they are the guardians, is wider than just the narrow diplomatic relationship with their host country; that it can include openness and better information and more public awareness as well as good, private bilateral links between governments. People like me can be a real embarrassment to these links, and if you are an ambassador you have to take a certain leap of faith and tell yourself that it is in the wider interests of Britain that the BBC should be helped.

At the same time, I much prefer it the way it is. The poor correspondents of the government-funded Voice of America have been obliged in the past to submit themselves to all sorts of indignities from the local US embassy, including having their reports checked by the ambassador before they are broadcast, to see that there is nothing embarrassing in them. I think any red-blooded BBC correspondent would resign on the spot rather than endure that, and I can't imagine there are many British ambassadors who would want to be involved in that sort of thing either. Our relationship with British embassies – when, that is, we have a relationship at all – is a completely personal one. I've noticed something about diplomats, though. You can have a perfectly good career if you keep your nose clean and just move on up the ranks year by year. But the ones who make it fastest to the top of the diplomatic service are usually those who are prepared to take a few risks.

'The most insecure people on earth,' Bertrand Russell once remarked, 'are those who are forever playing it safe.' It is as true for broadcasters as it is for diplomats. The trouble is, taking risks can get you into serious difficulty at times of national stress. Around 1968, a time when so many new phrases, expressions and clichés arose, people started using a particular formulation which was applied to all sorts of areas of human activity which seemed to need some kind of special policing. The template was 'Politics is too important to be left to the politicians', but it was applied in all sorts of other ways: 'Science is too important to be left to the scientists,' 'Policing is too important to be left to the police,' and so on. And in the spring of 1968, with Paris and Prague exploding with radical new ideas and Chicago and Los Angeles exploding with street rage, an unnamed member of the Wilson government was quoted by the *Guardian* newspaper as saying, 'Broadcasting is too important to be left to the broadcasters.'

It had to happen. Under Sir Hugh Greene, BBC television became the scourge of politics. Satirists who had mocked the absurdities of Harold Macmillan and Sir Alec Douglas-Home's tottering governments enthusiastically turned their attention after 1964 to the failure of Harold Wilson's government to deliver anything along the lines it had promised. Current-affairs programmes started exposing the sectarian nastiness of Unionist rule in Northern Ireland. Soon we began to get revelations about Britain's precautions in the event of nuclear war. The Wilson government's humble support for the Vietnam War came under closer scrutiny, as more and more people died there as a direct result of American tactics. Current-affairs broadcasting increasingly seemed to have taken on a left-wing tone; or at least it questioned existing realities in ways they had never properly been questioned before in Britain.

Party politicians, naturally enough, see everything in terms of partisan politics. They cannot understand people like myself, who may be interested in politics but don't approach the subject from the point of view of any particular party commitment. A Conservative government thinks that if it is being challenged by the broadcasters, that is because the broadcasters are instinctively pro-Labour. And when precisely the same broadcasters challenge a Labour government, the new ministers think it is either because the broadcasters are instinctively pro-Conservative, or because they owe their allegiance to the far left. It doesn't always seem to occur to any of them that the broadcasters might simply be doing their job.

You might perhaps expect that a government which claimed to be modernizing everything and throwing off the dead hand of the past might welcome a little enthusiastic questioning. The Wilson governments of 1964–70, however, were anxious to show the establishment that Labour could be trusted to become the natural ruling party. The Blair governments of 1997 and 2001, with their well-cut suits, their support for the Royal Family, and their closeness to the United States, have sometimes seemed very similar.

From the late 1960s on, the Security Service, which most of us call MI5, started proposing that more control should be introduced over the kind of people the BBC recruited and employed. In 1972, as a lowly employee recently promoted to be the BBC correspondent in Dublin, I found myself under a curious amount of pressure to sign the Official Secrets Act. No one actually said anything to me about it. Maybe they were embarrassed; they certainly should have been. I resisted, not because I had any intention of linking myself with some extremist group, or giving information to the IRA, or revealing national secrets, but because something inside me insisted that there was something questionable about it. I wasn't an employee of the state, and I didn't want to be. All I wanted to do was to report what was going on, fairly, freely, and in as unbiased a way as possible.

And yet 'security', which seemed to mean our political backgrounds and general trustworthiness, became more and more of an issue. Good people from outside the BBC were refused jobs in it because they had been involved in left-wing politics as students; or in one or two cases because some idiot read their file wrong. Obvious candidates within the organization failed to get the jobs they applied for. In some cases it embittered them and affected the rest of their entire careers. Wilson's Labour government lost the 1970 election, and Heath's Conservative government had replaced it, yet there was no discernible change; this was a policy the civil servants, not the politicians, were controlling. The pressures on the BBC were never stated publicly, and the BBC kept quiet about them too; but it was obviously getting worse.

At some point late in 1972 I came back to London and went to see one of the bewildering array of top BBC bosses – a man who had always been friendly and helpful to me.

'I'm a bit worried about this business of signing the Official Secrets Act,' I said. 'Do I really have to do it?'

'Any reason why you shouldn't?'

I didn't like the way he asked the question.

'No.'

'Then why not? It's just a signature. Doesn't commit you to anything, if you read the fine print carefully. I wouldn't worry about it, frankly.'

He was right: it didn't commit me to doing anything other than accept that I knew what the provisions of the Act were, and that they applied to me. The provisions of the Act were that if I was in possession of any official information I shouldn't pass it on to anyone who wasn't entitled to receive it. That, too, seemed perfectly reasonable. Yet the Act must apply to everyone, like any other law: why, then, should I particularly need to sign it?

It took me a long time to realize it was nothing more than a warning, a kind of threat: the British establishment's equivalent of a paramilitary leader in Belfast or Dublin telling you he knew where you lived. I resisted for almost another year, pretending I had forgotten about it or had mislaid the form. In the end, though, I received the bluntest of letters from the administration people in London: I seemed to have neglected to sign the Official Secrets Act. Here was a fresh copy. Would I kindly send it back, signed, by return of post, or else explain in writing why I was unwilling to do so?

John Hampden would have refused. So would Nelson Mandela. Andrei Sakharov would have sent it back with something scathing scrawled across it. I signed it. I'm not proud of the fact, but I was nervous in those days. If it happened now I would write about it for one of the newspapers, and create a noisy scene. But it wouldn't happen today. The great security scare had ended by the late 1970s: in spite of the satirical programmes on television, and the fact that broadcasters are always accused of being hostile to the government – any government – and the way John Humphrys and Jeremy Paxman scarcely let a politician get a straight sentence out before interrupting them, the state has somehow managed to stay afloat. I would say, of course, that it has stayed afloat partly because of these things. A society which is free to express itself, and where the government is seen to be the servant of the people rather than its master, is always going to be a healthy and confident one, and the country as a whole is more likely to be at ease with itself.

Slowly, too, governments understood that it was better to persuade the broadcasters, in much the same way as they tried to persuade the newspapers, rather than threatening them and trying to smash them. Margaret Thatcher, as Prime Minister, was a threatener – 'the original heavy breather', she was called. But after the 1987 election the steam went out of her warnings that if the BBC insisted on broadcasting the kind of things she and her ministers didn't like, the Corporation might be privatized. She had a falling out with her minister Norman Tebbit, who took a rigorously ideological approach to the BBC and wanted to get rid of it. She might have some authoritarian tendencies, but at heart she was a populist and knew that ordinary people wouldn't stand for it.

In 1990 John Major took over from her, and went out of his way to show that the long years of hostility between the Conservatives and the BBC were over. People like me, who had long been strangers to the roast beef and fine wines of the Downing Street dining room, started getting invitations again. And although his ministers complained constantly that the BBC was still run by a lot of lefties and needed to be controlled, there was never any question of taking them seriously. Indeed, the louder their complaints, the more it became clear they too were merely trying to influence the BBC by stirring up the anger of licence-fee payers.

Yet when Tony Blair came to power in 1997 and the flow of invitations dried up again, just as they had during the Thatcher years, I wasn't sorry. There is always a faint smell of putrescence, it seems to me, when journalists are made much of by politicians and invited round and petted and given a pull at a bottle of government port. Browning felt the same about poets, and wrote scathingly of Wordsworth, when he decided to join the establishment:

> Just for a handful of silver he left us,
> Just for a riband to stick on his coat.

Perhaps he would have been just as scathing about me for accepting a CBE to stick on my coat in 1991, after the Gulf War. I took it, firstly because I was told by the awarding committee that it was the civilian equivalent of a military medal, and secondly because it was plainly a part of John Major's keenness to show the BBC that he was no longer going to continue with Mrs Thatcher's hostility towards us. I thought it would be churlish to turn it down, and I can't say that I feel I have been corrupted by it, or am any more liable to say what British governments want. What are they going to do – take it away from me?

And yet there are real dangers. The more you hobnob with the people you are expected to report on objectively, the less objective you might find yourself being. And if you are proof against that, as many journalists are, the less other people might think you were capable of being objective. You have to be careful about these things.

It may be very civilized to be on good terms privately, like Balfour and Campbell-Bannerman walking into the House of Commons arm in arm, then separating to their opposing benches and yelling at each other angrily, but it detracts a little from the appearance of parliamentary opposition. These people, you feel, aren't paid to be friendly. Whenever the *News of the World* used to publish photographs of a detective chief superintendent holidaying in Spain at the poolside of some notorious London villain, people would nudge each other knowingly. Somehow, you don't want to be on good terms with the enemy. People would notice. You could even end up asking them soft questions.

So the danger nowadays seems to be from manipulation rather than from old-style heavying. Yet the manipulators can be remarkably threatening in their own insinuating way. It seems to be something which is mostly restricted to the BBC; as best I can find out – and these are things which competing news desks are understandably reluctant to talk about to people from rival organizations – the editors of big BBC programmes get the worst of it. Maybe this is because programmes like *Today*, *The World at One*, *Newsnight*, and the *Six* or *Ten O'Clock News* are the ones the politicians are

particularly anxious to influence. Maybe it is because in the past the
BBC often seemed more malleable, more nervous about political
pressure, and the manipulators were less likely to get the ripe
raspberry in their ear which they deserved; courteously delivered,
naturally.

Michael Cockerell, the author of many excellent and sometimes
ferocious television documentaries about senior politicians, once used
a wonderful phrase to express how the BBC used to approach general
elections; it went, he said, into a 'pre-emptive cringe'. We were so
nervous about the possibility of being criticized by any of the parties
for being unfair to them, that we became almost hysterically fair. In
1992, when I covered John Major's election campaign, I described it
in one of my reports as boring; which I though, in the circumstances,
was rather mild of me.

The Conservative Party's campaign chief, a man called Shaun
Woodward, blasted the BBC by phone that evening, and demanded
that I should be taken off Mr Major's campaign. It was then I realized
that, slowly and with some pain, the BBC had developed a backbone
in dealing with party politicians; up to that point I had sometimes
wondered whether it had been surgically removed some decades
earlier. Someone rang Shaun Woodward back and told him I was
staying. The next few weeks were difficult, because some of the
newspaper correspondents who were covering the Major campaign
seemed unhappy about my travelling with them in the battle bus;
journalists of this kind like to get on with the person they are
following, and I was regarded as a Jonah. But when things became
unpleasant I would transfer to the other bus, which contained the
cameramen and photographers, and they were much better company.
Shaun Woodward, by the way, having accused me of doing the
Labour Party's work for it by undermining John Major's campaign,
switched sides some years later. He is, at the time of writing, a
Labour MP.

As Ethelred the Unready found, the feebler your response to
outside pressure, the more likely it is that the pressure will be
increased next time. At last, it seems, the BBC has grasped this. It
shouldn't be on bad terms with the political parties: it should just say
to them, as the comedian Ali G puts it, 'Talk to the hand, 'cause the
face ain't listenin'.' In the past ten or eleven years, it seems to me,

the BBC has been a great deal better about this. There are reasons to hope that the pre-emptive cringe is now a thing of the past.

Yet there seem to have been some unacceptable goings-on. One correspondent says he noticed that when he wrote his script for the next news bulletin on the BBC computer, he would be rung up by Downing Street *before it was broadcast* and lobbied on a point or two. This didn't happen just once or twice. Downing Street has also rung *The World at One* programme to complain about the items it was planning to run.

The problem is, of course, proving that someone at Downing Street has broken the law by hacking into the BBC computer to read scripts and running orders of up-coming programmes. There have been investigations, but no final evidence has been found to make it certain. Nevertheless, I have spoken to several colleagues who are morally certain that it has happened.

'Either that, or they've got some pretty impressive psychics at Number 10,' one said.

If you know how to go about it, and what you are looking for, it probably isn't hard to hack into the BBC system. Nor does it matter all that much: no lives are at stake, and no real secrets. But it is illegal, and in order to get into the BBC system you have to pass a message reminding you of that fact.

Governments are perfectly entitled to put their case to the programme makers, and influence them in any way that is reasonable and will bear public scrutiny. It would be naïve to think we could ever get to a stage when the politicians no longer wanted to put pressure on the broadcasters – unless, that is, broadcasting no longer influences public opinion. My feeling is that the more insinuating ways of influencing the BBC's reporters and editors are an improvement on the old method of outright threat. In the past, governments put ferocious private pressure on the organization as a whole – sometimes, as during the Thatcher years, warning the BBC that it might be dismantled if it didn't change. Those days seem to be over for good. Nowadays the pressure is quieter and more subtle; and this is partly because the BBC has shown that it won't simply lie down and accept what the politicians tell it to do.

There is an absurd contradiction in attitudes towards broadcasting. On the one hand, the faithful supporters of any government are usually convinced that the broadcasters are their opponents. In the dying months of John Major's Conservative government, the accusations that the *Today* programme on Radio 4 was a hotbed of Labour sentiment became embarrassingly shrill; and Labour politicians dismissed the idea both publicly and privately, criticizing the Tories for being too thin-skinned. Within weeks the Labour government was accusing the *Today* programme of ingrained hostility. The same happened with *Newsnight* and *Channel Four News*. There is a strong element of ritual about all this, of course; the politicians know it isn't really true, but they want their supporters in the country at large to think it might be. It seems like the smack of firm government.

On the other hand, there are large numbers of people who assume that the broadcasters, and the BBC in particular, are under the strictest orders from the government, and actually obey instructions on a daily basis. This is fed by the accusations of politicians and their tame newspapers about the political affiliation of the topmost figures in the BBC, the chairman and the director-general. The chairman is appointed by the government, the director-general by the board of governors. When Sir Christopher Bland was appointed by the Conservatives, the immediate assumption was that he was privately a Tory. When Gavyn Davies succeeded him in 2001, everyone recalled that he had been involved with the Labour Party in the past.

It's perfectly reasonable to subject people like the chairman of the BBC and its director-general to the closest scrutiny about everything. But it's a complete misunderstanding of the way the BBC operates to assume that they give the organization its political colouring, which will be adopted all the way down the chain of command to the shopfloor workers who obey politely. There was a wonderful expression in a newspaper article about the BBC by Brian Appleyard of the *Sunday Times* in the spring of 2002; he spoke of the 'permafrost' within the organization which resisted the efforts of Greg Dyke to change the attitude and the culture to make them more responsive to the outside environment.

When you read, therefore, that Dyke is a popularizer who took TV-am so far downmarket that it finally disappeared down the drain, and that he is in the process of doing the same thing with the BBC, it would be a mistake to believe it; any more than you should necessarily have believed it when you read that John Birt, his predecessor, had instructed BBC News to give up proper, traditional reporting in favour of pre-ordained formulaic programmes which would be decided before the shooting had actually started.

My experience in thirty-six years of working for this strange, hugely powerful organization which is oddly lacking in confidence is that it stays very much the same, whoever is in charge at the top. The permafrost can be infuriating, but it is also a guarantee of sorts that the institution will remain recognizably the same. It has its ups and downs, of course: losing the rights to so many important sporting events in 2000 and 2001 seemed disastrous, until it slowly became clear that the television companies which had bought them had either paid too much or had problems in maintaining an audience. As I write, the BBC is undergoing a tremendous renaissance in its self-esteem. Some of Dyke's optimism has started to unthaw it; and as the results show up more and more, the optimism will grow.

The BBC is a constant, both in broadcasting and in British society. Sometimes it strives embarrassingly for the populist, and the schedules are packed with slick but low-grade quiz shows ('What "P" is the capital of France?'); sometimes it seeks to be worthy, with stiff costume dramas or dull attempts to reflect everyday life. Eventually, though, the buoyancy level reasserts itself. The BBC governors receive an unusual number of letters and start complaining, the board of management looks over its shoulder and gets nervous, and slowly the great dirigible will shake itself and adjust its level slightly as a result. The one thing that will not happen, assuming the BBC continues to be funded and governed more or less as it is now, is that it will sink irrevocably.

§

The BBC is a strange old outfit. Its huge, disturbed, self-righteous founder John Reith – 'that wuthering height' as Churchill, who disliked him intensely, called him – bequeathed us a set of values which still apply as strongly as ever. The balance he displayed during the BBC's first major crisis, the General Strike of 1926, when it reported the views not simply of the government but also of the strikers in a balanced and unexcitable fashion, remains our instinctive standard; so much so that I found it increasingly difficult to stomach references after 11 September 2001 to 'terrorists' and 'terrorism' on the BBC.

Reporting from Israel during the upsurge of suicide-bombings seven months later, in April 2002, I found myself, like the other BBC people in Jerusalem, under pressure from Israelis to use these words. We didn't, of course, because that would indicate to Arab viewers that we were taking Israel's side; and yet if the young men who flew aircraft into buildings in America were terrorists, why weren't the young men and women who strapped explosives round themselves and blew up their fellow human beings in Israeli cafés and markets?

We had, I feel, been sloppy in our easy acceptance of the word when it was connected with the United States, and we paid the penalty for it later. Stick to the rules: it's always better in the end. Personally, having witnessed the effects of a good many bombs in my time, I loathe the people who plant them, whatever their motives; and I think much less of the cause they support, accordingly. I'm not entirely sure what the difference is between an eighteen-year-old woman who straps explosives round her waist and goes in search of an Israeli market, or a young extremist who blows up buildings, killing dozens of people, and ends up as his country's political leader. But merely because I don't like people who plant bombs, I don't feel the need to call them names; and 'terrorist' simply means 'a killer whose cause I dislike'.

If you travel around in search of news, you are often aware of the pressure to cut corners like these – to ease up on the principle, for the sake of achieving some particular end. Mostly the pressure is from outside, of course, but there are occasions when you are tempted to hold back for a little, go quiet for the sake of some more important goal. Those are the times, it seems to me, when you should put your head down and go for it anyway.

An example: in 2002 I wanted badly to go back to Iraq in case of an attack by the Americans and British. The Iraqis had banned me for eleven years, and it hurt: I like Iraq a good deal, have made many friends there, and would (for reasons which are hard to explain) like to go back if the bombs started falling. I was just starting to get some indication that I might indeed be acceptable, when someone came to me with a proposal to make a documentary about Saddam Hussein's life.

There is no possibility of making a nice documentary about Saddam; not if, like me, you have seen the aftermath of his attack on the people of Halabjeh with chemical weapons, and have observed close up the fear every single Iraqi has of Saddam's security apparatus. And yet to say no would, I felt, have been a betrayal of precisely the kind of principle I am so good at spouting about. So I put my head down in the approved fashion and agreed. Interestingly, it seemed to have no effect on my hopes of going back to Iraq: and I had a clear conscience.

It's interesting: in the BBC, if you are called on to do something which you feel instinctively is unbalanced or unfair, you always seem to win your case if you appeal to Reithian principles. I suppose no one, however senior, wants to be seen to breach them. A long time ago, when I was the radio correspondent in South Africa and apartheid was still in full control, I received a letter from a senior BBC executive. Martin Bell, it said, was going to Washington as correspondent, and his job as diplomatic correspondent based in London was coming free; was I interested? It was the best job in BBC News, and I would have walked the entire length of Africa back to London to get it. After I had calmed down, I wrote back to say that, yes, on the whole, I thought I might be prepared to consider it. Then I tore up that letter and wrote another which said yes, I wanted it very much indeed; and that was the one I sent.

And then I heard nothing, for week after week. Worse, the man who wrote the original letter left, and someone else took his place. I found an excuse to write to the new man and asked if he also wanted me to take Martin Bell's old job. A long time later he wrote back. If you read the letter very carefully, you might just get the impression he did. But it clearly wasn't a done deal.

One day I had a phone call from the BBC in London. The man at the other end was clearly embarrassed, and took a long time to get to the point. Gradually, though, through the mists and evasions, I began to perceive the outlines of what was being proposed. A television correspondent, Mike Sullivan, who was a good friend of mine and a superb writer, was in South Africa reporting for television for a few weeks. He had just done a story on the education of black children, which emphasized some unwholesome facts: in particular, that very little government money was spent on schools and equipment for blacks. I had reported the same things myself for radio, several times; but the South Africans were much less interested in radio than in television.

The South African government spent four times as much on the education of my children, at Fairways Primary School in Illovo, than it did on the education of my black housekeeper's children. Even more offensive in some ways, my children had their textbooks provided for nothing; Caroline had to pay for her children's text-books – or at least she would have, if my then wife and I hadn't paid for them instead. But although the government of the unpleasant John Vorster deliberately ensured that black children had a worse education, it got furious if anyone pointed this out. My colleague had done precisely that, and the South African High Commission had duly complained to the BBC in the strongest terms. And somewhere in the lather of angry hypocrisy there was a threat that if the BBC wanted to have a television correspondent based alongside me in Johannesburg, it would have to do something to make up for Sullivan's crime.

The something was slowly revealed to me by the embarrassed voice at the other end of the phone line. By some miscalculation, apparently, the South African government actually spent more on black university students than on white ones. I was being asked to make a report on this. Everything in me rebelled against it. Of course, facts were facts, and if black students did benefit more than white ones it was certainly a point to make somewhere, when relevant. But to go out and make an entire television report which stressed the one solitary positive aspect of South African education seemed to me to be a political act.

'Ah, no, we wouldn't be asking you to do anything like that.'

I sat and thought about it. It looked as though this was precisely what I was being asked to do. And, although no one referred to it, I had the very strong impression that if I wanted Martin Bell's old job I was going to have to jump through this particular hoop for it.

Over the next few days I was given all sorts of assurances. Of course there was no question of my doing a piece of propaganda for South Africa; perish the thought.

'Well,' I said slowly, 'if I can simply report on what I find, and don't have to put in anything to please the South Africans—'

'Of course, of course,' said the voice at the other end. 'Absolutely. Quite. No problem.'

I didn't like it at all. My conscience told me that this was an invisible line, which I wouldn't be able to re-cross afterwards. The television correspondent was predictably and rightly furious, and I knew that if the result didn't turn out well there would be a long article about me, and the entire incident, in *Private Eye*. Any small reputation I might have built up would be destroyed. All I could do was to be as honest as possible, and avoid anything which looked remotely like propaganda.

I decided the report should be made at Fort Hare, the university for black students which was a byword for radicalism. The BBC camera crew, François Marais and his sound recordist Carol Clark, went with me. They knew what was at stake, and sympathized; it was their work, on a previous shoot in what was still Rhodesia then, which had put me in line for Martin Bell's job.

Fort Hare was rather pleasant. It reminded me of an American university constructed along old English lines: Gothic windows, plenty of ivy. The place was moderately well equipped, and the teachers seemed dedicated enough. You could see that it had benefited from relatively large amounts of state money. We filmed in a couple of lecture rooms; the students were working hard, and the lectures seemed good and interesting.

All of which meant that the report I would do was likely to be the kind of thing you might see in on the SABC, whose news reports broadcast nothing but the dullest propaganda.

'We need a final sequence,' François said.

My mind was blank from looking much ruin in the face.

'It's 12.15,' Carol said. 'Lunch time.'

'We haven't got time for food.'

'No – we could film the students having lunch.'

I couldn't think of anything else to film. Our guide from the university seemed nervous and asked if we were really sure we wanted to do this, and then agreed reluctantly.

Almost immediately we got into the dining hall, I saw why he'd been worried. The students had been quiet in their lecture rooms, because they were easily identifiable there. Here in the large dining hall they were all mixed up together. And because no one had bothered to tell them who we were, they assumed we must be from the SABC: agents for apartheid, therefore. They were deeply hostile.

The moment we appeared they started beating on their metal bowls with their spoons: it was like being in Sing Sing. The racket became deafening, and slowly it took on a distinct beat. That made it even worse. I grabbed the microphone out of Carol's hand and yelled at her to stand at the back, in safety.

'Let's get stuck in,' I shouted in François's ear.

He was a tough, stocky, fearless Afrikaner, and he didn't need any urging. We left our guide helplessly looking on, and headed off into the body of the hall. The students broke in panic and fury, hurling chairs and bowls of food at us, and leaping over benches in their determination to get away from our camera; they didn't want to be identified as trouble-makers. We were both hit a couple of times, but neither of us was seriously hurt. The pictures were, of course, spectacular.

If we hadn't turned up in the dining hall, lunch would presumably have proceeded quietly. Nevertheless there was a perpetual level of unrest at Fort Hare University, which often turned into rioting, and the atmosphere there was almost always tense. So our film properly reflected the reality of life at the university. It was broadcast that night, and the next morning there was another angry protest to the BBC from South Africa House in London.

I rang the boss soon after he took the call from the press chief.

'You agreed I should just report what I found there,' I said defensively.

But there was no need to defend myself. Mike Sullivan had made sure that everyone in the newsroom in London knew about the background to my report. There was quite a lot of feeling about it, and about the effort to placate the South Africans; which meant it was a relief to everyone that my report had taken the turn it did. And when the word went round that the South African embassy had complained about me as well, things seemed even better.

'Excellent piece,' the boss beamed. 'Glad you did it that way. Exactly what I was hoping for.'

As it turned out, the South Africans didn't stop us sending a permanent television correspondent to Johannesburg after all, and John Humphrys got the job. Our time working together in South

Africa started a friendship which has lasted ever since. Martin Bell's job became free soon afterwards, and I took it. It was, all the way round, a happy ending.

Still, as with the business of signing the Official Secrets Act, I should have refused outright instead of trying to get round it; and, as the outcome showed, if you stand by your principles (as the BBC has over the question of broadcasting programmes and interviews which the Chinese government doesn't like, for instance) you usually get what you want in the end anyway. Governments like the old South Africa and China may not appreciate what you do, but they understand that you will carry on doing it however much they try to stop you; and in the end they usually learn that it is better to let you broadcast what you want, and simply put in a strong complaint. If, on the other hand, you cave in under their pressure, they will simply pile on more next time, until in the end you only broadcast the things they like. And other governments will notice what you're doing as well.

This was the only time in my entire thirty-six years working for the BBC that anyone has ever asked me to report on something for a particular reason: in this case, in order to get a correspondent into Johannesburg. Apart from this incident, no one has ever suggested to me that I should favour one side above another, or emphasize one person or one party for any kind of political reason; nor have I ever heard of it happening with anyone else.

You will, I hope, notice that all the cases I have written about in my memoirs of the BBC's timidity and its willingness to have its arm twisted, relate to the past; usually the quite distant past. More than thirty years after Sir Hugh Greene was eased out for allowing the BBC to become a nuisance to the quiet, self-satisfied, unchallenged, potentially rather corrupt workings of government, his interpretation of the basic Reithian principles has become the settled policy of the Corporation. Maybe you remember what Greene said in Frankfurt in 1960: he wanted the BBC to be an honest mirror, 'held with as steady a hand as may be'. In the years since he said that, the hand has in my experience become remarkably steady.

9

Manhunt

Peshawar, Karachi, Delhi, Karachi, Islamabad, Karachi,
Dubai, Sharja and Dushanbe:
Wednesday 26 September to Wednesday 3 October

If we couldn't get to Afghanistan from Pakistan, our choices were restricted. Geographically, there were three possibilities: via Iran, Uzbekistan or Tajikistan. Politically, all three countries were difficult for journalists to get to, and the first two abutted onto territory held by the Taliban, with whom they both had hostile relations.

Like every empire, the Soviet Union had placed all the emphasis on establishing routes from each individual colony to the motherland. Just as you usually have to travel via London if you want to go from Uganda to Nigeria, so you have to go via the Russian Federation to get from one recently independent Central Asian republic to another. It was almost impossible to travel by air to the Tajik capital, Dushanbe, from anywhere except the Russian Federation; but you could fly to Tashkent, in Uzbekistan, from various places, including Delhi. Maybe, we speculated, we could then charter some old Russian military aircraft in Tashkent and fly across the border to Tajikistan.

That theory lasted until we spoke on a terrible phone line to Paul Simpson and David Shukman from the World Affairs Unit. They were still in Tajikistan after covering the drought which was affecting the whole of Central Asia. For one thing, they said, there didn't seem to be any planes for charter in either Uzbekistan or Tajikistan. Secondly, relations between the two countries were so bad it was unlikely that either of them would allow a charter flight across the border. So that was that.

We could, of course, have travelled the roundabout route from Pakistan to Moscow; but we would need Russian press visas, which would mean going back to London. I worked it out. Given the awkwardness of the airline timetables, it seemed to me, the earliest we might actually find ourselves inside Afghanistan, after the inevitable hanging around for visas and charters, would be in eighteen days' time.

We didn't have eighteen days. I knew a couple of well-placed people in Washington, one of them a friend of Peter Jouvenal's, whom I rang from time to time for information on all this. Neither of them knew precisely when the bombing of Afghanistan was likely to start, but both said it would happen any time after the next twelve days, on the first night that three different satellites could 'see' Kabul. I was determined to be in Afghanistan by then. Who knew, after all, whether the Taliban might not simply fold when the bombing began? (In fact, it started on the night of 7 October: fourteen days away.) I had the uncomfortable feeling that a wrong decision now would wreck everything. Yet we had to commit ourselves.

Only seven or eight years earlier, this would have been a much harder business. Throughout most of my career the BBC had not been particularly good at planning, largely because it lacked the money and the staff to do the job properly. After 1993, though, when it began to compete with CNN on a worldwide basis, the planning staff was slowly assembled and money became available.

Malcolm Downing was now in charge of planning. He was a close friend of mine from our days in Brussels together, where he had once been the Australian Broadcasting Corporation's European correspondent. Quick-witted, literate, deeply honest, very funny, abrupt to the point of gruffness and irritability, he was one of the best assignments editors I had ever been fortunate enough to work with; perhaps the best. Now, he had the thankless task of setting out the BBC's piece on the worldwide board in the wake of the attacks on New York and Washington.

His is a swinish job. You need great instinct to know when to send people to cover some story, and if you hold back for a day, or send too many people, someone will start complaining very loudly. If something goes wrong, which it often does, it's all your fault. When everything goes right, the credit is ladled onto the people on the ground, and no one remembers who sent them there.

Much, and perhaps most, of the credit for the BBC's success after

11 September 2001 belongs to Malcolm, and to the foreign editor Jonathan Baker. It helped greatly that Malcolm had a foreign correspondent's instinct for a story and the way it developed, while Jonathan had been the editor of the *Nine O'Clock News* and understood the demands that the vast range of BBC programmes were likely to make of the teams in the field. They and their staff of planners made a very good team indeed.

They went into action fast and well now. Someone got on the phone to Dubai and checked out the charter situation there. Someone else contacted Kevin Bishop from the BBC Moscow bureau, who was organizing a satellite dish and a full team from Moscow to get to Tajikistan. A third rang us back with what she had gleaned: we would have to get our own visas for Tajikistan and Northern Afghanistan. If we went to Delhi, the Russian embassy could give us a Tajik visa and the Northern Alliance would give us a visa for Northern Afghanistan. And Uzbek Airlines flew from Delhi to Tashkent every few days. It is hard to explain to you how much of a change all this help and advice represented, from the days (only ten years or so ago) when BBC correspondents and their crews were sent out to wander the world with scarcely any back-up at all.

Slowly, we worked out a plan. If we got ourselves to Tashkent, we might be able to travel to the Tajik border by road, and then on to Dushanbe; and then, somehow, we could get down to the river which marks the border with Afghanistan. Then – but we could cross that river when we came to it.

So at 7.30 on the morning of Wednesday 26 September, fifteen days after the attacks on New York and Washington, Paul Danahar, Peter Jouvenal and I left the Pearl Continental in Peshawar behind us and after an hour during which the clerk at the Pakistan Airlines office struggled with the hugely difficult business of writing out three tickets, we headed for the airport. We were all, I felt, thoroughly Pakistaned out. We sat back on the flight to Karachi, each with a row of seats to ourselves, and drank the Coca-Cola which was the strongest drink available on board.

At Karachi airport, where life takes on a Hobbesian dimension, we fought our way through to the departures lounge with all our gear and asked for the office of Uzbek Airlines, where our tickets from Delhi to Tashkent were waiting for us. Except they weren't. Where the Uzbek Airlines desk had been until two or three days before there was just an empty desk. Behind it was a picture of the Registan in Samarkand, and an advertisement suggesting that we would have a wonderful time if we visited Uzbekistan. On the desk was a notice informing the kind customers that for operational reasons the Uzbek Airlines office was now closed. We went into the CIP ('Commercially Important People') lounge, and Paul Danahar had to do some heavy work on the mobile phone.

We were committed: we had to go on to Delhi, because there was nowhere else to go. In the Cold War, when Pakistan's links were with China and the United States, India's were always with the Soviet Union. That meant that the best connections to Moscow and the former Soviet republics were through Delhi, not Karachi or Islamabad. Relations between Pakistan and India were strained, of course, and airlines and passengers between the two were treated coolly; but at least the flights left every day. We boarded the 2 p.m. PIA flight to Delhi. It was on time, and arrived on time. That was a relief, since we only had a two-hour layover before the Uzbek Airlines flight left Delhi for Tashkent. We would have to get all our gear through customs, buy our tickets for Tashkent, and check in. As we arrived at Delhi airport, we looked up at the departures board. '6.30 Uzbek Airlines to Tashkent. On time', it said.

Unfortunately we had no visas for India. We were in transit, we explained at the immigration desk, heading for Tashkent on the 6.30 flight. It could have been awkward, but India is a great centre of BBC-watching. Officials stopped what they were doing at desks some way off in order to come over and welcome us to Delhi. They hoped, they said, we would find some good guests for *Simpson's World* while we were with them. We were still talking about it when Paul looked up at the departures board again. '6.30 Uzbek Airlines to Tashkent,' it said. 'Cancelled.'

We had nowhere to go now. All we could do was stay the night in New Delhi, while the immigration people promised to sort out our visa problem. A couple of taxis took us and our equipment to a large, modern but rather tatty hotel where the service was vague and there was a faint smell of mould. My favourite hotel, the Imperial, was full. That night in my room I unpacked, made a few phone calls, and took a message from New York asking me to write an article for a well-known American magazine about our efforts to get into Afghanistan. I agreed.

'Maybe someone from the magazine could send me a text message to give me a time and number to call,' I said wearily, and switched the light off.

At four in the morning the phone rang.

'Hi. What time is it there? Oh, is it really? I'm so sorry. You see, someone asked me to send you a text message, and I don't understand what a text message is. I thought you could tell me.'

That rather defined our not very fruitful relationship. Three months later, after I had written them a 6,000-word article, the magazine closed down. It didn't altogether surprise me. At least they were decent enough to pay me.

At nine in the morning we were driving past the splendours of Baker's and Lutyens' architecture on our way to the Russian embassy. Ten years after the break-up of the Soviet Union the Russians still represented Tajikistan's interests in India and most of the rest of the world. This gives you some idea how important the outside world was to Tajikistan; and, I'm bound to say, vice versa. But the Russian embassy was hopeless; so hopeless, it seemed unfair that an American magazine should go under while Russian embassies like this survived.

After we had persuaded the man who spoke to us that Tajikistan was actually part of his responsibility, he began demanding all the impedimenta with which unwilling bureaucracy tries to dissuade the would-be traveller: letters of introduction from our organization in London, letters of invitation from the relevant state organs in Moscow and Tajikistan. We could wait for a very long time before we received them, and even then we would have to go to Moscow and then down to Tajikistan. He was a dull man, dressed in a thin, shiny suit of light grey, and he had the bulbous nose and thinning hair of the European Russian, and I found myself hating him very much indeed. After twenty minutes of this, we left. It was plain that the faithful servant of the former state of workers and peasants had no intention of helping us in any way; much better, we convinced ourselves, to try some other way.

We drove on to the Uzbek embassy. There we met a large, smiling, moon-faced man who, like his national airline, was enthusiastic about the idea of inviting us to his country but incapable of making it happen. He sweated a good deal in the heat, and explained that Uzbek law required us to have visas for the next country we were going to, before we could enter Uzbekistan. The next country was Tajikistan.

'No problem,' he said in a voice that was surprisingly high for a man of his size and weight. 'You just go to the embassy of Russia and ask for visa to Tajikistan.'

So that was that.

We got back into our taxi and decided to do the only thing that was remotely easy: get some Northern Afghanistan visas. The embassy in Delhi was in the hands of supporters of the Northern Alliance; and the Northern Alliance actively wanted Western journalists to come to their part of Afghanistan. Leaving aside the question of how this might happen, we relished the ease and pleasure of being in an embassy which merely required a smallish amount of money and three photographs from us, in order to give us permission to go somewhere. I looked at mine when it came back; it took up an entire page in my passport. The man who had stamped it had chosen the page opposite an old memento from one of my trips to Sarajevo during the siege of 1992–5. 'Maybe Airlines', it said: it was the stamp the UN put in your passport when they flew you out at the end of your stay. Now I had a Maybe Visa to a country I wanted to get to, but no way of travelling to it.

It was pointless to stay in India any longer, since we couldn't get to anywhere we wanted from there. By now, anyway, it was starting to become clear that the only possibility was for us to charter directly to Tajikistan, and argue our way in without visas. They wouldn't, we reasoned optimistically, turn an entire planeload of BBC people away. And if we weren't going to stay in India, there was only one place where I could be of the slightest use until the charter was arranged and ready to go: Pakistan.

Wearily, we put ourselves on the 21.00 flight back to Karachi that evening, with only a solitary stamp in our passports to show for all this expenditure of time and money. With us went two people from the BBC Delhi bureau – the correspondent Adam Mynott, and the bureau chief Tim Erwin. Tim was a Canadian with a particular taste for vegetarian Indian food, and he had brought an overwhelming number of packets of vegetable curry for use by the team heading into Afghanistan. (In the end the plans changed, and Tim didn't get to Kabul until much, much later; but we kept the vegetable curries, and were still heating them up and eating them for weeks.)

We arrived at around 1.30 in the morning in Karachi, tired and drained, and found that our troubles weren't over yet. In the previous few days, while we had been away, Pakistan had introduced a new system which meant that every foreigner entering the country had to have a visa: even the British, who had never previously needed one. We sat on hard wooden benches at the airport, waiting for the most senior immigration official to find someone on the phone to tell him what to do. At first, it looked as though he was going to deport us. He bustled around, his moustache bristling, while we made it clear that we would resist and that his name would feature with great prominence in the newspapers of a number of countries. In the end his moustache ceased to bristle, and he found a superior who told him to give us exceptional permission to stay for three days.

Outside at last, in the fiery heat of a Karachi night, the flying coach our hotel had sent for us developed a flat tyre. It took an hour to fix. Then, when we arrived in the hotel lobby, we found that Paul Danahar's suitcase and mine had somehow been left behind at the airport. Self-sacrificingly, Paul went back on his own to fetch them both. I just went to bed; age and rank, I thought, had earned me that much. It was just after 4 a.m.

Twelve hours later, we boarded a Pakistan Airways flight to Islamabad. The cabin crew made a great fuss of me, photographing each other with me. I put up with it all, posing like a performing bear with each of the group in turn, because I assumed this would earn us seats in the almost entirely empty business section of the plane. On the contrary; the staff showed us to our minuscule seats in the back of the plane, fed us what appeared to be cardboard sandwiches and milky water, and took no further notice of us. Behind their drawn curtains, though, they seemed to be enjoying themselves. It was nice that someone was.

The following day, Monday 1 October, was the first entirely positive day we had had in a long time. We found that Islamabad was one of only four places on earth where Tajikistan had its own fully-fledged embassy, and the man there, who seemed to double as press attaché, political secretary and deputy ambassador, gave us each a visa. This was possible because we already had visas to Afghanistan: the only achievement of our Indian trip. Better still, we thought up a way to avoid the long road journey from Tashkent (assuming we could get there anyway) to Dushanbe; Paul Danahar had found a charter company which would take us, and a lot more people too, from Dubai direct to Dushanbe. I told Malcolm how much it was going to cost – fifty thousand US dollars, which is a lot of licence fees – and held my breath. Malcolm thought about it.

'Fine. Let's do it.'

We were a sizeable step closer to getting into Afghanistan.

And so we left Pakistan once again, this time with twenty-nine pieces of luggage between us. We were travelling heavy, and it wasn't because we wanted to take dinner jackets and four changes of suit with us. Assuming we were lucky enough to get into Afghanistan, this would be a hard and long business. We needed a good deal of food and water, and a lot of television equipment – plus whatever else was required to get us through anything up to two months in a wild country: sleeping-bags, warm clothing, walking boots, and a great many books. The pile of cases and metal boxes in front of the check-in desk for the 07.00 PIA flight to Karachi made us look like explorers on an expedition; which, of course, is precisely what we were.

This time the jumbo jet was so full the cabin crew had no time to notice who we were, let alone photograph us. I'm not very fond of airlines from Islamic countries that refuse to provide their non-Muslim passengers with the comforts of life: among which are alcohol and halfway decent food. In this case I didn't even mind sitting in the back of the plane. I'm not a heavy drinker: two glasses of wine with dinner and a whisky before bed are enough for me, and I can perfectly well go for days on end with no alcohol at all. But because I travel so much, I like to make flying as enjoyable as I can; and therefore I object to having to make do with drinking some artificially coloured, artificially flavoured fizz for kids.

At Karachi they agreed to give us our passports back and allow us to leave the country, which was nice of them; and at last we caught the 22.30 Emirates flight to Dubai. Now Emirates is a real airline. It is owned and operated by good and devout Muslims who nevertheless realize that their service is so good that it will inevitably attract large quantities of non-Muslims requiring different treatment. And so, lounging in business class, we were able to select good-quality whisky and excellent claret, and eat food that tasted like food instead of dandruff. Beautiful women leant over us and offered more of all these things.

It was an hour and forty minutes of unalloyed pleasure – and a reminder of how good the real world can be. It came to an end far too quickly. If you are a real traveller, there always seems to be a correlation between comfort and the shortness of time available to enjoy it.

It applies to hotels as well: the better the hotel, the less time you will be there. I have lived for weeks on end in terrible places, with rump-sprung beds, drains that smell, cheap and uncomfortable furniture, and nothing decent to eat or drink; and I have stayed for a night, or sometimes only half a night, in rooms so grand you feel you need a sketch map to find your way to the lavatory. This, inevitably, was the case in Dubai. We were driven to an enormous marble palace, with a lobby big enough to take the Labour Party conference and still have enough left over for the Liberal Democrats. The lift was so swift and quiet that I pressed the button for my floor three times before I realized we were there already; and the room was almost as large as the Centre Court at Queen's Club. It was dark outside, but I could see there was a huge balcony with a large table and six chairs on it, overlooking what seemed likely to prove a glorious view over the sea when the dawn came up. The bathroom was a small spa, and the bed had all sorts of electronic gadgets that made it a pity to sleep. I looked at my watch: it was 2.12 a.m. We had to meet down in the lobby at 5.20, ready to catch our flight to Dushanbe.

My first thought, when the alarm went off, was, 'Who did this to me?' It took a little time to realize where I was, and to find my way out of a bed so wide, it didn't really matter which way I lay in it. I scraped my face with a razor, blinking red-eyed in the brilliant light reflecting off all the white marble. Downstairs, ten minutes later, I found a collection of BBC people who had gathered over the previous twelve hours from different places in order to take the charter to Dushanbe. The more recent the arrival, the redder the eyes. The women, who included a good friend of mine, Isobel Eaton, seemed strangely immune from this principle; but all the men looked as terrible to me as I must have looked to them. Isobel had two cameramen with her, Ian Pritchard and Frank Considine, but Frank (though he was one of the BBC's top men in the job) was there solely as a picture editor; neither he nor the other two wanted to talk about it, but it became clear to me that the programme they worked for couldn't find a picture editor who was prepared to go with them. Frank, a man I had always admired, volunteered to do it rather than allow the entire trip to fall through.

It seems to me that if you take a job there is a certain moral requirement to accept the bad side of it as well as the good. Of course it would be nice to concentrate exclusively on, let us say, in-depth investigations of the five-star hotels of the French Riviera. Some such opportunity does occasionally come up, but for every one like this there are weeks at a time in places where people fire guns day and night and have a morbid dislike of British television crews. So be it: if you don't like the job, you have a perfect right to refuse it. What seems to me to be wrong is to cherry-pick the nice places and leave someone else to do the rough stuff – which as a result, of course, then comes round more often than it should for everyone else. I've noticed, in particular, that men with families often seem to remember them at moments when something unpleasant is on offer. There is, I can assure you, much less talk of wives and children when a five-day trip to Rome to check on the health of the Pope is in the offing.

The BBC, though, seems remarkably forgiving. No one is shown the door for this kind of thing, no pressure ever seems to be put on anyone to forget their families and go. In fact, no one forces you to do anything, or condemns you for refusing to do it. The BBC glides on, regardless; I suppose that makes it a great and admirable organization. In fact the only thing it ever seems to punish its employees for is criticizing it in public.

Even this takes a long time to happen. What happens is that some senior figure who is beginning to find him- or herself increasingly sidelined or threatened by younger competition suddenly discovers that there is a principle at work behind the changes which are taking place. This principle is then announced to the press, which makes much of the critic; and the critic, believing that he or she has finally been understood and the people's love is at last finding expression through the press, is inclined to say it again. And again. And again.

For a long time, nothing happens. In one or two cases it never does. In the 1990s a famous old radio correspondent found himself under competition from a sharper, more competitive junior colleague who was good at television. The famous correspondent then declared publicly that the BBC had become Stalinist. But whereas Stalin was inclined to execute people who complained about him, the correspondent by contrast thrived. As far as I know, no one in the management of the vast organization even mentioned to him the slight moral contradiction that he had attacked the BBC to the world in the noisiest way imaginable and done it a certain limited amount of damage, yet seemed perfectly happy to keep on taking its money.

Other people have been less lucky – in the long run. Revenge often comes so slowly in the BBC that the original offence has long been forgotten by almost everyone except those who originally handed out the Black Spot in the privacy of some small management meeting; but it usually comes in the end. It reminds me of a Chinese novella I once read in which the lesser deities come in a deputation to the greatest of all the gods as he lies dozing away the millennia and beg him to punish some human evil-doer who has behaved with particular impiety. The great god explains lazily that this would be a bad idea, since in future he would be obliged to deal with every mortal who behaved badly, or else people would say he was losing his grip. Far better, he explains, to let things go their own way. Then, every time anything bad happens to a blasphemer, people would say 'You see? The gods always punish those who annoy them. It may take a long time, but justice is bound to happen in the end.'

§

We drove to Sharja Airport, along the Gulf coast, and saw our chartered aircraft for the first time. It was an Ilyushin 18, first designed in the 1950s, and it looked as though it hadn't had an overhaul since it was built. We made a lot of nervous jokes as we waited to get on board. There were, we noticed, thirteen of us.

It was a long time before we took off, and although we were due to leave at 7.40 the sun climbed higher and higher in the summer sky, until the temperature inside the Ilyushin must have been well over fifty degrees Celsius. We all sweated heavily, and, this being the tropics, the flies which had found their way onto the aircraft fussed about our faces in the most annoying way. The seats were as uncomfortable as only Soviet designers could make them: a third too small, and separated by skimpy little armrests which flopped up and down like a broken limb. The good thing was that we had two or three seats each to sprawl in. The bad thing – but there were so many bad things it seemed a little pointless to enumerate them.

It was a journey into the unknown. We had no way of knowing what kind of reception we would have, nor how we would make our way from Dushanbe to Afghanistan. And so, in order to manage our uncertainty and our hidden doubts, we fell back on making jokes: about the abruptness of the bosomy stewardess, who wanted to be like a Western flight attendant but could never quite forget the old Soviet ways with airline passengers; about the fact that we could see the pilot and co-pilot, through the open door to the flight deck, consulting their manuals; about the way one half of the aircraft had been left empty of seats, so that any Muslims among us could pray if we chose. There were, as it happened, no Muslims among us, but this didn't mean we didn't feel like praying.

And of course once the aircraft took off, we each kept half an ear open for any change in the engine-note; with furnishings as cheap and poorly looked after as these, what must the maintenance be like on the engines? Actually, according to an expert in such things whom I later consulted, the maintenance was probably excellent. Russians may not be much good at making things look nice, but they are experts in getting to places in spite of everything. I read a book, and wrote an article, and played a few games of patience ('I suppose it's the nearest thing to being dead,' T. S. Eliot once said to W. H. Auden, who found him sitting with a pack of cards) and laughed and joked with my neighbours. Sometimes I drank cups of scalding tea, and once I ate a meal reminiscent of *Antony and Cleopatra*: 'It is reported thou didst eat strange flesh / Which some did die to look on'. Sometimes I lay across the three uncomfortable little seats and tried to sleep. Even then I could still hear the note of the engines.

And sometimes I just sat and thought. The events of 11 September, less than a month before, had changed a great deal about the way we would see our lives from now on: the way we travelled, the way we built buildings, the way we saw our world. We had been shown a darker side of existence, which challenged the easy assumption that life must inevitably get better and faster and easier. And more peaceful. It was starting to dawn on some of us anyway. In 1969 I first saw Stanley Kubrick's film about the future which led us to believe that by 2001 we would be travelling to the Moon in rocketships like huge hotels; no red-eyes on them. The world has indeed become a smaller place in all sorts of ways, but we weren't shuttling to the Moon just yet. And down here on Earth it had already taken Peter Jouvenal, Paul Danahar and me longer to get to Afghanistan than Kubrick's astronauts needed for his entire space odyssey.

The modern world, I reflected, had come up against a barrier: not a technological one, but a barrier in human behaviour. Only a few years before, a largely obscure American academic became famous for telling us that liberal democracy had triumphed everywhere, and that history had therefore come to an end. Someone, unfortunately, forgot to tell the Taliban in Afghanistan. The Taliban were not big on liberal democracy: they preferred stringing up television sets at crossroads, closing down girls' schools, and forcing women to wear burkas.

The world's problems therefore have less to do with what we can achieve, and more to do with what we want to achieve; in other words, our attitudes and opinions and feelings – our passions – remain, as ever, more influential than our intellect; which, as Nietzsche pointed out with some satisfaction, is the servant of blind will. We have the ability to turn our world into the equivalent of Dubai airport, where everything looks good, the temperature is perfectly controlled, and no single piece of baggage is ever lost; but we are too unruly, too passionate, to do it.

And, to be honest, some of us anyway have a hankering for places which are chaotic, noisy, and usually hot; where the water is undrinkable, the insects are large and aggressive, and you can't get the BBC. I like my comforts, but on balance I would rather be in such places than in some kind of universal mall, where the shops sell identical goods to those in every other mall in the world. The events of 11 September showed us that something else exists outside the walls of our mall; that life cannot always be made risk-free.

So how do we respond? Do we stay at home, like the sporting heroes and movie-stars who think it's 'too dangerous', as Oprah Winfrey recently wrote to a South African television producer, 'to go from my territory to your territory'? Is it really safer to stay in New York or London anyway? Might it not be a great deal safer to spend your time in, say, Tehran, where there is twenty-five times less danger of being the victim of an unprovoked attack than in the United States, and eight times less than in Britain? Isn't it really that most of us are more frightened by the strangeness, the difference, of the outside world than by its real or perceived danger?

Our journey to Dushanbe passed in complete safety and quite reasonable, if rough, comfort. We even made a perfect landing in the middle of a sandstorm bad enough to prevent just about every other aircraft from landing. If we had been Italians, we would have applauded.

The arrivals hall at Dushanbe was a Soviet time warp. There was great confusion, people in carelessly worn uniforms called out incomprehensible demands, the clocks on the walls had all stopped at different times, and we breathed in that indefinable sweet smell which used to pervade every official building in the entire Soviet Union, and which seems to be composed of official disinfectant, perspiration, and cigarette smoke. Peter Jouvenal, who for various reasons didn't have a Tajik visa, had slipped off the plane without being noticed. His plan was that when the instant of our release happened he would be able to get through in the general crowd. He was watching for his moment. It came, of course, as it always does. At some indefinable moment the officials who had tried to hold us up all suddenly decided to let us through; and in the crush Peter slipped away without being noticed, just as he and I knew he would.

We were at last in Tajikistan, within fifty miles or so of the Afghan border; and we stood a reasonable chance now of getting across. Or so we thought.

§

As best I can compute it, there is forty-eight per cent more foreign reporting now on the BBC's domestic television news bulletins than there was in 1980. It's not surprising: the technology has improved beyond all recognition, the money we spend on foreign reporting has increased dramatically, and there are far more foreign correspondents working primarily for BBC television news around the globe.

To go back in the records and look at the old running orders of our news programmes then can be a little depressing: strikes, accidents, fires, an occasional murder, especially in Northern Ireland, some political stories – and a single item of American, and just occasionally Middle Eastern or South African, news. In the news bulletins I have checked through, from the early 1970s to the early 1980s, there were rarely more than two foreign news items in a single news programme.

I was particularly interested to find out how much reporting we carried from Afghanistan in those days. The answer is remarkably little. The overthrow of the King by his cousin in 1973 – the start of Afghanistan's descent into anarchy and terror – received a ten-second mention on the day it happened. After that I could find no mention of the country at all until 1979. No BBC correspondent visited Afghanistan for television, even when the Russians invaded in December of that year.

The first images of Afghanistan filmed by a BBC cameraman to appear in our news bulletins dated from January 1980. I was the correspondent; but we didn't actually enter the country, we merely filmed from across the border in Pakistan. We were with Lord Carrington, who was Britain's Foreign Secretary, and had been covering his long and quite arduous tour around the general area of the Gulf and Central Asia, reassuring Britain's allies and trying to get some idea of their likely reaction to this sudden incursion by the Soviet Union into new and strategically important territory. He began in Turkey, and went on to Saudi Arabia, Oman, India and Pakistan.

It was hard work for us: the Foreign Office, understanding little about television news and less about its importance, would only give the BBC three seats on Lord Carrington's aircraft, so I had to be my own producer and was obliged to find picture editors in every place we stopped. We stopped very briefly: one night in each country, except for Pakistan. There was no real time to get proper television pictures, and explaining this to the Foreign Office wallahs who organized the trip proved impossible. They, after all, had problems of their own.

In Riadh, a city I thought was probably the nastiest I had ever been to, though admittedly I had twenty years' less experience of nasty cities then, the Foreign Office man in charge of us said – like a schoolteacher allowing us a half-holiday – that we could have an hour and half to film in the town, but we would have to be back at the airport at the end of that time, or the plane would take off without us. Nowadays I would give a different and rather coarser answer, and anyway the Foreign Office wouldn't treat us so dismissively. Then I was nervous that we might not make the deadline, and the Foreign Office didn't care whether we did or not. It was the report in the next day's *Times* that mattered to them.

I bundled the poor cameraman and sound recordist into a taxi and shouted at the driver to take us to the *souk*. Which *souk*, he asked? The largest one, I told him. But the largest one was shut. So, we realized, was everywhere else; it was lunch time, and the streets of Riadh were entirely empty. Even the bad-tempered, arrogant drivers who normally filled them with their over-expensive cars had gone home for a meal and a siesta. Pictures of empty streets would not convey anything at all to the viewer; we would not have a decent report for that night's news on the most important diplomatic event for a very long time.

Panic lends you extra strength. In this entirely empty street I saw there was a tea house of sorts, and barged into it. There were about fifteen men lounging around inside in their dishdashas, drinking tea and soft drinks and eating some distasteful kind of stew. They looked like workmen. I jumped up on a table like a newsreel producer, *c*.1910.

'I'm from the BBC. I want everyone in here to go out into the street and walk around. Act normally. Don't look at the camera. Everyone got it?'

It would be surprising if they had, since scarcely any of them spoke English. But the owner of the place had a son who had studied for a year in Portsmouth, and he came out and explained to them what this madman was demanding. Obediently, rather nicely I thought, they left their stew and their soft drinks and wandered out into the savage heat.

I wouldn't, to be honest, have hired them as extras. They were extraordinarily wooden. They staggered around in the blinding heat.

They talked to each other and pointed at us. They stared directly into the iris of the camera from quite close up. None of it mattered to me: they were real people, this was a real street.

'*Shukran*,' I shouted at them all, and they trooped back to their stew. We just made it to the plane in time.

Oman was even worse. The BBC foreign desk had the number of a British expatriate who was said to be a picture editor there, but he didn't answer his phone. I jumped into a car and was driven round to his house, a beautiful old stone place overlooking the harbour. A cheap curved knife was sticking in the door, pinning down a piece of paper which was blindingly white in the sun. I had to screw up my eyes to read it: 'Patrick isn't in. He's gone shark-fishing. He'll be back around nine tonight. Why not come back tomorrow?'

I rang the office in London when I got back: I wouldn't be able to send them an edited report, but how about a live from the Oman television studio? They weren't enthusiastic – these things cost enormous amounts of money in those days – but we could try. That evening I made my way past the armed guards, found the entirely empty television suite, and got someone to turn on the lights. It was late. Nothing of any kind happened. With great difficulty, I managed to persuade a technician to let me make an international call, and spoke to the contact person at the switching-point in London.

'Oh yes,' he said cheerfully, 'got you down on the list here. Amman.'

'Oman.'

'Is that the same as Amman?'

'Not really.'

'Are you anywhere near Amman?'

'Not really.'

'How far away?'

'No idea – maybe fifteen hundred miles.'

'So you won't be able to get there in the next ten minutes?'

'Not really.'

'Oh well. Sorry about that.'

It was a different world in all sorts of ways, and I can't say I miss it in the least.

Pakistan was the culmination of Lord Carrington's tour. In Islamabad the camera crew and I were delayed by an interview with the President, General Zia ul-Haq. It was Zia who had staged a coup against the Prime Minister, Zulfikar Ali Bhutto, and later had him executed; who turned Pakistan into an Islamic republic; and who was later blown up in his aircraft in circumstances which have never been properly explained. He was, like every Pakistani soldier and politician I have ever met, extraordinarily charming.

The camera crew managed to get on board the press bus from which ever more irritated Foreign Office people were shouting at us, upset by our absurd behaviour in wanting to interview Presidents and the like. Unwilling to break away rudely from President Zia, I stayed on with him a little too long, though fortunately the crew got away. As I walked out of the main entrance to his headquarters, I saw the bus heading off. In the hurry and rush I had had no time to change my pounds into Pakistani rupees. I couldn't therefore pay for a taxi, even if a taxi had been able to penetrate the security of army headquarters. I couldn't think of anything else to do, so I went back and found President Zia.

'Of course I'll drop you off at your hotel, my dear fellow. It's almost on my way home.'

He did. As we drove he talked about Russia, and what a dreadful problem its old leaders were causing, and about Pakistan, and how he hoped to make a success of his presidency but how difficult that was likely to be. The street lights played on his saturnine face with its small, bristly moustache, and on his superb uniform with its red tabs. I don't think I spoke a word.

'Well, good luck, my dear fellow. It's been a great pleasure to meet you.'

The car with its escort drove off, while the hotel doormen were still at the salute. They looked at me as though I were a visitant from another world.

The next day Lord Carrington went to Torkham, at the entrance to the Khyber Pass, to be photographed looking into Afghanistan. At last, you felt the Foreign Office people must be thinking, these wretched television people can come into their own. I had the impression they saw us essentially as photographers whose pictures moved.

We lunched at the officers' mess of the Khyber Rifles, eating little pieces of lamb on skewers and drinking gin and tonic, and looking at the photographs of the officers around the walls: all European in the oldest, then partly European and partly Indian, then wholly Pakistani. Boar-spears crossed over the doorways. If I had looked under the official photograph of Jinnah, the founder of the nation, I daresay I would have found what an officer in another Pakistani border regiment, the Kurram Militia, showed me some years later: a darker patch on the wall, unfaded by the sun.

'That,' he said with what sounded to me like genuine reverence, 'is where the picture of the King-Emperor used to hang.'

At Torkham there is an observation platform from which you can look out across the wonderful mountainous landscape of Afghanistan, in the direction of Jalalabad. Lord Carrington dutifully looked there, deep into what was now Soviet-held territory, as the camera shutters went off. Every time he showed signs of wanting to stop, there were shouts of 'Just a bit longer, sir.' In the end, though the shutters were still clicking, he announced that he had had enough, and stepped down.

I was standing with the Reuters correspondent, a friend of mine of some years' standing. Something about the landscape and the numinous nature of the place we found ourselves got into me.

'What would you think if we just slipped away from this circus and got across the border? It'd make a great story.'

I hadn't thought it through in the slightest: it was just a sudden romantic notion. I could see something of the same emotion crossing his face.

'Don't suppose the office would let me,' he said.

I thought of my office, and my mortgage, and my family back in London. Later, when I asked them, the office did indeed tell me not to do it, as I had assumed they would; but by that stage I had given the idea up as impractical anyway. In the twenty-two years since then I have rarely been so sensible.

I wasn't to cross the Afghan border for another nine years, until the day the Russians withdrew from Afghanistan in February 1989. The BBC didn't exactly cover itself in glory with its Afghan coverage, unlike ITN, which was still in its heyday. Sandy Gall, the famously battered, gentlemanly ex-Reuters man who presented ITN's *News at Ten*, had made several forays into Afghanistan with the mujaheddin:

superbly effective television reporting of the best and most old-fashioned kind.

For reasons I cannot now quite understand, we never tried to imitate Sandy's derring-do at the BBC. Maybe we felt that Afghanistan somehow belonged to ITN in television terms, and that to follow him there would look merely second best. There were dark and rather unworthy mutterings at ITN that the BBC wasn't interested in going there because it was secretly pro-Soviet. Mrs Thatcher, the Prime Minister, appeared to believe this; though if someone at ITN had told her that people at the BBC cooked babies and ate them, she would probably have believed that as well. The fact was that the initiative for long and arduous trips like this always tended to come from an individual correspondent; the desk could only see these things in terms of length of time away and the cost of it all, and a trip to Afghanistan with the mujaheddin was always open ended and hugely expensive.

I suppose that, as BBC television's only roving foreign correspondent in those days, it never occurred to me to go there because there was always so much other work to be done; and if I didn't suggest it, scarcely anyone else would. These are not excuses, so much as an attempt to understand what went wrong. The fault lay quite heavily with me, but the reason was certainly not some hidden treason, some secret link with a paymaster in the Kremlin. The right moment never presented itself. What I failed to see was that there never is a right moment to spend two months or more out in the wilds of somewhere like Afghanistan: a long-running news story which has its major ups and downs, yet rarely comes to a crescendo. You have to make the moment.

§

I had never heard the name before, and for a moment I was thrown. I looked questioningly at the neat bearded figure in the white robes and the black turban.

'Who's that, then?'

'Commander Zardad. Your government knows all about him. Britain has given him political asylum.'

'And what has he done?'

'He is one of the worst bandits in Afghanistan's history. And he lives in your country, with the British government's agreement.'

It certainly took the wind out of my sails. The man in the white robes and the black turban was Dr Mutawakil, formerly the spokes-man for Mullah Omar, the Taliban leader, and now the Taliban Foreign Minister. I rather liked him: he seemed to understand what the BBC was about, and that it was an independent broadcasting organization and not merely the representative of the British govern-ment. This meant, of course, that he watched BBC World television, even though he was a leading member of a political group so fundamentalist that it believed television was sinful because it cap-tured people's images on videotape: graven images. Perhaps, as Foreign Minister, he had a special licence to view.

Our meeting, in the grand surroundings of the palace appropri-ated by the Taliban Information Ministry, had started off rather well. Dr Mutawakil was frank but unrepentant about the Taliban's record since it had taken power three years earlier. Yes, it had closed down girls' schools, but it was considering reopening some. (It never did, of course.) No, it didn't commit human rights violations; it had its laws, that was all, and people had to obey them. No, he didn't believe the laws were extreme, even though he agreed that some people in other countries might think they were insane. He himself did not. He believed the Taliban's policies were based clearly and properly on the laws outlined in the Holy Koran. He was the model of politeness and reason.

Then I started asking him about Osama bin Laden. This was a committed enemy of the West, a man who had been deeply involved in a number of terrorist acts; should he not be extradited to the West for trial, as the United States had demanded?

No, said Dr Mutawakil; he was a guest of the Taliban, and a close personal friend of the Taliban leader. It was the law of Islam to protect guests and if necessary defend them.

'Even though he is believed to have ordered a number of terrorist attacks?'

It was at that point that Dr Mutawakil raised the name of Commander Zardad. His timing was perfect. If the West was so concerned about terrorist crimes, he said, why had it given asylum to Commander Zardad?

Maybe, I thought, he has a point; and if he has, it should be acknowledged.

'I don't know anything about this man, but when I get back to London I shall do some investigating, and if what you say is true we'll ask the British government about his case.'

Dr Mutawakil nodded sceptically and folded his hands as much as to say, 'If you do, I shall be very surprised indeed.'

But I did. The *Newsnight* producer who was with me, Isobel Eaton, was as keen as I was to find out more about this Commander Zardad and run him to ground; if indeed he was in London. Somehow I doubted it. After all, the British Home Office was so anxious not to take in Afghan refugees that the Home Secretary, Jack Straw, had personally rejected a case I had brought to his attention of an Afghan gynaecologist who had worked as my translator in a series of reports on the Taliban, and had put his life in serious danger as a result. Was it likely, I asked myself, that the Home Office would reject a really deserving case and yet accept a man with a known career as an Afghan bandit? I should have known the answer to that one, of course.

Zardad, it transpired, had been the worst and nastiest of Afghan bandits in the years between 1992, when the mujaheddin had captured Kabul and taken over the country, and 1996, when the Taliban took power and chased them out. His base had been outside the town of Sarobi, two-thirds of the way to Kabul from Jalalabad. There the main road from Kabul to the Khyber Pass and Pakistan intersected a major north–south route. The territory was such that you couldn't get round Sarobi; if you wanted to go to the capital city or to its main supplier, Pakistan, you had to pass Commander Zardad's base.

At the height of his power he commanded more than a hundred men. Some would head out on raids, others would stay and guard the road. No car, no bus, no aid convoy could hope to pass without being stopped and searched – and, usually, pillaged. There is no reliable figure for the number of people who died there. Some people said dozens, some hundreds. That some deaths occurred at Sarobi seems unquestionable.

One of Commander Zardad's nastier refinements was the Human Dog, a naked, hair-covered madman who lived in a hole beside the road and was summoned out on a chain by Zardad to attack his prisoners. The Human Dog would attack them with his teeth and fingers, tearing them and trying to bite their throats. A number of Western aid agencies had suffered in this way, and when we made our film about Commander Zardad there was no shortage of interviewees prepared to come on camera and tell us about what they had seen at Sarobi.

It turned out that the Home Office had not given political asylum to Zardad, as Dr Mutawakil seemed to think, but it had certainly given him exceptional leave to remain in Britain, apparently on the grounds that his life would be in danger if he returned to Afghanistan. It probably would have been; but my translator's life would also have been in danger, and the Home Office had no qualms about rejecting his request for asylum on what seemed to me entirely flippant grounds. (Fortunately the Irish government was more enlightened; the then Foreign Minister, David Andrews, looked at the case and saw immediately that this was someone who thoroughly deserved asylum. Britain's loss, moral and medical, was Ireland's gain, since Dr Zekria is re-training to practise medicine there and has become an enthusiastic Irishman.)

It was the summer of 2000 before we could get everything together and go back to Afghanistan in order to find witnesses who were prepared to speak about Zardad's crimes. They were a small minority, and often they demanded the most elaborate protection against being identified. Most wanted to hide their face; some demanded that we should disguise their voice. As so often happens with Afghans, what they knew to be true and what they believed to be true tended to merge into one another, and this made them less than perfect witnesses. We knew we had to be careful: the BBC gets extremely nervous about these things, quite properly, and we had to reject several otherwise good interviewees because we weren't convinced about small details.

Absurdly, our filming in Afghanistan had to be done in secret. We might be working on a report which would please the Taliban Foreign Ministry, but the régime would never have considered relaxing their stringent rules about graven images for us. We had to find places where no one could see us, then collect our witnesses and drive them there. If the Taliban had been more efficient we could have been in trouble; as it was, of course, they never even noticed us.

The one thing we really wanted – because although I may pretend to be high-minded, I'm just a hack at heart, after all – was the Human Dog. Once before we had toured the slums of Peshawar trying to find him. At last someone told us where he was; but, like the man out of whom Jesus cast the devils in the Bible, he was nowadays clothed and in his right mind, and deeply unwilling to appear on the BBC. We decided that this must rule him out; our story was weaker without him, yet it seemed unreasonable to hunt him down when he was as much a victim of Zardad as the people he was forced to attack.

We had no qualms about revealing Zardad himself. Afghan exiles, as scandalized by his presence in Britain as Dr Mutawakil was, told us he was living in the south London suburb of Mitcham: an absurd place, somehow, for an Afghan warlord to come to rest. When we went there we found that Mitcham was a strange and complicated place, an old-fashioned outer suburb which had become the focus of much recent immigration. The new and old communities disliked each other intensely.

We cruised around and found Marsh Road, where Zardad lived: two lines of small, more or less identical Edwardian grey-brick villas, each with its own front garden. The garden of Number 3 was scraggy, and bits of cloth had been strung across the windows in lieu of curtains. Jouvenal had done a good deal of sleuthing here and had found a helpful couple nearby, elderly Conservatives who were unenthusiastic about immigrants in general and scandalized by the goings-on in the Zardad house. They had kept a particular eye on it, in the belief that something illegal might be going on there; our arrival confirmed everything they had suspected. Zardad employed and housed half a dozen young Afghans who left every morning and came back late at night. They weren't necessarily drugs dealers, of course; they could perfectly well have jobs at some local restaurant. He himself, the neighbours said, lounged around till noon, then wandered out for a few hours and came back later. After all, he was the boss; and that was how bosses behaved in Afghanistan.

Finding him had been no problem, but filming him might be. The BBC has become as obsessive about intruding on people's privacy and giving them grounds for complaint as it has about the portrayal of violence and putting its employees into danger. It's right, of course; for a great public corporation to behave with the intrusiveness of the tabloids would be completely unacceptable. Even so, we had to jump through quite a few hoops in order to get permission to confront Zardad. *Newsnight*'s lawyer was nervous about the entire project. How certain were we that this man was indeed Zardad? Certain, we said. But how was that possible? Had we seen him, or pictures of him? No; we had found out where he was on the basis of information.

'Information,' echoed the lawyer, as though it was a banned substance. He made a little sound that indicated his uncertainty and general lack of confidence in the entire procedure.

The BBC management was worried that we might break the law of trespass. How were we going to approach him? How were we going to get access to his house? How could we get him to confirm he really was Zardad? Journalists are expansive, it'll-be-all-right-on-the-night type of people; lawyers and managers are not. Once upon a time, when journalists ran the BBC, we would just have gone into an episode like this with a minimum of care and forethought. Not any longer. The lawyer could imagine the action that would be brought against us if we got the wrong man; the managers could imagine the questions they would have to answer if Zardad got himself a lawyer and accused us of forcing our way into his house unwanted.

Isobel bore the brunt of all this, and had to come up with answers. It was, I reflected, good for us; and in the end it helped us make a better film. Privately, though, she and I were nervous about the whole business: not that we would get the wrong man, but that we wouldn't get him at all. This had been a particularly expensive film to make, and if Zardad refused to come to the door and speak to us we wouldn't have any pictures of him. We could get away without the Human Dog, but without Zardad we didn't have a film at all; it'd be like making *The Beggar's Opera* and leaving out MacHeath.

And yet, as we edited the pictures we had got in Afghanistan, I could see what a good film it would make if we could indeed get some shots of Zardad. We had everything else: the witnesses, often very strong; the landscape; the context of his violence; the shock effect of showing a man who was the Taliban's enemy, and was even worse than the Taliban. At 10.30 that night, as we stood up aching and tired in the edit suite after one last look at what we'd done, I knew this was an excellent piece of work. It just needed, as a minimum, five seconds of Zardad opening the door to us, realizing who we were, and slamming it shut in our faces. We could freeze-frame and slo-mo that to our hearts' content.

The next morning, Wednesday 26 July 2000, was bright and sunny, yet I woke up to the leaden realization that I was loading the dice heavily against our success. Poor Isobel: she must have found working with me a distinct pain. We could only devote the morning to hunting down our Afghan mass murderer: by 12.30 at the latest I would have to be off to the Foreign Office, where I had to give a talk about the importance of human rights in foreign policy in the diplomats' lunch hour. It was a date I couldn't miss. Isobel had taken it on the chin. She was always a brave girl, but when, a year or so after all this, she announced she was going to withdraw from television for a while and go to live in the country, I wondered if I hadn't played a part in the process of driving her away.

My taxi driver wanted to chat on the way to Television Centre.

'In all my twenty-eight years as a cabbie, I've never seen . . .'

What it was he'd never seen I failed to take in: I was trying to prepare my talk for the Foreign Office.

The whole team for the bearding of Zardad in his Mitcham den met up in the *Newsnight* office, and went off to one of the BBC's gloomy, windowless cafés to finalize our tactics. Over bacon rolls (rather good) and coffee (irredeemably disgusting) we talked it all through for the last time. There were five of us: Peter Jouvenal, his friend and colleague Vaughan Smith, and the American John Jennings, plus Isobel and I. Vaughan I had known and admired for ten years, and worked with at various times; he was the cameraman who got the best pictures of the Gulf War by pretending he was still what he had indeed once been, an officer in the Grenadier Guards. He was also the one who, when his car was towed away in London, climbed into the pound at night, waited until someone else was leaving, and drove under the barrier before anyone had time to lower it again. Jennings, tall, thin and scholarly, was the ex-US marine who had worked so often in Afghanistan and would, sixteen months later, walk with me into Kabul.

John was particularly important to us because he had once been captured by Zardad, and would therefore be able to recognize him, and also because he spoke Farsi – Zardad's language. Peter would do the essential camera-work. Vaughan was our ace in the hole: the one who would get Zardad to admit that he was indeed Zardad. Faced with this barrage of checks and balances, even the lawyers and the BBC management had agreed we were taking all the necessary steps to avoid disaster.

We talked about the tiny camera which Vaughan would attach to himself, and the uniform he would wear, and the parcel that Peter had prepared for him. We were all, I think, a little nervous. Might Zardad be armed? How would he react? I looked at Isobel, and knew what she was thinking: the most dangerous thing of all would be if we didn't see him.

Isobel, Peter, John and I said goodbye to Vaughan and got into a white van with tinted windows, driven by an amusing, reliable man who was experienced at surveillance filming. Vaughan was travelling separately. It took us a long time to make our way through the long, slow high streets of South London. When we finally reached Mitcham we drove past the end of Marsh Road and turned into the next street, which ran parallel to it. There we organized ourselves. Peter fitted me up with a radio mike, which meant I could roam around without being connected to his camera. After that we sat and waited.

Isobel had gone to the neighbours' house to observe Number 3, and phoned us with dispiriting news: the neighbours, who kept a close watch on the place, thought Zardad had left the house the previous night and hadn't returned.

'They're saying the light's not on in the downstairs front room. He always has it on when he's home.'

I heard she was pretty despondent, though she wouldn't say so.

'We'll just have to go through with it,' I said, not being able to think of any alternative to our grand plan at this late stage.

'S'pose so,' said Isobel.

She was the boss, and she bore the ultimate responsibility for it all. I think by now I wanted it to work for her sake more than anything else.

'All right,' I told the others in the van. 'Time to go.'

I didn't tell them things weren't looking good; why burden them with our troubles?

The driver started up, and we eased slowly round the corner into Marsh Road. Inevitably, people had parked their cars all the way along the street near Number 3. The only available spot for us was a good forty yards away. The driver backed into the space. At least we could see the house from there.

There was a crackling in the ether, and Vaughan's voice came up on the walkie-talkie.

'Just reaching the corner now.'

It seemed pointless to tell him the operation would probably have to be aborted; we were too far committed now. I looked at my watch: 11.45. Absurdly, we only had forty-five minutes in which to catch Zardad; after that I would have to leave for my appointment at the Foreign Office. This was the only opportunity we would have to catch him today, or perhaps ever. After all, if we went through the entire operation and it misfired, someone would almost certainly warn him. It was strange: I was more tense about the pressure of time than I was about the fact that I might be about to confront a bandit and killer.

I watched Vaughan come round the corner. He was riding a scooter, and wearing black leathers and a domed helmet with the visor down. He parked, opened the box on the back of his scooter and took out a parcel wrapped in brown paper: Peter's parcel. It contained a particularly ugly set of Pakistani coffee pot and cups which we had bought in Peshawar with this exercise in mind. Peter, for the sake of verisimilitude, had even put the right amount of Pakistani stamps on the parcel.

'Approaching the house.'

These military men, I thought – they love this kind of thing. Then I remembered, in that brief instant of time, that although I had never been a military man I rather liked it too.

Vaughan rang the bell.

'Ringing the bell,' he told us unnecessarily.

Then nothing happened for a long time.

'Fuck,' I said out loud, with some bitterness.

Vaughan rang the bell again.

Again nothing.

'No good,' I said.

Vaughan rang the bell a third time.

'Look, we're wasting our time,' I said to Peter. 'Tell Vaughan—' I was going to say, not to bother.

But I stopped. The door was opening.

'Are you Zardad Khan?' Vaughan asked, in the loud, clear terms you might use to a child or an idiot.

There was an answering mutter over the walkie-talkie, which we could just hear.

'Zardad Khan? Yes or no?'

'Yes.'

'How do you spell it?'

'Z—,' Zardad began to say.

By this time we had the doors of the van open, and were out and starting to run the twenty-five yards down the pavement. Vaughan hadn't merely established that Zardad was in, after all; he'd got him to identify himself clearly enough to satisfy even a BBC manager.

Because I was out on the pavement first, I outran Peter and John and turned in through the open gate into the unkempt little garden. Zardad seemed sleepy and bewildered, and scarcely raised his eyes from the mysterious package which Vaughan was holding out to him. Inside the gate I had to stop for a second or two: no point in approaching Zardad until Peter and John could get into place, and Peter could start filming. Vaughan quietly slipped away.

'Hello, Commander Zardad,' I said. 'We're from the BBC.'

I meant it to sound neutral, but afterwards, when we looked at the pictures, the words seemed full of menace.

He rubbed his left ear, and looked at me. I realized then why he hadn't answered the door earlier, why the curtains hadn't been drawn in the downstairs front room: he'd been asleep. He looked at me, then at Peter's camera, then at John Jennings. His eyes remained on John for some time, as though he knew he had seen him before but couldn't quite place him. Perhaps he had held so many people prisoner, he was bound to forget some of them.

There was an awkward pause. Then Zardad stopped rubbing his ear and made a rather charming gesture that reminded me so much of the innate courtesy of the Afghan: he was inviting us indoors. Peter followed him in, and I took a quick look at the window where I knew Isobel must be watching. It was a look of sheer triumph, and she must have felt precisely the same thing.

The other two, used to the habits of Afghanistan, slipped off their shoes in the hallway. I didn't; for one thing this man was a murderer who didn't deserve the niceties of polite behaviour, and for another I might need to make a run for it if things turned nasty.

We found ourselves in the almost bare front room. A single light bulb hung from the ceiling. There were cushions around the sides of the room, and a tray on the thickly carpeted floor with old teacups on it: nothing else, not even pictures on the walls. We could have been in a cave in the Hindu Kush instead of familiar, suburban Mitcham.

Suddenly, Zardad slipped out through the sitting-room door and closed it behind him. I was afraid he might be doing the runner, not us; then I heard the stairs creak.

'Maybe he's gone for a firearm,' John Jennings said.

'More likely a knife.'

Peter said nothing. He was filming the room.

A few minutes passed, during which I thought of all sorts of possibilities, few of them comfortable ones. The stairs creaked again: Zardad opened the door, and shook hands with us. His hand was damp, and shook perceptibly. He hadn't gone to fetch a weapon, he'd gone to wash his hands: maybe to wake himself up. He was so nervous I almost felt sorry for him. Then I remembered the stories about the foot-burning, the Human Dog ripping people's throats, the random murders.

I looked at him properly for the first time: he was tall and gaunt, and much younger than I had expected – perhaps thirty. His eyes were close together, and he had a typical Afghan cast to his cheekbones and nose. His beard was neatly trimmed. He wore a combination of Western and Afghan clothes.

We sat cross-legged on the floor, while Peter knelt behind me. John Jennings translated in clear, unhesitant Farsi as I asked Zardad the inevitable questions: had he been the commander at Sarobi? Was he aware of the allegations made against him? Was he a murderer? What about the murders which had been carried out there? What about the torture and robbery?

He denied it all, of course – except for the fact that he had been the commander at Sarobi, which seemed inescapable now. He had done nothing except fight the Taliban. He was an honourable man, and no one had ever alleged these things against him before. He had never heard of any murders being carried out at Sarobi; I must be mistaken. In fact, since he had been there the whole time he could assure me that no murders had taken place there. The only people he and his men had killed were Taliban soldiers.

Weirdly, I still had the feeling as I sat opposite him that we had failed: it was hard to come to terms with the speed of the events which had brought success to a long plan. I looked at my watch: 12.25. If I was to get to the Foreign Office on time, I would have to leave now.

'I'm warning you,' I told Zardad through John Jennings, 'it will be very foolish of you to try to find the many witnesses we have against you, and to threaten them in any way. We found you here, and we will find you again.'

I swept out grandly, not waiting for the others to follow.

I arrived late at the Foreign Office, having come by tube and run across Whitehall from the Underground station. By the time I got there the diplomats had eaten all the sandwiches, so I was hungry as well as sweating. I doubt if my talk was a success; it was certainly quite offensive. Buoyed up by my success with Zardad and made bolder and more irritable by hunger, I lectured the diplomats about their duty to forward the cause of human rights wherever they were based. I also told them I thought British policy to China was supine and it was a disgrace that the Americans, who had much more to lose than we did, should be able to accuse Britain of being soft on China's human rights record. There was a certain harrumphing at the back – from, I later found out, several people deeply involved in making and implementing British policy towards China.

Then we went back to Mitcham, this time with a tremendous sense of achievement. We got more shots of Marsh Road, and I interviewed John Jennings about his experiences at the hands of Commander Zardad. He had, it turned out, been lucky to escape; if he hadn't been American he would probably have been murdered. While he was a prisoner at Sarobi he had witnessed enough atrocities to prove the case against Zardad thoroughly.

Then we returned to Television Centre. As I tried to get through the revolving doors which form a kind of airlock into the building proper, an officious, spotty young guard noticed that my pass was a week out of date.

'I'm confiscating this,' he said, as though I was a passenger on an Afghan bus and he was Zardad. It took me some time to get in.

We edited our report for *Newsnight* all evening, and finished only twenty seconds before it was due on air. The picture editor ran out of the edit suite and down the corner to the transmission room with the finished cassette faster than I have ever seen before.

'You're a genius,' I said to Isobel, whose calmness under fire had been remarkable as the deadline grew closer and closer. It wasn't just the effusion and relief of the moment; I meant it.

Nothing happened to Commander Zardad, of course. He got himself a lawyer, who made noises about suing the BBC for libel until he heard about the witnesses we'd interviewed. Well over a year later, a pleasant police officer rang me to get some more details about the case. After another six months he came to see me, and took down a statement. How likely was it, I asked, that Zardad would be brought before some kind of war-crimes court? Not at all likely, it seemed. And was he still at Number 3, Marsh Road, Mitcham? As far as the policeman knew, he was. But there were so many other cases, and he had had to spend so much time following up leads after the 11 September bombings, that it would be a very long time before a case could be brought against Commander Zardad. By the time it is, I expect he will have qualified for British citizenship.

None of it matters. We didn't go through the whole business of tracking Zardad down in order to have him arrested and put on trial; we just wanted to bring it to public attention. If the Home Office and the Crown Prosecution Service don't think there's enough evidence against him, that's their problem. We did our job.

10

Dumbing Down

Dushanbe was a small piece of well-preserved wreckage from the old Soviet Union, lying pretty much untouched on the Central Asian shore. After the Soviet collapse of 1991, republics like Tajikistan embraced their independence from Moscow with some reluctance, and did everything they could to keep things just as they were in the good old days when Stalin ordered the deportation of entire peoples from one time zone to another, and killed anyone who objected.

Hammers and sickles were positioned grandly on all the main buildings above the entrances and the pediments, or tucked unobtrusively into little corners from which they were impossible to remove: not that, here in Tajikistan, the new post-Communist régime wanted to get rid of them. It had put up banners and slogans and abominably bad statues everywhere, and in just about every respect it seemed to be a reach-me-down, poverty-stricken, less imaginative version of the old Soviet régime. As far as politics, the economy, and the secret police were concerned, nothing much had changed. Marxism–Leninism represented a suit of political and constitutional clothing that seemed just too good to take down to the charity shop and get rid of.

In the streets the older women hurried round in the bright fabrics of Central Asia with coloured scarves on their heads; the older men wore red or green skullcaps and dark suits. As for the younger people, they looked like younger people everywhere, except that these were poorer and less imaginative in their dress. The Tajiks predominated here; even driving through the streets on our way to the hotel, it seemed to me that the ethnic Russians we saw around us were starting to slip down the ladder, becoming poorer, taking on a lower status. This must have been what happened to the Hazaras, the

Mongolian soldiers whom Genghis Khan had left behind him in Afghanistan.

In some ways it wasn't a bad little place, I reflected: the trees were in leaf, the shops were Soviet in style but busy, the buses were made in China, and there were a few Russian or Japanese cars in the streets. If you liked the way Russia used to be (and I for one still have a certain hankering for it, as you might for old fashions, old books or old cars), then being in Dushanbe had something of that pleasant, familiar, slightly guilty feeling you experience when you put on a pair of slippers you had decided were too old and broken down to wear any more. But it was a place to pass through very quickly on your way to somewhere better rather than a place to stay. To have to live or work there must feel a good deal like being paraplegic.

There were two hotels of what would once have been called the Intourist class, the Dushanbe and the Tajikistan; names here seemed to be rationed like consumer goods. I could never remember which was which, and that brought on a dispute with a taxi driver once. The Dushanbe, or it might have been the Tajikistan, was better, but was entirely filled with delegates to some national conference; the Tajikistan, or it might have been the Dushanbe, was not so good and was entirely filled with Western journalists, desperate to get out.

As with a cult which has long since lost its force, and the rationale for whose rituals has long since faded, we had to go through all the old Soviet-style observances: getting accreditation, for instance. Forms had to be filled in, identity photographs had to be handed over, money had to change hands (a sufficient rationale for any ritual, of course) and after a lugubrious figure had read through my answers and taken my money he gave me a pompous piece of laminated plastic which I knew, and he knew, would be of absolutely no value whatever if I got into trouble with the local police.

It was one of those highly coloured things which you are glad to have only because it means you no longer have to go through this dreary ceremony any more; and as you put it in your pocket you look at it, thinking that it will go rather well with that collection of press passes which you keep on the wall of the downstairs lavatory, or in one of the drawers of your writing desk, mixed up with bits of shrapnel which nearly hit you, recording gadgets that have long since ceased to work and have been thoroughly superseded, and coins and notes from countries or currencies which no longer exist.

Armed with my useless press pass, I went back to the Hotel Tajikistan (or Dushanbe). It had become a kind of *salon des refusés*, filled with journalists who were hoping to get into Afghanistan but hadn't so far cracked the code. To me the code seemed to be perfectly plain: it was money. But the money had to be applied in the right direction, and that took information and contacts. Once again, I was glad to belong to a big outfit like the BBC with a good planning system. One team of ours had already crossed into Afghanistan, and the man who organized it was on the payroll. Strangely, perhaps, he wasn't in it for the money at all. He was an idealist, a journalist who believed in freedom of information and movement as a kind of religious faith, and was therefore something of a stranger in his own country; yet he knew all the ways that existed of bribing officials and slipping illegally through the gaps in the system, and he knew who was on the take.

Even so, it wasn't going to be easy. Possibly out of blind principle, like a donkey kicks, rather than for any clear or practical reason, the Tajik authorities seemed to want to stop anybody crossing into Afghanistan. Sometimes the Afghan Northern Alliance sent helicopters up here to pick up their own people, returning from some trip to the West. This, therefore, became the focus of everyone's desires. A Northern Alliance figure who Peter Jouvenal knew would come to the bar at the Tajikistan/Dushanbe and talk to us about this quietly for hours on end.

'So if we take the helicopter on Friday morning,' I heard myself saying with great earnestness, 'how long before we could be down in the Panjshir Valley?'

The Panjshir Valley was the Northern Alliance headquarters, fifty miles or so north of Kabul and not far from the front line.

'You would be there on Saturday evening,' said the man with the Northern Alliance connections reassuringly. 'Maybe Sunday morning.'

This I found deeply satisfying, as a child finds a story repeated again and again by its parents. It became an article of faith, something to hold onto in the turbulent waters of reality.

'And do you think we'll be able to get on the helicopter?'

'Yes, I do. The Northern Alliance wants the BBC to be there.'

There was a practical reason for wanting to go this way. If we flew down to the Panjshir by helicopter it would take approximately a quarter of the time needed to drive, and about a twentieth of the effort. I badly wanted to believe this man. I was as much in his power as if he told me he could get a twenty-fold return on my money. Conmen always tell you that their greatest asset is the desire of a mark to be convinced; this means the mark does most of their work for them. I know the roads of Afghanistan, if you can call a track composed solely of dust and boulders a road, and I was desperately anxious to believe there was a way to avoid days of ganglion-shaking unpleasantness. The helicopter was the thing; we would go by helicopter. I was turning into Toad of Toad Hall.

The BBC had managed to keep a number of rooms in the hotel, one of which was allocated to me. It was as ugly as a Soviet hotel-room could be, with wood panelling, skimpy curtains that scarcely fitted the windows and did nothing to keep the light out in the early mornings, a shower that didn't work properly, a handbasin without a plug and a lavatory with plastic fittings which stank all day and gurgled and fumed all night. The bed was too short for me to lie full length in, and almost too narrow to sleep on my back. The sheet was stained and had holes in it. No one did any laundry, and the fridge was empty. The television set would only receive Tajik TV, though I heard that people in other rooms were able to get foreign stations as well. Tajik TV is hard to watch for long periods, since its entertainment programmes seem to involve either violence or folk dancing. Sometimes, even, both.

Someone else had been living in this room: there were clothes in the cupboard and tins of food on the table. I tried to imagine who in the BBC would wear red Y-fronts, jeans jackets and Doc Martens boots, and eat tinned cheese and tinned sausage. During the night I found out. I had just fallen into a deep sleep at last, with the sheet wrapping its way uncomfortably round me like Gandhi's dhoti in the hot and airless room, when the door burst open and someone turned on the light and stood over me, saying something very loud about the ownership of the bed.

I told him to fuck off.

He was about to get unpleasant when the *dzhurnaya*, the house-keeper on night duty, came bustling in. She talked excitedly to the man in Russian: this room was now taken, she explained, but the BBC had another room for him, further down the hall. He snorted, but turned the light out and closed the door. We had apparently hired several Russian satellite engineers to move and operate our dish. This one wore red Y-fronts.

In the morning I realized that there were journalists everywhere in the hotel. Some I knew and liked, some I knew and disliked, most I didn't know and was thoroughly prepared to dislike. Like rats in an inadequate cage, we bared our teeth at one another and tried to guard our small pile of wood shavings.

Peter and I wandered out into the park opposite. Even at this early stage of the morning men were cooking *shashlik* over coals which they continually fanned like Chinese mandarins. We sat down and ordered sour ersatz coffee and talked the position over. According to the BBC World Service bulletin on short-wave that morning, there were still some diplomatic moves left before an all-out attack against Afghanistan began: but there were clearly only a few days left. I was getting nervy and anxious.

The morning air was thick and yellow and gritty on the teeth. The sandstorm which had stopped every flight the previous day except our Ilyushin 18 was still blowing, the sun was a pinpoint of brightness in the seething yellow sky. Even our coffee had a rasp to it.

'This helicopter's not going to fly in weather like this, is it?'

'No,' said Peter.

The gullibility cleared from my head instantly. There was no alternative to going by road, and we might as well accept it. The only question now was how we might be able to get out of Dushanbe, down to the south of the country, across the river which forms the border, and into Afghanistan. It wasn't going to be at all easy: there seemed to be some sort of ban on the movement of journalists, and crossing borders is hard in every part of the former Soviet Union. For that, at least, we had our contact.

Other things were becoming clearer, too. Paul Danahar, having come all this way with us, had run out of time before an unbreakable family commitment and would have to leave. Instead Peter and I would go to Afghanistan with the small radio team of Kate Clark, the expelled Kabul correspondent, and the engineering wizard Peter

Emmerson. Emmerson was a kind of broadcasting polymath, and we appointed him our travelling bureau chief, to organize things and be the paymaster.

We all wanted to leave at once; and yet somehow it got later and later, and nothing much happened. There were other demands – an outline for a *Panorama* piece on Afghanistan, a longish chapter for a BBC book on the 11 September crisis – which had to be addressed. The day passed, as such days do, and by the end of it we were still no clearer about when and how we might be leaving. Another meal of rice and uncertain meat and rough red wine from Armenia, so thick you almost had to beat the bottle to get it out, like tomato sauce. Another night in the inadequate ship's bunk that was my bed.

The next morning, Friday, there was no sign whatever of Jouvenal. The morning was a disaster, made worse by the news from London that the controller of BBC One wanted our *Panorama* brought forward by a week, so that it would go out on Sunday: in two days' time. There wasn't too much work for me, in that most of the programme was composed of passages from previous reports of mine from Afghanistan which some unfortunate in London had had to knit together. Even so, I had to write a connecting script and get it over to London in time for them to match it to the pictures.

Peter surfaced at 4 p.m., having been negotiating ways of getting to the border with all sorts of dubious characters. He was anxious to get off that evening, but it was clear to me that we would have to spend one last night in Dushanbe, while I laboured long and hard over the *Panorama* script. It ended up 6,000 words long, and had to be recorded that evening. Nothing Peter Emmerson could do to soundproof the room – not even putting the mattress against the window – could keep out the Friday night noise of a band playing Russian rock music quite badly and at a Soviet level of intensity: music-free distortion, as it's known. It was a long time before we managed to finish, and before Emmerson was certain that no stray sounds from the band had made their way onto the recording.

As we finished, Ben Brown, my colleague from the World Affairs Unit, arrived at the hotel. I am extremely fond of Ben, and have watched him develop from a young reporter, recently out of radio, to an accomplished foreign correspondent and then become one of the

best action correspondents in British television – perhaps the best.
His reporting from rural Zimbabwe, for instance, when Robert
Mugabe turned loose his so-called war veterans against white-owned
farms, was particularly memorable. Now I think both of us felt the
position here in Dushanbe was a little difficult. In our job you are
paid to be competitive, and it's hard to switch the reflex on and off
according to the circumstances of the moment.

Our agendas were clearly different. My task was to get as far
south and as close to the front line near Kabul as I could; Ben's was
to get to the BBC base at Khwaja Bahawuddin, across the river in
northern Afghanistan, where the satellite dish had been established.
Even so, it felt as though we were suddenly involved in a race with
one another, though we weren't at all, and he must have felt as
uneasy as I did.

§

There was a time in the BBC's development when a chance encounter
like this could have caused real trouble. Sometimes, indeed, you had
the impression that the editors in London used to like throwing two
or three of their big hitters into the ring without anyone to control
them, and let them fight it out between them like some kind of blood
sport. The result was almost invariably disastrous for the BBC – yet
another reason why ITN used to beat us on all the major occasions.
Slowly and painfully we began to adopt the ITN method, by which
the senior figure on any large-scale operation was not a correspondent
but a producer, who acted as a referee and would decide on the
ground which correspondent should do what. It was some time before
this began to succeed, but when it did our record started to improve
noticeably. We no longer fought each other, we cooperated; uneasily
at first, then more and more naturally as time went by.

Even now, it's difficult. As I say, television reporters aren't paid
to open the door for others, to make way, to be second on the story.
There is always an air of awkwardness until the various functions
and outlets have been assigned, and sometimes it is still necessary for
the producer in charge to police the division quite toughly. There are
correspondents who have such a dislike of the cooperative principle
that they won't discuss what they are planning to do; once, on the
biggest international story of the day, a correspondent from the

Newsnight programme and her producer, another woman, refused openly to tell the field producer in charge what aspect of the story they were intending to concentrate on that evening, and how it would fit in with the plans of the other two *Newsnight* correspondents working on the story. In the end, the producer only found out when their report was written and edited.

What made it all considerably worse was that a reporter from the *Independent on Sunday* newspaper had attached himself to the team and was writing an account of the way *Newsnight* handled a major story like this. The result was, of course, a pretty bad edition of *Newsnight* and an extremely funny but painful story for the *Independent*. If I had been the editor of the programme I would have sacked both the women for dereliction of duty; as it was, I was an outsider and simply looked on with growing embarrassment.

And, it has to be said, with a certain sense of familiarity. I don't remember a news story which was quite so dreadful as that, though they have existed; but there have been plenty of episodes when fighting the other people on your side has been more important than producing a good, well-controlled, coherent series of reports on a particular incident, which will complement each another and give the viewer a clear sense of what happened. It requires a central realization: that no one, either in the office or among the viewers, is likely to say, 'Unfortunately the BBC's effort was pretty disorganized, and I must have seen one set of pictures three or four times in different news reports, but So-and-so really shone. His report was head and shoulders above the others.' It doesn't work that way. No one much remembers one particular report in these circumstances; all they remember is that the reporting was all over the place, and that you played a part in the general disaster.

The difficulty, of course, lies in the egos of the people who are doing the job. Television news has to be a cooperative effort if it is to have any chance of success, and yet some of the fiercest personalities around can be involved in the operation. What is needed is a clear set of instructions and good, firm leadership. If your task is properly delineated and you stick to it, there is less likely to be a problem. And if you don't stick to it, and insist on encroaching into the areas which it has been agreed belong to one of your colleagues, then someone has to have the authority and the determination to make sure the original agreement is properly policed. In the sometimes difficult circumstances and general lack of time, this can be a real problem; yet on it depends the success (or failure) of the entire enterprise, and the use (or waste) of tens of thousands of pounds. Television news is not a cheap business.

I am striving, of course, to give you the impression that I am somehow a quiet, gentle sort of chap who will always hang back and allow the other fellow to go forward and take the limelight if it's in the general interest. Well, I have done it, certainly – and then again there have been times when I haven't. Sadly, egos are not like physical stature; they do not shrink with age. It may be mildly disgusting to see some elderly, much-respected figure behaving with the aggression and competitiveness of a seventeen-year-old, but it certainly happens a good deal: in politics, in higher education, in acting, in literature, in science, and of course in broadcasting; everywhere, that is, that older people compete on a basis of equality with younger ones. The old are, alas, no less foolish than the young; merely better at hiding it. It used to be fashionable to say that if only women had full equality with men the world would be a more sensible place. Not a bit of it. Given the power and the scope, women behave in precisely the same foolish, aggressive way as men.

I have written elsewhere about the two ageing BBC correspondents who almost came to blows over who should record a piece to camera in front of a headless body lying in the street during a civil war. (The producer on hand successfully proposed a compromise: one should stand in front of the body and the other should stand in front of the head, which lay a little way off.) There have been other equally embarrassing examples of indecent exposure of the personality over the years. A famous one happened near the scene of a famous accident, where only a blanket strung across a piece of rope divided a BBC television correspondent from her radio colleague: also a woman.

The television correspondent was falling dangerously behindhand in the lengthy process of editing her report for that night's news. Yet when she heard the radio correspondent doing a live question-and-answer session down the line to a programme presenter in London, and giving what the television correspondent thought was the wrong cause for the tragedy, she stopped her television edit and stamped furiously around the blanket to put the radio correspondent right.

'It wasn't like that at all,' she stormed. 'What happened was . . .' And she told her, at some length.

This was difficult for the radio correspondent, who was still on the line and was still being interviewed, live, by the programme presenter. She did her best to take no notice of the loud explanation going on beside her, but it cannot have been easy. She apparently considered the alternative, which was to put the phone down and shout at the television correspondent to shut up and go away; but that had its problems too. In the end the television correspondent stamped angrily back to the other side of the blanket, but by that stage too much time had been lost and they failed to get their report onto the satellite in time: the greatest crime you can commit in television news. (It happened to me for the first time in my life in Jerusalem not long ago, and – believe me – you do not feel good with yourself if it does.)

Competitiveness can lead to some very strange behaviour. In 1982, when Israel invaded Lebanon, the fighting in Beirut, the capital, was terrible: the worst I have experienced, and the most personally dangerous for me. Israeli planes came over again and again, hitting buildings in West Beirut which Israeli spokesmen claimed were Palestinian terrorist centres. How they knew this was never clear, and often when we went to see the site of the attacks we would find old women and their families living there. They were as likely as not to be Lebanese Muslims.

Somehow, though, the danger didn't seem to unite us and our colleagues. In August 1982 I found myself in Christian East Beirut, while a colleague of mine was across the Green Line in the west of the city: the more dangerous part. Maybe I was jealous of him for having a better (or at any rate a fiercer) story than I had. Maybe he felt, as a younger and professionally more junior man, that he had to resist the intrusion of someone like me. One way or another, we found ourselves competing irritably in the area where East and West Beirut came together. (I should say that now, twenty years later, I have formed a considerable liking for this man, and always enjoy meeting him; and I cannot quite think why I disliked him before. Too much competitiveness, I suppose.)

Shortly after that, I had to leave for home. My replacement, a famously noisy but extremely effective correspondent, wasn't able to come in for a day or so after I left. I was nominally his boss, but since he was older, more aggressive and much more experienced than I (at this stage I had been in television news for only four years), this wasn't a relationship I insisted on. Yet at that time we were going through a rather friendly stage; and so I wrote him a long hand-over letter, which I left at the hotel for his arrival. In it I explained the situation, and told him to watch out for the correspondent in West Beirut; he was, I said unjustly, inclined to be a snake. Sometimes, between colleagues, you do say these things.

It was a very considerable error of judgement. As I heard it later, the new arrival had scarcely reached the hotel and read my letter when he told his crew he was going to West Beirut alone to see the correspondent on the other side. Going to West Beirut meant going through the Green Line at the Museum crossing point: probably, at that stage, the most dangerous spot in the world. I used to cross it as rarely as I could: it frightened me too much. Every day the militiamen who controlled it would take people they didn't like out of their cars and shoot them by the side of the road. They particularly didn't like Westerners, though you could usually get by if you had a television cameraman with you. The correspondent didn't have a cameraman with him, but being a man of considerable courage as well as quite fanatical mischief-making, this did not stop him. He drove straight to the famous Commodore hotel, where our opposite number was staying, and thrust my letter in his face.

'You've got problems,' he said. 'Look what Simpson thinks about you.'

It wasn't to ingratiate himself with the other correspondent that he had come all this way and faced all this danger: it was in order to make trouble. Then he got back into his taxi and was driven back through the most dangerous spot in the world, his mission accomplished. He had made trouble.

He has long since left the BBC, and the other correspondent has matured into a quiet, gentle, successful figure who has never mentioned the letter to me – probably out of sheer good manners.

Pure mischief-making aside, the worst example of destructive competitiveness I ever came across was a few years ago during a major international crisis. It was a difficult and tense period, when those of us who were there felt deeply uneasy about our security. Maybe that played a part in the small-time but ferocious contest which unfolded among the people from one particular television station. It wasn't, I'm glad to be able to say, the BBC.

The correspondent in question was a tough, hyper-aggressive figure whom I had cordially disliked for years. His competitiveness seemed to me at times to amount to the level of psychosis, and stories abound in the television business of his threats and occasional violence. Here, however, he was doing rather well. He got a number of big stories before I did, and seemed to me to be altogether more effective. His office clearly didn't think so. Quite late in the crisis they decided to recall him, and sent another correspondent to take his place – a man I had known and admired for some years.

The first correspondent was outraged, and refused point-blank to leave. And because he had good contacts in the city, he was able to do something about it. In particular, his staff of local people had excellent relations with the police.

During that entire period the police ruled our lives, and they were particularly difficult. Every ten days or so we had to go to their office to renew our permission to remain in the country. The man responsible usually demanded a bottle of whisky as part of his fee. He was a strange, vulpine character whom my colleague, the local BBC correspondent, aptly gave the nickname 'Wolfman'. You were obliged to sit round the table with him at police headquarters, drinking other people's whisky and laughing at his jokes. As it happened, I quickly opted out of this business and preferred to wait outside in the hall. Nor did I bring him any whisky; and the curious thing was, he still stamped my passport. But it was a long and distasteful process, and it could wreck half the day even if you didn't drink anything with Wolfman.

The correspondent who was resisting orders to leave arranged it so that his replacement had to go to see Wolfman and get his visa renewed every single morning. This made it impossible to do any serious work whatever. Day after day he would have to go down to police headquarters, returning only in the afternoon. In the end he couldn't bear it any longer, and told someone senior in his organization what was happening. Even then the original correspondent wouldn't leave, and one of the most senior figures of all had to be sent out from headquarters, fly in to the capital of the neighbouring country, make the long and possibly dangerous journey to the city where we were, and face the chance of further violence there, merely in order to sort out someone's psychological problems.

There are, of course, those of us who feel it never does any harm for senior managers to see what life is really like at the sharp end; but if I had been the editorial figure I would have sacked the correspondent on the spot, and handed him over to Wolfman for punishment. As it happened, the correspondent kept his job and Wolfman was later sacked. But senior managers are not mocked. I hear the correspondent rarely appears on television nowadays.

Like all of us, I have had my ups and downs with my own colleagues too: Kate Adie, for instance, who is one of the most famous figures in British broadcasting, and extremely popular with the British public. Once, buying a couple of CDs in a shop in Oxford Street, I was asked by the salesman if he might have seen me on the news. He might, I said modestly, though I had to tell him my name.

'So what do you do, then?'

'Foreign reporting mostly.'

'What, wars and that?'

'If I can't avoid it.'

'Still doing it, then?'

'Well, I really prefer doing other things.'

'So – a kind of Kate Adie of your day, were you?'

There is something which touches the British psyche about a gutsy, slightly schoolmistressy woman who is prepared to act tough and do anything for a cause: think Elizabeth I, think Mary Kingsley, think Florence Nightingale, think Edith Cavell, think Margaret Thatcher. Kate Adie was the first British woman broadcaster to cover a war from the dangerous side: the side the bombs are falling on. Overnight she became famous for her reports from Libya, when President Reagan bombed Tripoli and tried to kill Colonel Gadhafi in revenge for a terrorist attack against American soldiers in Berlin. This was actually thought to have been carried out on the orders of the Syrian government, but Syria was too big and dangerous for President Reagan to attack; Libya, by contrast, was a small, eccentric, unimportant little country which had needled the West for years. And Kate Adie was there when the Americans hit it.

Later, she was lucky to escape with her life during the Tiananmen Square massacre. I was there at the same time, and the cameraman who was with her that night told me she had behaved with remarkable courage. Nowadays women are as likely to report on wars as men are, and some – Maggie O'Kane, Marie Colvin, Janine di Giovanni, Orla Guerin among others – do so with real distinction. The Hackette in the Flakette Jackette, as the satirical magazine *Private Eye* calls them, has become as familiar as the Hack at scenes of grief and trouble. But Kate Adie set the standard, and is admired accordingly.

Kate is, in her way, magnificent: one of the very few genuine characters that BBC News has thrown up in my time. What's more, in writing of her, I cannot forget that I spent one of the most enjoyable days of my entire life in her company. It was in the mid-1980s, and Kate and I were in Delhi for the Commonwealth conference, she covering the Queen's visit, I the conference itself. At the end we found we had a free day, and three of us – Kate, Mike Davies (a picture editor who was a particular friend of mine) and I – decided to go by train to see the Taj Mahal the following morning. We were staying in different hotels, so we agreed to meet by the ticket desk of the railway station in time to catch the 7.30 train. Somehow, things went wrong. I thought it would take much longer to get to the station than it did, so I was there forty minutes early. I stood waiting for the other two, who were coming from the same hotel, and watched the station clock tick closer to 7.30. I waited another ten minutes, but they still didn't show up. Furious, I went back to my hotel.

When I phoned Kate, we went through one of those irritable 'Where were you . . .?' conversations. One or other of us had gone to the wrong station, clearly, and we each thought it was the other. Yet at the last moment, before putting the phone down angrily, I remembered from some previous argument between us how charming Kate could be if you said to her, 'Why don't we just forget this?' So I did. I suggested that since we must all be quite hungry, the other two should come round to my hotel and have breakfast. We could decide what else we should do then. There are some people who would

simply keep the argument going; not Kate Adie. She has a willingness
to be peaceable and agreeable, which her detractors don't seem to
notice.

Over breakfast the three of us were very jolly. The unspoken
decision not to hold an unpleasant post-mortem about the morning
had cleared the air entirely. One of us – it may have been Kate herself
– suggested that we should still go to the Taj Mahal, but not by train:
we should hire a limousine and do it in style. We did; and it made for
a delightful day. We stopped for lunch at a place where there were
tame monkeys and a snake-charmer, and spent hours roaming over
the Taj Mahal itself: one of the few great buildings of the world
which never disappoints. This being India, extraordinary and sometimes terrible things happened. We watched wild dogs swim out into
the river and attack the partially burned bodies that floated past from
a funeral pyre; we saw a woman giving birth in a ditch on the way
back, and an army lorry knock a bullock-cart full of people off the
road. Several of them looked very dead to me, and others were clearly
injured, but the army lorry and the driver of our limousine both
refused to stop and help them.

It was, altogether, one of the most memorable days I have ever
spent, and it was entirely due to a basic niceness of character which
Kate has always retained. I saw her most recently at the Royal
Festival Hall in London, at a celebration for the sixtieth anniversary
of the programme *Desert Island Discs*. She made one of the most
amusing speeches about her choice of record, and the audience
probably showed more affection for her than for any of the other
luminaries who had been invited to speak. Watching her and listening
to her, I remembered that day in India; and it seemed to me that she
was still fundamentally the same person, despite the fifteen years of
intensive fame she had enjoyed since then. Fame doesn't always do us
any favours; but it can't change anyone entirely.

§

On a newspaper, there is never any question who has the real power:
it lies with the editorial team. No matter what the correspondents in
the field send in as copy, this can be changed, rewritten, and added
to by the sub-editors in the office. A newspaper is a construct which
follows the basic blueprint of the editor and his various deputies.

An effective television news operation is completely different. Since most of the reports arrive shortly before the programme goes on air, an editor in television news is much more in the hands of the teams on the ground; it isn't possible to rewrite or add to a finished and edited report from the field. The editor has to discuss the shape of the report, its scope and length and general approach, hours beforehand, and only when it finally arrives will it be clear how the correspondent has carried out the brief.

So if a newspaper is a settled monarchy, television news is more like a state of constitutional conflict. There is a quiet, polite, unspoken battle between the editorial centre and the staff on the road over who precisely is going to control each particular news item. A programme editor has the ultimate power, of course, but has to exercise it by agreement. In the past, before the BBC got itself properly organized, there would often be shouting matches down the phone to London, as the correspondent demanded to use one particular set of pictures which were wanted for someone else's report, or required greater length for the final edited report. Sometimes, no doubt, such things still happen; but in a properly run organization they are so much wasted breath.

At the same time, there has to be a proper balance between the perceptions of the people on the ground and the demands of the editors back in London. It is always a bad sign when editors use expressions like 'The way we see the story here is . . .' It is the function of an editor to put together the different elements of the day's news into a coherent form, not to dictate to correspondents on the ground how to present the news from their part of the world.

There has to be a partnership, a balance of views, a two-way discussion; if an editor insists on a particular interpretation or a special treatment of a news event which clashes with the instincts and understanding of the person on the spot, then something has gone wrong with this fundamental relationship. We send out people of independent mind and wide experience to make up their own minds about what is going on in a place; if we then start to tell them how the newspapers, or other television organizations, are interpreting events, and insist on being given the same interpretation, then this detracts seriously from the independence and the experience that we expect correspondents to show. These should be matters for discussion and debate. I don't mean that the correspondents have the right to close off their minds to perfectly reasonable suggestions, or to alternative ways of viewing a story. But it would be completely wrong to oblige them to imitate tamely the reports of the correspondent for some other organization.

These things are always a tug-o'-war, and rightly so; with luck, when the tug-o'-war is finished, the rival pressures will have been exerted and the position will be more or less right. But it is essential for both sides to listen carefully to one another well in advance, before the ensuing report has been committed to tape and is virtually unchangeable. Anything else can make for bad broadcasting. Television is very different in this respect from newspapers, and it's important to appreciate this difference. In broadcasting, correspondents require a lot more trust; if you can't give them that, you should recall them.

The extraordinary thing about television news is that the first time the editor of a television news programme usually sees a report in his or her programme is when it is being broadcast. The report may be inept, it may be wrong, it may be libellous (because even though the words on television or radio are spoken rather than written, a lying report technically constitutes a libel rather than a slander), it may be irresponsible, it may be treasonable; it may be all of the above. But the editor of the programme, the person who has shaped it and commissioned each of the items it contains, mostly sees the main items at the moment they are being broadcast: that is to say, at the moment everyone else sees them. This is something which astounds and terrifies print journalists, who come from a tradition in which the editor and his deputies shape the paper, or at least the news pages, with some care, checking them for libel and for general acceptability.

Because the technology exists for television to be a live or near-live medium, that's exactly what it is: as close to live as possible. Not in China, or Iraq, or (I dare say) North Korea; in such countries the boss's first duty is to make sure the content of their news programmes accords with the ruling ideology, otherwise there will be trouble. What matters there is to be acceptable in the eyes of authority, not to give the viewers the latest news. But in Western countries television news is a knife-edge occupation, in which the most important thing is to be as up-to-the-minute as possible. And since it is technically possible to send a report by satellite only five minutes before the start of the news bulletin, that is when we send it. A lively, well-funded television news operation will probably have four or more reports coming in at the last moment like this. And since neither technology nor the human brain has yet advanced to the point where one person can simultaneously watch four news reports, each of them two and a half minutes long, the programme editor can't do it.

As a result, he or she has to entrust the task of watching each news report to a news producer. Yet even then, there isn't much that can be done about it if the report is badly wrong. At two minutes to ten there is rarely time to cut a passage out of the report and none at all to replace it with a different set of facts. The only weapon left in a television editor's armoury is the ultimate deterrent: to drop the report altogether. The choice is as inflexible as the old logic of nuclear stalemate. You either broadcast it, faults and all, or you have to broadcast another report on the subject, made for a different news programme, which may not be so up to date.

For this reason, the team on the ground has to be entirely trustworthy. Maybe it makes us all a little more cautious than we ought to be. If you can't be certain of a fact, during those two heated hours when you sit in front of the two editing machines ('the edit pair', to use the current jargon, though soon no doubt the technology will improve to the point where we only have to carry one), and if you have no way of checking it, then the chances are you will leave it out; even if it makes your report that much blander and less specific. In my experience you often feel the responsibility of the organization's reputation weighing on you as you scribble your words down and record them onto tape. Maybe it makes you more timid, less forthright, safer. It certainly makes you less opinionated. There is a kind of television effect on reporting, therefore, which is induced by your awareness that there is no one between you and the audience: it often blunts the sharpness of comment, and it makes for a greater emphasis on demonstrable fact.

If you watch the reporting of Sky News, ITN, CNN or the BBC, you will often be struck by the similarities between them rather than by the differences. None of these organizations provides its correspondents with any editorial guidance or 'line'. The correspondents on the ground may have all sorts of different views and expectations, but they also have complete freedom to report what they see. There is a statutory or institutional requirement on each of them to provide balanced news, and it is anyway a matter of common sense: their worldwide audiences are broad and are often likely to have conflicting opinions about a variety of subjects, so the correspondents are obliged to look at a situation from a wider, broader perspective, and concentrate on providing a properly rounded view, rather than a purely national one.

Now that all the main television networks in the United States are owned by large parent companies, there is sometimes strong pressure on them to tilt their reporting in the commercial interests of the group. Correspondents covering an outbreak of Ebola in West Africa in the early 1990s were encouraged, for instance, to mention the Hollywood feature films on the subject of a mysterious epidemic which breaks out in Africa which were made by movie studios owned by the parent companies.

'It's actually very similar to the situation described in the current motion picture *So-and-so*, which opened recently in the United States,' an American friend of mine found himself obliged to say on air. He didn't feel good about it, but it wasn't the result of a request; it was an instruction.

Political interference in American television is far less obvious, and seems to happen very little. There is certainly nothing to match the heavy pressure from the main political parties in Britain to get more favourable coverage at critical moments. Americans would react with as much disapproval of that as British people would of the commercial pressures on American television.

In January 1991 President George Bush personally rang the head of news in every American organization with a correspondent or crew in Baghdad, begging each of them to pull their people out before the bombing of Baghdad started. It was never entirely clear whether Mr Bush's main motive was the desire not to have the blood of Americans on his hands – that was the official version – or whether he wanted to clear the foreign journalists out of the Al Rashid Hotel, where we were all staying. Saddam Hussein had a bunker virtually underneath the hotel, and it may be the Americans wanted to get a clear shot at it. CBS pulled its staffers out and sacked their freelance cameraman, who came and worked for me. NBC withdrew their American staff but left the non-Americans there. ABC left. Only CNN, to their great credit, refused altogether to withdraw.

Even the BBC tried to order us out. One night we received a warning which originated in Washington that the Americans were going to bomb the hotel despite our presence there. The Iraqis heard about it too, and soldiers forced us at gunpoint into the altogether inadequate shelter underneath the hotel. I spent an uncomfortable few hours there, imagining all too clearly what a penetration bomb would do to us all. Then, accompanied by a cameraman, I slipped past one of the guards who had fallen asleep, and made my way back to our office upstairs in the hotel. Better, we reasoned, to ride the hotel down than to sit underneath it when the bombs came.

They never did come, of course. And if they had, they wouldn't have caught Saddam Hussein anyway. Years later his head of military intelligence told me after he had defected to Britain that Saddam never spent any time in his bunker under the Al Rashid once the attack started. Instead, he used to live in small safe houses out in the desert, and held meetings with his staff at different places every day – none of them anywhere near the capital.

The worst example of political pressure I have heard of in the United States occurred in the 1980s, and came not from Washington but from Israel during the first Intifada. The correspondent in the Middle East for one of the big networks heard that Israeli soldiers were capturing boys who threw stones at them and breaking their arms. It was done out in the open in a particular field at night-time, and the correspondent was told exactly where he could hide and get the best pictures with a night-sight. Sure enough, when it was dark, the soldiers dragged the boys out, forced them to rest their right arms on a boulder, and smashed a rock down on them.

The correspondent's report, understandably, caused a sensation, and his pictures were shown around the world. In the United States there was an outcry. As far as I know, no one ever suggested that the pictures were faked, or that they didn't show what the correspondent claimed they did. The anger was simply that the pictures should have been shown at all, since they did so much damage to Israel. In the end, the vice-president of the network was obliged to travel to Israel and apologize humbly on television for having broadcast them.

§

My first appearance on network television came in 1977, when I had just started as the radio correspondent in South Africa. I was in Cape Town, reporting on the passing of some dreadful new piece of apartheid legislation in parliament, and was asked by the foreign duty editor in London to do a report on it for the early evening bulletin on BBC Two. We had one in those days. I had to go to the studios of the SABC, on the seafront at Clifton: a glorious place. (Seventeen years later, accompanied by my future wife Dee and the cameraman Nigel Bateson, I went back to the same studio to do a live broadcast for the *Six O'Clock News* about the forthcoming election of 1994, which swept away the last remnants of the apartheid system and the political party which had created it. We had been walking on the beach barefoot, and the studio staff were surprised to see that the legs of my trousers were rolled up and my feet covered with sand; all that showed on television, though, was my upper half, encased in a dark jacket, a white shirt, and a striped tie.)

I was extremely nervous about this first appearance of mine, back in 1977. I prepared for it endlessly, learned my words to perfection, sat on a high stool and stared sincerely into the camera. That camera lens, until you come to like it and it comes to like you, can be a very off-putting object indeed. I was duly put off; but the report had to be delivered live, and there was no autocue: just me, my memory, and the camera lens.

I got through it. I'm not sure how good it was – not very good at all, I imagine, though I tried not to display any of the obvious signs of nervousness: no drying-up, no flickering of the eyes, no shaking in the voice. Afterwards I rang the foreign duty editor (Dennis Donovan, who later became a good friend) and asked him with the kind of quaver I had managed to keep out of the broadcast if it had been all right.

'Fine,' Dennis answered. 'One minute, twenty-seven.'

'No, I really meant the content.'

There was a slight pause.

'Yes – one minute, twenty-seven,' he said.

In a way, I suppose, it was a compliment. He assumed that the content would be fine anyway; only the length was in question, and since I had been asked to provide a minute and a half, there was nothing much else to talk about.

The fact that so many news items come in at the last minute is the clearest indication imaginable that there is no heavy editorial hand at work in the BBC. In Soviet television in the distant past a correspondent would have satellited the report a good two hours early, so the news editor of the day could watch it and order any cuts that might be necessary. The correspondent would also have telexed or faxed the script well in advance, so that it could be examined for any heresies or inaccuracies which would get everyone into trouble. Only after an editorial committee had examined the script from all angles would the word go out to the correspondent to proceed.

Which is, depressingly, precisely what happens today with American television network news. One or two favoured and much-trusted correspondents are allowed to write their scripts as they choose, and feed over their edited report to New York without all the preliminaries. The rest have to email their scripts well beforehand. That, in a fast-moving business like television news, can be a real problem. You always hear stories from network correspondents about how the editorial committee has sat on a script for hours, then announced it wants major changes when there is almost no time left to make them.

Worse, it means that a team of people who are sitting in New York, and know nothing of conditions in Baghdad or Belgrade or Kabul apart from what they read in the newspapers and see on television, presume to dictate to the person on the ground how he or she should describe events there. It is the precise opposite of reporting; it means that everyone involved is drawn into that dreary, mindless round by which the same few facts and impressions are cycled and recycled around the system, regurgitated in homogenized form and specially pre-digested so as not to challenge the audience's expectations or understanding in any way.

An American producer I know was once working on a report from London about marriage. She had written the script for her correspondent (quite a few correspondents in American television need this kind of help) and included the word 'matrimony' in it. She emailed it to New York at about five in the afternoon, London time.

At nine o'clock she had a phone call from the foreign desk in New York, insisting that the word 'matrimony' be dropped from the script in favour of 'marriage'.

'Nobody uses words like that,' said the foreign editor reprovingly. 'You've got to use words that people can understand.'

And not just words, but concepts they can understand. Nothing difficult. Nothing out of the ordinary. Nothing which makes them pause to think. Given that more than fifty per cent of Americans watch television but never read a newspaper, it isn't surprising their comprehension of the world around them is shrinking and decaying. The United States, thanks to the diminishing effect of appealing to the lowest common denominator, is turning into an Alzheimer nation, unaware of its own or anyone else's past, ignorant of its own or anyone else's present. It is an ugly and shameful betrayal by the very people who should compete the most in bringing the world to the American viewer: the managers who control the television networks. Instead, they have persuaded the American viewer that the world is of no account.

The big network news programmes in the early evenings often nowadays contain large numbers of prearranged features, most of them about aspects of life in the United States. The events that are happening in the world around them often seem of less significance than the carefully packaged items about health and insurance and old-age homes: each the result of research among focus groups and target areas of the population. The fundamental business of explaining to people what has gone on in their world today, the task that Ed Murrow and Walter Cronkite recognized as being fundamental to their function in life, has long been set aside. Instead, 'reality TV' has taken over.

The desire to know what is happening, which is present in all of us, has been transferred from the complicated world of real life to the stripped-down, easy-to-understand issues of a fireman's or a policeman's or a fighter pilot's or a nurse's life. We watch them facing real fires, real criminals, real targets, real emergencies, and we feel we have seen the real world. The trouble is, television dresses up everything it deals with, so that in the end real people start behaving as television expects them to behave. The complexity of real life is varnished over and smoothed down yet again. It ceases to be real life at all, it's reality as entertainment, easily digested, lacking in any roughage. You know the outcome before you switch the programme on.

It's infotainment, it's sociotainment, it's militainment: empty, silly, meaningless perhaps, but it's what control groups say they like. What else can they say, when they don't have anything better to watch?

The word may sound antiquated, Reithian, imperialist, arrogant in our ears, and it is rarely used nowadays; but the broadcasters in any society have a duty to fulfil. They have access to all the information in the world, and it is their duty to pass it on faithfully to their audiences. Suppose surgeons consulted focus groups before they carried out an operation, or asked their patients what kind of treatment they would like; imagine if judges had the benefit of an opinion poll before deciding on a sentence. But television executives have grown up in an environment where it is acceptable to bend and mould reality.

And so, in a world where people always seem to feel the news is likely to be bad, there is a temptation to create a little good news, touching up the facts and encouraging positive, happy, cuddly events to take place. Once you begin this process, there is no end to it. If the eighteenth-century playwright Nahum Tate could rewrite *King Lear* to give it a positive ending, why should we not rewrite the news as people tell us in the focus groups that they would like it to be: Prince Charles happily married to Princess Diana, Osama bin Laden marched in chains through the streets of New York?

The enemy of proper information and good reporting is not stupidity but insipidity. The men and women who work on the US networks are intelligent, able, competitive people; but the context within which they are obliged to work is a Nahum Tate one, where the viewer must not be stretched or challenged. I would say the quality of many network people is at least as high as that of their equivalents in British television news. I doubt, for instance, whether Britain can produce a programme presenter to match the quality of Peter Jennings, the Canadian who presents the main news on ABC TV. I have known Peter for years, and used to admire his ability as a foreign correspondent, in the days when ABC had a proper range of foreign correspondents. Now I admire him as a newscaster.

One night, when I was watching ABC News, both the tape machine which was supposed to play in an item about the Middle East and its back-up failed to function. For the networks, which rate smoothness of production above any question of journalistic or picture quality, this is just about the worst thing that can happen. But Jennings, who acts as a kind of honorary programme editor and has a particular interest in the Middle East, apologized gracefully, and then told us with perfect fluency what the correspondent's report contained. I applauded the screen at the end of that bravura perform-ance, and felt that whatever enormous sum of money Peter was getting for his work, it wasn't nearly enough.

Yet Jennings, possessed of all that ability and of all the kudos of being one of the most senior figures in ABC News, cannot raise the quality of the material which is broadcast, even though he must know most of it is otiose and unchallenging. The system makes these things very hard indeed to change; and the system which obtains in Ameri-can television news – the domestic variety, certainly – discourages difference and hard thinking, and encourages homogeneity and con-ventionality of thought.

The pressures on British television are almost equally strong, but there is a great deal more resistance. Some of the responsibility rests on government, which creates the framework within which the various television companies have to operate. The rot began to set in during the last years of Margaret Thatcher's premiership, when the commercial companies successfully persuaded the government that there was no need for such stringent rules about maintaining a relatively high level of factual and current-affairs programmes. The Thatcher government had no objection, especially if it helped the commercial companies compete better with the BBC. When Carlton Television, with its determinedly populist approach, was given its franchise, it meant the beginning of the end for responsible factual broadcasting on independent television. From now on, entertainment ruled. The last gritty, sometimes irritating but usually provocative current-affairs programmes were abandoned in favour of the down-market, anodyne *Tonight with Trevor MacDonald*.

Carlton may be a lost cause as far as decent factual programmes are concerned, but other broadcasters are not. They have constantly to defend themselves against the dumbing-down charge, and that is good for them. It means that the central issue in news broadcasting is always the quality of what is broadcast. Like the geese on the Capitol, a lot of the complaints are just imitative hissing and cackling; yet when the time comes and the barbarians are finally getting ready to storm the city's heights, there is a respectable chance that the hissing and cackling will awaken the citizens. That's the hope, anyway.

'Dumbing down' is usually taken to mean the process by which television becomes ever more stupid and irreflective. Maybe this is true for entertainment programmes, but it isn't the main problem in news. There, the real enemy isn't so much stupidity as slickness of presentation, which irons out the detailed and interesting in favour of the bland and unexceptionable. Form takes over from content, and all that counts is presentation. Of course presentation is important: if it's clumsy and amateurish, the quality of the reporting becomes obscured. But it is the facts, and the context they exist in, which really count. Debase the facts, neglect the context, and your entire operation begins to go downhill.

Sometimes public criticism about dumbing down is misguided. In 1981, when the BBC finally got rid of the last of the actors who read the television news, there was a national outcry. Kenneth Kendall and Robert Dougall were superb performers, confident, urbane, reliable. But that is all they were: performers. The sense of knowledge and understanding they radiated seemed impressive, yet they would never have been able to write the news themselves and knew little about it. They were excellent actors, and as a result they convinced the viewers thoroughly. It was some time before John Humphrys and Michael Buerk (I had been dropped because I was much less good at reading the news than either of them) reached the levels of confidence and smoothness of presentation that Kendall and Dougall had long achieved, and for years the BBC was heavily criticized for making the switch. But imagine what would happen now, if the BBC announced that Michael Buerk and Peter Sissons were to be replaced by actors: dumbing down would be the kindest expression that people used.

As viewers, we transfer our own wishes and judgements to the people we see on the screen. We regard the emptiest-headed presenters as serious intellects because we like their faces, and we regard someone as dull or pompous merely because we never see them smile on camera. It's not reality, it's appearance. I was once invited to the

American embassy in London to see a preview of an excellent film about the Cuban missile crisis, which starred Kevin Costner. He was superb as President Kennedy's chief adviser: tough, masterful, dominating the screen. And then at the party afterwards the man himself arrived: smaller, feebler, clearly nervous of speaking to an audience of diplomats and journalists. Having only a few moments before persuaded us by his screen presence that his intellectual courage was enough to prevent an international crisis, he now told us hesitantly how grateful he was that the American embassy was here, because the world was a dangerous place and he only had to climb its steps to be in complete safety. This was in Mayfair.

Appearance isn't everything, therefore. There has to be some substance somewhere. As with Peter Jennings of ABC, this substance must be united with the art of television presentation; without the art, the substance isn't much use. More than one famous expert has been brought into television from the real world, has stared louringly into the camera and barked gruffly at it a few times, then disappeared for ever. 'The face for radio and the voice for newspapers' isn't just a broadcasting joke, it's a warning. You don't have to be beautiful to appear on television, God knows: if that were true, few of us would ever have made it. But you have to have a certain liking for the camera, and a certain appreciation of why it is there and what it wants. And the camera has to reciprocate.

11

Crossing the Oxus

Late that night in my room at the Hotel Dushanbe, I set my alarm for 1.45 a.m., and got a couple of hours' fitful sleep. We were supposed to be leaving at 2.30, heading for the Afghan border. I can't say I really believed it: this entire trip had been so full of false starts and false hopes, it seemed unlikely we would ever get anywhere; something else would come up, some other circumnavigation would be required. I lay on my inadequate bed and read a few pages of E. M. Forster's *Howard's End*; including this passage, which seemed to sum up everything that had happened to us:

> Actual life is full of false clues and signposts that lead nowhere. With infinite effort we nerve ourselves for a crisis that never comes.

Time was unquestionably running out. I didn't know how many satellites were visible over Kabul by now, but it couldn't be much longer before the Americans and British started their bombing of Afghanistan. Nor did I have a great deal of belief in the Russian who was supposed to get us to the border. He sounded altogether too good to be true.

I dressed and packed, and heard the *dzhurnaya* grumble from her makeshift bed in the open area near the lift as I lugged my gear down the creaking wooden floor of the passage. This was the only time of the day or night when the lift could be relied on to work properly, and it came up slowly, clanking and wheezing. Downstairs in the lobby the hotel was dark and silent. A small group of BBC people was starting to gather. Paul Danahar was there, looking depressed: he had decided he couldn't come with us, since he wouldn't be able to make it back to South Africa in time for an important family occasion. I was sorry, because he and Peter Jouvenal and I had got on well, and it felt bad to let a team break up. There were all sorts of other BBC people around, who were only going as far as the satellite dish camp at Khwaja Bahawuddin, just across the river in Afghanistan.

We needed to get our equipment out of the hotel's luggage store, but the man in charge refused to open up without being paid a sizeable amount in US dollars. Someone, somehow, raised the cash. Then there was a new problem: our fixer had undertaken to get us three big vehicles: the minimum we would need to get everybody in. Instead he had only got us two ordinary cars. It wasn't enough, and he had to go out to find another. I was annoyed, because I felt we had all been hauled out of our beds much too early in the morning, on false pretences. If I had known how good Anton would prove to be, and how difficult it was to get any kind of vehicle in Dushanbe, I would have been much more understanding. Somehow, though, shortage of sleep and too many people milling aimlessly about always makes me irritated.

'Just go and get another car, and don't bloody come back till you've got it,' I said; quite unnecessarily, since that was precisely what he was heading off to do.

Fortunately his English wasn't up to the job of understanding my precise meaning, though my manner and tone must have translated pretty clearly. I speak annoyance fluently, and in my business I find I get a lot of practice. In this case it was a mistake, and I imagine he needed all his professionalism as a fixer when he headed out into the darkness to find another vehicle.

As for me, I went and lay down on a seat in the lobby, near the night porter, who lay covered in a blanket nearby. Too near, as it turned out: every time he shifted position his blanket would lift momentarily and let out the stink he had generated. Don't believe the people who tell you that smells can't keep you awake; for me, they're as bad as loud sounds. The smell was very loud indeed – deafening at times.

By 4.30 everything seemed to be in place. We even had a larger vehicle, and all our gear was loaded into it. I shook hands with Paul Danahar, and joked that I'd probably see him in a few hours' time, when we arrived back at the hotel with our tail between our legs; but I prayed it wouldn't be true. Peter Jouvenal had gone on ahead of us, catching a ride down to the border. He still had visa problems, and didn't want to have to show his passport to anyone.

My vehicle was a taxi, and I shared it with Kate Clark, the BBC correspondent who had been thrown out of Kabul the previous March. She based herself in Pakistan and spent her days ringing dozens of contacts around Afghanistan every day, often finding better stories and more urgent and important news that way. We had a pleasant time as we drove southwards over the Tajikistan mountain ranges, talking about studying English at university and the British class system and what it meant nowadays to be British. She was a brave woman, and completely devoted to the cause of broadcasting to Afghanistan. It always surprises and delights me that the BBC can find people with her degree of dedication. I only hope it is sufficiently grateful to them.

The roads were remarkably good for this part of the world – another achievement of the old Soviet Union – and we made good time. I had a variety of pressures on me that day: to get into Afghanistan, first and foremost, but also to record four or five pieces to camera when we got there, to link the edition of *Panorama* which several producers were slaving to put together back in London for broadcast the following night, Sunday. It was a look back at what had happened to Afghanistan during the past quarter-century through the eyes of Peter Jouvenal and myself – a record of our trips there at key moments: in particular, the withdrawal of Soviet troops, the rise of the Taliban, their consolidation of power, the growing significance of Osama bin Laden.

All this was being assembled in London, and I had recorded the commentary and sent it the previous night. But this collection of reports from the past had to be linked together with pieces to camera from inside Afghanistan; and we had about eighteen hours, realistically, in which to cross the border and record them. Would we get there? And when?

The third pressure on me was more immediate. My weekly column for the *Sunday Telegraph* was due every Saturday morning, and even though we were still travelling, this was the only time I would have free to write it. So directly it grew light I pulled out my small Psion computer and started work on it; the deadline was only four hours away. We bumped up and down along the road and I hit the wrong keys again and again. But I was on a mission; I wanted to make some things clear. This is what I wrote:

> The downward spiral which began in this country when the King was overthrown nearly thirty years ago seems to be approaching absolute rock-bottom. Presumably the long-awaited strikes against Afghanistan will begin soon. Having watched Taliban forces fighting their own countrymen, I don't imagine they will put up much resistance.
>
> The Taliban are good at beating up men in the street who have trimmed their beards, or whipping women for accidentally showing their faces in public. But they aren't up to much when it comes to facing bullets. 'Their élite, battle-hardened forces are on full alert,' one Pakistani newspaper trilled last week; I don't think we need to worry too much.
>
> The only Taliban fighters I have seen in Afghanistan since 11 September were lounging in the sun by a roadside position, so unalert they didn't notice the sound of the generator which was powering my portable live broadcast unit, a short way away. It is a fairly safe assumption that they will be a pushover. Whatever happens, the Americans have got the twenty-first century equivalent of the Gatling gun, and the Afghans have not.
>
> Our myths about the Afghans go back a long way. One is that they always defeat their invaders. In fact a long succession of invaders has been quite successful in Afghanistan, from Alexander the Great and Genghis Khan to the British in the nineteenth century. But they have been successful only when they have carried out a series of quick hits, then staged a well-planned withdrawal. When the invaders think of staying on, like the British in 1839 or the Russians in the 1980s, the Afghans eventually overcome their own differences long enough to see them off.
>
> If the Americans, with British help, attack the Taliban hard from the air, put in special forces to help the Northern Alliance take Kabul, and then rely on old-fashioned treachery for someone to turn Osama bin Laden and his associates in, they ought to do really well. Lord Roberts, the victor of Kandahar, would approve.

But what happens afterwards? Logic requires that the Americans should get out fast, leaving the country in the hands of the Northern Alliance. Yet that is the approach that got us into all this in the first place. Leaving Afghanistan to its own devices while simultaneously meddling in its politics from the outside helped to foster the savage civil war which has gone on ever since the Russians pulled out in 1989.

These are ideal waters for other people to fish in. The United States and the Soviet Union fought out their proxy war here in the 1980s; India and Pakistan express their rivalry over Kashmir now by supporting opposing factions in Afghanistan. There are always groups prepared to take other people's money and do their dirty work.

The only conceivable force which can take over from the Taliban is the Northern Alliance. Yet this is essentially the same grouping which the Taliban chased out of Kabul in 1996, cheered on by large numbers of people who were sickened by the Alliance's gross corruption and mismanagement in government. And that was when they had the services of the most effective politician and military leader in the coalition, Ahmad Shah Massoud. He was murdered three days before the attacks of 11 September, presumably by bin Laden's men.

What is needed is the most delicate of tactics: encouraging the victors to form a government which will keep the peace, give everyone a reasonable chance whatever their religion or ethnic background, and resist both revenge and the insidious growth of corruption. It will be very hard indeed, but they must be held to it.

The Taliban arose in the first place only because Afghanistan became a kind of international black hole, where any lunacy could flourish. Let's hope the Americans are thinking beyond the coming battle to the new Afghanistan which will follow. Otherwise we will be faced with something like the old Afghanistan, as violent as ever.

Months later, as I read this, it doesn't seem to me too bad. (I hope if I'd got it all wrong I would still have printed it here; there's no point in writing memoirs like this if you're not honest.) The most obvious mistake was to think that someone would hand over Osama bin

Laden and his associates; as I write these words now, months afterwards, that is starting to look distinctly unlikely.

I am proudest, though, of having stuck my neck out about the uselessness of the Taliban as a fighting force. This idea of mine may have raised some eyebrows at the *Sunday Telegraph*, and it certainly did at the BBC when I started pontificating about it. You must remember that in those early stages of the attack on Afghanistan most Western journalists had fallen for the Pakistani notion, essentially generated by the Taliban themselves and by their supporters in the Islamic world, that the Taliban were dedicated Islamic fighters who were not only willing but anxious to sacrifice their lives for the faith. But neither the Pakistani journalists nor the Western ones had seen the Taliban in action. I had.

§

First of all, you have to understand who the Taliban actually were. Their name means 'religious students', and the word is plural; instead of talking about 'the American Taliban' when they meant an individual volunteer who came from the United States, the American newspapers should have spoken of 'the American Talib' – but hey, who cares about this kind of foreign trivia? The movement started out in the *madrassehs*, religious schools, attached to the Afghan refugee camps along the Pakistan border.

Here the children of Afghans who had been forced out of their homes by the Russian invasion were taught an angry, defiant faith which would one day take them back across the border to cleanse their forefathers' country of the evils of godless Communism. President Zia ul-Haq of Pakistan, the genial army commander who gave me a lift to my hotel after I had interviewed him back in January 1980, gave this movement great encouragement; he also set Pakistan on the path to becoming an Islamic republic – of a kind.

That wasn't all they were taught. In some ways these Afghan refugees were brought up as Pakistanis, and they took on various Pakistani notions, including a liking for cricket. I have watched them several times, playing on level patches of dusty earth with a ball that is no more than a round stone wrapped in cotton and taped up thoroughly, the batsmen equipped with cheap bats of white wood bought in the local bazaar, and the wicket-keeper wearing gardening gloves. The most devout of the Taliban were taught, as the Holy Koran says, that riding and archery are the only godly sports; but plenty of Afghans who drifted into the movement were fervent cricketers.

In those days, the Taliban had other godparents as well as the Pakistanis. Under President Reagan, the CIA was under instructions to make life as difficult for the Russians as possible in any way, and Pakistani military intelligence, the ISI, always seemed to have an extraordinary sway over the CIA; which obediently gave its blessing to the growing Taliban movement as well, on the grounds that it was likely to fight the Russians harder than any of the other mujaheddin groups. The CIA never seems to have checked out this concept very carefully; the ISI's word was good enough for them. As for Ahmad Shah Massoud's fighting force in the Panjshir Valley, which withstood everything the Russians could throw at them, in major annual offensives, the ISI told the CIA that they weren't worth supporting, and the CIA obeyed. What the ISI really meant was that Massoud was hostile to Pakistan.

And so the Americans sent money and weapons and some training effort to the Taliban. If the CIA noticed that they were inclined to be a little extreme in their attitude towards Islam, they took no notice. It doesn't seem to have occurred to anyone in Washington that this might cause trouble afterwards. But then the American governmental machine has a habitual failing: it throws everything it has into today's battle, without bothering too much about tomorrow's. Maybe this is because each President and his staff have, at the most, two short terms in office, and can't get a third; so what happens in the future will be someone else's problem – on the next President's watch, as the slightly tedious phrase has it.

In the years immediately following the Soviet withdrawal, the Taliban gradually turned themselves into a fighting force. But they had a particular instinct for public relations, which made me suspicious of them right from the start. When they swept across the Afghan border and captured Kandahar, they wore flowing white garments to give the impression that they were avenging and destroying the dirt and evil of the past. It was a little too well thought out, too pat, too forced, I felt; what my old English supervisor at Cambridge, Arthur Sale, talking about writers who strove over-hard for a particular effect, used to call *voulu*.

Yet they convinced plenty of Afghans, especially when they began clearing the crooks and robbers and bandits, the Commander Zardad types, out of Kandahar and the other places they captured. More and more groups of Afghan fighters came over to their side, and the Taliban almost invariably accepted them, asking few questions about their behaviour and political orientation in the past. The Taliban needed an army, and they slowly picked one up as they went. Soon they were persuading groups right across Afghanistan that they represented the winning side, and that the old mujaheddin groups which had captured Kabul in 1992 and overthrown the pro-Communist leader Najibullah were on their way out.

When I went to Afghanistan in 1996 to report on the Taliban, they controlled nearly two-thirds of the country and were just starting their big push on Kabul, which they duly captured a few months later. We visited their main base, Kandahar, and found the weird society which they had established there: the television sets strung up like hanged men at the main street intersections, the occasional frightened woman scurrying around, wrapped like a parcel in her burka, terrified of showing an ankle or a wrist, the closed-down girls' schools, the bans on whistling and singing and on music of any kind. Outside the Taliban Foreign Ministry in Kandahar, when we arrived to get our accreditation, we found a group of Taliban gunmen quite unlike any soldiers I had seen anywhere else in the world.

For a start, they were often stoned. The ferocious laws which the Taliban enforced against the use of alcohol certainly hadn't been extended to dope. They leant on each others' shoulders, giggling at us like schoolgirls and reeking of the stuff. And they had a hallucinatory look to them in other ways. Kandahar is famous in Afghanistan for the homosexual proclivities of its inhabitants, and these men were painted up like Karachi tarts. They had used mascara liberally, which (together with the dope) gave their eyes a strange, deep-set, soulful look, like Theda Bara in a 1920s movie about vamps and their conquests. Their hair was tousled but brushed up into a bush around their heads. They had painted their fingernails and toenails an orange-red, and they had high-heeled gold sandals on their feet. They also had long shaggy beards and AK-47s. I don't think I will easily forget the sight of those dirty forefingers, those chipped red nails, curled around the triggers. You might not want to come across a group like this round the back of the bicycle sheds, but ranged in the trenches opposite they were unlikely to give you much cause for anxiety.

Characters of this sort weren't of course the only troops the Taliban had; they weren't even necessarily typical of their forces. But I realized then that what we had come, lazily, to call the Taliban army was really a large cluster of different groups around a smallish central group of genuine Taliban fighters; and only a smallish percentage of the Taliban army, therefore, shared the ideas of the volunteers from the *madrassehs* along the Pakistan border. The great majority were just time-servers who had changed sides at the key moment and gone over to the winners. Directly it became clear that the Taliban weren't the winners any longer, the loyalty of large numbers of their soldiers would immediately be in question; and it wouldn't be long before the gold sandals would start walking and the mascara and the nail polish would be applied on the other side of no man's land.

Later, around Kabul itself, we saw Taliban troops besieging the city. They were pretty feeble, sitting out in the late afternoon sun and talking and laughing idly, poorly trained and distinctly inadequate. They were fine if the opposing troops were as useless and unmotivated as themselves, but when it came to standing up to twenty-first century weapons and a properly disciplined First World army, they simply wouldn't hang around and fight.

So it wasn't all that much of an act of faith to write all this in my *Sunday Telegraph* column; nor was it particularly far-sighted of me to forecast the utter rout of the Taliban in front of Kabul in my various broadcasts during the following weeks. And if the other journalists, Western and Pakistani, who spoke in such nerve-racking terms about fanatics and would-be suicide troops and ferocious Islamic discipline had ever troubled to come to Afghanistan and see the Taliban army for themselves, they might not have been quite so ready to chill our blood.

The fact is, though, that this view of the Taliban fitted into a pattern which is at least as old as the Crusaders: the ferocious armies of Islam, whose faith is stronger than their fear of death and who will take as many *firangees* with them as they can on their way to Paradise. Of course, you only have to think of the events of 11 September or read the newspaper accounts of suicide-bombers in Jerusalem or the towns and cities of Israel to see that this isn't entirely a Western fantasy. But it also evokes a certain highly predictable shudder in the comfortable European mind.

The horror stories about the Assassins, drug-crazed followers of the Old Man of the Mountains, who went out, fortified by hashish (hence their name) to murder political leaders, both Christian and Muslim, evoked precisely this kind of reaction. If there had been a *Daily Mail* in the early Middle Ages you could imagine it getting worked up into a rage about the subject while its writers flicked through the Latin dictionary to find synonyms for 'fanatic' and some medieval equivalent of Peter Hitchins frothed over his parchment and demanded controls on immigrants from Outremer in order to protect our women and children.

Marco Polo, who was almost certainly a fraud and who surely cannot have visited China (can you imagine someone travelling there at any time in the last three thousand years and never once mentioning tea?), nevertheless had a very good notion of what made Europeans' blood run faster; and his stories of the Assassins, with their themes of drugs, Islamic fundamentalism and suicide-killers, did the trick perfectly. Neither he nor anyone else ever quite explained how the dose of hashish which the Old Man gave his followers managed to last for months on end. But of course that's the beauty of tabloid journalism, ancient and modern: as long as you don't ask too many questions and don't know too much about the subject, it can easily scare the pants off you.

This, then, was why I was in such a sweat to get back to Afghanistan. The bombing could start any day now, and it wasn't at all clear to me how intensive it was going to be or how quickly it would work; but that it would work, and bring about the collapse of the Taliban, I was quite clear in my mind. And directly the collapse took place, the Northern Alliance would attack Kabul and, I knew, capture it almost without a fight. In the meantime I was here in the mountains of southern Tajikistan: not even in the same country.

As it turned out, of course, I got the timescale hopelessly wrong. True, the bombing was about to start, but it was so slow and leisurely and Afghanistan was so wretchedly poor, that it scarcely made much difference for a long time. On 6 October there were actually another thirty-eight days before the big push on Kabul began; but I was quite right in thinking that the bombing could start at any moment. There genuinely was no time to be lost.

§

It was morning, and we were getting close to the frontier. The villages had that indefinably transitional quality that border areas have, still recognizably of their own country yet beginning to take on the atmosphere of the country next door. The farmers in the fields were wearing turbans and Afghan clothes, even though the roads here were still good and there were Soviet-era schools and even occasionally clinics in the villages we went through.

According to our arrangement, Peter Jouvenal should by now have crossed the river and be waiting for us in Afghanistan. But as we drove fast down the dusty road, a figure suddenly ran out from the garden of a house to our right, waving his arms and shouting. It was Peter; for some reason, this was as far as he had been able to get. He had been waiting for us for several hours. It looked like a problem, because anyone who stamped his passport as he left the country would see he'd entered it without any kind of authorization. In a place like Tajikistan that was likely to cause a good deal of trouble.

I turned to our fixer and told him all about it. I also explained that there could be no question of delay, because Peter was the only cameraman we had and I would have to record a number of pieces to camera for our *Panorama* that afternoon, directly we reached Afghan soil. There are two kinds of fixer. One type – by far the majority – makes a big song and dance about this kind of problem; maybe it protects them in case of failure, and looks more impressive in case of eventual success. The other type, in the words of my wife's *voortrekking* ancestors, makes a plan, simply adjusting to the changed circumstances and working out a way to avoid the new difficulty. That is what our fixer did now, and I respected him for it greatly.

'No problem,' he said. 'We go by secret road.'

Yet it must have been something of a problem, since we already had an army vehicle with us, to escort us to the border. The fixer went over to talk to the driver and explained things to him, and came back.

'Your friend travels with me,' he said, and our convoy lurched off.

Soon we came to a fork. The main road, metalled and reasonably straight, continued off into the distance, but there was a smaller dirt road off to the left. This was the secret road: an army track which ran along the border for a long way, and which only military vehicles were supposed to use. For this reason there were no control posts along it.

Our fixer's relations with the army were interesting. He was a Russian who had spent a good deal of time in this area as a reporter. The army here was Russian too: as part of the agreement at the break-up of the Soviet Union, Moscow agreed to defend the external borders of any former Soviet republic which requested them. Tajikistan, too small and poor to able to run an army of its own, was one of the new states which asked for help. He knew every Russian along here. We drove a long way along the border fence, actually in no man's land, and when we reached an army camp Anton jumped out and went to talk to the soldiers.

This is the difficult bit, I told myself. If we are stuck here, or sent back, everything starts to collapse around my ears. Tomorrow's *Panorama* will be a disaster. We'll never get to Kabul in time for the attack. I tried to seem impassive and confident, for the sake of the others; but a good deal of defeatist nonsense was swirling around in my brain.

And then the fixer came walking back, turning every now and then to wave at the soldiers, and smiling.

'No problem,' he said.

'But what about my friend with the passport difficulty?'

'No problem, no problem,' he said again. And he was right.

The river lay shimmering in between the open sandy dunes, on its long way to the rapidly disappearing Aral Sea. The ancients, and the not-so-ancients, called it the Oxus; its present name, much less musical, is the Amudarya. On this side lay difficulty and passport controls and officialdom and bureaucracy; on that side lay the wide open spaces of Afghanistan, where money and determination could get you anywhere you wanted to go.

'Is there still no problem?' I asked, scarcely able to believe that my troubles were over.

He looked at me patiently; he must have been getting very sick of all my nervous witterings.

'John,' he said, putting extra Russian consonants into the word so that it came out as 'Dzhon'. 'I promise. Everything will be good. Anton tells you so.'

He gripped my hand, and this time, at last, I believed him. The promised land lay a quarter of a mile away, across the Oxus, and I finally accepted that, after twenty-five days of hard and unsuccessful grind, I was going to get across. And instead of fussing around any more, I went and got myself a self-heating packet of curry, the kind of thing you buy in camping and expedition stores.

Weeks of living on these things lay ahead of me, but this was the first one I had experienced. It was a flat silver-foil packet, with a separate plastic sachet of water and a larger plastic bag. You put the silver-foil packet in the plastic bag and pour in the contents of the water sachet, then fold up the plastic bag and leave it for twelve minutes. As time went on and the food supplies grew smaller, those twelve minutes became the longest of our lives.

Against all experience we imagined that the finished product would look like the picture on the front of the packet, and taste like a real curry; and the longer we had to wait for it the more we salivated. To be honest, the quality of the food wasn't at all bad, and it was superb to be able to get a hot meal without needing to light a fire or do any cooking. But the choice of dishes was limited to four, and the chemical which reacted with water and heated the food made a nasty stench as you opened the packet. I suppose you always hope things are going to be perfect until you actually experience them. Reality has its own flavour, and it isn't always very appetizing.

On this first occasion, though, I enjoyed the meal hugely, ladling it down with a large white plastic spoon and staring across the river to see if there was any movement on the other side. We had been told that a ferry would come across and pick us up, and there was indeed a ferry beached on the Afghan bank of the Oxus. People were even wandering about near it, but in true Afghan fashion no one seemed to be doing anything very active about bringing it over to us.

'Dzhon,' said Anton, gripping my arm and pointing in an altogether different direction. 'Your ship.'

But our ship wasn't a ship. It wasn't even much of a boat; and yet my heart leaped at the sight of it. All it was, was four large tractor tyres bound together with rope and supporting a wooden frame which was covered with straw. Four men, one at each corner, plunged a paddle into the churning water and guided it towards the shore. A fifth stood in the middle and directed them. His was clearly the job to have.

The reason I was so delighted to see it was that this was very much the kind of craft which Alexander the Great's men had made when they crossed the Oxus hereabouts in 329 BC; only they improvised. I had brought the Greek historian Arrian's book on Alexander's campaigns with me on the trip, because it seemed likely that we would cover some part of the route he travelled in Afghanistan and Central Asia. This is how Arrian describes the scene at the Oxus:

> When Alexander first tried to cross it, the task seemed impossible. The river was about three-quarters of a mile wide and much deeper than you would expect, given its breadth. And because it had a rapid current and a sandy bottom, it was impossible to drive piles securely into its bed: the piles could get no grip on the soft sand, and were quickly swept away by the force of the water. Timber was scarce round there, and it seemed a complete waste of time to wander off in search of sufficient wood to construct a bridge. And so Alexander gave orders that all the cowhides which the men were using as tents should be filled with wooden chips and other dry waste, then tied and sewn up carefully so they would be watertight. And when they were filled and sewn like this, they were sufficient to get the men across the river over a period of five days.

Nothing much seemed to have changed here in 2,300 years: the river itself, the surrounding sandy desert we could see on the far bank. The Macedonians were travelling in the opposite direction from us, from Balkh to Samarkand (or as they would have put it, from Bactra to Maracanda), and had got bogged down in the desert. They had run out of water, and the only way they could quench their thirst was by breaking into the wine supplies; not altogether the ideal solution.

When they saw the waters of the Oxus – these waters – all discipline broke. The Macedonians charged wildly for the river bank, threw themselves in, and drank deeply from it. Some of them suffered badly as a result. Alexander's enemies had burned all the available river-craft, which is why they had to make their own: hence the ancient equivalent of tractor-tyres. Typically, Alexander the Great didn't hang around while they did it; he just headed across the Oxus with his own personal guard, the Companions, and left the army to follow.

I had brought another book with me, by a much later traveller who had passed this way: Sir George Scott Robertson, the British Agent at Gilgit in what is now Pakistan, published *The Kafirs of the Hindu-Kush* in 1896. 'Kafirs' is the Arabic word for infidels, and we would nowadays call the people whom Robertson wrote about the Kalash. They claim descent from Alexander the Great's soldiers, and it was they who made the objects I bought in Chitral when we tried to get into Afghanistan from Pakistan. Robertson's book is one of the best late-Victorian accounts of travel I know, full of passion and excitement. Here, for instance, is part of the contents list for one of the chapters:

> The narrative continued—My escort behave abominably—Utah's tact—My illness—Temporary desertion of escort—A crisis— Shtevgrom—My tent rushed—I am declared a prisoner—My escape—Manage to get clear of Shtevgrom—A perfect hiding-place—Return to Kamdesh—Hardships on the road—I get the whip hand . . .

And so on. By comparison, these memoirs of mine seem pretty flat. In a long career of roaming some of the wilder places of the earth, my tent has never been rushed, and I have only twice been taken prisoner by bandits. Robertson was the kind of man who could scarcely cross a river without having his boat sink; and although he had a great affection for the people he met and travelled with, he was always particularly taken up with his own concerns, and rather less with other people's:

> Not the least of my misfortunes was the fact that, with the
> exception of a light pair of lawn-tennis shoes, which I was
> wearing at the time, every pair of boots I possessed was lost in
> the river. Shermalik lost some of his treasure . . .

With these experiences in mind, I thought the raft on its tractor-tyres
looked very unsteady indeed. But at least it was here, and the ferry
was still stuck firmly on the mud opposite, with the same people
milling unproductively around it. If Peter Jouvenal and I took our
gear across, we could at least make a start on our pieces to camera
for *Panorama*; and if I am really honest with myself, I suppose I
thought we ourselves would be sure of getting to Afghanistan, even if
something happened to prevent the other BBC people we were
travelling with. Like Sir George Robertson, my thoughts were firmly
on myself and my fortunes; and like Alexander the Great, I was
prepared to leave the others and head on if necessary. Not very
impressive or very altruistic, I grant you. But when I glanced round I
could see that none of the others seemed particularly anxious to trust
themselves to this insecure raft anyway. I looked at Peter.

'I think we should take it,' I said.

The raft wobbled badly as we climbed on it: the four tractor-tyres
didn't make for stability. The others handed us our gear. We settled
it around us on the straw, and sat on it. The rowers pushed their way
out into the current, and the boat spun round and headed for the
other shore. We were crossing the Oxus at last.

The only problem was the Northern Alliance commander who
was with us. He was a thoroughgoing Dismal Desmond, a jobsworth
who kept insisting that we should head straight for the Alliance's
Foreign Ministry when we reached the other side, in order to get
ourselves accredited. He would accompany us there, he said, in his
jailer's voice. We had no intention whatever of going with him, but it
looked as though it was going to be hard to brush him off.

By now we were in the middle of the Oxus, and the full force of
the current was almost too much for the four oarsmen, yet never quite
bad enough to sweep us away. I looked round the raft anxiously. All
Peter's television gear was with us, and if the raft tipped over we
would be in real trouble. Like Robertson, I could just be left with my
tennis-shoes. The grey-green water ran faster and faster, and bits of

trees and wreckage flowed by us. The oarsmen, skinny but strong, sweated and grunted with the effort as they dug their paddles into the current. We seemed to be making no progress against it at all, and the far bank was as far away as it had been five minutes earlier; we were just a little farther downstream, that was all. The only good thing was that the tension had made the jobsworth shut up.

And then, slowly, the rowers started to make a little more headway. The parabola of our passage across the river flattened out, the current had less effect on us, the far shore started to come closer. We were, I decided, going to make it. By now the rest of our team, half a mile away, were getting their stuff together to load onto the big ferry which had finally made it across. In the end, we reached the other shore only a few minutes before the rest of the team. But theirs was a more boring, if more stable passage; we had, after all, crossed like Alexander the Great – even if in the opposite direction.

By now there was no perceptible current at all, the rowers were relaxed and laughing as they made their strokes, and the jobsworth had started up again about our duty as journalists. I could see the faces of the people on the other side, and the little flowers on the river bank, and the thick mud of the foreshore which reached out towards us. There would be no avoiding that, clearly. But the mud was Afghan, and I almost felt like gathering a great handful of it and kissing it. We had arrived at last, after all this effort and all this time. And the great thing about Afghanistan was that there was no officialdom, no immigration, no one who cared enough to throw you out. We were back, and we were back to stay.

I jumped out, up to my ankles in the glutinous stuff. The temptation to kiss it evaporated very quickly. Even so, it felt extraordinarily good to be here. There would be plenty of obstacles, plenty of Robertson-like hardships on the road, plenty of despair; but I wasn't going to leave this time until I had got back to Kabul, no matter what it took. That was the promise I made to myself as I stood there in the early afternoon sun, looking out at the desert hills and delighted to be back. Then I remembered the boatmen.

'Have you got any money to give these poor sods?' I asked Peter.

He hadn't, any more than I had. We had no Tajik money left, no dollars, no pounds. Our colleagues had all the cash, and they were a long way away down the river bank.

'I don't suppose Pakistani money's exactly what they want,' I said; Pakistan being the Northern Alliance's big enemy.

I pulled out a wad of it and showed it to them. I was right: it wasn't at all what they wanted. The moment was an awkward one. Eventually they allowed us to take our gear off the raft, though they wouldn't help us. I couldn't blame them for that.

It got rid of the jobsworth, though; maybe he felt it wasn't a good idea to be seen around with us. Instead, we headed off in the direction of the local military commander, whose tent stood on the top of a nearby hill. He turned out to be charming and relaxed, completely unlike the man on the raft. His shaven chin and moustache proclaimed him to be an old supporter of President Najibullah and the Communist system.

Afghanistan is a country where men wear their allegiance on their faces: shaving, or growing a beard, are political acts. Yet it is also a very forgiving country. Nowadays the commander was fighting for the Northern Alliance and against the Taliban; that was all his comrades cared about, not his past history. Afghans accept each other at face value – literally. They switch sides, and expect everyone else to. Yet each change of heart is taken seriously, while it lasts. Everything depends on the relative confidence of the different parties, and directly that starts to leak away the defections begin. This was the process which had stripped the mujaheddin government of power in 1996, and allowed the Taliban to take over from them. Soon, the Northern Alliance hoped, the same process would start to bring down the Taliban.

The commander invited us into his tent and talked to us about the military situation. The front line up here was a few miles away, and was mostly quiet; apart from the occasional exchange of artillery fire. But already, he said, sitting cross-legged drinking his tea and eating the little dried and sugared mulberries which Afghans love, they were starting to get secret enquiries from the Taliban commanders on the other side: enquiries such as, what would be the Northern Alliance's response if they changed over? What positions would they be given? What would happen to their men?

I explained to him that we had a television programme to finish by the evening: would he object if we did some interviews and recorded four pieces to camera around the area of his camp? The commander waved his hand with Afghan courtesy: the camp was ours, we could do what we wished, and he would move out immediately with his officers. What would we like to eat? We declined the meal as politely as possible, but I was grateful for his kindness.

That was the good side of being back in Afghanistan. A slightly more irritating side was to show itself very quickly. Peter was filming the commander and me from outside the tent, and I pointed out the line of shoes at the entrance; could he, I asked, get a shot of them? He was just focusing on the shoes when a thoughtful aide moved across and started collecting them up.

'It's that bloody gene,' Peter Jouvenal called out to me.

His theory, after working for twenty years in the country, was that Afghans have a highly developed gene which warns them when a television cameraman has spotted a good shot – and they come and wreck it.

A jeep drove up in the desert, throwing a huge cloud of yellow dust into the air. It was Paul Simpson, the London-based producer I most often work with, looking remarkably dashing with a black and white Afghan scarf round his neck. When he and my wife Dee and I travel together as the Simpsons, the relationships confuse everyone: since he and Dee are the same age, most people assume I must be Paul's father and she must be his wife. It freaks them out thoroughly when Dee and I go to one room and Paul to another.

He had come to welcome us and take us to the BBC camp, forty-five minutes' drive away, but I got him involved in our filming; Peter Emmerson too – the radio engineer and news organizer who was to spend the next month and a half with us. I had to interview Jouvenal for *Panorama*, which meant that Emmerson and Paul Simpson had to do the camera-work. The role-reversal was extensive.

I asked Jouvenal about the time he had interviewed Osama bin Laden for CNN. What was he like? Peter repeated the line he had used to me some days before.

'Cold, withdrawn, a bit like a bank manager.'

And he pulled out his photograph, which he held up for the benefit of the camera. In it, Jouvenal and bin Laden were sitting side by side, together with the CNN correspondent Peter Arnett and the producer. Aside from the beard, bin Laden did indeed look rather like a bank manager reviewing a stubborn overdraft.

With everyone's help, we finally got through the pieces to camera. It was still only five in the afternoon, and I had fulfilled each of my three commitments: we had got into Afghanistan, I had written and sent my *Sunday Telegraph* column, and we had recorded the necessary inserts for *Panorama*. They still had to be satellited to London, but that was the easy bit. The BBC had a satellite dish at its base at Khwaja Bahawuddin, where Paul was the boss. He drove us there through the sand which had caused Alexander the Great's Macedonians such problems.

Khwaja, which everyone pronounced 'Hodge', was a mushroom of a town which didn't appear on any maps I had seen. A couple of years earlier it had just consisted of a few houses; but its position so close to the Tajik border meant it was a useful place to establish a headquarters, and the Northern Alliance had done just that. Various of their departments, including the Foreign Ministry where the jobsworth had wanted us to register, were here.

So was the BBC. We had been the first organization to get a satellite dish into Afghanistan, and for some reason the dish had stopped here, a mile or two inside the border. There was, it was true, a front line not too far away, and later on this became pretty active. But the real action lay a long way south, twenty-five miles from Kabul; up here, Hodge was so distant it scarcely seemed like Afghanistan at all. Yet once the BBC had settled down, all sorts of other news organizations did the same, and Hodge became the main broadcasting and journalistic hub for covering the war.

To be honest, I didn't like the whole idea. True, when we reached the BBC compound, I could see how impressive it was: a big walled area with proper gates to deter thieves, and an open space in the middle of a square of buildings where tents were pitched. It wasn't permanent, since the aid agency which owned it had rented it to us for a fixed period of time, and would soon afterwards reclaim it. Nor was it a soft option. The facilities at this particular place were quite good – people came to visit the BBC just in order to use its sit-down lavatory – but after the aid agency came back and needed the compound back, times were very difficult for the BBC team. They had to move out to another compound, where things were very much more crowded and difficult; especially as regards the lavatories. Or lavatory, since there was only one for the entire team: the kind of

long drop with a curtain of sacking across the entrance, where the
flies buzz, the smell is appalling, and at night you pray you won't
drop your torch.

The reason I didn't like it had nothing to do with the sanitary
arrangements. There is a tendency in today's television journalism to
create these big broadcasting hubs wherever you go, with a satellite
dish and working areas and a mess tent and people who can give you
medicine for your ills and protection against everything from ants to
AK-47s. It's entirely necessary if, like the BBC and Sky News and
CNN and the others, you have to broadcast twenty-four hours a day.
But there is a danger that what should be the most sinuous and
flexible business on earth will somehow become ossified. Journalists
find it distinctly harder to go and see what is happening in the world
outside the compound walls if everything they need seems to be inside
it: electricity, water, contact with the office in London, phones,
computers.

When the idea of introducing a 24-hour television and radio news
service was first mooted, Charles Wheeler, Martin Bell and one or
two other leading broadcasters, all famous for their ability to roam
off the beaten path and find out what was really going on, issued a
strong warning: there was, they said, a danger that journalists would
in future be chained to the microphone, and wouldn't be able to
break away long enough to find something to report on. Partly
because they were so forceful in expressing these anxieties, it didn't
turn out like that at all. The new services were given the proper
funding, and plenty more correspondents and producers were hired –
enough to make it possible for some real reporting to be done. Even
so, the gravitational pull of the hub is very strong, and when
conditions outside are tough you really have to force yourself to leave
it. For that reason I much prefer not to get involved in the first place:
if you don't have anywhere to hang around, you won't find yourself
getting stuck.

Still, I was in a much easier position than the others. I had *carte
blanche* to rove around, and no one was relying on me to provide the
day-to-day, bread-and-butter reporting from Hodge; or 'Northern
Afghanistan', as the broadcasters in London were calling it. When I
started strutting about and announcing in a loud voice that I was
planning to get out of there as fast as possible I could see how envious

the faces around me were. They would have been only too happy to get away too.

How we were to do it, I still had no idea. But we were all too tired to care, after being on the go since the early hours of the morning. We gave the pieces to camera we had recorded to the Russian engineer in charge of the satellite dish, and he played them over to London. I looked at my watch: eight o'clock at night here, four-thirty in the afternoon in London. Kabul is confusingly three and a half hours ahead of London, which makes every time calculation difficult and open to error. *Panorama* easily had enough time to stitch the pieces to camera into the edited structure of the programme by tomorrow night. As the tape played out I had a final view of myself on the monitor, wandering around the desert and gesticulating. The last of my commitments for the day had finally been discharged.

There was no room in the BBC compound for all of us, so Peter Emmerson, Peter Jouvenal and I were taken off to the Associated Press compound, where we (well, certainly I) snored away the night on the floor of an empty, dusty room. I dreamed of boats and rivers and, inevitably, of sinkings.

§

In ancient Greek drama there was generally a moment where the chorus stepped forward and started speaking the views of the playwright himself about the action, or the chief character, or the general state of Athens, or the way the gods had been behaving recently. It was called the Parabasis, and this business of the piece to camera in television news is rather similar: the key, in a way, to the entire performance.

It doesn't always have to be this important; at CNN, for instance, they often regard the piece to camera as a useful way of linking two different sequences of pictures, and when they do it they call it a 'bridge' – the equivalent for a newspaper writer of expressions like 'meanwhile' or 'in other developments'. But in its most basic form it is the moment when we finally see the person who has been orating to us behind the scenes. He or she steps out and appears before us, and gives us some idea of the issue at the heart of the report. The American networks call it a stand-up; the French a *plafond*, a platform; and in most other European countries it is known, more simply and more obviously, as a statement.

For all sorts of reasons, this moment is an awkward one. It breaks the attention of the viewer, who has been getting used to the story which is unfolding, and it intrudes all sorts of other considerations into what should be a straightforward recital of events. The viewer starts to think, 'What a strange-looking man,' or 'What's she done to her hair?', or 'Isn't he getting fat?', or 'She looks just like my auntie, and her name was the same before she got married. I bet they're related.' So the important thing about a piece to camera is to integrate it into the action as much as possible, by shooting at the same time as the rest of the action, or by continuing to run the pictures of the action over the first few words of the piece to camera.

The two best pieces to camera I have ever seen were from a couple of famous World Affairs Unit alumni, Ben Brown and George Alagiah. By chance, both were recorded in Zimbabwe. George was reporting on the rural unrest, and was driving round the countryside from one trouble-spot to the next. It seemed the most natural thing in the world when we saw him face to face. He talked to the camera as though we were actually there with him, and ended up telling us where he was going next. Then he climbed into his vehicle and started to drive off. There was nothing remotely artificial about it, as there so often is about a piece to camera. It was a completely integrated part of the action, and you felt when you watched it that you were part of it too.

Ben spoke to camera when he was under siege from a violent, yelling mob of so-called war veterans in a farmhouse in Zimbabwe in 2001. The 'veterans' had orders to attack them, as part of President Robert Mugabe's campaign against white Zimbabweans, Britain, and the BBC. It seemed to Ben and his crew that the mob was going to break in and kill them at any moment – and Ben realized this was the opportunity to record a piece to camera. It was superb television: you could feel his own nervousness coming through, and your heart went out to someone who could, as it were, take the time out to speak to you at a moment like this. The Royal Television Society made him its Reporter of the Year for his report, and it was thoroughly deserved. I'm biased, because the early 1990s, when Ben and George and Brian

Hanrahan and Jeremy Bowen and David Shukman were members of the World Affairs Unit were some of the most enjoyable of my entire career. I used to enjoy merely walking into the office in the morning, and taking them all to lunch from time to time was a real pleasure.

Most pieces to camera aren't recorded in life-or-death circumstances, of course, and the problem is usually how to make them more interesting. Nowadays there are determined efforts in most big television organizations to liven them up. The fashion is to gesticulate meaningfully, and to walk and talk at the same time. All to the good, of course, though this too can become as formulaic as merely standing in the middle of the screen and barking words at the camera. Nowadays you see reporters waving their hands like Italian waiters, one movement every four words, or walking a few awkward paces from one place of no significance to another place of no significance. Personally, I prefer not to wave my hands about too much, and only to walk when it reveals something about the background; but that's only because I am stuck in my ways, and know, like President Gerald Ford, how difficult it is to walk and talk at the same time.

There aren't really any rules, except to be as natural as possible. The closer your words and actions are to everyday life and conversation, the better the result will be. That's why some of the more stilted characteristics which we television news reporters occasionally exhibit appear so ludicrous. Here are three examples, each taken from a news broadcast. Only the names have been changed to protect the embarrassment of the reporter concerned; I could perfectly well have done all three myself.

1. A reporter is standing in front of a building, which is very clearly a supermarket. It says so in big letters which seem to be passing through the reporter's right ear and out again through his left. 'The men drove up in an unmarked estate car' [unmarked in this context meaning what? Showing no signs of having been in a collision?], 'jumped out, and ran into the supermarket behind me here, firing a shot into the air.' The last six words, which are ill-explained – was the shot fired outside before they went in, or inside? – are difficult to hear, because the reporter turns his head away from the camera at the key moment to look at the enormous supermarket which fills the frame behind him and whose name appears in very large letters; in doing so he moves out of audio range of the little

Dee in England . . .

. . . and at work with Andrew Kilrain ('Killa') in the streets of Kabul, June 2002

Bob Prabhu, who developed the camera style for *Simpson's World*

John Jennings and I discuss our meeting with Commander Zardad. I am wearing a suit, not for the Commander's benefit but because I have to make a speech at the Foreign Office immediately afterwards.

Commander Zardad bearded on his doorstep in Mitcham. He is holding the trick parcel which Vaughan Smith has just handed him.

Rahman Beg, the best and grandest member of the BBC house-staff.

Hajji Bari briefs us on the assault on Kabul. From left: Nick Springate, Peter Emmerson, Hajji's bodyguard, Peter Jouvenal, Hajji, Joe Phua

Bombing along the front line

24 October 2001. Possibly the first video report live from a battlefield. The streak of light between the two Northern Alliance soldiers is a Taliban rocket.

The battle for Kabul begins.

I do a piece to camera on the Taliban's second defensive line, captured only twenty minutes earlier. A bad idea: there is no sense of action, I look far too neat, and it could have been filmed hours after the Northern Alliance had moved on.

William Reeve on the receiving end of some American friendly fire in Kabul

Rageh Omaar records a piece to camera in newly liberated Kabul.

A Pakistani volunteer for the Taliban gives himself up in the grounds of the Hotel Inter-Continental.

Fearful yet defiant: a captured Arab volunteer, possibly Egyptian.

Nelson Mandela wows the dons of Magdalene College, Cambridge, May 2001.

Simpsons' World

microphone which has been pinned on his lapel. It's a completely unnecessary gesture which was once fashionable among television reporters; they would often accompany it with the phrase 'Behind me as I stand here . . .'

2. A reporter is standing in a street with firemen moving around in the background, a large ladder visible, and a building which has been burned. She is talking to camera in the middle of the frame, but is weirdly angled so that her right side is turned almost entirely away from the viewer and her left shoulder is pointing towards us. It must take a considerable muscular effort for her to be able to keep looking at the camera. The whole thing is extraordinarily unnatural; the reporter would never think of standing in someone's sitting room talking to them in a strained position like that. The original purpose of this kind of thing, which we copied from American television news, was to make it clear what was happening in the background, and it is of course important to see that that the reporter is right there at the scene of the action. A slight angling of the body is necessary to draw the viewer's eye into the picture; but this much angling merely looks odd.

3. A reporter is standing in a foreign city, answering the questions of a news presenter in London. The presenter is relaxed, informed, pleasant.

'We heard you a moment ago saying you didn't think the government there would take any immediate action, John. Why do you think that is?'

The reporter's eyes are glassy, and he is standing stiffly to attention. His very first word shows the unnaturalness of the whole business.

'Michael, the situation here is becoming more and more confused by the moment.'

When do you ever hear anyone answer a question by starting off with the name of the person they are speaking to? Most of us never call people by their names at all in normal speech; but to use it at the start of the answer gives the whole exercise a stilted, awkward tone from which it never recovers. In this case, John does it because he watches a lot of CNN, and in the early 1990s some CNN executive issued an instruction that first names should be used as much as possible because it sounded matey. Fine; but correspondents sometimes had a problem remembering to put them in later in the answer, and saying the name first got that particular duty out of the way.

CNN reporters doing these 'two-ways', or 'down-the-lines' seem to be under less time-pressure than BBC ones are (on CNN you never hear that dreadful studio chop-off 'We must leave it there,' which sounds as though the presenter has become thoroughly bored by the correspondent's obsessive rabbiting on) and they are usually allowed to complete their answers. When they have done so, they say the presenter's name with a little question mark attached to it, as a clue to the director in the gallery that it is time to cut back to the studio:

'So now they are saying here that it could be war. Urethra?'

Habits like this are as natural as a bad toupee, and the mere sight of them diverts almost all the viewer's attention to the one area the reporter doesn't want anyone to notice. The more natural, the more relaxed, the easier you are with the camera, the better the viewer feels.

We all have our King Charles's heads when it comes to these things – in my case, the way BBC presenters ask questions like 'What's the mood on the streets?' – though many of them are perfectly harmless and it is only the frequent repetition which makes then irritating. But anything which savours of awkwardness and the formulaic really has to be excised.

One afternoon twenty years ago, during the period when I was reading the news, an old newsroom hand came and stood beside me in the gents' lavatory on the sixth floor at Television Centre. He was a marvellous character, of the old-fashioned, colourful kind you never seem to find in television newsrooms nowadays: a former RAF fighter pilot and theatre director called Sandy McCourt, as fat as Falstaff and with Falstaffian appetites and humour and an absurd little moustache and beard, as sandy as his name. He was a lot older and more worldly wise than I, and I was always a bit in awe of him.

'You know,' he said, emptying a capacious bladder at interminable length, 'you and the camera are a bit nervous of each other at the moment, aren't you?'

I mumbled that it was true.

'I'll tell you what. If you stick at it, you'll come to love the camera, and when that happens the camera will love you. But you've got to stick at it.'

It was as good a piece of professional advice as I've ever been given. It took several more years before it started to come true, but the more I stuck at it, the more I began to regard the camera first as a companion, and then slowly as a friend. And even more slowly the camera seemed to change its mind about me. It didn't show me up as being quite so awkward or stiff or nervous any more. It seemed to want to listen to me; and as I stared into its lens, while I did my pieces to camera, I no longer saw an unforgiving, unblinking, hostile piece of technology staring back at me.

Instead, I started to think of it as being like a little tunnel, a little hole in the wall, on the other side of which were my friends and relatives and well-wishers, and large numbers of ordinary, unprejudiced people who really wanted to know more about the place I was in. All this probably sounds grotesquely sentimental, and in a way I suppose it is; after all, there must be plenty of other kinds of people, bored, ignorant or hostile, who are also watching. But it showed me how important it was to cultivate an affection for the camera, and it helped me to spot the people who have established this relationship with it: Jon Snow, Michael Nicholson, Matt Frei, Ben Brown, Andrew Marr, Mark Austin and Bill Nealy of ITN, and at least four Jeremys – Bowen, Paxman and Vine of the BBC, and Thompson of Sky. There are plenty of others too.

Sandy McCourt died long ago; but his advice will stay with me as long as I am able to stand in front of a camera and speak to it. Maybe, for me, the camera has become Sandy McCourt.

12

Hard Travelling

Khwaja Bahawuddin, Rustaq, Faisabad, Baharak,
Ferghamu, Sar-i-Sang, Anjuman and Panjshir Valley:
Sunday 7 October to Friday 12 October

I was stiff and aching from lying on the concrete floor and the place was cold, but it wasn't enough to damp my spirits: it still felt good to be back. Afghanistan is one of the places which has this effect on you, I find. I felt like John Buchan's relentlessly imperialistic hero, Richard Hannay:

> The tonic weather reminded me of South Africa, where in the Boer War I used often to go to bed supperless on the wet ground and wake whistling from pure light-heartedness.

As it happened, there didn't seem to be anything much to eat or drink for us either. Jouvenal, Emmerson and I sat for an hour or more on the veranda in the weak sunshine, gradually thawing out and waiting for someone to drive us back to the BBC compound. When we got there, I talked things over with Paul Simpson, gratefully warming my hands on a mug of scalding Nescafé. Of course I would have liked it if he had been able to come with me, because we had worked together in so many bad places and I knew how reliable he was. But he'd been sent here to be the boss of the whole complex Hodge operation, and the office wouldn't take kindly to his simply drifting off. I couldn't prevent myself from letting the suggestion hang half-expressed in the air, though, knowing that he disliked these big set-piece efforts as much as I did. Then we talked about something else.

As we sat there, friends and colleagues from BBC bureaux in

different parts of the world wandered round the compound. And there were others I knew slightly, including a tall, rangy, pleasant-faced Singaporean called Joe Phua who wore a yellow and black scarf round his head and looked extremely piratical. I had worked with his cousin – they belong to a large and famous tribe of cameramen, the older members of which worked for Australian television during the Vietnam War – and inexcusably got the two of them mixed up. Joe didn't seem to mind. He had a pleasant, relaxed disposition which I would come to depend on heavily in the weeks that followed.

Standing in the middle of the compound, like quartermasters in a commissariat, were a couple of security advisers the BBC had hired for this operation: former Marines, or maybe members of the SAS or SBS. The Special Boat Squadron is the naval equivalent of the SAS, and according to legend is even tougher. It was never entirely clear to me, or I think to them either, what their precise function was supposed to be, except to make sure we didn't come to any harm. As things turned out, they were mostly in charge of logistics, from organizing vehicles to getting accommodation; but they also helped out as sound recordists, lighting men, drivers, advisers, cooks, and good companions. Here at Hodge they seemed to be in charge of supplies too; there was a magical tent in the middle of the compound where you could get virtually anything you might need for travelling and living rough, from sleeping bags and torches to packets of processed cheese.

If you are the boss of an outfit like this, you are always tempted to keep as many of your people and as much of your equipment as you can. It was my great good luck that Paul should be in charge of Hodge, because he was prepared to give me anything and anyone I needed for the expedition to the front line outside Kabul. I explained to him as we sat there that it was madness for me to stay in Hodge for another night. The attack on Kabul could come at any moment – I repeated what the man in the Pentagon had said about 'seeing' three satellites – and I wanted to get going directly I could arrange the necessary vehicles.

'But will it be enough just to have Peter Jouvenal? Won't you need an editor as well? Why don't you take Joe Phua?'

I jumped at the chance, of course. Joe wasn't just an editor, he was a distinguished cameraman as well.

'And you ought to have a security man to go with you. It could be really difficult where you're going. I think you ought to have Tony Rippon. He's some kind of Royal Marine.'

He pointed to a tough-looking character with sandy hair who was lifting a heavy box with some ease and carrying it over to the main tent. I was old enough to be Paul's father, yet Paul was the one looking after me. I asked him if he was sure he could spare Joe and Tony.

'I'm sure we can get London to send someone else in.'

And so, in this chance way, one of the best teams I've ever been fortunate enough to work with was assembled. I didn't realize at the time how much I would need the extra two people, or just how good they would be.

There were now going to be six of us: Kate Clark, the radio correspondent from Kabul; Peter Emmerson; Joe Phua; Tony Rippon, the ex-Marine; Peter Jouvenal; and me. We gathered together in the compound, and I explained that we had to get going that afternoon. We worked out that we would need four Russian jeeps for the journey: small, uncomfortable vehicles, but tough enough for the mountains we would need to cross in order to get to the front line outside Kabul.

I asked Peter Jouvenal to outline the two hundred-mile trek for us: it would, he said, run down through the mountains to Rustaq and on to Faisabad, then over the 12,000-foot Anjuman Pass, into the Panjshir Valley, through that to the town of Jabal Saraj where the Northern Alliance had its headquarters, and on finally to Charikar, twenty-five miles north of Kabul, where the front line was. The only time we would find a metalled road surface, Peter said, was the twenty miles from Jabal to Charikar. The rest would be mountain tracks, the beds of rivers, boulder-strewn plains. It sounded pretty tough. At that stage, fortunately, none of us knew quite how tough it would turn out to be.

'And how long will it take?'

Jouvenal said he thought about three days. 'But it all depends on the conditions. Anjuman could be snowed in. Anything can happen in Afghanistan.'

I didn't really care: I just wanted to get going. Every instinct in me said that if I even stayed here to do a single broadcast from the satellite dish, we would find ourselves stuck for good. The magnetic force would start to operate.

But we had to get hold of the four jeeps first, and this in a town where journalists were continually passing through and looking for transport. We had the promise of one through a contact of Jouvenal's, but the rest could be a problem. Fortunately, at the compound of Associated Press Television News there was Suroj.

Suroj was an excellent young producer, half Indian and half Iranian, whom Paul Simpson had come across a year or so before in Tehran, working rather disconsolately as a waiter at an hotel. At that time we had needed a translator, and Paul had asked him if he would work for us for a couple of weeks. He jumped at the chance. It had turned out to be the making of him: his English was perfect, he was an adventurous, can-do kind of person, and he was desperate to travel. After we had left Tehran, APTN needed a local producer, and on the strength of our recommendation Suroj got the job. Now he travelled the globe for APTN – and at present was here in Hodge. Suroj was generous and extraordinarily helpful. He went out immediately and started finding jeeps.

It took all afternoon. In the meantime we went out to the small bazaar, a muddy area with converted shipping containers as shops, and bought the kind of things we would need: thick cotton quilts for sleeping on, dreadful synthetic blankets which crackled with static electricity every time you rubbed them against something, thermoses, fruit. In one shop I saw a *chapan* – a long, thickly quilted winter coat in green stripes with a psychedelic kind of lining, which Uzbeks in Afghanistan wear over their shoulders so the sleeves hang down. For some occult reason the sleeves are always extraordinarily long, as though *chapans* are made to measure for orang-utans. I tried it on, and put my arms in the sleeves. It fitted very well except for the arms, which made me feel like Cro-Magnon man. It mightn't look good in the King's Road, I reasoned, but who knew what I might need on this trip of ours through the mountains?

There was a good deal of only half-smothered amusement at the expense of the Englishman who thought you put your arms into a *chapan*, and the owner indulgently let me have it for ten dollars and thought he'd gypped me. I don't think there was a single night for the next six weeks when I wasn't grateful for the impulse that had made me buy it.

The jeeps were starting to arrive: rickety, rusted, with windscreens crazed by the heat, or cold, or bullets, and with drivers who looked like cut-throats, but jeeps all the same. It was like herding cats to get them all ready at the same time: they needed petrol, or tools, or oil, or tinkering with, and as the evening wore on I grew more and more afraid that they would just melt away for the night.

Suddenly I heard a flurry of conversation from one of the buildings in the compound, and a group of people gathered round a woman who was sitting on the steps, a satellite phone in her hand. She worked for one of the US networks.

'That's funny,' she said, 'the guys in London have just had a call from New York to say they've got to stay at their desks and not leave from four o'clock this afternoon London time.'

People debated what this might mean; but I knew. That was precisely what had happened at the start of the bombing of Baghdad in 1991. The networks had had a roundabout tip-off from the Pentagon, but no one wanted to say over an open phone line what was going to happen. I told Paul about it quietly.

'I've really got to get going,' I said.

If London knew that things were about to start, and realized I was still at Hodge, they'd never let me leave; and we might well miss the big ground attack on Kabul as a result. Four in the afternoon, London time, was 7.30 in the evening in Afghanistan. It was 5.45 now, and getting dark; and things might start happening in an hour and forty-five minutes. Time to go.

We loaded up the vehicles. It seemed to take an eternity, and now I was in a real sweat. With a certain amount of difficulty I forced the drivers to stand in front of their jeeps and rounded up our party; Kate was making a long phone call, and was reluctant to break off. Then we shook hands all round, settled ourselves in the jeeps, and moved out through the compound gates into the dark, our headlights cutting deep into the surrounding darkness. At long last we were off.

§

It was, of course, an anticlimax; in my experience these big leaving scenes usually are. We were only a hundred yards or so from the gates of the compound when we realized the fourth jeep hadn't left. In spite of all the checks I had made the drivers take, it couldn't even start. We spent twenty minutes waiting impatiently by the roadside in the dark before we saw headlights emerging from the compound gateway and heard the bronchial sound of its engine.

'Gearbox trouble, I should think,' Tony said tersely.

And at the start of the hardest journey most of us will ever make in our lives, I thought. The sensible thing would be to go back, get it properly sorted out, and leave in the morning. But the most sensible thing of all would be to have stayed out of Afghanistan altogether. Common sense had played very little part in the genesis of this expedition, and I saw no reason to introduce it at this late stage.

'We'll head on,' I said.

I had the feeling that everyone agreed, though I didn't put it to the vote. Maybe it was just that it would have been such a let-down to go back those hundred yards now.

Outside Hodge we raced across the desert in the near darkness, all four jeeps sounding and looking fine now, throwing up fine plumes of sand into the night sky. There was no road, just a line of tracks. Ahead of us lay the mountains. So far so good; but I didn't say that out loud, knowing how Peter Jouvenal dislikes any breach of the ancient Greek principle of *aidos* – walking humbly before the gods, that is, and not getting above yourself. Personally, I regard it as rank superstition; and yet which of us, at times when our lives are going really well, likes to say so, just in case? But in case of what, it would be hard to say.

In the light of the newly risen moon we could see the mountain track ahead of us. It was very steep. We had reorganized the convoy, putting Kate, Joe, and Tony in the jeep which had had engine trouble so it would not simply fall back and get lost unnoticed. The two Peters and I were in another, and the other two carried our gear. Normally you wouldn't send gear with just a driver, of course, but here in Afghanistan there was nowhere for a thieving driver to take our things if they stole them; the wild terrain meant that all four jeeps had to keep together. And anyway I had to have Peter Jouvenal and

Peter Emmerson travelling with me, in case the bombing started; Emmerson had to operate our videophone so I could start broadcasting, and Jouvenal would have to do the filming. It seemed better and more companionable for the other three to travel together, too.

We stopped at the foot of the mountain track, and decided that the faulty jeep carrying Joe, Tony and Kate should go first in case it developed problems. With a great deal of roaring and dust, the driver raced his engine and headed up the steep slope. The jeep ground on, getting slower and slower, and then it stopped altogether. The brakes failed. It started rolling back towards the black precipice on the left, and towards the next vehicle in the line, which was stopped.

Inside, Tony shouted, 'Jump! Jump!'

Joe threw himself out, and came rolling down the slope. Kate refused to get out, and Tony felt he had to stay with her as the jeep came closer and closer to the edge. It was horrifying to stand there, watching: and I felt it was all my fault for forcing the pace and insisting on leaving in the dark.

Somehow, the jeep's driver managed to keep control of the steering-wheel. They missed the other jeep, and stopped short of the precipice. Joe was shaken, and had hurt his elbow and hip. The hip was just a bruise, but the elbow started swelling up fast and would need proper care. Still, when Tony tested it out it was clearly not broken. We were only an hour out, and we had already come close to utter disaster.

I have had some hard journeys in my time, but the next five days were the worst I have ever experienced. Group after group who made it down to the plains north of Kabul told us similar stories. For instance, two journalists were dozing in the back of a jeep when its brakes failed on the steepest part of another mountain pass. The driver jumped out and abandoned them, and the jeep rolled backwards towards the precipice – then stopped, with one wheel hanging over the edge and another stuck on a bit of rock. The temptation to point out to the driver the error of his ways must have been pretty strong; but of course they had no alternative but to keep him on.

Nervously, and with much less of our original enthusiasm, we headed in convoy up the mountainside. By now Peter Emmerson was holding our satellite radio out of the window with its little dish pointing at the sky, and we listened for any news that the bombing of Kabul had started. We switched between the BBC World Service and CNN, which broadcasts the audio of its television service for radio listeners. No one is a greater admirer of the World Service than I am; and when I was told recently that a superannuated Conservative government minister from the early 1980s, Sir John Nott, had argued in the Thatcher cabinet for the World Service to be closed down by withdrawing the government grant-in-aid which keeps it going (apparently because there were no indications it achieved much in the way of sales for British companies, and because the BBC in general was 'unpatriotic' during the Falklands War) I was furious. Margaret Thatcher didn't like the BBC either, but at least she realized that dismantling one of the nation's most prized treasures would be a great deal more 'unpatriotic' than asking hard but perfectly reasonable questions of here today, gone tomorrow politicians.

All the same, the World Service has its foibles; one of them being that when it is broadcasting a play it is unwilling to break into it and announce any item of breaking news short of all-out thermonuclear war. As we bounced over the boulders at the top of the mountain pass and started heading downwards, it was broadcasting a play: something gritty about life in Manchester, I think. Cursing, I asked Peter Emmerson to retune to CNN. He held the dish out of the window, pointing it at some small piece of hardware up there among the densely packed stars, and we listened to an empty interview with an American politician about the aftermath of the 11 September attacks which avoided any awkward questions whatever. How nice it would have been if Larry King had asked him what he thought of the CIA's early support for the Taliban; but no, it was all about grief and loved ones and the need for the entire nation to stand together at this difficult time. Anything else would, of course, have been 'unpatriotic'. John Nott would have relished it.

But CNN did at least break into this to tell us that explosions were being reported from Kabul. The Americans and (to a far lesser extent) the British were firing missiles at a city whose infrastructure was so primitive it might have been easier and a great deal cheaper to have left it unbombed. How would we have noticed the difference? This was not, however, an easy moment for me. I was in the middle of nowhere, neither in a good position to broadcast nor in a place which counted. I was just in the mountains somewhere north of Kabul.

'Go on, get past the other jeeps! *Burru! Burru!*' I shouted; '*burru*' being the word you yell at an Afghan driver when you want him to go faster. If you are being more polite, you say '*Burru bukhai.*'

Stupidly, I had allowed us to fall to the back of the line. The others wouldn't know that the bombing had started because they had no radios, and therefore they couldn't tell that we needed to stop and do some broadcasting. Our driver pulled out on the narrow track, sped up, and tried to get past the others; who, being Afghan, also speeded up to stop him overtaking. It took a good deal of yelling and arm-waving to get them to stop.

This was the first time we had used the videophone as a team, and it wasn't a quick business setting it up. I raved up and down, shouting that we couldn't lose time like this. Jouvenal set up the camera and the tripod, Joe put up the lights, Emmerson linked up the satellite. They had to dig the equipment out of boxes buried deep in the various jeeps, some of which had been thrown around by the accident. The surprising thing was that they managed to get it all working so quickly. Within a maximum of ten minutes, we were standing on a freezing mountain-top in northern Afghanistan, able to go on air.

'Just give me a word or two for level,' said a calm voice from the London studio. 'Are you hearing our output?'

I was. The only problem was that I was shaking with the cold; and although I wouldn't normally have cared, I was worried that my shivering would be visible on the screen. Kate had to lend me her bright blue down jacket, and I started broadcasting: gleaming out through the Afghan darkness like some enormous bird in brilliant blue plumage.

When the last interview was finished and we were just starting to pack up, a call came through: would we re-record two of the links we had sent to *Panorama* yesterday, in order to give the programme more immediacy? I had forgotten about the programme in all the rush, but I reflected now that it was going out that night – a piece of inspired timing from the BBC's point of view. Tony produced another down jacket for me in a more sober dark green, and I re-recorded the links. I rarely seem to manage the good broadcaster's trick of getting the words out properly the first time, especially when I am freezing cold and standing in a place where no one has ever broadcast from before. In the end, though, we got them recorded; and although when I look at the tape now it looks hurried and nervous to me, maybe that gives it precisely the immediacy *Panorama* wanted. I was impressed by the calmness of the producer at the London end, who had so little time to stitch the whole thing together.

Nowadays, the means of communication often seem to define a great news event. In the Gulf War of 1991 it was the satellite phone – by today's standards an enormous affair the size of a sideboard, with a huge umbrella-like dish which you put up next to the sideboard. How the much-missed Brian Hulse (who later died of cancer) managed to smuggle all this past the vigilant customs men at Baghdad airport shortly before the war began, I have no idea. But having a satellite phone of our own revolutionized our reporting, and came as a tremendous and highly satisfying shock to CNN and the Iraqi government when I announced to them that we had it; between them, they had cooked up a thoroughly dodgy deal which was intended to ensure that only CNN would be able to broadcast from Baghdad.

But scuppering the deal didn't do us all that much good in the long run, since everyone apart from CNN was soon thrown out of Baghdad by the authorities; with the exception of a good friend of mine, a Spanish newspaper journalist, who somehow managed to persuade the Iraqi Ministry of Information that if it hadn't been for a chance historical occurrence at the end of the fifteenth century the Spanish would be Arabs too. It was some time before the Iraqis got annoyed with CNN and invited other news reporters (including Jeremy Bowen of the BBC) back in to cover the rest of the war.

The means of communication which defined the war against the Taliban was the videophone. It had already been in use for well over a year, but only *in extremis*. To be honest, everyone in television looked down on the poor old videophone. The picture quality was ropy, and the restrictions on the images you could reasonably show were considerable. No doubt when we watch our videophone recordings in the future we will be deeply embarrassed by their crudity.

We transmitted our recorded and edited reports via a machine called the Toko, which sent pictures down a phone line with excruciating slowness: a two-and-a-half-minute report took about forty minutes to send. The picture quality was a little fuzzy, but otherwise perfectly acceptable. When you stood in front of the camera and orated live down the phone line, however, the loss of quality was considerable. If you moved as you spoke it resulted in all sorts of jumps and awkward breaks in the picture; and if you turned your head or pointed to something in the background it was video disaster. Even standing rigid and motionless, as though you were appearing on television in 1954, wasn't all that good: they had to shrink the picture down to a third of the screen in London so the viewers couldn't see the bad lip synch so easily.

I didn't care. I didn't have to watch myself back, which is one of the most painful things about working for television, and I didn't have to drive to any studio or run up the stairs to a hut on any roof to do my broadcasting. We could set up the camera wherever we wanted. By the time of the next great international crisis, when they open the lid to my coffin, give me a quick infusion of virgin's blood, and let me loose on the world again, the videophone quality will no doubt be perfect: as good as a portable studio and feed-point. But though in Afghanistan it wasn't fantastic, it was certainly good enough; and as we stood there in the darkness and the freezing wind of the Hindu Kush mountains, packing up the gear, we knew we had done a good job; but I had a certain amount of apologizing to do for having been so ferocious to everyone as they were setting the gear up.

We raced on to the village of Rustaq, where we were planning to spend the night. We reached it at one in the morning, Afghan time, and were just able to set the gear up in the darkness of the main street, and do a live interview for the main news at 10 p.m., plus the other habitual television customers on every live link to the BBC: World Television and News 24. The extraordinary thing was that no one in Rustaq showed any interest in us. The entire village remained asleep. No one came down to see what this sudden flood of light was, or why people were calling out to each other in a strange language. Not even the dogs barked. We had to beat heavily on the door of the little guest house outside which we had set up our broadcasting studio, in order to get anyone to let us in.

The drivers slept in one small room, and against all the accepted norms of Afghan behaviour the five Western men and one Western woman slept together in another, laying out our sleeping bags on the earthen floor. I wrapped myself up in my *chapan*, and was deeply grateful for its remarkably thick padding. It was 3.00, and I slept briefly but heavily: so heavily that, although no one liked to say so when we woke at 5.45, I could see I must have snored loudly.

Poor Joe's elbow had swollen up to the size of a tennis ball, and it was giving him a lot of pain. He claimed, of course, that it didn't hurt at all, and wouldn't give him any problems if he had to do some filming. Joe Phua is one of those cameramen whom no amount of physical pain can stop. It doesn't even seem to spoil his temper.

The jeep which had caused the problem was, however, irreparable. Its dull, resentful driver was paid off, and we found a replacement at once: a pleasant, sharp-faced driver who was the only one to stay with us for the next six weeks. His name was Sharif, but he looked so much like a friend of mine (despite the turban, the beard and the general clothing, that is) that I always thought of him as Noel. Sharif-Noel had, he later confided to us, driven a tank for the Communists in the war against the mujaheddin; and when encouraged, as long as there were no heavy-duty mujaheddin supporters around, he was inclined to boast about the numbers he had killed. He loved his tank, yet he treated his Russian jeep with the utmost carelessness. It was missing a window, it was always disgustingly dirty, and there was one place where you could see the road through the rusted floor.

'Did your tank look as bad as this?' I once asked him.

'Oh yes,' he replied; which was honest, at least.

We brought the drivers up to breakfast in the caravanserai, and ate badly cooked eggs and flat, unleavened Afghan bread.

'*Toshnab?*' I asked, remembering the word for lavatory in Farsi.

The caravanserai owner pointed to the field outside the village: the universal toilet.

Kate was sitting in one of the jeeps, writing and then broadcasting a dispatch for the World Service, surrounded by a crowd of several hundred people. Her time in Afghanistan had taught her that crowds always gather, and that the best thing is to ignore them completely. For these people, in their remote village, the BBC World Service was an important presence in their lives, with a large majority of the entire population of the country at that time listening to the BBC's news bulletins in Afghanistan's two main languages, Farsi and Pashtu. You could always tell when the news was on, because the streets became empty.

One of the bad things about working for television is that you start to reckon your surroundings solely in terms of pictures; and if you can't film it you feel annoyed. As we drove westward out of Rustaq in the early morning light, dozens of people were pouring into town with their produce for market: carts piled high with apples and lettuces and onions, superb characters in turbans and *chapans* more colourful than mine perching on the backs of tiny donkeys, women in blue and white and yellow *chadooris* walking in line astern balancing baskets of fruit on their heads, and each of them throwing up clouds of golden dust with their feet, which hung in the brilliant morning air and intensified the sharpness of the sunshine. I felt somehow that the whole of this wonderful show was wasted, because we didn't have time to stop and get the cameras out.

There had been an earthquake here, and the ground was frighteningly fissured. The rents in the earth's surface were immeasurably deep, and often too wide to jump across. At this point one of the jeeps developed a problem, and we all had to stop. The sun rose higher and higher, warming up the world; still the jeep wasn't fixed. I got increasingly impatient. Who knew how quickly the Taliban would collapse? There would be more missile attacks on Kabul directly it got dark; the big push by the Northern Alliance could come very soon.

I persuaded myself that we couldn't afford to wait for the driver to fix his jeep. Tony agreed to stay with it, and Joe, who didn't like to leave Tony on his own, decided to stay too. We agreed to meet that night in the town of Faisabad, though the arrangement was inevitably vague. As we drove away I didn't feel too good about it. After all, when someone had suggested on the last stage of our journey through Tajikistan that we should leave Peter Jouvenal behind because his lack of a visa might imperil the rest of us, I launched into a long and self-righteous lecture about never leaving colleagues behind. Now I was leaving two of them behind.

The road became harder. Much of it lay along a dry river bed, with the tyres bouncing off the boulders and making things for us very unpleasant indeed. Sometimes we would leave the river, and drive along in dust that was deeper and more pervasive than the waters of any river. There had been plenty of fighting here at one stage. Twice we saw unexploded bombs embedded in the track, and had to edge round beside them carefully. It was typical of the breakdown of life in Afghanistan that no one troubled to dig them out and get rid of them. The rusty skeletons of Russian troop-carriers and tanks like Noel's lay beside the road for children to play on.

It was 3.15 by the time we reached Faisabad. I hadn't originally wanted to stay here, feeling that we should try to make it to Baharak. But that would mean we would lose all contact with the other two, and the drivers were settling down into that comfortable business of fiddling with their engines that showed they wanted to stay here the night. By the time we had set up the camera on the outskirts of the town and I had been interviewed several times by television programmes in London, and Kate had done her stuff for radio, it was plain we weren't going any further. Anyway, one of the drivers had gone off to do some repairs, and it was dark before he came back.

A stream of passers-by had stopped to watch our strange proceedings, and no fewer than four of them had offered to put us up for the night; such being the hospitable impulses of the Afghan. But Peter Jouvenal had already headed off to see if we could stay at the UN compound: not necessarily easy, given that all the foreign staff had been evacuated from it. When our other driver came back, Peter Emmerson, Kate and I drove into the centre of town where we had agreed to meet Peter.

Another long wait: but at the end of it, laughing and talking loudly with excitement, Peter Jouvenal had brought Tony and Joe Phua with him. As they were driving through the town in complete darkness, their headlights had swept across the front of a vehicle, and in the few milliseconds available Joe recognized Jouvenal. So we were reunited. I felt a great deal better, and Tony insisted that their jeep was now in reasonable shape.

We headed round to the UN compound, where the local people in charge had agreed to let us stay the night. After what we had been through for the last couple of nights, it seemed remarkably civilized. We ate kebabs and small, sweet dark grapes, drank quantities of Afghan tea, and stumbled upstairs. I found a real bed, with a real electric light, and read for a while before falling asleep and sleeping for a blessed seven hours. The next time I would sleep in a bed would be in Kabul, after the Taliban had been overthrown.

§

I went round waking everyone up at 5.15, and we were on the road remarkably quickly. But the unusual burst of speed didn't last. The two middle jeeps kept stopping, and every time they did the entire convoy would be halted. All four of the drivers would then lift the bonnets of their vehicles and start messing around with the engines. There was a kind of passive resistance on their part, and, I came to believe, on the part of their jeeps, to all this hurry of mine. It offended their notion of the proprieties. They didn't mind getting up early, but they did like to pause for reasonable periods during the morning and at midday, and they preferred to stop all together at around four in the afternoon. Afghans are highly sociable people, and the drivers enjoyed spending time in each other's company. They couldn't see the point of rushing, and there were always mechanical reasons to slow everything down.

The best speed we ever made on the entire journey was about eight miles an hour: not too bad, considering the terrible nature of the track. When it was at its worst, it would probably have been easier to walk: sitting jammed into our hard, unsprung seats and gripping onto the window-frames to keep ourselves steady as the jeeps lurched and bounced and jerked, we were acutely uncomfortable. I have done a lot of driving in Afghanistan, but never for this unrelenting amount of time and never, it seemed to me, over such bad terrain. Peter Emmerson and Joe Phua were coming down with bad colds. It amazed me that they could stay lively and cheerful under circumstances like these.

We made it to the next town, Baharak. There, the drivers staged a kind of mutiny. We stopped in the centre, and they demanded large amounts of money to make the repairs on their vehicles.

'Let's get this straight. These jeeps of yours are in a dreadful condition, and we have to pay to put them right?'

But neither Kate's nor Peter Jouvenal's Farsi was up to expressing the angry irony. The drivers just nodded their heads: that was the position. And of course it was. Take any four Russian jeeps in Afghanistan and you would have found the same faults; driving for days on end over boulders and fine dust would destroy the coachwork, suspension and engine of any vehicle. It was only because Russia builds its jeeps like it builds its foreign policy and its old women that they had made it here at all. And since the drivers had no money, there was no one else to pay for the repairs except us.

I strode angrily around the area off the main street where we had parked, consulting the others and making up my mind: this was a good place to find a better vehicle and get rid of the worst of the jeeps, which was driven by the worst of the drivers: a weaselly little man with stained and ragged clothes and a dark, suspicious face. He was always the first to stop and the last to get going, and he spent more time than anyone else under the bonnet of his vehicle. I looked his jeep over, and saw all sorts of things that might soon go wrong with it, from a tyre that was split to a loose exhaust pipe. It certainly wasn't up to tackling the mountain range which we could already see in the distance.

He didn't like it, of course, and his mate, who drove one of the other jeeps, didn't like it either. That was a pity: his mate was one of the better drivers, and his jeep was probably in the best shape of all. But if his weaselly friend was forced to stay behind, he said, then he would stay too. This was no time for me to cave in and accept the weasel's terms: we would be stopping every ten minutes and paying through the nose for the rest of the journey if I did.

All negotiations take a long time in Afghanistan, which is a society without clocks or deadlines; and we were at a real disadvantage, not being able to express ourselves clearly enough in Farsi. At this point Kate came back, bringing with her a tall, gentle, pleasant-looking, well-educated young man. Khalil was a tremendous find: his English was good, he had been a medical student until the war intervened, he seemed to have no fear whatever, and he was good and easy company. His meeting with Kate in the main street of Baharak was to change his life permanently. He stayed with us throughout the battle for Kabul and its fall, and eventually Peter Emmerson (who is noted for his generosity in these matters) organized it so he could travel to Belize on a scholarship and resume his medical studies.

With Khalil's help we found a red twin-cabin Hi-Lux and paid off the other two drivers. By this time the one who had wanted to stay with his friend as a way of putting pressure on me had changed his mind, and was begging to come with us. But there seemed no point. We had the best combination of vehicles now, and it seemed to me that three vehicles were twenty-five per cent less likely to break down than four; but then I have an unmathematical mind.

I wanted to get away fast, both on general principle and because hanging around a small Afghan town when you have mortally offended two locals and are known to have fabulous amounts of money on you seems like a generally bad idea. But of course the Hi-Lux now needed all sorts of small repairs, even though the driver had promised me it was ready to go. I wandered off through the town, being stared at by everyone as though I was a being from another world – which in Afghan terms, I suppose, I was – and buying things like scarves and pillows to make the journey more bearable. But I held onto my walking stick; you never knew what might happen.

We had a pretty good set of drivers now: the Hi-Lux man seemed reasonable enough, and the two jeep drivers were Shah Mohammed, a (relatively) shaven former Communist whom I'd taken a liking to, partly because he had a large thermos of tea in his cab which he kept stocked up, and the former tank-driver I called Noel, who had shown himself to be thoroughly reliable and had taken our side against the two mutinous drivers. Our equipment and gear was packed onto the back of the Hi-Lux and covered with a tarpaulin. It was a remarkably clear case of putting all our eggs in one basket, certainly – what on earth would we do, I wondered, if the Hi-Lux went over a precipice? – but it lightened the loads of the two jeeps and made travelling in them marginally less uncomfortable.

By 12.40, at long last, we were ready to set off again. The parking area where all our negotiations and repacking had taken place was now occupied by all sorts of heavy trucks taking Russian shells and ammunition from the Tajikistan border down to the front line north of Kabul: yet another sign that the big offensive was about to start soon, and that we must get a move on. As we drove out I half expected the mutinous drivers and the group of sympathizers who had gathered round them to do something to us, but they merely spat on the ground and turned away.

Outside Baharak the road continued south-east. Ahead of us were some of the great peaks of the Hindu Kush range, which we would have to climb soon. Now, though, we were back in a kind of dust-desert. The dust flared up all round us, lighter and softer and more insidious than any sand, and seeping through the gaps in the windows and up through the floor of the vehicle. Our faces became caked with it, and it stayed in the pockets and seams of our clothes for weeks afterwards. Even Shah Mohammed's tea had a little residue of dust floating on its surface when we pumped it out of the flask.

Although this area of Afghanistan is close to the Pakistan border, it is in some ways the most desolate, under-populated and remote-seeming part of the entire country. The Hindu Kush derives its cynical name, meaning 'Hindu Killer', from the days when the Islamic tribesmen would force their way down to the soft, warm plains of India and bring back slaves who died of cold and malnutrition by the thousand in these unforgiving mountains.

I had a map, but like all maps of Afghanistan it seemed to show a different terrain altogether from the one we were passing through. There was no mention of Khwaja Bahawuddin (Hodge), nor of Rustaq or Baharak, and the road through Faisabad seemed to go east–west. But of course it wasn't a road anyway; it was just a direction; an aspiration, you could say. All I knew for certain from the map was that we were in the province of Badakhshan, which is part of an enormous area spreading into four countries: Afghanistan, Tajikistan, Pakistan and China.

That rang an immediate bell. At some point in my schooldays, for no reason I could understand then or can understand now, I had been forced to learn part of a poem about Afghanistan. Then, twenty years or more later, I found a copy of the book it was printed in, as I was rooting through a dusty old second-hand bookshop. I have it in front of me now, a slender green volume called *Verses Written In India* by Sir Alfred Lyall, a late Victorian Anglo-Indian administrator. Flicking through its pages, I came across the passage I had committed to memory all that time ago, and hadn't entirely forgotten even now:

And far from the Suleiman heights come the sounds of the
    stirring of tribes,
Afreedi, Hazara, and Ghilzi, they clamour for plunder or bribes;
And Herat is but held by a thread, and the Usbeg has raised
    Badukshan;
And the chief may sleep sound, in his grave, who would rule the
    unruly Afghan.

Doggerel, of course; yet it now seems to me to sum up the absolute essence of Afghanistan and its politics as well as it did more than a century ago. As a child, this and other bits of poetry (and even a hymn, of which I have forgotten everything except that it had something in it about desert plains) instilled a longing for strange places in me, and I suppose I should be grateful to whichever dry-as-dust old pedagogue hammered the words into my mind. Now that I have actually visited Badakhshan and Herat, and crossed the Suleiman Heights, I've found the Afghans just as unruly as Sir Alfred Lyall did, and just as interested in plunder and bribes. Who said a school education never teaches you anything worth knowing about real life?

I needed these reflections. There was nothing else to think about, as we bucketed along, our vehicles breaking down with predictable regularity every mile or so. We changed our driving companions from time to time, and for this stretch mine was Peter Emmerson. I asked him with growing interest about the sky-blue Morgan which he drove in London: a startling break-out from his rather donnish personality. You would be able to pick Peter out of an identity parade immediately if you were told to look for a BBC engineer. He doesn't have the open-toed sandals, but he does have the studious air of a man who understands mechanical complexities. What you can't see from the quiet exterior is the spark of adventure which leads him of his own volition to take part in absurdly uncomfortable expeditions like this, and makes him buy the most romantic and authentic of sports cars.

And so for mile after mile, through the choking dust, stopping every now and then for some problem with one of the vehicles, he told me about the lore of the Morgan; so much so that I, who don't even possess a car and think very little about them, became convinced that I should put my name down for one when I got back to London. If I ever did get back, that is, and could gather together the money. The big problem is that there is a five-year waiting list; not exactly instant gratification. Yet I became so keen on the idea that I used the satellite phone to ring Dee in South Africa from one of our enforced stops, in order to break the news to her.

She is a great deal more interested in cars than I am, and was immediately taken with the idea. And later, of course, like me, she dropped it. A Morgan is not exactly the kind of car you can leave parked in the street for months on end, if you travel as much as we do. And there is something mildly ludicrous, perhaps even pathetic, about an old boy racing round the countryside at the wheel of a young man's sports car, chasing after his lost youth. But that didn't stop me thinking about it. After all, in day-dreams as in night-dreams you are never old or sick or burdened; just your young, unfettered self.

That night, as we pressed on in an attempt to find somewhere to spend the night, we saw a bonfire by the side of the road and four men with guns standing in our path. The one who spoke to us was beardless and had a nasty, high-pitched eunuch's voice. His neck was adorned with plasters as though he was suffering from boils. They didn't point their guns at us; they didn't need to. They just wanted money.

'It's all starting again.' Peter Jouvenal sat in the darkness, watching them.

This kind of official lawlessness was what had brought the downfall of the Northern Alliance in Afghanistan in 1996; now, even before they had recaptured Kabul, they were up to their old tricks.

'Fuck off,' I said angrily to the eunuch, and turned away from him.

Noel, our driver, thought otherwise, and maybe he was right. He handed over a 100,000-afghani note: just a few pennies in the real world. For such a small price I suppose there was no point in delaying us and possibly getting into real trouble. But it felt like a bad principle.

We drove on and on in the darkness. There were no villages, no houses even. It was 10 p.m. before our headlights lit up the walls and ranch-like wooden gates of a caravanserai in the desert. It was, the drivers said, called Ferghamu. A big scared dog came out to look at us, then ran off nervously; dogs get broken in pretty roughly in Afghanistan. Its master proved harder to waken, and we had to beat on the gates for a long time before they were opened. I went in with him to check out the sleeping accommodation, and he lifted up his paraffin lamp to reveal a dozen or more bodies stretched out under blankets. As the light fell on them, the bodies came to life and sat up uncomplainingly, full of advice about where ten new arrivals could be laid to rest. I didn't like the idea at all; the room stank. Beside the gate there was a storeroom, dry and warm, where the drivers could sleep. The rest of us couldn't all get into that, though, and so we settled for an open cowshed across the road: a bit breezy, more than a little smelly, but after a long day's jolting we lay down and slept at once.

At 5.00 the next morning there wasn't even a cup of tea to get us going: the caravanserai didn't seem to run to it. Peter Emmerson cut up a Mars bar with mathematical care and handed us each a piece. The daylight showed us how close we were now to the mountains. Peter Jouvenal and I knew this bit of road quite well; we had come this way three years earlier when we made our film about the lapis lazuli mines at Sar-i-Sang. I had never thought to come back; yet here we were again. The fan broke on our jeep as it took a difficult hill, and we got out to walk. I went behind a bush to have a pee, and saw on the ground a beautiful little piece of gem-quality lapis, a brilliant dark gold-flecked blue. I put it in my pocket.

The scenery here was magnificent. Deep in the valley, a hundred or more feet below us, ran the jade green waters of the River Kowkcheh, while the mountains reared up behind, 18,000 feet or more, with the first snows of the autumn lying on them, orange in the weak early morning sun. The village of Sar-i-Sang, when we reached it, was unchanged from when we had seen it last. Around it lay the ruins which could easily have dated back to the fourth millennium BC, when the lapis mined in this mountain was already starting to reach every centre of civilization in Asia, Africa and Europe. It was from here that the inlay for Tutankhamun's funerary image was produced, and court ladies from Babylon, Ur and Jericho to pre-imperial China wore the bright beads of Sar-i-Sang around their necks.

The miners had finished their night-shift, and were hanging around in the street calling out 'Lazhwa, lazhwa' – Farsi for lapis. We went into the *chai khaneh*, the tea house, where photographs of cool, alpine scenes had been fixed on the ancient stone walls; and beside them, there, mysteriously, there was a picture cut out of some magazine of the city centre of Newcastle, in England. Time seemed meaningless: we were just part of some wider continuum. The chances are that the *chai khaneh* had been here since Pharaonic times; and we were looking at a picture of 1970s Newcastle. We drank a lot of green tea, bought quite a lot of lapis, and Peter Jouvenal pulled out a self-heating packet of sausages and beans and shared them around.

I have made a lifelong habit of eating local food and drinking, where it seems sensible, the local water. Too many people bring their own food and water with them, then get sick when supplies run out and they suddenly find themselves obliged to rely on the local stuff. Without having the faintest idea of the scientific and medical realities, I have persuaded myself that I have built up a resistance to bad food and bad water over the years. Certainly I have thrived in places where colleagues of mine have gone down with stomach troubles, and I can only think my strange habits have something to do with it; together with a small nightly dose of Laphroaig. The last time I threw up from food poisoning – forgive me for being so personal, and so graphic – was in 1978.

Much of this is, I suppose, a matter of self-suggestion. During the 1982 war in Lebanon, when camera crews were extremely hard to come by, I was obliged to work with a young and completely inexperienced sound recordist from the mid-west of the United States, who had never left America before. (How he regarded the outside world after his two weeks in the nastiest place on earth, one can only surmise.) His mother had made him promise that he would only drink bottled water, and he had kept his word. After a hot morning's work we got back to our hotel, and I asked the sound recordist to go to the kitchen to get us some soft drinks. He came back white-faced: he had found the waiter filling mineral-water bottles from the tap, and sealing them. That night the poor little chap was as sick as a dog.

We left Sar-i-Sang with real regret, and eventually reached the hauntingly beautiful Skazar Valley, where the lakes were as jewel-like as anything from Sar-i-Sang and the birch trees were turning to gold. The Anjuman Pass, 13,000 feet, was somewhere above us in the chain of mountains, and we were hoping to get over it this evening. But when we stopped at another tea house, our drivers got talking with the driver of a military truck, who told them that unless we were over the Pass before it got dark we would be in real danger. The road was so steep and the precipices so great, you had to do it in daylight. It would, the truck-driver said, take us five hours to get there. Now it was three in the afternoon, and the sun went down at around six.

I hurried the drivers on; even if we couldn't make Anjuman before dark, we could at least camp out underneath it and cross the pass early the next morning. Now we came across a series of frighteningly dangerous bridges over the rivers which came rushing down from the mountains: loose planks, the gaps between them filled carelessly with rocks and bits of wood, and often only a couple of inches wider than the wheels of our vehicles. The trucks which also had to take the route over Anjuman ploughed through each of the rivers as they came to them, but the waters were often four or five feet high and our jeeps would be swamped.

At last we came to a bridge which was so rickety and narrow that Mohammed Shah, who was game enough, felt he could only be certain of getting over it in reverse. The river lay ten feet below. He tried, with a great roaring of his engine, but it was no good. It was six o'clock, and getting dark. All we could do was to start again at first light. We ate a disconsolate meal, then wrapped ourselves up and stretched out in a field in the lee of a stone wall. Up here in the mountains it was savagely cold, and even my *chapan* didn't help much as I lay and watched the magnificent stars wheeling overhead. Only Tony, the ex-Marine, enjoyed himself; he used to go on winter exercises each year in Norway, which seemed to have made him impervious to the cold. All he wore was a T-shirt and tracksuit bottoms.

Mornings, of course, always bring a sense of new hope and rejuvenation. Aching and frozen though I was, I felt better for the thin air and the slow rising of the sun. But the Hi-Lux was clearly in a bad way, and was unlikely to make it over the Anjuman Pass. So for the second time on this journey I did what Alexander the Great had done at the Oxus River, and decided to press on with a smaller group. It didn't feel any better than it had before, but it seemed to me once more that the most important thing was to get the group who would be involved in broadcasting into position for the big attack. When it came down to it, our gear and Tony could wait a little longer; the rest of us couldn't. I explained all this to Tony, who would be left alone in the mountains of northern Afghanistan with thousands of pounds' worth of gear to look after, and no way to get it across.

'No problem, I'll just stop a lorry.'

Once again I shook hands with him and abandoned him.

In the bright early light Mohammed Shah ran his jeep over the wooden planks as though it were as wide and as safe as the bridge in the picture of Newcastle. But we quickly ran into new trouble: the bolts holding the jeep's engine kept giving way, and the thread on them was rapidly becoming stripped. Now it was stopping every hundred yards or so, and each time it took Mohammed Shah twenty minutes or more to get it going. The other driver, Noel, came hurrying up carrying a heavy old-fashioned jack, and keeled over with altitude sickness and breathlessness. He was admittedly a bit of a drama queen, and maybe some of it was put on. We fed him a self-heated meal, and he eventually recovered enough to drive again.

Mohammed Shah, meanwhile, was in something of a state. He kept playing a tape with a wailing voice on it, and weeping. After a while we found out that it was a song about the troubles in Afghanistan. But it wasn't a song about grief and loss, so much as about revenge; very Afghan.

> We should do to Pakistan
> What Pakistan has done to our country.
> Pakistan has ruined Afghanistan.
> Afghanistan should turn and destroy Pakistan.

Or something like that. Gloomy stuff for a difficult journey.

At last we reached the foot of Anjuman. It reared up magnificently above us, its head streaked with snow. I found I couldn't keep my eyes off it: it was the key to all our futures. In its shadow we stopped at the inevitable lonely tea house, miles from any habitation, and found a Northern Alliance commander there who was also passing through. He assured us he had had orders to be ready for the big push on Kabul in three days' time.

'No problem,' said Mohammed Shah, which usually meant there was a very big problem. 'We'll be in the Panjshir Valley by eight o'clock tonight.'

'Yes,' I said, 'and I'll be a millionaire tomorrow if I win the lottery.'

I had to explain to him what a lottery was, and how much a million pounds was worth; a million afghanis represented a few pounds, so in itself the figure didn't impress him greatly.

And so we started up the Pass. I was nervous: not because the route was so dangerous, though that played its part, but because I felt we wouldn't get across, and would somehow be stranded up here in the mountains when the big attack took place. If ever I'd prayed in my life, I prayed now. All our competitors were already in place on the front line: CNN, ITN, maybe Sky, and a slew of newspapers. And thanks to my faffing around in Pakistan and my inability to realize early enough that the right road lay through the former Soviet Union, we were still crawling towards them in a set of vehicles that wouldn't make an awful lot of money as scrap. I stood to be humiliated, and so did the BBC; and at that moment I wasn't certain which I wanted less.

'In two hours we'll know what's going to happen, one way or the other,' I said.

The two Peters, Emmerson and Jouvenal, stayed silent. What, after all, was there to say?

Slowly, Mohammed Shah's jeep, with its cracked windscreen, its unsecured engine, its thousand other faults, mechanical and structural, and its habit of breaking down every twenty minutes, ground its way up the worst mountain pass in the whole of Afghanistan. It did it without stopping once. On either side of the road you could see the places where other vehicles and teams of pack-animals had come to grief over the years: the rusting wrecks on the terrifying, mile-long slope which lay to our left, the whitened bones of horses and donkeys scattered around the verge of the track we were following. Somehow, we were winning.

I took an aspirin, the all-purpose traveller's friend, to cope with the effects of the altitude. I have been higher than this, to about eighteen thousand feet in the Himalayas, but even fourteen thousand was difficult. My heart thumped and I tasted bile, while the jeep's engine coughed and wheezed in the thin air, like an old man in the post office on pension day. Still it carried on upwards. Sometimes the road was so steep that we had to get out and climb the path on foot, gasping for breath and trying to draw enough oxygen into our lungs to keep us going. The view was sensational. I felt I was looking out at all the kingdoms of the world; but somehow there was too little mental capacity, given my anxiety and my breathlessness, to take in the beauty.

Back in the jeep Peter Jouvenal said something I couldn't hear. I was too stressed to ask him to repeat it, but he did anyway.

'We've done sixty per cent of it.'

The jeep kept on going until it reached the top of the pass. Mohammed Shah must have expected a more excited reception from us, given all the angst of the past few hours, but all we felt like doing was shaking hands and clapping him on the shoulder. Then we and the group in the other jeep got out, and laughed, and stretched ourselves in the sunshine, and took happy snaps of each other. Although we still had a long and uncomfortable journey ahead of us, our chances of being utterly humiliated seemed to be receding; and extraordinarily Mohammed Shah's jeep seemed to have taken on a new life. What had happened to the stripped bolts and to the thousand other failings wasn't at all clear to me, and Mohammed Shah himself couldn't explain. No matter: we were on our way downhill now, and could go into Mexican overdrive if all else failed.

We stopped for a while at a solitary tea house beside a fork in the road – the place where Alexander the Great and his men, heading in the opposite direction from us, from south to north, once took the north-westerly route which led him among other things to his future wife, the beautiful Roxana. We set up the satellite phone and I called the desk in London to tell them we had made it over Anjuman. I could hear the relief in Malcolm Downing's voice: he too would have been humiliated if we had failed to make it to the front line in time.

I looked around while I was speaking to him. Nothing, I reflected, except the tea house itself, the truck parked outside it, and our two jeeps, could be in any way different from the scene Alexander would have seen. The rest was just unchanging mountains and rocks and shale and dust.

We headed off down the road to the Panjshir Valley. At long last, things seemed to have turned around for us: the Northern Alliance soldiers at the checkpoint looked at the letter we had brought with us from the Foreign Ministry in Hodge, explaining that we were foreigners, six in number.

'But you are only five; this man is Afghan.' He pointed to Khalil.

We explained about Tony; and almost immediately we came across the UN cars which Kate Clark had summoned up by phone some hours earlier to meet Tony and pick him up, together with all the gear. We simply weren't used to things going this much according to plan.

There were still six or more hours of driving to go down the dark grandeur of the Panjshir, with the river running beside and below us to the left, and the high walls of the valley rising sheer to the right. This wasn't the kind of road where you wanted to meet anyone coming in the other direction. But there was no one to meet. Our drivers slumped over the wheel and drove in a kind of catalepsy.

At last, as I was beginning to think we should stop and sleep in the vehicles, we reached the village of Basarak. In the impenetrable darkness some uniformed character at a checkpoint tried to insist that we should go and spend what was left of the night at a Northern Alliance Foreign Ministry house, but we were too tired and too sick of Afghan officialdom to do any such thing. We told him so, and drove off into the night.

Anyway, we knew where we were going: Hajji's house. Hajji was a friend of Peter's and mine from previous trips here. He was a rich man, with a large compound outside the village. It took a lot of pounding on the gates before his old, grumbling servant came and opened them, but Hajji himself, in an enormous dressing gown, and huge bare white feet with dark brown toenails, embraced us and welcomed us; and he plied us with tea and listened to our stories with genuine interest. Mohammed Shah had been right: we did after all spend the night in the Panjshir Valley. I slept stretched out on Hajji's floor cushions. For the first time in many days I felt entirely relaxed, knowing we had made it.

In the morning, everything seemed fine at last. Tony had joined us after various adventures, and we hired a wonderful old lime green Soviet Moskva limousine, in which Peter and I drove around town as though we were Politburo members going to the Kremlin to pick up our latest Order of Lenin. The suspension wasn't up to much, after long years of being driven around Afghanistan, and the bodywork wouldn't last much longer; but it was an experience.

We drove in it to the bazaar in Jabal Saraj and found that prices for just about everything any Westerner might want were going through the roof. Clothes, tins of food, blankets, sleeping mats, carpets – they were all at least double what we had paid in other places on our way down. Then we headed on to the villa where the

Northern Alliance Foreign Ministry had based itself, in order to get accredited and find out what was going on. Dozens of journalists from almost every Western country (though I didn't see any Americans I recognized) were milling around inside the compound and in the street outside.

There were a few friends of mine among them, including Maggie O'Kane of the *Guardian* who had done what we had signally failed to do, and made the journey over the mountains from Pakistan. It had clearly been a rough experience, but she made light of it. Just to listen to her in this hot, dusty, fly-infested place made me homesick for my quiet, peaceful flat overlooking the sea near Dublin; Irish voices always do.

'Dreadful place, this. A place to get out of as soon as you can.'

Maggie isn't a journalist who follows the crowd.

Many of the people there were wandering around in strange remnants of Afghan dress. We were too; journalists seem to like dressing up. They were apparently waiting to put their names down for trips to the front line, or get an interview, or find out a fact or two from someone. It was like Hodge, only a great deal worse. I agreed with Maggie: it was a place to fly from in horror. I was irresistibly reminded once again of *Scoop*, which I had fortunately brought with me. Later, when I was fully reunited with my gear, I dug it out and found the passage I wanted:

> Terrific deals were done in the bazaar in tinned foodstuffs; they were cornered by a Parsee and unloaded on a Banja, cornered again by an Arab, resold and rebought, before they reached the journalists' stores . . . Everyone now emulated the costume of the Frenchmen; sombreros, dungarees, jodhpurs, sunproof shirts and bullet-proof waistcoats, holsters, bandoliers, Newmarket boots, cutlasses, filled the Liberty [hotel]. The men of the Excelsior Movie-Sound News, sporting horsehair capes and silk shirts of native chieftains, made camp in the Liberty garden and photographed themselves at great length in attitudes of vigilance and repose.

Quite. I looked inside the Foreign Ministry: the CNN team had made camp in the garden of the compound, and their satellite dish was up and apparently running. Whether they also wore horsehair capes and photographed themselves at great length I had no way of knowing; though if they were like us, they probably did. I badly missed the Russian satellite dish we had had at our camp in Hodge, but there was always a resounding silence from London when I suggested that it should be brought southwards to join us. With hindsight I'm grateful it wasn't. Hodge was pumping out all the hour-by-hour stuff which I was so keen to get away from. If it had come down to join us we might have turned into the slaves of the dish as well, instead of being able to get on and do our own thing. And when we needed it later, it turned up at precisely the right moment: one of the best bits of timing I have ever seen.

That afternoon we took the Moskva to meet General Hamid Gul, who had formerly been the head of the police under the old mujahed-din régime, before the Taliban captured Kabul. General Gul was a gentle, smiling character who looked strangely like an elderly land-owner from the Scottish Highlands; perhaps it was his Harris tweed jacket that gave him the resemblance, and as it happened General Gul had a couple of children who were being educated in Britain, so maybe it wasn't altogether fanciful. He had won great respect in Afghanistan because he had resigned from his post on a point of principle: his men hadn't been paid for a long time. Resigning on such an issue was unheard of in Afghanistan at the time.

He might not have an official job nowadays, but everybody dropped in at his compound in Jabal Saraj to see him and exchange gossip. Over the plump, sweet red grapes of the locality and endless cups of tea, General Gul told us the latest: the Northern Alliance now had ten thousand troops on this sector of the front line, and the Taliban only had three thousand. The big push would start in three or four days. I was fine about that, now that we were here: we would have a couple of days to get over the journey and relax, and be ready for it when it came. All I wanted, though, was to stay as far away from Jabal Saraj and the journalistic circus as I could manage.

§

If I had only known it, the most dangerous part of our entire Afghan experience was over. There would be others, as you will hear; but more BBC journalists have died in road accidents over the years than in combat. Speed, bad roads, carelessness, tiredness, have taken the lives of too many good people. One of the things I thought about when I was jolting and bucketing around in the jeeps on the way down was that if I got out of all this alive I would campaign within the BBC for a monument to the people who had died in the Corporation's service. Still, I reflected, it would need to be carefully designed: no good making it like an honours board at school, with lots of room for more names at the bottom. Imagine how that would make you feel as you glanced at it on your way to the airport for yet another conflict. It'd be like marching the soldiers up to the front line in the First World War, past the labour battalions digging the mass graves for the coming battle.

The only thing wrong with the idea of a memorial, as far as I can see, is that it might somehow glamorize a profession which is altogether too keen to glamorize itself already. This business of danger annoys me. No one, after all, forces any of us to do the job we do. I don't think there is a single newspaper or a television or radio organization anywhere which orders its employees to head off to dangerous places. On the contrary, they often seem to throw all sorts of obstacles in the way of your doing something or going somewhere.

Nowadays there is a positive fetish about putting people through courses run by ex-soldiers to teach them what it is like on a battlefield. I confess that I have never been on one of these courses, getting out of them by alternately pulling rank and keeping my head down at the key moment. I maintain it's because I have been through the real thing so many times that I don't have to have it simulated for me; but in fact it's because, as a rather unhandy, bookish kind of person in middle age, I dread the thought of being made to run up and down hills and throw myself flat in the mud while people shout orders at me that I cannot understand and fire off blank rounds around my ears, while everyone else laughs at me. It's bad enough when the real thing actually happens to you, it seems to me, without having to pay thousands of pounds for a lifelike imitation.

On the other hand my wife Dee, who was told she couldn't come to Belgrade to join me as my producer during the NATO bombing of 1999 unless she went on one of these courses, assured me it was hugely enjoyable, with good food, plenty to drink, good companionship, and plenty of bored and lonely men trying to get off with her.

No one, she said, had tried to humiliate her, and I can well believe it. Even so, I think I shall continue to pull rank.

There is something embarrassingly look-at-me, something distinctly self-referential about the idea of journalists in danger. Of course, real danger is genuinely enthralling if you survive it, and it makes excellent pictures – if, that is, you are lucky enough to catch it on camera. Unfortunately, such moments are pretty rare: either the camera isn't running at the time, or else it isn't pointing in quite the right direction at the key moment. Television can sometimes be the most frustrating business on earth.

And so there is always a temptation to underline the sense of menace by, say, kneeling down to do your piece to camera (which gives the feeling that you might be shot if you stood up) or waiting to begin it until a gun goes off nearby, in case there are no other shots or explosions while you are talking. These are tricks of the trade, not necessarily false or illegitimate at all, since the bangs are real enough and so, often, is the sense that you might get your head blown off if you peer out of your shelter. But whenever you are watching a television news report and there is a bang immediately followed by a television correspondent talking to camera, you know it's being done for effect. Especially if I'm the one doing it.

The wearing of a flak jacket – Evelyn Waugh's 'bullet-proof waistcoat' – on camera is sometimes done for effect too. This is a difficult area to be judgemental about, since the BBC is at its most auntyish when there is danger around and insists that you must always wear a flak jacket if there is the remotest chance of your getting shot or bombed. I read a newspaper story recently about a former BBC correspondent, which quoted him as saying he had never worn a flak jacket in his life; which was fine for him, since he worked very largely for radio. No one knows what you are wearing: a flak jacket doesn't make a different sound. Directly you appear in front of the camera in some place which is even only moderately dangerous without wearing body armour, the phone rings and emails of complaint start arriving from the office. Once, indeed, I was hauled up before a senior manager and given a thorough ticking off, after I had been incautious enough to write somewhere that I had deliberately not worn my flak jacket. But it's all meant in the best possible way, and it isn't simply because if you get shot someone will have to fill in lots of forms and pay your family large amounts of money; it's because, just like your auntie, they genuinely worry about you.

I don't like flak jackets. They are heavy and cumbersome, and often difficult to zip up. They make you unbearably hot in the tropics, they give you (well, me) the figure of a tall Mr Pickwick or a monster pouter pigeon, they slow you down and they make it harder to do the thing that usually gets you out of trouble: run like mad, or else find a ditch to throw yourself in. The protection they offer is pretty limited. Those two plates of protective Kevlar, one in front and one at the back, seem awfully small when you slot them into place; what about all the rest of you, you ask yourself as you put it on. I have seen the body of an aid worker in Sarajevo, dressed in a state-of-the-art flak jacket of a type I had been considering getting myself. A chance high-velocity bullet had struck her sideways on in the shoulder, where there was no protection, and had travelled into her heart. On the other hand, of course, there is the famous story of the cameraman Vaughan Smith – the one who delivered our dummy parcel to Commander Zardad from Afghanistan – who was hit by a bullet in Kosovo. It struck his mobile phone (not, as some versions had it, his wallet). Vaughan was wearing his flak jacket, and might well not have been in a position to turn another frame of video or deliver any parcels again if he hadn't been.

There is a wider issue than safety, though. Not long ago I was wandering with a camera crew through the streets of a town in the West Bank which was under occupation by the Israeli army. There was a curfew, and Israeli soldiers are famous for shooting at journalists at such times, on the perfectly correct but scarcely very comforting basis that they aren't supposed to be there. A good case for wearing a flak jacket, if ever there was one. And yet I began to feel more and more uncomfortable as we stopped and interviewed several furtive old ladies and little kids who had been sent out to get food on the basis that the Israelis were less likely to shoot them than a man.

Why, after all, was my life so much more important than theirs, that I should be wearing a flak jacket which probably cost as much money as these people had seen in their entire lives? I promise you, it doesn't feel good; and it's remarkable how rarely ordinary people suggest that, like a raincoat in a storm, you might care to lend your armour-plating to them. The idea that I should have special protection when I make a living reporting on the troubles of people who don't is not one that I feel at all comfortable with.

In the past, whenever I travelled to Beirut, I used to be driven around by a tall, rather macho Lebanese called Abed Takush. He had been inherited by the BBC from our former partners, NBC News from the United States, and had worked for the two of us for a quarter of a century. I grew very fond of Abed. In particular, I liked the way he loved his job. I would listen with pleasure as he told me all the exciting stories he had covered with Jeremy Bowen and other correspondents; getting him to drive Dee and me to Tyre for lunch and a look round seemed pretty feeble by comparison.

Abed would laugh loudly, his eyes disappearing in his long face as he would repeat, with a certain amount of exaggeration, what everyone had said when the Israeli shells started falling on the coastal road during Operation Grapes of Wrath.

'We never minding what happen, Mr John. Is our job. We going everywhere, doing everything. Mr Jeremy say, "Fuck it, and keep driving."' Abed would roar with laughter again. '"Fuck it, and keep driving."'

On 23 May 2000, Abed was driving Jeremy Bowen through the celebrating crowds close to Lebanon's border with Israel. Israel was finally withdrawing its soldiers after eighteen years of military occupation. Jeremy and his cameraman got out of the car and started filming an Israeli kibbutz on the other side of the border. Their car was clearly marked 'Press' and 'TV', and the nearby Israeli tanks must have seen the cameraman getting out with his gear. No matter: one of the tanks opened up from close by and hit the car, with Abed in it. Poor boastful, brave, willing Abed was killed instantly.

Israeli civilians from the kibbutz had brought their children to watch from the other side of the border, and they saw the whole incident. It wasn't altogether unexpected: four Lebanese civilians died in that area during that period of twenty-four hours. Israeli tank crews aren't usually careless about their firing, and it is hard to dismiss the suspicion that they were teaching these foreign camera crews a lesson: something similar had happened some years before, when an entire CBS crew were killed by an Israeli tank. Since they were Lebanese, not American, the resulting fuss was pretty minimal. Later I took up Abed's case when I met the Israeli chief of staff. He was a decent man, and very apologetic. It was, he said, a tragic mistake; and he wouldn't accept that it was anything more. If and when we get our memorial, Abed Takush's name will have an honoured place on it. I think there is a good chance that, like quite a few others, he died for the BBC.

Whenever a journalist is killed or injured, there is usually a fuss about it. If the journalist was a prominent one, there will be articles in the press questioning whether any story is worth getting killed for, and whether things have gone too far. If he or she was a television journalist, the articles will question whether the competition in television news is so great nowadays that reporters are risking their lives unnecessarily. Of course, journalists write the newspapers, and they are more interested in what happens to other journalists than most of the rest of the population is. It's a little like those news items which tell you breathlessly that two Britons were slightly hurt in the Andean earthquake/Bangladeshi flood/Australian outback fire which killed hundreds of other people.

But it isn't simply that our own mean more to us than any number of others do. There is a sententiousness which hangs over the violent death of any journalist, as though democracy itself has been injured. Special meetings are convened, statements of condemnation and principle are drafted, voted on and adopted, hot air is released in large quantities. I'm not in favour of journalists being killed, of course; but whoever said reporting was supposed to be a safe profession?

If anything of this sort were to happen to me, I should be most offended if I became the subject of some pompous meeting about the dangers to free speech in the modern world, and I would strongly advise my friends not to attend it. I have done my utmost to avoid being killed for the BBC, and intend to keep it that way; but if by some malign chance it were to happen, the responsibility would be mine, and mine alone – not the BBC's, nor television's. A jolly get-together, a few familiar hymns to belt out, and then a quick adjournment to some place where food and alcohol were freely available, on me – that would be the height of my posthumous ambition, as it would be for most journalists who are getting on in age. It might be sad for some, but you couldn't remotely call it a tragedy.

Of course, when a young man like my BBC radio colleague John Schofield, with his wife expecting their child, is killed by vicious, trigger-happy Croatian soldiers, or when a man in the prime of life like Nick della Casa, the cameraman who worked with me in Baghdad during the Gulf War, is murdered by bandits in Kurdistan, it is altogether different. I still don't believe these things constitute a threat to democracy, but they represent a personal tragedy in a way that the death of some elderly character like myself wouldn't be.

The position of journalists who travel abroad in search of news is altogether different from that of journalists like Veronica Guerin, who was murdered by the Irish gangsters she was investigating, or Daniel Pearl, who was executed in the most disgusting fashion by religious lunatics in Pakistan while he was trying discover more about the secret funding of Al Qaida, or all those who have been injured, imprisoned or killed in Serbia, Russia, Colombia, Peru, Zimbabwe, Burma, China, Hong Kong, and a dozen other countries because their writing or broadcasting upset some powerful, potentially violent vested interests. They deserve all the concern and honour that the outside world can accord them, and attacks on them are indeed an affront to decent people everywhere.

For the most part, the job of the foreign correspondent may carry immediate risks, but these tend to fade away once the assignment is over. Sometimes, though, there is trouble afterwards. I have been followed around and shouted at by the supporters of various causes when I have come back to London after being away. Serbs screamed at me after I was thrown out of Belgrade in 1999 (and some ghastly woman academic did the same thing in print, though she accused me of being part of the pro-Serbian lobby), Israelis have sent me hate-mail after I have visited the West Bank, a couple of angry Palestinians pestered me when I did a story on the corruption surrounding Yasser Arafat, some Peruvian officials followed me round Britain when I wrote a book criticizing their President, and in the more distant past Iranian dissidents sometimes ran after me in the streets of London, shouting insults, after I reported on revolutionary Iran.

Soviet officials occasionally used to make heavily threatening phone calls, but only to the office. The Czechoslovak secret service once set an extremely attractive young woman onto me to trap me after I had upset the Communist government there; so there are some benefits. None of these things seemed particularly worrying, either at the time or later, though they were occasionally annoying; and when I was a rate-payer in the Royal Borough of Kensington and Chelsea, it was more than a little irritating to be pursued by foreign activists down Kensington High Street. But it's extremely rare to get anything worse than a few insults. As the former head of Saddam Hussein's military intelligence apparatus told me after his defection to Britain, he felt completely safe in London – even though the Iraqis, and others, have killed various dissidents in the West from time to time. My BBC colleague Georgiy Markov, a Bulgarian dissident, was killed by a poisoned pellet fired into his leg on Waterloo Bridge in the 1970s, after he had poked fun at the ludicrous Bulgarian dictator Zhivkov for a German radio station; the KGB supplied the Bulgarian secret police with ricin to do the job. Markov's name, too, belongs with Abed's and John Schofield's on the monument to those who have died in the BBC's service.

There are, of course, also stray lunatics: stalkers, fantasists of different kinds, outright psychotics. The assumption is that one such murdered the beautiful and charming Jill Dando, whom I worked alongside for some time. Appearing on television attracts such people, and they construct their crazy notions around you accordingly. Once I walked into the office to find that a woman had called me four times that morning. When I rang her, she shouted down the phone, 'You are the father of my daughter's child.' We discussed dates for a while, and I proved to her that this was unlikely since I would only have been twelve at the time of conception.

'Oh well, it must have been someone else on television,' she said. 'Bye.'

I get plenty of strange letters, but the worst was a single typed sheet of paper:

> You told me you didn't know Pete Smith. I saw him standing beside you on television last night. Now I know what to do.

For some time I left this in the drawer of my desk at work, in case something happened to me. But it never did.

For journalists, a certain amount of what the BBC bureaucrats call negative feedback is inevitable. Since you can't please everyone, you shouldn't even think of trying. And if you don't like getting nasty letters or phone calls, find another line of work. But stay away from sport or politics: it's far worse there.

13

Teamwork

Water gushed down over my head, my shoulders, my chest. I gasped with the cold, but it felt exhilarating. General Hamid Gul's bathroom was more of a storeroom, really: full of sacks and old tools, with a galvanized-metal water container at one end and a drain in the middle of the floor. It was the first time in eight days that I had been able to wash and change my clothes. The dirty ones were disgusting, and I thought of throwing them away; but that seemed unbearably wasteful in a society like this, where everyone probably wore their clothes for much longer than eight days.

As the water ran off me, things felt good for the first time since I was packing my gear at the Pearl Continental hotel on 11 September in preparation for going home, and heard the BBC news presenter say they were starting to get reports of a plane hitting a building in New York. Peshawar was only 165 miles away as the crow or the cruise missile flew, but it had taken me thirty-two days to get here. Idly, pointlessly, I did the mental arithmetic as I rubbed the shampoo into my dust-encrusted hair: 5.15 miles a day, 0.2 miles per hour. Not exactly great going, even for Afghanistan. I could have walked there in my burka in a tenth of the time, as long as no one noticed my boots.

There weren't any towels, but I didn't care. I let the pungent air dry me off while I whipped up the shaving soap with my brush and peered in the mirror. Being able to shave is something you scarcely think about back in the real world. Here, it had an existential significance: this was my resurrection from dirt and self-disgust. My face burned afterwards and the blood flowed freely, but at last my cheeks and chin felt smooth. I was slowly finding my way back to the civilized norms again.

I looked down at the rest of me. With only one meal a day, washed down with half a gallon of tea instead of half a bottle of red wine, the weight had been dropping off: another reason to feel good. I peered at the ugly scar on my thigh and knee. It was a memento of the NATO attack on Serbia in 1999 and the operation I had in a partly bombed hospital in Belgrade after I fell and injured myself; the knee had stood up extremely well to the punishment I had been subjecting it to, here in Afghanistan. At that point there was a polite noise outside the door, and I shouted out that I was just finishing.

General Gul's house was rather more deficient in the lavatory department; so was Afghanistan as a whole, of course. To get to the jakes – only an Elizabethan word would do to describe it, I felt – you had to walk across the courtyard and climb an appallingly rickety ladder, twelve feet high, to the upper storey. One of the steps habitually gave way under you, but in my experience you only remembered that as you put your weight on it. A completely inadequate piece of torn sacking hung over the entrance, and inside – apart from the flies – was a very distasteful hole in the mud floor: the long drop. Only, without wanting to go into too many details, it wasn't nearly such a long drop any more.

When you were *in situ* for the first time you realized how completely inadequate the piece of sacking was; and afterwards, when you looked up from the courtyard to see if anyone was in the jakes, you could see that the curtain hid nothing at all. Anyone up there was almost totally visible to everyone in the courtyard, twelve feet below.

The previous day Peter Jouvenal had disappeared, as he so often did, and had come back hours later to tell us about the place in the nearby town of Charikar which he had found for us. It was excellent, he said: a modern building, with plenty of rooms, and windows which looked out over the front line. It had once been the municipal headquarters for the town.

'There must be something wrong with it. I mean, this is Afghanistan.'

'Well, it's not in very good shape.'

'What, it's been bombed or something?'

'A bit, yes.'

A pause.

'And people have been using it as a latrine.'

'We're going to be living in a public shithouse?'

'Well, Hamid Gul will give us some policemen to clean it up.'

'So when can we move in?'

'Tomorrow. We can go to see it tonight.'

'It's not going to be ready, is it? They can't clean it up that fast.'

'I think it will be.'

Peter's confidence won us over. Personally, though, I found it hard to believe.

Both Peters, Joe and I drove out that night to do our first television report from our new home. The road between Jabal Saraj and Charikar was the first paved surface we had so far encountered in Afghanistan on this trip. It was badly chewed up in places by shelling, because this whole area had been fought over for years, but the drivers could do speeds along it which we had almost forgotten were possible.

Charikar was dark and silent when we got there at nine in the evening, and as we turned right at the traffic policemen's post beside the bazaar and headed for the municipal building, our headlights lit it up. It was a smashed and apparently deserted official building of Soviet design, three storeys high and fifty yards long. Not a single window remained in it, and it seemed to have taken some direct hits from shells or rockets. I don't know what we'd expected, but this wasn't Television Centre.

By the thin light of a torch, I stepped through the smashed door and up the concrete stairs inside. The entrance hall smelt of some rotting substance: things had been stored here, and forgotten. My torch lit up the long corridor on the first floor, then more stairs. In the utter silence my breath seemed very loud. This was where we would base ourselves: it seemed pretty unprepossessing. I shone my torch down the infinitely long corridor, and the beam simply seemed to peter out in the darkness.

It stank up here. All the rooms on both sides of the corridor had obviously been used as a public latrine for a very long time. You had to be careful not to gag, and it was clearly impossible to set foot in any of the rooms: the torch showed that. But at least the corridor, by common consent, had been left untouched. It was just dirty from years of neglect.

A gaping window at the far end of the corridor opened out onto the valley where the front line ran, a mile or so in front of us in the darkness. On our way here we had seen red and white tracer going up, and what looked like flares. Now, as I stared out, it was entirely silent. I couldn't see anything except some looming mountains on either side of the dark valley.

'There are more Taliban up there.'

Peter pointed to the mountain on our right as we looked out. They seemed extraordinarily close to me: close enough, certainly, to have seen our headlights and now our torches.

The others set up the equipment, and we did our first live videophone two-way interview from Charikar for the *Six O'Clock News* and all the other programmes from the place which was very soon to be our home.

But there seemed no point in staying here breathing in the appalling stink, until our next appointment with the *Ten O'Clock*, so we packed everything up and went back to Jabal for a meal and a quick nap, then reluctantly turned out again in the darkness with all the gear at 1 a.m. This time, just as I was in full flow, answering the questions of a News 24 presenter, I became aware of some ghostly characters looming up in the darkness behind the camera. My colleagues said nothing to them, because they were worried it might disrupt the live broadcast, and I tried to ignore them and concentrate on the questions from London.

Irritatingly, given that we had expended so much effort to get down to the front line, it was clear that some of the questioners in the studio thought we had strayed away from the scene of real action – which in their minds was Khwaja Bahawuddin. How to explain that we were now where things were happening and that Hodge was merely a useful place to set up a satellite dish, without undermining the hard work of all the people up there, defeated me completely. So I just left that particular question hanging unanswered in the air.

But it helped me forget about the ghosts, until the interviews were over. Then I saw that they were Northern Alliance soldiers. They were standing round with their blankets over their heads and their AK-47s in their hands, giggling and relaxed. They were thoroughly stoned. Close up, I could smell it on them; it even drowned out the lavatorial stench from the rooms nearby. They seemed to have some point they wanted to make to us, but were too happy to be able to speak about it. Maybe they'd seen our lights, and had come in to investigate. It wouldn't be surprising: the Taliban on the far side of the front line must have seen our lights too. They were shining brilliantly down in the direction of the Taliban, which had made me feel a little uncomfortable between the shoulder blades as I stood with my back to the valley.

In the end, since they had nothing intelligible to say to us, we shook hands with the hopheads and drove back to Jabal.

The next morning the whole team made the journey down the tarred road to Charikar. By day it was a busy commercial centre, with shops lining the roads in and out and bicycles and trucks choking the streets. Even so, everyone and everything stopped as we went past: God knows who they thought we might be. In daylight the municipality building (which I privately named Bin Laden Mansions) was rather impressive – apart from the war damage, which was extensive. It certainly dominated the town, and the valley behind it. Perhaps a little too much: you couldn't fail to see it, or indeed fail to hit it if you were shelling the place.

It looked neater and better in every way than it had the previous night: and when we went upstairs we found to our surprise that it no longer smelled bad. Instead, there was a rather pleasant odour of disinfectant everywhere. The policemen and their skivvies had cleaned up all the rooms at our end of the building, though you didn't have to investigate too many doors down the corridor before you found rooms that were untouched by the cleaners.

At that moment there was trouble.

'This commander, he want speak with you.'

Our current translator, trying to silence a flow of passionate Farsi from someone, looked troubled. I turned to see who the flow came from: it was a short, tough, bearded character with kohl-rimmed red eyes, dark brown *peran tomban*, and a gun. I wondered whether it was the kohl which made his eyes red, but I decided in the end it was anger. I got that right, anyway.

'Name, Hajji Bari,' said the translator.

I shook hands with Hajji Bari; he seemed less enthusiastic. There was another flow of Farsi.

'Saying, why come here with no permission?'

I explained about the police.

'Saying, nothing for police here. Hajji Bari is here.'

That I couldn't question. It was disturbingly clear that he wasn't just a passing visitor. Hajji Bari was a military commander, and this was his base. We had moved in and started cleaning the place up – his private toilet, for all we knew – without asking him. It was an awkward moment.

I knew I had to do a number on him. This was a useful and important place to be, and it was essential that he shouldn't throw us out. So when he invited us down the far end of the corridor, a long way away, to what I now realized was his office, I put on my concerned, friendly, we're-all-bit-part-players-in-the-great-events-of-our-time face, and went with him. I couldn't of course know that this was one of the critical moments of our entire expedition: more important, probably, than crossing the Anjuman Pass quickly. But I think I guessed it.

I had to stifle an involuntary gasp of dismay: Hajji Bari's room was painted a hauntingly repellent shade of pink. A number of heavy-bearded men were sitting on cushions around the walls, and the tea-kettle was being passed around as freely as poteen at an Irish country wedding. They were Hajji Bari's sidekicks, and they looked at me without pleasure. But I was into smiling in a big way by now and greeted them as though we were friends of the groom. At the far end of the room were three silent, gloomy characters I had seen before: the police chiefs who had assured us there would be no trouble about our coming here. I was less forthcoming with them.

There was nothing for it, I decided, but to go into auto-grovel.

'If we have moved in here uninvited, all I can say is that I am deeply apologetic. I wouldn't have intruded on your headquarters like this for the world.'

'Saying, very sorry,' said the translator.

I could see I would have to do a bit better.

'You see, your soldiers were so good that when we came here last night we didn't even see them. Fine body of men: you've got them well trained. Congratulations.'

I thought of the useless, giggling pot-smokers of the night before, their heads covered with their blankets like old Irish market-women; God forgive me for the lying, crawling bastard I am, I thought.

But Afghans have little interest in the unglazed truth. They like a bit of schmooze, and I was schmoozing them with every fibre of my being. The stern characters with the beards melted first; I was going down well in the peanut gallery. But the boss's eyes still matched the fuchsia walls. Time for some more grovelling – and for the first real hint of business.

'If there was any way we could ask you for your help and protection,' I said, cutting the poor cops adrift after they had done so much to help us. 'I understand, of course, that it wouldn't be possible for this kind of thing to done entirely free . . .'

My words hung in the smoky air. Translate that, you bugger, I thought; but it was clear to me that he wanted to improve on it.

'We are rich and willing to pay,' I understood him to say.

The whites of Hajji's eyes began to fade back to their normal yellow. Beards around the wall bristled and were stroked. Now we were talking.

By the time I walked out, Hajji Bari was the BBC's best friend. He would provide us with carpenters to put in doors and windows; with his finest soldiers (whichever they might be) to act as our guards; and with vehicles to take us wherever we wanted. Since he was the commander in charge of this entire stretch of the front, we could go and film his soldiers there at any time without needing permission from anyone else, even at the height of battle. He would supply us with cooks, food, and experienced people to do our shopping. No one said anything about payment for all this, but I reckoned it would all be marginally cheaper than staying at the Islamabad Marriott, and a damned sight more interesting. We sealed the agreement with a smelly embrace.

So this became our home for the next five weeks. The stories about an imminent attack on Kabul fizzled out to nothing; the Americans weren't willing to let the Northern Alliance have their head for a while, in case they spoiled everything. It was quickly clear that we would be staying at Bin Laden Mansions for some time. The self-image of the British is that they are at their best when times are hard and conditions are rough, and it is largely true. We turned this Third World toilet of ours into a liveable if spartan base, cold enough for us to have to wear our warmest clothes, but clean and tidy and almost homelike. As the weeks stretched out the artists among us – chiefly Joe Phua and Peter Emmerson – drew on the walls the creature-comforts we missed most: a drinks cabinet, which we stocked from our imaginations, a television set, a really expensive Bose sound system, and dozens of CDs with humorous names. Also three flying ducks.

Peter drew his piano from home and, in a charming gesture to me and to Dee, whom I was missing a great deal, drew the music for the old song *I Like a Nice Cup of Tea*. On the journey down I had told them how, when Dee and I were on a desert island in the South Pacific to record the (allegedly) first sunrise of the new millennium – the BBC, like everyone else, was a year too early – the President of the island group of Kiribati, to which Millennium Island belonged, turned up there with a large entourage and held a big party. Every national group was expected to sing their national song, and Dee, as a South African, got irritated with my dull English pretensions about *Jerusalem* and said we should sing *I Like a Nice Cup of Tea* instead. It was, she said, the true national anthem of Britain.

Belts had to be tightened at Bin Laden Mansions. There wasn't much edible food, and no alcohol at all. We lived off eggs, hard boiled or sometimes fried, large quantities of Afghan bread, fruit and vegetables of various kinds from the market, disgustingly fat, greasy and tough meat (though most of us turned aside from this with revulsion), gallons of tea, and the vegetarian curries which we had brought with us from India. Our communal meal took place around 6.30 every evening, and selecting which particular packet of curry to eat bulked surprisingly large in our minds from about five o'clock onwards.

Later, Peter Jouvenal summoned an old servant of his, Rahman Beg, who had lost a leg in a mine explosion and had received a wooden one at Peter's expense, to be our cook. He didn't know much about cooking.

'I am farmer,' he used to say, in his orotund English.

With his turban on one side of his bald head, his ogling eye and his peg-leg, he reminded me irresistibly of Robert Newton playing Long John Silver in the film of *Treasure Island*; Rahman Beg also had an extraordinarily camp way of speaking English, putting his techni-colored head on one side and holding out his hands with the index fingers pointing upwards.

I grew very fond of him. Perhaps it was because he seemed so amazingly out of place, a foreigner among all these British, and much too grand and theatrical for the local low-lifes whom we hired to clean and wash up. He was our butler, I suppose.

'Don't be angry with poor Rahman Beg,' he implored me once when I shouted at him, and I never said a hard word to him again.

Except once. It was early in the morning, and I was sick of the thought of another hard-boiled egg. People were walking out of the kitchen eating fried eggs with Afghan bread, and I asked for one too.

'Oh no, sir,' said Rahman Beg. 'No fried egg.'

'Don't give me that, Rahman Beg. I want one.'

'No fried egg, sir. I am sorry. No is fried egg today. Have nice cup of tea.'

My temper, never very far from the surface in the mornings, especially when I am hungry and haven't yet had a cup of tea, nice or otherwise, exploded.

'Don't be so fucking stupid, Rahman Beg. What do you think all those people are eating out there? Sheep's testicles? I want a fried egg and I want it now.'

Rahman Beg's camp old head was already turning to the side, and the index fingers were putting in an appearance.

'Very sorry, sir. Rahman Beg is thinking you are saying "Friday". Is Thursday today, sir. Have nice fried eggs, sir. You will like.'

In a strange, monastic way we rather enjoyed ourselves. The windows were covered with clear plastic, the doors were re-hung, black-out curtains were hung. This was one of Tony Rippon's finest moments, and he oversaw the various workmen superbly. Later, he left us and was replaced by a quieter, gentler yet possibly even tougher security adviser called Andy Faulkner, who had been in the SBS.

'Aren't the SBS supposed to be the best there is?' I asked him.

He made the kind of modest noises you do make under such circumstances.

'Better than the SAS?'

This was, Andy explained, only to be expected. The SBS were drawn from the Royal Marines; the SAS from all the various regiments of the British army. It was only to be expected that men from one unit and one tradition would work better together than a mixed group like the SAS.

'And the American Navy Seals?'

'Ah well,' Andy said, anxious not to sound boastful or unkind, 'you have to make allowances . . .'

Kate and I each had our own rooms, while the others shared a room. They got quite annoyed, I noticed, when they realized that our translator Khalil was sleeping in the drivers' room, too polite to come and share with the Europeans. They insisted that he join them. Having passed through the long journey over Anjuman, Khalil was one of our own.

Eventually, when other people came, we had other rooms cleared out for them: David Loyn, to whom I was unpardonably rude when he arrived, accusing him of poaching on my territory, arrived with Vaughan Smith and Mardan, a senior figure from the Farsi service at Bush House, who was famous in Afghanistan and was treated with enviable respect everywhere he went. Within half an hour, of course, David and I were back on our usual friendly terms. I suppose I felt I owned the story here, which was stupid and unreasonable of me, and not true anyway. Anyway, David is one of the best examples I know of the wandering journalist who finds his own stories, and he must have regarded Bin Laden Mansions with the kind of distaste I showed for Hodge or the Foreign Ministry compound at Jabal.

We were joined, too, by Phil Rees from the *Correspondent* programme and his crew. Phil did a famous report from both sides in the Algerian violence of the mid-1990s, which attracted a great deal of admiration. Jonno, his cameraman, had blond hair, was clean-shaven, and attracted a good deal of attention from the gay element among the Northern Alliance troops. They were inclined to pinch him and touch him up; not a good move, given that Jonno was a former Royal Marine.

Later, others arrived: Nick Springate, one of the chief news producers, who took over as bureau chief and released Peter Emmerson, Tony Rippon and me from the burdens of managing the Mansions; Ian Pannell, who came to work for domestic radio; and a crew from ABC Australia. Between them, they cheered us up no end. Our new septic tank, dug in the courtyard by a team of wondering Afghans was ready just in time.

We slept fairly rough on the concrete floors, though we quickly got used to it. My *chapan* now did duty as a blanket, and a very effective one. I bought a couple of rather attractive local carpets for the floor, and on the wall I hung a British-made musket, as supplied to the Afghan army in the 1850s and also, Peter Jouvenal informed me, sold (characteristically) to both sides in the American Civil War. A row of books on the table Tony had found for me, a late Victorian military camping chair which Peter Jouvenal had bought in Peshawar and carried round with him (it fell apart once and dumped me on my Afghan carpet), an electric light powered by the generator which Joe Phua and Peter Emmerson cherished like a child, and my small computer to write on: I really had been worse off in some five-star hotels.

In some ways the best thing about Bin Laden Mansions – especially in comparison with the way most other Westerners had to live in Afghanistan – was the lavatories. Because this place was Russian-designed, it had proper sit-down toilets. The flushing system didn't work, of course, but you could pour water down them from a bucket; and Tony laboured to make sure our local help kept the galvanized containers full. I even had my own private lavatory: one of those hole-in-the-floor efforts, with porcelain footholds on either side. It reminded me of being in my favourite café in Paris. As time went on, we had a sanitary engineer on almost constant call, unplugging lavatories that were blocked. It was he who supervised the digging of the septic tank in the grounds outside. Until that was completed, we found that the waste pipes from the lavatories sometimes merely emptied onto the floor of the rooms below. Not exactly ideal.

I liked the evenings best, when the work was over for the day and we used to sit round after our meal and drink the everlasting tea and talk and joke idly. Sometimes there would be explosions down on the front line, or bombing in Kabul itself, and we would gather out on the balcony beside the camera which was set up on a tripod there, and peer companionably out into the darkness.

There were very few personality clashes. Almost all of us were thoroughly used to the strange business of working on the road, which means living side by side under conditions of the greatest intimacy with people you often scarcely knew beforehand, from totally different backgrounds and nationalities, and getting on with them for the sake of the job. If you don't get along, the job suffers; and it soon starts to show on air. Fortunately, we did get along, and very well too. Again and again I missed Dee, because she has a sense of fun and enjoyment which, I have noticed, ties a disparate group of people together.

At around ten o'clock the party would start to break up, and we would move off to bed. A line of smelly paraffin lamps stood in the corridor outside our crew room, and we would take each one and head off to our rooms. Then Joe or Peter Emmerson would switch off the generator for the night, and the electric lights would go out. I would shut the door of my room with a brick as a doorstop, and climb into my sleeping bag with the *chapan* over me. After reading for a while, I turned down the wick in the lamp and fell asleep on the hard floor. As time went on, it came to seem more and more natural and comfortable.

I would also put in a pair of earplugs. This was a difficult decision at first, because it always seemed to me an outside possibility that the Taliban, who knew exactly where we were, might sneak up the largely undefended road from the front line one night and take us prisoner. It was perfectly likely, too, that our building might take a hit from the Taliban position up on the mountainside. They fired a couple of rockets just over our roof on one occasion (the second one exploded about ten feet from Joe Phua as he was filming the casualties from the first). And then, around dawn one morning, there was a gun-battle between two different Northern Alliance commanders, one on one side of our building and the other on the other. If you are wearing earplugs, these are things that can pass you by until it is too late to do something about them.

On the other hand, there were the dogs. Charikar had hundreds of them, mangy, broken-spirited creatures which lived to bark. At night one solitary dog would wake up and start to make a noise, and others would take it up until the entire dog population of the town seemed to be barking. Then, slowly, the noise would move across into the Shomali Valley, away from the town, and disappear into the distance; and things would be quiet again until the next time a dog woke up and started the entire process again. I am a light sleeper, and without the earplugs my nights would have been disturbed continually.

Then of course there were the occasional bombing raids which the Americans carried out on the Taliban lines at night. With earplugs I couldn't hear the explosions, but I could sometimes feel the concrete building quake and that was enough to wake me. Of course it wasn't a perfect solution to block myself off from the sound. Still, I got through my time in Charikar without any serious problems. But I kept my flak jacket and the essentials of my existence – torch, boots, walking stick, knapsack permanently packed – beside my bed, just in case.

The corridor was still our studio, as it had been on that dark night when we first arrived. Eventually we got our carpenter to put up a wooden screen to protect whoever was doing the broadcasting from casual onlookers and people wandering down the corridor from the mujaheddin quarters at the far end. It had the only south-facing window on our floor, which meant that it looked directly out over the front line in the direction of Kabul. The city itself, twenty-five miles away, was hidden from us by some low mountains. I must have stood in front of the open window for hours on end, talking to the videophone. The full extent of the glorious Shomali Valley, the richest agricultural land in Afghanistan, lay behind me. Sir Alexander Burnes – 'Bokhara' Burnes, whose adventures in Central Asia made him a best-selling travel-writer and earned him a knighthood at the age of thirty-five, and led to his unpleasant death at the hands of a Kabul mob in the uprising against the British in 1842 – came this way, and wrote glowingly about the area; for instance, in his book *Cabool*, published only months before his death:

> On our return journey from Istalif we passed through Isterghich, Sinijet-dura, Tope-dura, Si-yaran, and Chareekar, the last a large bazar-town of about ten thousand inhabitants. . . . They are a

succession of separate valleys at the base of lofty mountains, glowing and rich in foliage, which forms a striking contrast to the bleaker ground by which they are divided, and the still bleaker hills that rise above them. Wherever nature or the hand of man has conducted water, there are to be seen gardens and orchards; and the surplus water, which runs down lower into the valley, nourishes rich crops of grain.

To the east of the valley was Bagram airbase, which had fallen into the hands of the Northern Alliance some time before. There was often fighting around there. I liked to go to Bagram, partly because there were usually good pictures to be obtained of the wrecked airport, and there was always the chance of action. I also liked it because it was the site of one of Alexander the Great's colonies. I got out my Arrian and checked on the details:

> Alexander's route now took him to the Indian Caucasus [i.e. the Hindu Kush]. Here he founded a city and named it Alexandria.

No surprise about that: Alexander was fond of the sound of his own name. The settlement was later known as 'Alexandria-by-the-Caucasus', to distinguish it from all the other Alexandrias he founded around the Near East and Central Asia. He put in a Persian called Proexes as governor of the district, and left Neiloxenus, one of his Companions, in charge of military affairs. Neiloxenus also had a contingent of soldiers to garrison the settlement. But in the spring of 327 BC Alexander came back, and found that things were not as they should be.

> He dismissed the governor, whom he had earlier appointed, for incompetence, and he increased the settlement's population by putting in families from the neighbourhood, together with his own men who were no longer fit for service. Nicanor, one of the Companions, was left in charge of the settlement itself.

I could never find anyone around Bagram who knew anything about the ruins of Alexandria-by-the-Caucasus; but that didn't mean much, since every building in the Shomali Valley, inhabited or not, looks as though it could be a ruin from Alexander the Great's time. The mud-brick from which everything is built degrades fast, but only to a certain point; after that it is as strong as steel, and largely indestructible. The ruins must be there somewhere.

I found myself staring, day after day, at the valley and the front line, and at the hinterland which the Taliban controlled. This was forbidden territory, and it exerted a tangible attraction. At night-time we would see the headlights of vehicles bringing up reinforcements and supplies to the Taliban positions: spears of light in the darkness, pointing directly at us. With binoculars, you could make out the road that led to Kabul. Would we ever travel down that road?

Sometimes it seemed as though an attack was close, sometimes as though it might be postponed indefinitely. Whenever I rang Dee in South Africa, we would speculate endlessly about it, but to no purpose whatever. These big events have a logic of their own, which takes no cognizance of people's illnesses, or their loneliness, or their need for a decent night's sleep and a glass or two of single malt whisky. All I knew was that I was here in Charikar for the duration; so were Peter Emmerson and Peter Jouvenal, who were both determined to see it through; so was Joe Phua, who refused to go even when the BBC told him it was time to leave; so was Kate Clark, who wanted to get back to her old job in Kabul once again.

The work kept us fully occupied. Sometimes I used to slip out in the morning to the local barber for a shave, sitting in his chair with my head back, having soap smeared over my face, and enduring the scrape of the razor.

'Make sure he gives you a new blade each time,' Jouvenal warned me. 'They're perfectly capable of using old blades in this country, and you can catch all sorts of unpleasant things that way.'

I did; but it was a moderately restful experience, and enabled me to think about the day and what we should be reporting on. I would have gone there every morning, but the barber was annoyed when I came back the second day in a row, and rubbed my chin harshly. He thought my coming back represented a complaint about the way he had shaved me the day before: most Afghans, if they wanted to be shaved at all, would only have it done once a week.

At other times I would roam around the bazaar on my own, not really looking for anything to buy because there wasn't much, apart from food and some interesting spices; though I did pick up a harsh, grandfatherly button-up cardigan in dark greens and browns, made in Iran, to keep out the increasing cold. The shops and stalls buzzed with insects, especially the ones which sold butcher's meat, honey and Afghan sweets.

Mostly I just went out to greet people and, if I could manage it, talk to them. Once, perversely attracted by the hand-coloured portrait photographs in one of the shops (they reminded me of the pictures people used to display of Iranian martyrs in the war against Saddam Hussein), I had my portrait taken by an ancient figure with a large wooden box camera. But every time I went to see if the prints were ready, his assistant had some excuse I couldn't understand, and after ten days I stopped going back.

I liked Charikar. For a brief time I became a familiar figure around town, and was habitually greeted by the cooks who stood outside the dozen or more restaurants, cooking kebabs and nothing else over their stoves. As a group we became curiosities, watched and sometimes followed wherever we went. Yet we were never troubled by anyone. Even when I went to the money-changers and came back with enormous and undisguisable wads of 10,000-afghani notes, no one tried to take them off me.

It was only after we left that I discovered our headquarters had been built on the site of a British fort during the disastrous occupation of Afghanistan by the British Army of the Indus from 1839–42, which ended in the chaotic, murderous retreat from Kabul. Apart from the fall of Singapore a century later, it is the worst defeat the British have ever suffered. Two of the heroes of the episode fought here in Charikar: Eldred Pottinger, a young Ulsterman who saw the trouble coming but failed to persuade 'Bokhara' Burnes or his superior officers that he was right, and Lieutenant Haughton, who was in command of a contingent of Gurkhas based at Charikar.

The day after Burnes was murdered in Kabul, four thousand Afghans attacked Pottinger's tiny outpost at Lughmanee, just outside Charikar. Everyone else in the post was killed, but Pottinger managed to escape to the town. The next day the same group of tribesmen arrived to attack the British fort there. The commanding officer was killed, Pottinger was wounded in the leg, and when a group of Punjabi gunners began to desert, Lt Haughton tried to arrest a couple of them. One of the Punjabis lopped Haughton's hand off, and with another blow severed the muscles on one side of his neck, so he couldn't hold his head up.

Nevertheless, under Haughton's leadership the garrison at Chari-kar resisted for several days, hopelessly outnumbered. They hung curtains on top of the fort's walls so the Afghans couldn't see them or aim at them, but eventually the water ran out and they decided to retreat to Kabul under cover of darkness. It was some hours after dawn before the Afghans discovered they'd gone, because the bugle-major, who was too badly injured to escape, had managed to sound the morning call as usual. But in the darkness the fugitives from the garrison had become separated from each other as they tried to cross the Shomali Valley, and in the end only five of them reached Kabul: among them Pottinger and poor Haughton, who had to support his neck with a cushion.

Both survived the massacre of the Army of the Indus, and got back to British territory. Pottinger, a gentle, modest man of whom it was said you could sit next to him at dinner for weeks and never think he'd heard a shot fired in his life, died in Hong Kong of typhus at the age of thirty-two. Haughton recovered from his terrible wounds, and went on to become Governor of the Andaman Islands, Commissioner of Assam, and later of Cooch-Behar. Yet his coura-geous defence of Charikar was never acknowledged by the British authorities. The entire business was so terrible they probably didn't want to be reminded of it.

Opposite Bin Laden Mansions stood the town's disused cinema. Charikar had been fought over by the Northern Alliance and the Taliban for years, and the Taliban had captured it twice. Those were bad times for the townspeople, and the Taliban had gone through everything, murdering, torturing and (their own speciality) destroying all images of living beings. The cinema, of course, drove them wild, and they wrecked it. I sometimes wandered round it, looking at the places where they had set fire to the cans of film, and peering into the damaged projection room. The frames of the seats were still in place, facing the smashed and empty stage where the screen had once hung, but the cushions had been looted. One eve-ning, as we talked, it became clear that while our lavatories were unusable we had each made our way quietly across to the cinema and used the stalls instead, not realizing everyone else had had the same idea.

§

You can't really do anything much in television news without having a team behind you. There are one or two distinguished reporters who travel around entirely alone and do their own camerawork; but that is usually for a particular story in some hostile or otherwise difficult place, and they will bring the pictures back and edit them somewhere more comfortable. In the case of an operation like ours in Charikar, I could never have done the job alone or with just one other person. There was simply too much work to get through, day after day, and it was too complex. Normally I would take a producer with me on a big trip like this, to work with the cameraman as a director and make all the technical and practical arrangements, while I could get on with the journalism. Best of all was when a bureau chief like Nick Springate arrived, to sort everything out and deal with the demands from programmes in London.

In our case it was different. Paul Danahar would have been the producer, but he had had to leave us in Tajikistan. Paul Simpson would have been the bureau chief, but he couldn't leave Hodge. But one of the main functions of a bureau chief is to ensure that the different correspondents in a big operation carve up the work equitably and efficiently between themselves; and in Charikar there was no need for that. Our spheres of operation were all clearly demarcated: Kate Clark did everything for the World Service, and eventually Ian Pannell looked after the demands of domestic radio. Peter Emmerson acted as a bureau chief for radio, parrying, accepting and sometimes fending off the huge demands for two-way interviews, live shots, dispatches and so on.

That left me with television, until David Loyn turned up and took some of the load off my shoulders. But one of the many pleasures of being in these strange and difficult places is that you can set your own schedule; and although the two Peters, Joe and I were obliged to stay up till two o'clock most mornings to report live for the *Ten O'Clock News*, it was always possible to turn down the less reasonable demands.

There is a fine balance between having too few and too many people on a trip like this. I think we could have managed better if we had had at least a couple more people early on. When the reinforcements eventually made the dreadful journey south from Hodge and joined us, life became a great deal easier. But too many people can be a nuisance as well. The best way, it seems to me, is to have a bit too much work to do, but not too much. And if you have too little work, especially in a place like Charikar where there was absolutely nothing else to do, there can be real trouble.

Everyone knows, or assumes they know, what correspondents and cameramen do; but producers? You never see their work directly on screen, yet the fact that anything appears there at all is a tribute to their abilities. A producer does everything from ensuring that everyone gets on the aeroplane and the tickets are paid for, to going out with the cameraman, finding the story, directing the correspondent (not always an easy task, with those of us who are older and more prickly), negotiating with the programme editors in London, overseeing the editing of the report, taking the edited cassette to the feed-point, and making sure it gets to London properly. I have done all these jobs myself, but if there is someone to do them for me it enables me to speak to useful news sources, travel round, and think about what I am going to write.

And it means there is always someone else to bounce ideas off and ask advice from. Not every correspondent welcomes the presence of a producer on the road: some, indeed, seem to have problems about the very idea. But in my experience a good, intelligent, pleasant producer is the best ally you can have. (I married mine, so I suppose that proves the point.) When you sit in the edit suite it can be a comfort to have a third opinion on what you are doing. It also means that when you are editing, you can concentrate wholeheartedly on writing the script while the producer and the picture editor between them decide how best to lay down the pictures.

The correspondent sits alongside the picture editor, watching the pictures and writing the commentary ('the track') at the same time. Every two or three sentences the correspondent stops writing, records another section of the track onto the edited cassette, and the picture editor lays down the requisite pictures to the words.

Not everyone does it this way. Some correspondents still apparently write and record their entire track first, sometimes not looking at the pictures at all. This usually makes for pretty bad television, and you can tell just by watching the result that the correspondent had no interest in the pictures whatsoever. Others have particular idiosyncrasies; Martin Bell, who may possibly have been the best reporter there has ever been in British television news, eventually got to the point where he wrote nothing down on paper at all. He would look at the pictures, work out the words of the next sentence in his head, walk up and down the room a couple of times fixing the words in his mind, then grasp the microphone and record the sentence. I doubt if anyone else could do that, or indeed would want to do it. The great advantage was that it sounded natural, like the rhythms of his speech. It didn't sound as though he was reading it off a piece of paper, one of the more depressing features of a lot of television news reporting.

It is a serious offence to take so long with the editing process that you miss a satellite feed. A slow picture editor or a slow correspondent can make it happen; and the producer, unable to do anything serious to hurry either of them up, has to sit and watch helplessly as the clock ticks on towards the deadline. The rule of thumb is an hour's editing per minute of edited material, so a two and a a half minute report will take something like two and half hours. Sometimes it can take very much longer, particularly if there is a lot of intricate editing of the sound to be done. Paul Simpson, working with me recently in Jerusalem on some long and complicated reports, devised a system of timing which allowed him to tell whether we were getting badly behind ourselves; and it saved us at least twice from disaster.

Producers, lacking the ego of either the correspondent or the cameraman, are the sheet-anchor of the team – the one entirely sane member of the trio, with no interest to defend except that of the final product. At the same time, the producer can occasionally achieve an extraordinary measure of success. The one television interview Pope John Paul II ever gave was in 1982, to a BBC producer who had become lost somewhere in the recesses of the Vatican. The producer, Courtenay Tordoff, had gone with a cameraman to get some shots of the Pope at a photocall. The Falklands War had recently started, and no one knew whether the Pope would carry out his plan to visit Britain, or whether he would postpone it until the war with the predominantly Catholic Argentina was over.

On their way out afterwards, Tordoff and the cameraman became separated from the other journalists. They wandered down a corridor or two, and for some reason opened a particularly imposing door. The Pope was inside.

'Go on, ask him a question,' urged the cameraman; these things seem easier to cameramen than they do to the person who actually has to do the asking.

Tordoff is a bluff, unfazable character: 'Excuse me, Your Holiness,' he said, and the interview was on.

It was only brief; but during the course of it the Pope made it clear he would indeed be coming to Britain as planned. Courtenay Tordoff's exclusive interview was broadcast right around the world.

ITN was understandably desperate to match the papal interview in some way, and the following morning the Pope was due to meet some pilgrims in St Peter's Square. Ignoring all the normal protocol, the ITN reporter and his famous old Italian cameraman, who had once worked for Mussolini, broke through the pilgrim ranks. The reporter called out some question to the Pope relating to the Falklands War and his proposed visit to Britain; the BBC might have got its interview a day earlier (a rare phenomenon in 1982, when ITN was still a much more effective organization than the BBC) but capturing the Pope's heavily Polish English on the subject was well worth doing.

Surprisingly, the Pope was happy to speak to British television for a second day running. He explained, as he had to Courtenay Tordoff, his reasons for going to Britain. But it all came to nothing. Mussolini's cameraman, overwhelmed at seeing the Pope so close, had immediately gone down onto one knee. ITN had an interesting close-up study of the cobbles of St Peter's Square, and nothing more.

I have dealt elsewhere in my memoirs with the subject of cameramen: they can of course be tough or nervous, intelligent or dopey, sensitive or irreflective, quick- or slow-minded – exactly like the correspondents and producers they have to work with. The old television news tradition, deriving ultimately from the newsreel days, encouraged cameramen to think independently and be able to work on their own. This was less true of cameramen from current-affairs programmes who had to work with producers and directors, because the producers and directors usually wanted to do the thinking for both of them.

Derek Collier was a prime example of the older type of news cameraman: a former naval petty officer, he was tough, excellent company, and with his fiercely broken nose and white hair he was a particular favourite with susceptible women all over the world. Margaret Thatcher adored him.

'There's Derek,' I once heard her say at a Conservative Party press conference. 'Move back, Geoffrey' – this to the foreign secretary, Sir Geoffrey Howe, who got her arm in his chest – 'so he can have a good shot of me.'

A few weeks before the Gulf War began in January 1991, Derek Collier and his sound recordist and I were in Baghdad. The future Russian Prime Minister, Yevgeniy Primakov, flew to Baghdad as President Mikhail Gorbachev's special envoy for last-minute negotiations with Saddam Hussein in the hope of avoiding war. The talks went on much longer than expected, but when they were finished no one knew the outcome. The Iraqis and the Russians outdid each other in their unwillingness to say what had happened. The plane which had brought Primakov to Baghdad was waiting for him at the airport.

'Go and see if you can get a shot of Primakov,' I told Derek. 'Only be very careful. You know what they're like here about airports.'

I wanted to go with them, given the likelihood of their being arrested, but I had a report to edit for the lunch-time news. Anyway, if anyone could take care of himself and talk his way out of trouble, Derek could.

They followed a line of official cars into the VIP side of the airport, where no Westerner and certainly no camera crew had probably ever been, and managed in some occult way to get onto the apron. There they found the Deputy Prime Minister, Tariq Aziz; a fierce little man with a nasty temper, who made it clear to me a few weeks later that if I didn't stop asking him questions about some urgent issue he would have me liquidated.

Derek went up to Tariq Aziz and did an interview with him,

calling out the questions round the camera. Such was his charm that Tariq Aziz smiled at him like Margaret Thatcher, and thanked him for coming.

Then Derek and the sound recordist went and stood in the shade, and Derek checked the tape. There was scarcely anything on it; even the best cameramen occasionally get 'out of phase', as they call it, and switch the camera off when they think they are switching it on. This is very disconcerting, since nothing of the interview is recorded – just the steps to and from the interview. Derek had got out of phase.

So he and the sound recordist went back to Tariq Aziz, who was still standing waiting for Yevgeniy Primakov to arrive. And instead of telling Derek he would have him liquidated, Tariq Aziz nodded understandingly when the out-of-phase concept was explained to him, and agreed to give them a second interview.

As it came to an end, Derek – who was of course the only cameraman at the airport – turned round and saw Primakov's car arriving. He filmed him saying goodbye to Tariq Aziz, who didn't know himself how the talks with Saddam Hussein had gone. And Derek realized that if he didn't ask Primakov a question about it, no one would know what had happened. As Primakov walked up the steps to the open door of his Ilyushin, Derek called out to him.

'Did your talks go well, sir?'

Primakov, looking as sour as ever, paused a few steps from the top.

'No,' he said, very distinctly, looking straight into the camera lens.

Derek Collier had obtained a one-word, major world exclusive.

His sometime sound recordist, Don Nesbitt, was every bit as bold as Derek, but rather more accident-prone. I was very fond of Don, who volunteered for everything on the principle that he wanted the BBC to be the best. Once I worked with him in Hamburg, when Helmut Kohl was Chancellor. A hostile left-wing element had rather cleverly got themselves onto a walkway above the Chancellor, and started throwing bottles down on top of him. The crew and I hurried forward through the crowd to film it, and poor Don took a bottle right on the head. He went down as though he was dead.

I remembered that he had been blown up by a landmine a few weeks earlier, and that he had had some shrapnel in the scalp. Unfortunately, though, I was fired up.

'Never mind him,' I shouted above the general noise of shouting and the crash of bottles, 'I'll pick up the sound gear and we'll carry on.'

We got some good material, before we came back and found that Don had already been taken off to hospital. The camera had been running when I said not to mind him, and there was a bit of hostility towards me from Don's colleagues. Not from Don himself, though.

'Quite right,' he said. 'I'd have done the same myself.'

And he explained to me why it was a good thing that he had gone to hospital: they'd found some extra bits of shrapnel in his scalp from the landmine, and taken them out.

Some years later, Don was working with Derek Collier in some town in provincial France, where a man with a handgun had taken over a bank and was holding everyone inside hostage. It was a long siege, on a hot day; and during the afternoon Derek went off to find a lavatory while Don took over the camera. No sooner had Derek gone round the corner than the man came out onto the steps of the bank and fired several shots – one of which went straight towards Don's camera. The bullet buried itself into the lens, and left Don with something of a black eye.

'Look what happens when I leave you,' said Derek when he came back.

Camera crews like the two of them were the finest flowering of the old newsreel tradition. The BBC and ITN crews used to be older, and worked their way up through the system. They started as lighting men, or sometimes as dispatch riders, and it took them years to be promoted to camera-work. The temptation is to say something along the lines of 'They don't make cameramen like that any more', but the fact is that they do. The old generation of British cameramen has been replaced by a new generation of young, active and easy-going Australian, British and South African cameramen, clever, educated and equally resourceful. I often think that the real pleasure of working for television is the companionship of the cameramen.

But I do sometimes miss the sheer ability of people like Derek

Collier and Don Nesbitt to take over the entire show themselves and do everyone else's work; including mine. And I miss their company too.

§

There are, of course, all sorts of other people who play their part in a successful shoot. In several places the driver has been critical to our success, and just occasionally to our survival. I have worked with some excellent drivers, from Colombia and Lebanon to China at the time of Tiananmen Square. I have also worked with some strange ones. In Peru, for instance, we hired a Skinnerist psychiatrist called Johnny who, though charming and amusing when everything was quiet, was inclined to go crazy if anyone mentioned the words 'fast' or 'hurry' or 'late'.

He would almost froth at the mouth, mounting the pavement and scattering pedestrians, screeching round corners on two wheels, blowing his horn incessantly and – if he were stuck at a traffic light and couldn't unbox himself – leaning out of the window and beating menacingly on the door of his van. We found ourselves using all sorts of codes if we were getting short of time, so as not to light Johnny's blue touchpaper. Once, when we were on our way to a highly sensitive meeting with a key contact from the Shining Path guerrillas, I let slip that we might be a minute or two late.

We hadn't of course told Johnny the sensitivity of what we were doing, so he duly went crazy and we arrived outside the contact's house with a squealing of tyres, our brakes screaming. No fewer than four newspapers were lowered in the parked cars of police spooks who were watching the house.

Having trouble with the police, getting arrested, and being questioned at the station are a familiar part of the job if you work in difficult places. I notice, when I talk to pleasant, comfortable groups of people in Britain or elsewhere, that they find this difficult to comprehend. They like hearing my stock of stories – how Colonel Gadhafi broke wind continually during my interview with him in his tent in the desert, how Ayatollah Khomeini refused very politely to shake my hand, how the cannibal Emperor Bokassa stocked his deep-freeze, and Osama bin Laden offered someone the disappointingly small amount of $500 to kill me. They particularly enjoy any story with bullets, shells or rockets in it, and they tut-tut sympathetically when I tell them about being forced to kneel in the Beirut dust while someone pulls the trigger of the gun he's holding to the back of my neck, then laughs because it's unloaded. They're with me all the way on this.

When I start to tell them about getting arrested, though, they shift uncomfortably in their seats. Crazed dictators and cruise missiles are one thing; falling foul of the law is altogether different. Yet for those of us who work in television news, this is nothing unusual; and the nastier the place the more likely it is to happen. For a start, you are horribly noticeable wherever you go: two or three Westerners, tall and differently dressed, stand out in any crowd you are in. Directly the camera goes up on the cameraman's shoulder, it's like the Grand Fleet hoisting the battle-flag: you're committed, and everyone can see it. It gathers crowds. It also gathers policemen. And when trouble starts, policemen everywhere seem to like sticking their greasy hands into the lens of a television camera.

During my thirty-six years in broadcast news I must have been arrested dozens of times. Usually it's no more than a brief questioning. Sometimes it's the full monty: a roughing up, a trip to the cells, threats, an eventual, grudging release. The offence is being around when trouble starts. If they can't stop the trouble, there is a certain kind of policeman who prefers roughing up the camera crews instead.

Late on the night of the presidential election in Iran in June 2001, I was standing in a park in northern Tehran with Paul Simpson and a freelance cameraman, Steve Lammiman – a Londoner. We knew the result already: President Mohammad Khatami, the country's (relatively) moderate leader, had won by a landslide of eighty-four per cent against his conservative rival. Around us, several thousand young people were milling about, trying to start up a demonstration.

Things in Iran are frequently weird, and this evening was weirder than most. The would-be demonstrators wanted to celebrate the re-election of their President, and the police – who were almost exclusively of the secret variety, plain-clothed and nasty – were out to stop them. In Iran, the secret police are part of the old conservative system which clings to power and influence even though it is clear that the vast majority of citizens want the kind of change President Khatami is always promising but can't deliver.

Paul, Steve and I didn't look anything like young Iranians out for a celebration. Even in the hot darkness of the park we stood out; like a camera-crew in a crowd, you might say. Steve had the camera by his side and we tried not to get into conversation with the would-be demonstrators, because we wanted to let the situation develop a little before we got ourselves into trouble. But it didn't matter. The secret policemen had seen us long before, and were just waiting for the moment to do something about us.

They gathered round us now in the sticky heat and moved in suddenly, trying to grab the camera from Steve's hand. Paul and I stood defensively in front of him, all three of us resisting hard. But there were quite a few of them, and only three of us; and slowly, like a loose maul on a rugby field, they pushed and dragged us down to the main road where the police cars were parked, punching and grabbing us.

Why, exactly, did we fight back? It was obvious we were going to be arrested, and this would probably only make it worse for us. Yet we had done absolutely nothing wrong. We had full official press accreditation which allowed us to be there; this was an open space, a public park, with no restrictions on the use of cameras or the presence of foreigners; and we hadn't turned a frame of tape because nothing had really happened. And anyway there is something in every free man and woman that makes them resist treatment which is unfair and unreasonable. Especially from secret policemen. There are grades of unpleasantness, and secret policemen in places like Iran come quite high up on my list.

It wasn't quite accurate of me to say earlier that there were three of us in the park. There was in fact a fourth member of our team, a man I have known far longer than Paul Simpson or Steve Lammiman. His name was Mahmoudi, and he had been driving me around Iran ever since I first went there in 1978: my Iranian equivalent of Aziz in Peshawar. There wasn't – there isn't – anything I wouldn't trust to Mahmoudi's care, and he has got me out of more trouble than I can remember. He is older than Aziz, and only a little younger than I am, I should judge, with short grey hair, a grey moustache and round steel-rimmed spectacles. He looks tough and effective, and he is. Mahmoudi was never a great enthusiast for the mullahs, and showed it by refusing to grow a beard, even when times were hard in the early days of the Islamic Revolution. As I say, you can't really do anything much in television news without having a team behind you, and Mahmoudi was an important part of our team.

I had told him that we expected some sort of demonstration in the park, and asked him to keep an eye on us. I was absolutely clear about it: he mustn't at any stage get involved, because the trouble would be much worse for him, as an Iranian, than it would be for us. But he must stick close, see what was happening to us, and do something afterwards to get us out. Mahmoudi didn't need to be told any of this; he and I had been in this sort of situation plenty of times before.

So when the cops descended on us, Mahmoudi was circling round us at a distance, keeping a discreet and very careful eye on what happened to us. And even as the scrum developed and we were being gradually forced towards the police vehicles and our inevitable arrest, I got a quick glimpse of Mahmoudi walking close beside us and then heading off purposefully. I knew he wasn't getting away to save his own skin; that's not the way Mahmoudi does things.

There was a great deal of screaming and shouting beside the long line of police cars, with their lights flashing blue and red and gold in the hot summer night. We were pushed and shoved and punched, but Steve, like a good scrumhalf, never let go of his camera.

'They're just a load of stupid bastards,' he said to me, his face sweating in the hot night. I grinned back.

Mahmoudi, by this time, had sought out the police general who was in command of the uniformed men at the scene. The uniformed police in Iran are a relatively moderate lot, prepared to support the general principles of law and order and not too concerned about all the extremist business which the conservative clergy insist on. For the most part, they were just standing round uncomfortably, watching the secret police lay into anyone they didn't like the look of: any man, that is, without a beard, and any woman who showed her hair. And television crews.

Secret policemen always outrank ordinary policemen, but a general is a general; and this general was an enthusiastic watcher of BBC World. In particular, it turned out, he liked my programme, *Simpson's World*.

'They have arrested Simpson of the BBC,' Mahmoudi told the general grandly. And he added, for good measure, 'I think there will be a big fuss about it.'

'O God,' moaned the general, wiping the sweat off his large but rather pleasant face, 'now I shall be in trouble.'

And he ordered his uniformed policemen to take the three of us, still struggling and shouting, away from the custody of the secret police and put us into a marked police car for our own protection.

We had no idea what was happening, and fought the poor uniformed policemen who were only trying to help us with as much fury as we had fought the secret cops. I should have realized, though: the secret cops were furious, and tried to get at us as we were pushed into the car. One of them, a particularly unpleasant-looking character with a face scarred by burned-out acne, jabbed his finger at my eye before the uniformed police got the car door shut. I saw it coming, and turned enough so he couldn't stick his finger into the corner of my eye and put it out as he wanted. But I took the full force of his long, dirty fingernail in the white of my eye, and it hurt badly.

We didn't realize it, but our problems were over. A circle of uniformed policemen formed around the car to keep the secret cops away, and it was just a matter of waiting for someone in authority to take notice of us and process us. This, however, took some time. I suppose we sat huddled together in the heat of the police car for almost another hour before we were driven to a police station. There we had to identify ourselves, make a statement, and fend off first the spitefulness and then the crawling attention of the police detective in charge. (A friend of mine, Edward Chaplin, who was a senior diplomat at the British embassy in Tehran, was once attacked by Iranian secret policemen who beat him up, then took him to a cell. He told me afterwards that the worst thing about it was that the man who had beaten him most savagely came and sat next to him and asked him for a visa to come to Britain.)

At one stage, walking idly around, I went over to the window. There, in the car park, stood Mahmoudi. He was looking up and waiting for the moment when I might see him. He waved and grinned: it was his way of telling me that everything was fine and that he hadn't deserted us. As though it would ever have occurred to me for a single moment that he might.

14

Live from the Front Line

Charikar: Sunday 14 October to Monday 12 November

I hung out of the window at the end of our corridor, peering at the Shomali Valley, where the front line ran, through my expensive new Minolta 15 × 35 binoculars. I had bought them at Dubai airport eleven days earlier in that extravagant frame of mind which has cost me so much money on the way to dangerous places, when the outcome of the episode seems so uncertain that there seems no good reason not to spend a little. The binoculars were already dusty and stained from travel, and looked as though they could have done service in the Western Desert during the Second World War.

At seven in the morning, children were already gathering below the window to stare at the strange beings who had taken over the Municipality Building.

'Hello Misterr.'

'Wherryoofrrom?'

'How arr yoo?'

Where, I wondered, did they get their weird English from? Who, anywhere in the English-speaking world, ever says 'Hello, mister' to anyone else? I smiled and waved, and they went into ecstasies of excitement and embarrassment. Old men pushed wheelbarrows piled high with clothes or bricks, or tried to coax tiny little donkeys to pull unreasonably large loads. A few women in burkas scurried around like beetles in the bright light. A few men lounged around smoking and chatting, with only the AK-47s to show they were soldiers. Their uniforms, American-supplied, wouldn't arrive for some time yet.

'Hello Misterr.'

'How arr yoo?'

Soon, of course, we wouldn't notice any of these things at all, and would start cutting the everyday pictures of Charikar life out of our reports, in the belief that they weren't of any interest. Sometimes I think that first impressions are the only things that count, because they show you how extraordinarily different and exciting life in a new place is. All too quickly you become used to them, and after a while you fail to notice them at all. Turbans, burkas, donkeys, AK-47s: they all become part of the ordinariness of life instead of its extraordinariness.

Sometimes, though, this descends into outright Gee whizzery, and you have to be careful. When CNN opened its new bureau in Delhi it held a big party for dozens of Indian dignitaries and notables, and showed them a composite video of CNN reporting on India which began with a sacred cow crossing the road. The dignitaries were deeply irritated. For them, India was an exciting new centre of world business and technology, and they regarded pictures of a sacred cow ambling through the traffic as a deliberately patronizing First World view, something to be regarded with embarrassment and impatience; whereas for Americans or Europeans it is a symbol of the strangeness, the excitement, the otherness, of life in the East. I can sympathize with both sides; I just hope that if I put pictures of a sacred cow into one of my reports I would remember not to show it to an audience of well-heeled, Western-minded Indians and expect them to be impressed.

We decided to go back up the road to the Panjshir Valley and interview Dr Abdullah, the Northern Alliance Foreign Minister, for that evening's news. His press spokesman, whom we saw briefly on our way through Jabal Saraj, advised us not to go and disturb Dr Abdullah since he would be too busy. A couple of days earlier this spokesman had instructed us not to set up our base in Charikar, but to stay with all the other journalists. There is a certain atavistic pleasure in ignoring the instructions of such people, whose interests almost never coincide with those of the journalists they deal with.

So we went anyway. There probably are times when you should heed the voice of press spokesmen, though I cannot think of any offhand. But in Afghanistan, unlike most places on earth, you have a freedom of action which enables you to go pretty much where you like, and do pretty much what you want to do, whatever the authorities say. There seemed no serious reason not to go.

The Panjshir Valley is very long and very beautiful and runs for fifty miles or more, and every few hundred yards of it are marked by the rusted wreckage of Russian vehicles which invaded the valley seven times or more during the ten-year Soviet occupation, and still never managed to subdue it. There is a magnificence and a freedom to the Panjshir, and the air itself, clear and cold, seems to breathe resistance.

The man who led the defence of the Valley was Ahmad Shah Massoud, the dominant figure in the Northern Alliance: a dour, thoughtful man with deeply lined cheeks, whose authority had been badly damaged by the four years he spent in government in Kabul, between the collapse of the pro-Communist government of Najibullah in 1992 and the victory of the Taliban in 1996. Those years were spent mostly fighting other leaders of the mujaheddin, some of whom were paid to attack each other by the Russians and some by Pakistan. There was corruption and great incompetence, but it never attached itself to Ahmad Shah Massoud himself.

His problem was always a political one. He had the strong support of the British, who had, during the 1980s, sent him a million dollars in gold by a British agent; but the Americans, who listened far too much to the Pakistanis and were half-inclined to favour the Taliban, didn't trust him. In November 1996, after the Taliban had captured the town of Sarobi, Ahmad Shah Massoud packed up everything he had and fled northwards to his old stronghold, the Panjshir.

I had interviewed him several times, and was always impressed by his quietness and his intellect. I wanted to interview him again, but while I was heading to Kabul in September 2001, trying to persuade the Taliban to let the BBC back into Afghanistan, he was murdered, here in the Panjshir.

Now, as we started speaking to various survivors of the attack in which he had died, the purpose of his murder became clear to us: it was intended to be the signal for the attacks on the World Trade Center, the Pentagon, and the White House. According to the survivors, an Arab television crew had been hanging around Massoud's headquarters in the Panjshir for three weeks or more, hoping to get an interview with him. Arabs would normally be regarded as enemies of the Northern Alliance, but these men were very persuasive about wanting to put Massoud's views across to a Middle Eastern audience. This being Afghanistan, no one thought to check their equipment.

At last the moment came for the interview. There were, as there usually are at such times, several people in the room when it was recorded. The questions were straightforward enough, and though they were mildly hostile there was nothing to make Massoud or his associates suspicious. They didn't know that the battery pack belted around the cameraman's waist was full of plastic explosive.

Then the reporter started asking a question about Massoud's likely policy if he captured Kabul: what, for instance, would he do about Osama bin Laden? The mention of the name was the signal for the cameraman to detonate the explosives; and the reporter instinctively shrank away from him. Massoud guessed instantly what was going to happen and tried to throw himself onto the floor, but he took much of the force of the explosion and died of terrible injuries some time afterwards. The crew were killed outright; several of the onlookers survived. The murder was the pre-arranged signal for the Al Qaida agents in the United States to synchronize their hijacking of the four planes; and one of the best and brightest leaders modern Afghanistan had produced was swept off the board.

We filmed Dr Abdullah, one of Massoud's closest friends and allies, as he spoke at a council of war attended by all the main survivors of the attack. He stood out by reason of his appearance, which was modern, Western and neatly groomed, while the others were traditional Afghan warlords, turbaned and bearded. Among them were the men who might have been expected to order that foreign camera crews should be properly searched. Nothing had changed, no lessons had been learned: we ourselves had been able to walk into this room, which contained all the remaining leaders of the Alliance, without being checked.

It was clearly a difficult moment for the Alliance. They assumed that the moment for the big attack on Kabul would be coming soon, yet there was no sign, at this stage, that the Americans were going to bomb the front line near Charikar – the key to the capture of Kabul. The Americans seemed to be as worried about the Northern Alliance, with whom, thanks to the influence of Pakistan, they had never had particularly close links, as they were about the Taliban.

That was what the council of war was about; and as soon as it was finished Dr Abdullah came bustling in to see us. (Like Najibullah and plenty of other leading Afghans, he had only this one name: when the Western media, uncomfortable with this and plagued by urgent questions from their desks, asked him about this, he suggested they should call him 'Abdullah Abdullah'. 'Then I will answer, "Yes, yes",' he said.) You can usually spot what a politician wants to tell you in an interview, and in this case it quickly became clear: the Northern Alliance council of war had decided to calm the anxieties of the Americans about a possible bloodbath in Kabul – something that would never actually have taken place, as anyone who knew Afghanistan and its ways could have told them – by offering to stop its forces at the gates of the city and allow a trained force of police to enter and take control.

It made a good report that evening, combined with pictures of the continued air attacks on Kabul itself. Although it was only twenty-five miles away, it was hidden from us by the intervening mountains; from Bin Laden Mansions we could see the flashes of the bombs as they landed, and the fires that were started. They lit up the night sky. But what about the Taliban trenches in front of us? When would the Americans start to bomb them?

The next afternoon there was a little action: occasional mortar rounds were lobbed from one side to the other, and you could hear the sound of rifle shots. In the magnificent amphitheatre of the Shomali Valley, with the mountains on either side of the green plain before us, every sound was magnified. We were anxious to get down to the front line and see for ourselves what the situation was. So I went down the dark corridor which linked our part of the building with Hajji Bari's, and sought him out.

Now that our relationship had been cemented with hard cash, Hajji Bari was delighted to see me. There would be no problem about our going down to the front line; in fact, we could leave straight away, and he would show us round. He was more than a little proud of it. Hajji was, after all, the man in sole charge of the most important section of front line, straddling the main Kabul road. I thought of the problems the journalists back at the Foreign Ministry in Jabal Saraj had in trying to get permission to reach the front, and once again blessed our good fortune in fetching up here with Hajji.

We gathered our gear together, and climbed into his jeep. On its windscreen someone had pasted a large picture of Ahmad Shah Massoud, edged in black.

'I can't film with that there,' Peter said.

I told Hajji. He made a gesture as though to say it was of no importance, and the driver pulled the portrait of his revered and murdered chief off the windscreen. I think that was the moment when I realized we would be able to do anything here we wanted, within reason. We drove out through the town, with the children laughing and capering around our two cars, and headed south down the paved road in the general direction of Kabul. The good surface didn't last long; there were constant shell-holes and tank-ruts in it now. A few farmers kept on working, in spite of everything, but otherwise the fields and vineyards were empty and deserted, and the vines were a sad, uniform brown: unwatered, untended, for the years the fighting had gone on here. What made the Shomali Valley good for growing grapes and apples also made it good tank and trench warfare country; and that had destroyed the vines faster than any outbreak of phylloxera.

Close to the front line there were concrete blocks across the road, and we turned sharp left onto a dusty farm track, our vehicles jolting up and down in the way we had grown used to on our journey south. It ran along the front line and behind it, and was used to supply it. But the entire area, by three in the afternoon, seemed utterly somnolent. The farmhouses were the soldiers' bases, and they lounged around there in twos and threes, drinking tea and chatting in a slow, desultory kind of way. To me, used to more strenuous wars, it was surprising how little weaponry there was on show and how few soldiers there were manning the trenches.

This was a very different type of conflict, carried on at quarter speed on both sides. Entire stretches of the front line were entirely empty of men. And even when there were three or four gathered together in one place it was hard to think of them as soldiers. They wore no kind of uniform whatever, just the usual rather grubby robes of the Afghan civilian. Rank was indicated by equipment: a sidearm, a walkie-talkie. The ordinary soldiers were an unimpressive bunch; some were just boys.

In every war there is a strange, unspoken relationship between the soldiers on both sides. They do things at set times, and they refrain from doing other things at all. Any violation of these tacit rules is regarded with particular anger and hatred by the other side. It was as true here as it was on the Western Front in the First World War, though it is hard to think of a greater contrast between the horrors of trench warfare then and this half-hearted, half-time conflict in which there were very few casualties and neither side had much in the way of weapons.

War in Afghanistan at the start of the twenty-first century was very much what it must have been in Europe in the Middle Ages: groups of ill-disciplined troops ranging around the countryside, more like bandits than like regular armies of trained soldiers. Yet they weren't bad men by any means, and we were never robbed or threatened at any stage by the front-line soldiers. As in any civil war, they knew the men on the other side quite well. Often they had fought alongside each other in the past; sometimes they were personal friends. There was certainly no question of hatred; at least for the Afghans among the Taliban. The foreigners – Pakistanis and Arabs – were a different matter.

Hajji Bari grunted an instruction to his driver to stop, and we all climbed out. Peter Jouvenal and I were wearing our flak jackets in the afternoon heat, and attracting the attention of every *mujahed* there. Wearing body armour when you are with unprotected soldiers is always, I feel, a difficult business. They often feel, quite understandably, that they need it more than you do; and there is also an instinctive desire among them to check out in a practical way how well it keeps out bullets. In other words, you are always vulnerable to the possibility that they might either rob you or shoot you. You just have to hope they can control the temptation.

With Hajji there, though, no one would be trying anything. He was a tough character, assertive in spite of his lack of inches. One glare from those kohl-rimmed eyes would be enough to quell any nonsense. His men all understood that we were under Hajji's protection, and that anyone who interfered with us would have to take him on. We followed him up to a low wall of sandbags, facing across no man's land. Hajji was turning out to be a good television subject. He didn't need to be told that he mustn't look at the camera, he liked the attention, and he seemed to have an instinct for what would make a good shot. God knows how; one or two wealthy Afghans, like General Gul, had satellite dishes and the generators to make everything work, but even so it was hard to make out a picture through the snowstorm of poor reception. I think Hajji was a natural: he would have made a good television correspondent, if only he could shave and lay off the eye make-up.

Now he leant on the sandbags, looking searchingly across the open stretch of land opposite: just as Peter Jouvenal would want. Then, without being asked, he lifted his walkie-talkie and started speaking into it – still staring out across no man's land.

'What's he doing?'

There was a confused babble of electronic shouting from the walkie-talkie.

'He's calling the guys on the Taliban side.'

Not just the guys, but the Taliban commander. It turned out that he and Hajji Bari had known each other for a long time, and had fought side by side with each other against the Russians. There was a good deal of banter.

'Things must be pretty bad on your side. Not much food, not enough guns. And the Americans are coming.'

'Ah, your paymasters. You'll be getting your dollars soon.'

'Yes, and you could be getting them too if you come over to our side.'

The Taliban commander opposite used an expression that meant something along the lines of hell freezing over first. There was a final exchange of jovial insults, and the walkie-talkie went dead.

'So what impression did you get from him about morale on the other side?'

'Things aren't good there. I can tell. I know him well, you see. Life is difficult, and they are getting worried about the Americans coming.'

'What are you trying to do by talking to him? Is it just psychological warfare?'

'I would like him to defect to our side.'

'And do you think he will?'

'Yes, in the end. He is thinking about it already. You will see.'

We moved on. Hajji Bari tuned in to another frequency, and held his walkie-talkie up in the air where we could all hear it.

'You hear this? It is Arabs speaking. They are over there.'

I peered over the lip of the trench. All I could see was a shattered house.

'You must look again.' He pointed, and I thought yet again what an excellent performer Hajji Bari was on television; it was as if he was giving Peter Jouvenal time to follow the movement of his arm and hand with the camera.

'How good are they as soldiers, these Arabs?'

'Better than Afghans. Osama has trained them to fight Russians, and now they only have to fight us. For us it is a problem, because they will fight and they have nowhere else to go. But it will not be a very big one. They are not very many, and some of them are not very well trained.'

I was learning real respect for Hajji Bari. His judgements seemed to me to be clear-minded and calm.

He led us stooping along the narrow trenches, their parapets only five feet high, to a disused water pumping station: the highest structure in this part of the valley. It was an eerie feeling, climbing the exposed earth steps cut in the side of the hill. And when the steps turned round the front of the hill towards the Taliban lines, only a couple of hundred yards away, you could feel the eye of the enemy sniper, sense the pressure of his forefinger on the trigger. But although it felt bad, it probably wasn't dangerous at all. There was relatively little sniping anywhere along the front; after all, if one side raised the general temperature it would be bad for everyone. Afghans are sensible people, who wherever possible take a live-and-let-live approach towards each other.

There were three Northern Alliance soldiers guarding this position, the most prominent along the entire stretch of front line, and when they stood up to greet us it was obvious that one of them had a wooden leg.

'How did this happen?'

The one-legged soldier made a curling motion round the top of his head with his forefinger: the universal sign in Afghanistan for a turban, and therefore for the Taliban.

'A Taliban mine?' He nodded. 'How long ago?'

'One year.'

It was impossible to think of all this happening anywhere else but Afghanistan. Only two and a half active soldiers stood between the Taliban army and a pre-emptive attack on the Northern Alliance lines before the Americans got more involved. And yet it was perfectly clear to us, to the Northern Alliance command, and no doubt to the Taliban themselves, that there would be no pre-emptive attack, any more than there would be a commando raid on Bin Laden Mansions to take us hostage.

As we drove back up the road with some good pictures of life on the front line, I was turning all these things over in my mind. I was certain now that the Taliban wouldn't put up a serious fight when the Americans finally gave the Northern Alliance the green light to attack Kabul. That wasn't the way the highly orchestrated business of warfare worked in Afghanistan: it was like a confrontation between two lions, where the weaker accepts it has no chance of winning and surrenders to superior force.

When the Russians left in 1989, they continued to support President Najibullah, which meant that the mujaheddin were the weaker side; until 1992, that is, when the Soviet Union had collapsed and the mujaheddin became dominant. Then in 1996 the Taliban swept through the country and the mujaheddin abandoned Kabul and took to the mountains north of the city – becoming known in the process as the Northern Alliance. Now, five years later, the events of 11 September 2001 brought American support for the Northern Alliance, and everyone knew the Taliban wouldn't be able to resist. Including, of course, the Taliban themselves.

Nine days earlier I had suggested in my *Sunday Telegraph* column that the Taliban were unlikely to stand and fight. That is what a column is for: to float suggestions, to propose ideas. Now, after listening to Hajji Bari and walking the front line, I was convinced this view was indeed the correct one. It was time to come out into the open with it, on television.

That night, in a live 'two-way' interview with Peter Sissons on the

Ten O'Clock News, he asked me a question about the strength of the Taliban as I had seen them from the Northern Alliance front line. Casting round for a suitable simile, I remembered the misshapen little hen's eggs Rahman Beg had bought in the market and hard-boiled for us that morning.

> I don't think the Taliban will put up much of a fight. I think that when the time comes and the Northern Alliance make their big push on Kabul the Taliban will simply crack like ... like you break the shell of an egg. I simply don't think they'll resist very much at all.

I could sense the scepticism at the other end: not necessarily in Peter's voice, but in the minds of everyone a long way from Afghanistan who believed all the stuff in the British and American press about war-hardened fighters getting ready to sell their lives dearly. It wasn't, I now understood, the way Afghans did things.

And what about the Arabs and Pakistanis, and all the other foreign volunteers for the Taliban? I thought they would fight a little harder, as Hajji Bari expected, and they certainly wouldn't sell themselves or surrender easily. But there weren't enough of them to make the difference. Kabul was there for the Northern Alliance to take, any time the Americans chose. The only people who didn't seem to realize this were the Americans, and their British allies and supporters. Perhaps they shouldn't read the newspapers so much, I reflected. We were all of us – governments, soldiers, journalists, experts of a dozen different and questionable kinds – much too inclined to believe our own myths, and disregard the clear signs in front of us.

From now on we spent part of virtually every day on the front line. I didn't always go myself, and sometimes we relied on our friends from Australian Broadcasting; but we made sure we had pictures of what was going on; especially after the Americans finally began bombing the Taliban positions opposite us on Sunday 21 October. That morning we were awoken by the Charikar dawn chorus: barking dogs, braying donkeys, the clattering of wheelbarrows as the shopkeepers took their goods to work, the hammering of carpenters, the sound of gunfire. But something seemed to be up; and as we stood on our balcony, looking out over the Shomali Valley and cracking the shells of our hard-boiled eggs, we decided who should do what: Peter Jouvenal and Tony would go to Bagram airbase, and Joe and I to a farmhouse that formed one of the key points of Hajji's front line.

It turned out to be our best front-line coverage so far, especially since Peter got some very enjoyable shots of General Babar, one of the top military commanders of the Northern Alliance, turning up to watch the start of the American bombing from the ruins of the Bagram control tower. He hadn't expected to find Peter there, and his contortions as he spoke on his walkie-talkie to some American forward spotter, while trying not to let Peter hear what he was saying, were very entertaining. Possessing all the politeness of an Afghan and knowing Peter well, he didn't feel able to do what any Western commander would have done, and throw him out.

The bombs themselves were remarkable: immensely accurate (as far as I know, only one American bomb went astray during the next twenty-three days in the Shomali Valley) and throwing up enormous columns of smoke and dust into the air. I am not fond of the whole tactic of aerial bombardment, having spent much too much of my life being shown round the ruins of people's houses which have been hit by accident. The pathetic heaps of bloodstained clothes lying under the dust and rubble don't somehow make you feel better about the pilots who do these things from the safety of fifteen thousand feet up.

But there were no villages, no civilians under these bombs: just Taliban fighters. To be honest, it's never a good feeling to watch as the bombs fall, no matter who is underneath them. The Taliban were no different from the Northern Alliance forces; chance had taken them one way, and the Alliance soldiers the other. They might have been terrified and demoralized by the explosions – except for one thing. Contrary to the impression our reporting gave, the bombing was very light; so much so, that Dr Abdullah complained to the Americans that they weren't doing nearly enough to break the Taliban's will to resist. For the first ten days or so there were often only a couple of bombs dropped a day; and because of their accuracy it was perfectly possible for Taliban troops in one position to be entirely safe and untouched, while another position was utterly destroyed.

So, far from terrifying the Taliban, the bombing actually encouraged them to believe that the Americans were too cowardly to attack them properly; were too nervous of them, perhaps. The only real experience Afghans had had of aerial bombardment, after all, was during the Soviet occupation, when the Antonovs and Tupolevs and the helicopter gunships would come over in force and blast an entire area to rubble. The purpose was to kill and injure as many civilians as possible. There was no such thing as precision bombing, and no intention to achieve it. The Americans, dropping a few perfectly aimed bombs a day, seemed very mild and ineffectual by comparison.

Yet at the same time some of the journalists who were further back from the action reached into the recesses of their memories and started producing expressions like 'carpet-bombing'. Perhaps it was the B-52s that did it, enormous silver tridents in the sky which flew thousands of miles to deliver two or three bombs. It was B-52s which carried out genuine carpet-bombing in Vietnam and Cambodia, plastering entire areas with as much high explosive as was used in a month's raids on Dresden or Berlin during the Second World War. The Americans had no great concern about civilians then: they died like flies.

But the world had turned away a little from the naked brutality of the 1960s and 1970s; and now the greatest military power in history seemed to be pussy-footing around, unwilling to smash the Taliban lines when it could do so there and then. It would have been so easy, and it could have been done with a relatively easy conscience. Public opinion in the United States, which had been prepared to watch hundreds of thousands of civilians being killed, injured and displaced in Vietnam, was now more tender. And in the thirty years since then, American military hardware had become immensely more powerful and precise. Yet there is such a thing as being too sophisticated for your enemy, and watching the bombing of the Taliban front line was like watching the RAF bomb John Ball's army in the Peasants' Revolt of 1389. It was a ludicrous mismatch.

The basic problem, of course, was that Washington was deeply reluctant to send in ground troops to Afghanistan. The US army is not as impressive a fighting force as people think; like the British secret service, MI6, it benefits hugely from its reputation in the movies. Its ordinary soldiers are well below the level of the British or French armies, its Marines are noticeably less good than the Royal

Marines, and only its special forces are really first-rate. Yet even here the best of the American special units, the Navy Seals, are only on a par with the SAS; as Andy Faulkner hinted, they aren't as good as their exact equivalents, the SBS. Still, they have first-class equipment, and behind them is the US Air Force, which is unquestionably the best anywhere.

Altogether, then, it would be much easier to bomb the Taliban from a height and then get the Northern Alliance to do any of the unpleasant hand-to-hand stuff.

The strategy worked well; yet it was interesting to see how quickly, after the brief war in Afghanistan was over, some analysts decided that air-power alone had beaten the Taliban. Not so; and if the Northern Alliance hadn't existed and no one else had been prepared to put ground troops into Afghanistan, the Taliban might well have clung on to power, like Saddam Hussein in Iraq.

Personally, I was getting nervous about the length of time this whole business was taking. I felt I was needed in South Africa, where Dee's mother was seriously ill. In London, meanwhile, a member of my own family had just died. Long satellite phone calls aren't enough; sometimes your physical presence is required. And yet I felt I couldn't just walk out of the story, because I knew better than most how hard it would be to get back into it again. Did I really want to go back north, over the Anjuman Pass, and then out to London, only to face the whole journey all over again later? I knew what would happen: I would get stuck in London, or maybe in Islamabad, feeding the broadcasting monster without having anything new to broadcast about. There are some people who are superb at analysing a situation from a distance, but I'm not one of them. I need to see things with my own eyes.

The stresses and strains of the past few weeks started to show, now that we had begun to relax after reaching the point we had been aiming for over such a long period. I developed some ugly and painful mouth-sores and a bad cold, and generally showed all the symptoms of over-exertion; it's strange how you can keep going for weeks, but quickly go downhill once the worst of the pressure is off. For a couple of days I shut myself up in my room, listened to my selection of mini-discs as I lay on my hard bed on the floor, and gradually recouped. Occasionally, blinking in the light, I would shuffle out in my *chapan* and get myself a cup of tea or some hot curry. The others were sympathetic, and made me things if I wanted them; but mostly, they could see, I just needed a bit of rest.

On the third day, I rose again. It was Tuesday, 23 October, and we were planning something rather new in television news: genuinely live coverage from a war. You often used to hear in the Vietnam War about pictures being beamed 'live' from the battlefield into American homes, but of course it wasn't true: the pictures which Americans saw on their nightly news broadcasts were a good twenty-four hours old, and had been heavily edited. In the Falklands War, thanks to the lack of self-confidence on the part of the British senior commanders, there was a built-in delay of five or six weeks before the pictures of the fighting reached London and people could finally see them. It was a serious public mistake, which they have acknowledged and will, we hope, never make again.

In the Gulf War there was no lack of self-confidence on the part of the American military, but the technology didn't quite exist to broadcast live from the battlefield except by phone. And although the sound alone was fine, it didn't make up for the lack of images. During the nasty little genocidal wars of the 1990s in the former Yugoslavia and Rwanda there were rarely any front lines to report from: most of the 'military' action consisted of groups of thugs with guns and axes murdering civilians. Even in 1999, during the NATO bombing of Serbia, we relied on our mobile phones more than on pictures.

But in 2001 the videophone finally came of age. It was far from perfect, of course: I'm sure that in the future we will be as amused by the ludicrously bad, jerky quality of the pictures as we are by the Lumière family's efforts in 1895 at the Salon Indien. Finally, though, we had the technical ability to take a camera out into the front line and broadcast the pictures live: 'live' meaning simultaneously, so that what the viewer sees is what the correspondent is seeing on the ground.

And so, with the sense that we were breaking new ground, we headed out in two teams: Peter Jouvenal and Tony Rippon, Joe Phua and I. Peter would get pictures on the front line for use in our edited reports that night, Joe would shoot the live interviews – 'two-ways' – with London, with the action going on in the background. We reached one of Hajji Bari's main positions (by now we were so well-known to them that we didn't even need to ask for permission to come in) and set up our cameras. Gratifyingly, the American planes came over exactly on cue; and for once the raid was a heavy one. We went over three times to BBC World as the explosions crashed behind us. It was, in a small way, an historic moment.

Services like BBC World and News 24 are used to live events, and are prepared to accept a little roughness round the edges and a little uncertainty. The people in charge of the big domestic news bulletins have been trained to believe that a good news bulletin is a tidy news bulletin. So when it came to crossing live to the news on BBC One, the programme's running order had been set in concrete half an hour or so beforehand, and nobody wanted to change it. The news could have been the first British domestic programme to carry live pictures of a war; instead, the running order was sacrosanct.

As the bombs fell, quite close to us, I called in on the satphone, and listened to the news. First there was a long discussion about whether Britain faced a danger from anthrax (it didn't, as things turned out); then there were reports about the latest in Washington. It was only ten minutes later that the programme came to me to ask me what was happening on the front line. But the last bomb had fallen a good six minutes earlier, the planes had all turned for home, and even the fires on the front line opposite had died down; so there wasn't a huge amount to report.

By now Joe was getting ill – suffering, perhaps, from the same thing I had. But he carried on, and that evening we had an excellent edited report to send over. At midnight, our time, we had the added benefit of being able to go live into BBC World from Bin Laden Mansions with another air raid going on behind us in the darkness. We knew now that we could do it. We just needed the people in London to put us on the air.

It is, of course, very easy for people like me, who have only our own little segment of the world to consider, to complain about the stupidity, short-sightedness and timidity of everyone else. This is one of the many diseases that news correspondents are prone to: the belief that we, out here, know everything and are infallible, while everyone else fouls up and lets the organization down. If you examine these things objectively, you find it isn't usually true in the slightest.

So the following morning, Wednesday 24 October, was to be the big moment. Peter Jouvenal and Tony had already gone on ahead, to the area we had filmed the day before. This seemed to be a particularly good place, because the trenches opposite the Northern Alliance positions were manned almost entirely by Arabs and Pakistanis – the foreign volunteers whom the Americans were particularly targeting. The previous day Peter and Joe had got some good pictures of some of these foreign Taliban, whom we were now learning to call Al Qaida members. (Wrongly, in fact. These were just low-grade cannon fodder; Al Qaida only recruited the very best.)

Joe, Khalil and I headed off to find the others. We drove through the narrow lanes between the dead vineyards, with high mud-brick walls on each side – a perfect battleground for partisans, I thought, and the despair of tank-drivers, who would be vulnerable to attack from every corner if they tried to get through here. Afghan mud-brick is extraordinarily strong and impressive stuff. I have seen a tank-round hit the wall of a house at fairly close range, and leave nothing but a large splat in it: the mud-brick simply absorbed the explosion, and wouldn't allow the shell to penetrate more than a few inches.

There were still farmers living here, determined not to abandon their land to anyone; and in the end they turned out to be right, because the war in the Shomali Valley was only a couple of weeks away from its end now. They waved at us as we went past, or greeted us with a solemn *asalaam aleykum*, and their children giggled and fled through doorways and into fields at the sight of us. When the lanes grew too narrow for our vehicle we parked and walked along parallel to the front line for half an hour, guided by one of Hajji Bari's men whom we came across. He knew where Peter and Tony were, he said, and lumbered off leaving behind him the unmistakable whiff of Afghan marijuana.

But of course he got it wrong. When we got to the house he meant, I could see there was no chance that Peter would be here: it was too far from the front line, a good two hundred yards back from it. There were several photographers here, French and Italians, who had been brought there by their Foreign Ministry minders; but this was another clear sign that Peter wasn't there. There is a fierce war between television cameramen and newspaper and magazine photographers, who each think the others are an unnecessary nuisance and get in the way of a good shot.

I couldn't seem to make our guide understand that we were in the wrong place, and he wandered up the mud-brick stairs to the roof where the photographers were grouped. By now I was really irritated. The day was getting on, the American planes would soon be coming over, and we still hadn't linked up with Peter. Angrily, I shouted at the guide and thumped my walking stick – the one I had bought in Chitral – on the wall to get his attention. Not realizing the strength of my anger and the hardness of the mud-brick, I brought the stick down again and it shattered into four pieces, leaving me holding just the crook in my hand.

'They'll be further on, close to the front line,' said Joe quietly.

It was impossible to imagine him doing anything so violent or stupid as I had just done. He still wasn't feeling particularly well, but that didn't stop him – any more than a broken bone in his foot would later.

I agreed; and we ploughed on together across the open field, carrying the videophone, the satellite phone and the camera equipment.

'Be very careful, John,' shouted one of the French photographers.

I looked up and realized I knew him. I waved, and we headed on. Obviously, the Foreign Ministry minders had filled the photographers with fear about the dangers of being so close to the front. To be honest, I didn't think it was particularly dangerous there; as long as the Americans kept hitting their enemies, that is, and not their friends.

In a building which formed part of the front line, and was as smashed as a Flanders farmhouse in 1917, we finally stumbled across Peter and Tony. They were sitting side by side on a bench in the sunshine, looking glum and saying little; and when I looked round and saw the mujaheddin soldiers they were with, I could understand it. Unusually for Northern Alliance troops, these were a nasty-looking bunch, lazy and hostile. But their position was a good one, right opposite the Arab trenches, and I knew that Peter was waiting there, putting up with the stupid insults and the mockery, until such time as the bombing started. Then the soldiers would be too preoccupied to take any of notice of Peter, Tony and the camera, and they could get the pictures they wanted.

But it wasn't any good for Joe and me. We needed freedom and cooperation if we were to be able to do our live broadcasts. Peter pointed out another shattered house nearby: you couldn't see the Taliban positions so clearly from there, but it was actually slightly closer to the Taliban front line. The soldiers who were manning it were a lot more friendly, Peter said.

It was a nasty, exposed walk, with nothing between us and any snipers who might be stationed on the Taliban front line, about eighty yards away, and it seemed to take much longer than the distance merited. It was a bad idea to hurry, though: that can give snipers unnecessary ideas. Eventually, we reached the lee of the damaged farmhouse and I beat on the ancient wooden door. If we hadn't known that there were soldiers here, we would have thought the whole place was just ruined and abandoned.

Rank bushes and trees grew unchecked around the walls, and there were signs of past fighting everywhere: empty boxes of high-velocity rounds, discarded pieces of clothing, the occasional bullet-hole in the walls. Eventually there came the sound reluctant feet, and the door was opened a crack. A boy of fifteen peered out at us, listened to Khalil's explanation of who we were, heard the magic name of Hajji Bari, and opened the door wider.

Inside was a gatehouse with dark little rooms opening on either side. I got a quick glimpse of blankets and teacups on the floor. This where the soldiers slept. Straight ahead of us lay the courtyard around which the farmhouse was built. It was all more than ever like the First World War: at least a couple of artillery rounds must have landed here at some point, and everything was churned up and wrecked: bits of farming equipment, furniture, clothes, shoes, the bones of long-dead animals lay everywhere. The buildings themselves were spectacularly damaged; and on the rooftop, up a flight of damaged steps, stood half a dozen soldiers like survivors of some terrible disaster. Peter had been right; there was no hostility here, just a great deal of nervousness. They were in the firing line, and it frightened them.

We walked carefully up the broken steps. I felt the need of the walking stick I had broken; we all have our fears, and mine was falling down and damaging my leg again, rather than the artillery fire from the other side – which, after all, I had no control over. This is not to say I wasn't experiencing fear. I was feeling quite anxious, and

I daresay Joe, who among his other achievements was a sergeant major in the Singaporean army reserve, was anxious too, though he wasn't showing it.

People who aren't nervous when they are in difficult places always worry me, because that means they are capable of doing any stupid thing. When the guns are going off, I like to have people around me with a proper sense of their own vulnerability. But we had a job to do, and we were here to do it. It isn't, I think, courage that makes you go on in cases like this, it is a sense of duty. I knew that Joe, like me, was anxious to get a really good series of broadcasts going when the action started, and that this mattered more to him than being certain of his own safety. What, after all, was the point of coming all this way and suffering all this discomfort, if we didn't push the boundaries a little?

For the most part the Northern Alliance soldiers here were really just kids. But they were excited to see us, and enthusiastic to help – as long as it didn't mean standing out in the open too much. And when I saw their firing positions, I could see why. We were unnervingly close to the nearest Taliban position, and must have offered the Arabs on the other side a most tempting target.

Both Joe and I could see where the best broadcasting position was: a wing of the farmhouse, opening out onto no man's land. The walls had been smashed by shells and bullets, and you could see the short intervening stretch of no man's land through the holes. There was also some suitable military equipment in the background: all perfect as the background for a live appearance by me. The only problem was that the garrison had been using this particular area as their toilet. And as I looked, there was stirring in the dust and broken lathes and excrement, and a dark, smallish rat came out and started nibbling away. I don't mind shells and bullets all that much, but I do draw the line at human crap and coprophagous rats.

'I think I should be somewhere over here,' I said firmly, pointing elsewhere. Joe agreed.

As it turned out, the position was rather a good one. Joe framed me with a broken, empty window behind me, and although it looked out along no man's land rather than directly at the Taliban trenches, a flash of reddish light shot across the gap and there was a loud explosion almost immediately afterwards. We had found ourselves in the middle of an exchange of fire between Northern Alliance and Taliban tanks; and now the afternoon's bombing by the Americans was just about to start. As long as no one hit us, we would be fine.

Time was getting on: one of the main bulletins was about twenty minutes away, so I gave it a ring.

'But is there anything actually happening?' asked the voice at the other end. London suddenly seemed a very long way indeed from this smelly, noisy, nerve-racking place.

'Nothing except a tank battle and some bombing by the Americans.'

'Then I don't think we'll take anything, thank you,' said the voice, as though I was trying to sell it double-glazing.

Editing a news bulletin is a mystery which I have never been inducted into, and would probably be bad at. It is also very difficult, and needs a good deal of nerve, especially when the unexpected happens. Anyway, we were free now to concentrate on the kind of customers who would be more interested; and after yesterday's experience World and News 24 were both enthusiastic.

For the next three hours, as the news approached, the two services crossed to us again and again. Suitable bangs and explosions took place each time, and as the evening wore on the flashes shone brighter and brighter in the encroaching darkness. There seemed to be a kind of alleyway next to our building down which passed the shells from the two sides, while the Americans returned three times altogether to bomb the Taliban line. Tracer fire, red and white, went up into the sky; and although it was all on the videophone, which meant that movement of any kind was a little awkward and jerky, the interviewers in London clearly relished the action that they could see.

Sitting on my camera-box talking to camera, with the excrement on the floor close beside me and Joe peering into the viewfinder, I felt surprisingly good. I long ago learned not to shut my eyes, flinch and hunch down when there was a loud bang close by; at least when I'm on camera. George Bowling, the hero of George Orwell's *Coming up for Air*, says he knew that a shell was coming for him during the First World War:

They say you always know. It didn't say what an ordinary shell says. It said 'I'm after you, you b——, *you*, you b——, YOU!' – all this in the space of about three seconds. And the last YOU was the explosion.'

I have great respect for Orwell as a writer, particularly on this kind of war, which must have had strong similarities with the Spanish Civil War in which he was a volunteer. But he's completely wrong about this. Sound travels much slower than light, and by the time you hear it, the bullet or the shell has missed you. It's the ones you don't hear that get you. So for the most part, what frightens you on the battlefield is the loud explosions of shells which have already gone past you. Looked at in the right way, this thought can almost be a comforting one.

As for the soldiers around us, they had long ago lost their nervousness, and were excited by the spectacle and by their grand-stand view of the whole thing.

'This is what television news should be all about,' Joe said happily when he finally decided the light had become too bad to do any more filming, and packed up the videophone.

He was right. There should be more to television news than a string of well-crafted but essentially static and safe reports; especially ones which contain too many glib spokesmen. Live reporting is the hardest and most rewarding broadcasting you can do, and live reporting from a battlefield is harder than any other kind. I don't flatter myself that anyone will remember what happened on 23 October 2001, but in its small way it was a first.

§

Audiences for television news and current-affairs programmes have been dropping slowly for the last fifteen years and more. They rise dramatically, of course, when important events occur, and there seems to be a lower limit below which audience levels are unlikely to fall: there will always be an irreducible number of people in any country with a genuine interest in what is happening in the world around them. But the signs are not particularly encouraging. People from eighteen to thirty watch television news the least, and the indications from the United States are that it is relatively rare for people to gain an interest in the real world in their thirties or older. If they don't have it when they're young, they may never have it at all.

In the 1950s and later (sometimes much later), watching the news was regarded as one of the things you had to do. It was part of being a British citizen, like voting or standing to attention when they played the national anthem in the cinema at the end of the evening's showing. The news induced a certain sense of respect in you: people wiser than yourself were telling you things you needed to know, and you had to listen politely to them even if you didn't really understand what it all meant. Watching the news was like taking a small homeopathic dose of Britain itself: respectful, accepting of authority, serious-minded, concerned.

That kind of response is fading out. Everything has changed. People consult their own wishes more, and are less concerned with what others think of them. Authority is no longer regarded as something which is valuable or admirable in itself. There are so many other competing interests and attractions in life, and even when you are sitting in front of the television set there are often plenty of programmes which are more exciting to watch than the news. Nor do you have to wait for the scheduled news bulletins to find out what is going on. There are several 24-hour channels which will give you the news now, without your having to wait. What's more, they will tell it to you in greater depth and at greater length than the conventional bulletins can. So the big news programmes aren't only losing the people whose interest in news isn't particularly strong, they're also losing the people who are really enthusiastic about it.

Still, things change. Each of the different news services which the BBC has introduced, from Radio 5 Live to News 24 to BBC World, has been a real success. In overall terms, more people are watching and listening to news than ever. BBC Online has become the most visited website in Europe, and half the hits on it are from the United States. 2001 was the year when, for the first time since the start of the 1960s, more people in Britain listened to BBC radio than watched BBC television. Back in the 1970s, when I worked for radio news, the advice of the older people there was to get out of radio while it was still possible, because there was no certainty radio would even exist in a quarter of a century. The quarter of a century is now up, and radio audiences are actually larger than television ones. The situation has rarely seemed healthier and more encouraging.

The same pattern has shown itself in the BBC's international broadcasting. Until two or three years ago there was considerable gloom in the radio World Service, as BBC World television gained more and more attention and respect internationally. Here too the radio people felt they had no real future, except in the foreign-language services. But all sorts of developments, not least the arrival of cheap satellite radio receivers for the developing world, have changed the position in the same way and at the same time. In 2001 the World Service achieved its highest audience figures ever, at around 150 million – very similar to BBC World's audience levels.

So when I go to Television Centre nowadays, I don't find despair – far from it. The news business is booming as never before. What I do find is puzzlement; no one has any clear idea how we can win back audiences for the big formal news programmes on domestic television.

The viewing figures for our main evening news went up when we changed its time from 9 p.m., partly because 10 p.m. is a better time for news anyway, and partly because the disastrous decision by ITV to move ITN's main bulletin around provided the BBC with extra viewers.

It was a bad mistake by the ITV companies, and the BBC won't be doing the same thing. The board of governors, who are put there to protect the overall public interest, wouldn't allow it anyway. But there is pressure from the programme chiefs on the news programmes to look for ways of increasing their audience figures. Nothing wrong with that, of course: the editors of news programmes should constantly be trying to attract more viewers. One of the reasons that news is declining in every Western country is that television stations have habitually relied on old, conventional formulas instead of looking for new ways of persuading people to watch.

But there is a danger. Teams of audience-research people scour the country asking viewers what sort of news they want to see, and in the absence of any particularly inspiring idea (because none of us really knows what sort of news we would like to be told, apart from England winning the World Cup, crime figures imploding, Osama bin Laden taking a career break, and all those cloned American coffee shops in our high streets closing down) they tick the boxes which say they would like to have more local news, consumer news, and news about entertainment. If there were a box that said 'no more gloomy news about depressing things we can't do anything about', they would tick that too.

Yet this is quite clearly no way for television news to go about trying to attract people back to their bulletins, or else it would have succeeded long ago in the United States, which has gone through all these processes far more intensively than Europe has. Instead, American audiences for news programmes are dropping even faster than they did when the broadcasters gave them at least some semblance of proper information.

No; the wrong questions are being asked. People have an urgent need to know if their lives are going to be changed by economic issues, by politics, by terrorism, by ecological factors. They need to be given the facts to make up their own minds on questions like 'The War against Terror' and English devolution and the euro. This isn't arrogance or a belief in the right of broadcasters to tell people what to think, it's actually the reverse: the most arrogant approach is to say that all people can understand is news about crime and traffic and consumer affairs and the weather and show business, so that's all they'll get. The world is a difficult, dangerous, highly complex place, and unless we help people understand it to the best of our ability, we are failing them in the most shameful manner. And – as happened with American audiences after 11 September – they will turn on us angrily and demand to know why we let them down.

The American example is an important one, because it shows us what we must avoid. Viewing figures being the life and death of commercial television, all that counted was to provide information which appealed to the lowest common denominator. That emphasized the local: regional news in the first instance, American news in the second. Everyone who has been to the United States and switched on a television set at news time will have had the experience of listening to the introduction about 'Here with the national and international news is . . .' and then watched headlines about car crashes, light aircraft crashes, local disasters and local crimes.

A depressing downward progression has followed. The less people were told about the outside world, the less they could understand it.

The less they could understand it, the harder it was to tell them. The harder it was to tell them, the less it became possible to tell them. So they knew less, and could be told less, and knew even less and could be told even less. The circles of ignorance and dereliction of duty became smaller and smaller, until in many cases no one is telling anyone anything of real importance whatsoever.

It isn't even as though it costs so much nowadays to tell people what is going on in the world. Foreign news, which used to cost so much compared with domestic news, is getting cheaper all the time, as the technology for getting pictures and sending them back shrinks and becomes less expensive. The picture agencies, Reuters and APTN, have reached remarkable new levels of quality, and their reach is global. The world comes to every television station hour by hour each day, as the agencies offer up their material. There is nothing to stop them from informing people better, except their own reluctance.

Early in 2002 I spoke to an informal group of BBC News people about our news coverage. In the course of the meeting, I argued strongly that the domestic news bulletins should be taking more foreign news; especially the *Six O'Clock News*. It is, after all, my job to argue for more foreign news on the air. Someone in the room rang up a magazine with an inaccurate version of what I had said, and the magazine, not understanding what it was all about or troubling to speak to me first, made further mistakes in reporting it. Over the next fortnight, such is the speed of modern newspapers, *The Times* and the *Independent* printed the story with even more mistakes – and of course without speaking to me either. I was presented as a dissident, criticizing the entire direction that BBC News was taking.

It annoyed me, not only because it wasn't true, but because if I had wanted to criticize the BBC publicly I hope, as I have said before, that I would have had the decency to stop taking its money first. I certainly believe there should be a lively debate within the BBC about the future of its broadcasting, but I don't think the right place to conduct it is in the pages of magazines and newspapers that can't get the argument right.

I'm not a dissident. On the contrary, I'm very proud of the way things are going in the BBC. As it happens, I don't think there is a problem about the direction its news is taking. Memories are very short, and it has become so fashionable to speak about 'dumbing down' that no one seems to recall how uninspired the quality of our television news programmes was in the 1970s or early 1980s. Our radio programmes, too. Some were so parochial, so dull, that I used to find them unbearable to listen to. Now anyone in Britain who needs to know what is going on has to listen to some part of the *Today* programme every morning. That is in great part the work of the cantankerous John Humphrys.

Humphrys is the kind of star you only really get in journalism. He is often gruff and not always in the best of tempers; though ever since he and his beautiful wife Val – one of the presenters who questioned me over the videophone in Afghanistan – gave birth to their son Owen, he has been a changed man.

It is a long time now since he and I bumped into one another in the sixth-floor corridor at Television Centre, and he told me the management were suggesting that he should present *Today* instead of the *Nine O'Clock News*.

'Do you think they're trying to get rid of me?' he asked me.

It's the kind of question we tend to ask ourselves in the Corporation.

As it happened, I knew they weren't. I also knew he didn't have any choice but to accept, so I told him he would enjoy *Today* hugely and could let his personality off the leash there. His success wasn't immediate, but it was quite extraordinary. And it has made him one of the top broadcasters in Britain. That's worth pausing over for a moment: a grey-haired man in his late fifties appears on a radio current-affairs programme and becomes one of the most famous people in the country. It's not, you must agree, altogether predictable.

Today has gone counter to the depressing decline of news programmes. It gave up the unchallenging, the relentlessly jolly, the small-town, the easy-listening approach of twenty years or more ago, and it has taken on the big issues of the day without making any concessions other than to explain things carefully and sensibly. Politics, which according to the currently perceived wisdom among broadcasters is dull and a switch-off, is the *Today* programme's lifeblood. Hearing some leading political figure being given the once-over by a *Today* interviewer is fascinating and revealing listening.

The success of *Today* shows that not a single one of these gloomy notions – that people aren't interested in politics, that they don't care about the outside world, that they are tuning in to news programmes less, that they can't handle difficult subjects and must be fed a diet of consumerism, local crime and notable accidents – is necessarily true. All you have to do to have a successful news programme is to pitch interesting things to people at the right level. You have no right whatever to bore them, or make them feel stupid, or talk over their heads. It isn't, in other words, the news *per se* which is a switch-off; it's dull, unchanging, unimaginative conventions which some news programmes employ – the formulaic approach, which is as lively and varied and changeable as the hieroglyphics on a temple wall in Egypt.

Let's look at some of the elements which are involved in this: the presenters, for instance. The tradition, when a programme needs a makeover, is to bring in younger presenters to replace the old ones – and, in particular, the old male ones. But where does that leave John Humphrys? He, after all, is a major reason why more people than ever are listening to the *Today* programme. And if you think that's simply because Radio 4 listeners are middle-aged, middle-class Southerners (the type of audience, incidentally, which any advertising agency would die for) then how do you explain the fact that the most popular news presenters in the history of British television were the ITN duo of Sandy Gall and Reginald Bosanquet – rather grand characters, each in their fifties, the latter of whom was not entirely a stranger to the bottle?

It seems to be the case that viewers of all ages like to watch news presenters with a bit of character; the kind who look as though they have knocked around a little and know the world for what it is. Anna Ford has triumphantly disproved the notion that women can't continue presenting news programmes with style much after the age of forty. What counts is her personality and her ability; we want to hear the questions she is going to ask. Character, intelligence, experience: people like to be told the news by presenters who are clearly interesting in themselves, and who know what they're talking about, regardless of age.

It should be the essence of a good news programme that it seeks to attract and interest everyone. We need good, attractive young presenters and reporters, and we need good older ones too; it's not the age that counts, it's the quality. And if you're thinking to yourself that at the age of fifty-seven I would say these things as a matter of course, I must tell you that I'm not eyeing up a job reading the news myself. I did it in the past, not very well, and found it hugely boring and unsatisfactory. I'd never go back to it, even if it were offered to me; which it never will be.

As it happens, the BBC has a good variety of news presenters. But what about the unbreakable formulas – the suits, the studio desks, the headlines, the set-piece introductions, the goodbye smile and the shuffling of papers at the end? If you have a hundred satellite television channels, you can watch news presenters right across the known universe doing precisely the same thing. Sometimes the news items are different, sometimes they're the same; but the presentation is almost identical. That either means it's perfect, or else we need a change; and the falling audience levels across the world suggest it may not be entirely perfect.

In Britain the BBC, ITV News, Sky, are all puzzling their heads nowadays about how to make their news programmes more attractive. There are no easy solutions; it isn't enough, for instance, to say that since political news bores people, we should have less of it. That certainly isn't an option for the BBC, at any rate. Instead, we have to find more attractive and absorbing ways of presenting political news to people. And not just politics. The longer I work for television news, the more I realize that we need to offer people a more varied set of choices in general: more news about the environment, more insight into crime and fashion and entertainment and nuclear weaponry, more investigations into corruption and price-fixing at home and abroad, more adventure. The world is a big, complex and very exciting place: why doesn't that come over more on television news? Why do most of the reports on domestic television news come from the same few, predictable places?

The editors, the producers, the correspondents, the cameramen and the studio staff in British television news are of better calibre nowadays than they have ever been. That needs to be reflected in the quality and variety of the stories we broadcast in our news programmes. And we need to free up our techniques too.

It was with some such idea that, back in 1997, I proposed a new type of programme, which would be less restricted and formulaic, and would allow people to see something of a place for themselves, instead of having to view it solely through our eyes. BBC News 24 and BBC World, being new themselves, were both enthusiastic. I was fortunate enough to have the backing of a dynamic and imaginative set of bosses, Tim Orchard and Bill Taylor (now both, unfortunately, lost to the BBC), and they encouraged the whole idea and acted as its godfathers.

It was simple enough: we would take a camera out onto the streets of wherever I happened to be, and interview some interesting guest as we walked around. It would be entirely unscripted, and we wouldn't edit it; we would simply show the viewers what happened to us during the twenty-five minutes the programme lasted.

Our first programme was filmed in Algiers, at a time of considerable tension. I interviewed the BBC North Africa correspondent, with a group of twelve armed policemen standing round us to protect us – they said – from attack. I never knew how likely such an attack was, though I soon came to believe that the greatest number of murders were being carried out by the Algerian government itself, determined to stamp out fundamentalism.

Paul Simpson was the first producer – suitably enough, for a programme known as *Simpson's World*. It proved very difficult for the cameraman, and was made more difficult still when a crowd of about two dozen young Algerians mobbed us, in spite of the efforts of our police guards.

'I can't get them out of the shot,' the cameraman grunted, going almost down to the ground in an effort to avoid showing the excitable kids as they jumped around us.

It was then that I had the defining idea for the way the programme should develop.

'Don't bother,' I said. 'They're here, so you might as well show them.'

So he straightened up, and was able to concentrate much more on showing the streets and the people surrounding us; though our police guards did their best to keep out of the picture. Instead of trying to pretend that the crowd wasn't there, we made a virtue of showing it, and interviewed several of the young kids around us about the conditions of their lives. One in particular stays in my mind to this day, a tall, stringy young-old character of around seventeen, studious and desperate.

What is there for us here? Nothing. No jobs, no money, no future. And if we try to go to Europe, Europe doesn't want us. We are prisoners, prisoners for ever in our own country. Can you tell me what will happen to us? Of course you can't. You will go away, and forget what you have seen here. And when you are a long way away, we will still be here. We will still be prisoners.

It wasn't a very good programme, because it was so rough and uncertain; but I felt this one interview provided such an insight into the minds of people who had to live in a country which the outside world saw so little of, that it alone justified the entire twenty-five minutes.

My wife Dee, who was a freelance film producer in South Africa for some years and was taken onto the BBC's staff in Johannesburg at the time of Nelson Mandela's election there in 1994, became the producer of *Simpson's World*, and started travelling with me wherever I went in order to produce it. And in case you think this must be a nice little earner for the Simpsons, I should tell you she gets less than the equivalent of Supplementary Benefit for her work on it; but this doesn't matter to us, because the BBC pays for her travel, and it means we can stay together.

The cameraman who established the basic techniques for the programme is a good friend of mine, Bob Prabhu, with whom I have worked for twenty years. He grasped the concept immediately, and started developing it. Cameramen who have spent their entire careers trying to keep the camera straight and keeping extraneous elements out of the shot find it hard to understand that we don't mind if it wobbles, and bystanders stray into view. The more bystanders the better, I feel. Once, in the Old City of Jerusalem, when Bob was walking backwards down those lethal wet limestone steps, he lost his footing and fell into a large rubbish bin. It took two of us to pull him out – and we left the whole sequence in when we broadcast it.

In Moscow we made a *Simpson's World* in the Metro, and were arrested because we had decided not to go through the impossibly bureaucratic business of getting an official permit to film. We carried on with the programme while our fixer, Olga Mesherikova, talked her way and ours out of trouble. (Olga, who had the dignity and bearing and beauty of a Tolstoyan heroine, died in 2001 at a depressingly early age of heart disease: a victim of the system which stole her family estates after the Revolution, killed her parents and grandparents, and left her an outsider in her own country. But at least she had the pleasure of watching the corrupt old system collapse, and could explain everything about it to her daughter Anya before she died.)

In a nasty little drugs town in Colombia we wandered around talking about the way the cocaine trade had affected the entire country; and while we did so, Bob broke away to film a machete fight between two thugs which broke out alongside us. That was, we all felt, vintage *Simpson's World*. We have wandered round some difficult places in our time: the Tehran bazaar, the streets of Belgrade during the NATO bombing (this was one of Dee's best programmes), and Bethlehem during the Israeli army incursion, when we weren't entirely sure we would survive. Colonel Gadhafi was interviewed for *Simpson's World* in his desert tent, and King Abdullah II of Jordan, a charming young man, showed me round the portraits of his ancestors and answered some difficult questions with great skill while his press secretary kept hissing at me to stop.

Some of my BBC colleagues think it is far too rambling and unstructured, and wince at the amount of verbal stumbling (mine and others'). But when it is on form, I believe it can illumine things a great deal better than the highly polished, perfectly edited reports we see all the time on television. I want it to be as natural as we can make it: a 25-minute section cut out of reality, unretouched and unpolished. Above all, I want to allow people to make up their own minds about what they are seeing; I don't want to dictate to them what they should think. Chekhov once wrote a letter to Olga Knipper in which he likened his work of a playwright to that of a trial lawyer. It was his job, he said, to lay the facts before the jury, not to tell them how to react to them. I agree completely.

And, I have to say, the programme has an extraordinary following. It is only broadcast twice a month, but its audience has been estimated at 140 million. That number includes, I am told, Saddam Hussein (who has apparently had his criticisms of various editions; it sounds disturbing), Colonel Gadhafi himself, and all sorts of leading politicians who are, perhaps, a little more mainstream. The Emperor of Japan (to name-drop further) is an enthusiast for it: he told me so when I met him at the palace in Tokyo, before his visit to London. Once, when we recorded an edition in an Israeli settlement, talking to the settlers, a man ran down the road from his house fifty yards away, calling out my name. I am used to a certain amount of occasional abuse, so I prepared myself for something unpleasant. Instead, he said he had recognized me by my walk, and wanted to shake hands with me.

'What can we refuse to *Simpson World*?' asked a shopkeeper in Isfahan, when I asked him if we could come in and film his carpets; and the programme's mere arrival in places from Hong Kong and Singapore to Stockholm and The Hague has been enough to make newspaper headlines. Forgive me if I boast about it, but I love it as fiercely as though it were my own slightly ugly, not very clever child; and I feel it proves that a cut-price television show with minimal back-up and resources is capable of opening windows.

There isn't room for more than one or two programmes on television as unstructured as this, but somewhere in our perfectly crafted schedules there ought to be room for a shaggy, unprescriptive, uncut look at real life. And perhaps it has one thing to teach the rest of television news: the virtue of relaxing a little, of becoming a touch more natural. And of looking at the world with new eyes.

15

Finishing the Job

Charikar and Kabul:
Sunday 11 November to Tuesday 13 November 2001

Five o'clock on Sunday morning: I woke up believing that, at long last, the big attack was going to happen. Hajji Bari had told us the previous afternoon to be ready to leave for the front line at six. I switched on the BBC: at the United Nations President George W. Bush and President Musharaf of Pakistan had both called on the Northern Alliance not to enter Kabul. Some commentators were interpreting this as a warning to the Alliance not to *attack* Kabul; they forgot that in politics and diplomacy you have to look at the use of words very carefully. The Northern Alliance had already said quite clearly they wouldn't enter Kabul; so Bush and Musharaf were merely telling them not to do something they weren't planning to do anyway.

But it all seemed deeply confusing, and the mood among the journalists based at the Foreign Ministry in Jabal Saraj was gloomy. Some of them, indeed, had decided that nothing was going to happen until the following spring, and had left for home a couple of days earlier. I didn't think they were right, but nothing that was happening sounded like the prelude to an immediate attack.

At six o'clock there was no sign of Hajji. He eventually turned up at around ten, complaining that we had hired a new driver from someone other than him. He didn't even mention the possibility of an attack. We covered our deep disappointment as best we could, and took refuge in Rahman Beg impersonations: 'Why not?' and 'Is finish?', with forefingers in the air and eyes rolling. It didn't help much.

A couple of weeks earlier we had hired a new translator and local fixer, Khair Mohammed. This had brought us a lot of grief from the

Foreign Ministry, who claimed the sole right to hire out translators to foreign journalists. We suspected that any translators we hired from them would be useless, and would only be there to keep an eye on us and report back. Khair Mohammed, anyway, had other advantages: his father was the top man in Northern Alliance military intelligence, who seemed to be passing messages to us via his son.

Now Khair Mohammed arrived, as neat and well-groomed and quiet-spoken as always. I walked up and down the corridor with him for greater security, as he told me the latest.

'My father say, America only seeming to say no to Northern Alliance to please Pakistan. Attack will take place tomorrow, as I told you. Don't have worries.'

It was true: Khair Mohammed had told us the attack would happen on Monday; it was just that Hajji Bari had seemed so certain it would be today.

We had been invited to lunch by General Anwari, the head of the mostly Hazara Harakat-e Islami group. We were quite a big party: apart from our immediate group there was another new translator whom Nick Springate had found. He had been the professor of English at Kabul University, and was charming, studious and strangely bird-like, with a thin beaky face and an odd cowlick of hair across his forehead. Others in the group were Tony Davis, the Australian journalist who knew Afghanistan well, John Jennings, the American ex-Marine who had been with Peter Jouvenal and me when we tracked down Commander Zardad in London, Anthony Loyd, *The Times* correspondent, and his photographer friend, Seamus Murphy, both of whom I had come to like very much indeed. In particular I admired their way of going off quietly and finding good, untold stories by simply meeting different people around the front line and staying with them for long periods at a time. You can't do this kind of thing very easily for television, but it seemed to me to make the best kind of newspaper reporting.

Anwari greeted us with considerable warmth at his headquarters, a little way from Jabal. Peter Jouvenal and I had, after all, put his organization on the map back in 1989 by going with them to Kabul, and Anwari had been a senior figure in the mujaheddin ever since. We owed him and his top men a great deal, too. Abu Faisal, whose courage and toughness had saved our lives back then in Kabul, was

there too, and our meeting became quite emotional. You could see
the effect of the injuries he had suffered as a result of helping us. He
was still a big man, but he seemed thinner and slower and quieter
than before.

We all sat round the tablecloth on the floor, which was covered
with good things: fresh vegetables, fruit, yoghurt, bread, great
mounds of rice flecked with berries and spices, and a dozen different
dishes of varying heat and ferocity. After the scanty diet at Bin Laden
Mansions it was unforgettable. Anwari still had many complaints
about the Americans, their closeness to Pakistan, the suspicion with
which they continued to regard the Northern Alliance, their unwillingness to throw everything into the attack on the Taliban, their
unceasing caution and slowness. But the Northern Alliance, under
General Dostam, an Uzbek leader of great ferocity, had recently
captured the vital town of Mazar-e Sharif from the Taliban, and that
was clearly the beginning of the end. Anwari was a very happy man.

So, by the end of lunch, were we. I had learned to believe
everything that Khair Mohammed told me, because it invariably came
true; but it was good to have Anwari's endorsement of his assurance
that the big attack would take place tomorrow. The food cheered us
up, too, and so did the English of one of Anwari's top assistants, who
(together with John Jennings) did the translating. In particular, he
found it difficult to say the words 'terrorism' and 'terrorists'; they
came out as 'tourism' and 'tourists'.

'Anwari says absolutely essential to stamp out tourism from the
world. Any tourists should be arrested and put on trial. He says
tourism is the great evil of modern times.'

'I absolutely agree with him,' I answered. 'I don't feel that
Western governments are nearly tough enough on tourism. They
should stamp it out once and for all.'

It was turning into a good day altogether. As I sat writing in my
room at Bin Laden Mansions, there was the roar of a lorry engine
outside, and a good deal of hooting and excitability. I kept on writing
because I had a deadline, but when I heard the sound of loud,
cheerful conversation and some new voices, I went out to see what it
was all about. The satellite gear had arrived from Northern Afghanistan, with its Russian engineers and its BBC producer. Dumeetha
Luthra, bright and enthusiastic despite her awful journey, had been

with us on the charter from Dubai. I marvelled that someone as delicate as she looked could have endured the trip down from Hodge and looked so good on it.

The timing of the dish's arrival was as good as it could have been. The engineers were able to get everything up and running just in time for the big assault. It was an extraordinary success for us, and owed a great deal to the planning skills of Nick Springate and the determination of Dumeetha. Her journey over Anjuman with the truck, in snow and freezing temperatures, sounded far worse than ours.

She and the others had brought all sorts of things with them: cold-weather clothes, gadgets like head-torches and tin-openers, some medicine I needed, some really powerful painkillers, some excellent cigars, and – best of all – sizeable quantities of alcohol. Somebody, knowing my weakness for Laphroaig, had put a bottle in for me: an act of great thoughtfulness and charity. There were also some books, which I badly needed too: Dickens and Trollope; but, through a rather charming misunderstanding, the Trollope wasn't Anthony, as I had expected, but Joanna. No matter: I read that too, and enjoyed it.

At this point, when it seemed that Christmas had come early, General Gul Haidar, the one-legged raider who had been put in overall charge of the assault on Kabul, came bursting into Bin Laden Mansions, shouting greetings, accepting all sorts of food he had never eaten before, and eyeing up the bottles of booze speculatively. It was, he said, all on for tomorrow; and the Northern Alliance had been approached by a very senior commander on the Taliban side, who promised to come over to them directly the fighting began.

That night those of us who were going to Kabul with the attackers got all our things ready for the morning and left them in the corridor outside our rooms. I was just taking a rucksack and my flak jacket. Everything else I had with me – the carpets, the heavier gear, even the *chapan* – would be shipped down to Kabul once we arrived there. Nobody doubted that we would. I lay down on the floor and went straight to sleep, too tired even to speculate about the coming dangers or where I might spend the following night.

At six o'clock I was up, and we loaded our gear into the jeeps and headed down to the front line. There were already columns of smoke going up, and violent, jolting explosions. We got as close as we could to where the actual fighting was just starting. Joe and I went into a bombed and wrecked farmhouse to set up the camera and perhaps the videophone; though at the moment we were far ahead of London time and couldn't do any live broadcasting for the different programmes. The half-dozen Northern Alliance troops who were based there were too stoned to stop us, or even take much interest. We hoped they weren't typical of the rest of the army.

Joe found a niche on the top floor, overlooking the front line, with a wrecked piece of wall to lean against. But after two bullets went by so close that we could hear them crack nastily in the air as they passed, I told Joe to pack up his equipment and go down again. This was going to be a long day, and an important battle. I didn't want anything to happen to him or me which might stop us reporting it. A major rocket and artillery duel was starting up. The Chinese rockets of the Northern Alliance were seeking out the Taliban's Russian rocket-launchers, and vice versa. They arched through the sky over our heads and crashed into the hilltops a couple of miles or so on either side of us. Then the tanks opened up. The Taliban tanks, which were mostly being used as mobile artillery, had taken a considerable beating from the American bombing, yet there seemed to be plenty of them around still; as the Iraqis had proved in 1991 and the Serbs in 1999, air power alone cannot take out everything.

By now we could hear the deep rumbling of aircraft engines coming down the valley. It was a sound we had become thoroughly used to over the past few weeks, and soon the silver crosses of a couple of B-52s showed in the sky, leaving their huge four-track vapour trails three miles above us. They wheeled majestically around, and brown and grey smoke boiled up out of the ground quite close to us, mounting into the sky, and the shuddering sound hit us again and again. More American planes were flying down from Uzbekistan to join them, their vapour trails crossing one another, and the smoke went up and we were jolted by more explosions, and then more. Joe and I walked past Peter Emmerson and Kate Clark as they were trying to put over a report to the BBC World Service, who are notorious sticklers for good quality of sound. I could hear Kate apologizing to the studio engineers down the satellite phone.

'It's just that it's very noisy here,' she was saying.

They had asked her to do it again, without the unacceptable background sound.

Fortunately, the television bulletins were rather more in favour of that sort of thing, and we were able to supply it. We set up the videophone on the lip of a trench, and called *Breakfast News*. Jeremy Bowen, who had covered so many battles himself over the years, was the ideal interviewer. He seemed to know precisely the right questions to ask, at precisely the right moment; and he left me free whenever I wanted to break off and describe the action that was taking place thunderously all round us. At the end of our interview he said, 'Enjoy yourself!' It was vintage Bowen. I knew how much he would have enjoyed it too, if he had been there alongside me.

I heard later that some of the more politically correct elements rebuked him after the programme, on the grounds that it was unacceptable to suggest that anyone should enjoy reporting on a war. That seems to me like Pecksniffian humbug. I don't like wars in the slightest, and regard them as fundamentally evil – especially when the people who are being killed are mostly civilians. But this was, by contrast, a very different kind of war, in which the casualties were numbered in dozens rather than hundreds or thousands, and very few civilians died.

It would be dishonest to deny that there was a certain excitement at being so close to the action, and at getting such magnificent front-line pictures; and Jeremy understood that. It wasn't the prospect of blood that was attractive: far from it. But there was an undeniable excitement in the air, now that the culmination of all our efforts had arrived; and the personal risk involved in getting the results we wanted gave me, and I'm sure the others with me, a heightened sense of anticipation and – yes – enjoyment. I don't think there is anything to be ashamed of in that. Jeremy Bowen said what he did because he understood from his own experience what we were likely to be feeling.

We needed to get on now; the Northern Alliance forces were starting to push forward and take some Taliban positions. In order to make our way forward we had a long and rather nerve-racking walk of a quarter of a mile along the road which ran through no man's land, parallel to the Taliban front line. We were outlined clearly against the sky, but no one shot at us; maybe they were too preoccupied by the American air raids and the continuing rocket attacks. We set up the videophone in seven different places altogether that morning, reporting each time for three or more programmes.

Not all the live shots were successful: several times the presenters at the other end seemed to think I was still in Northern Afghanistan, and I had to explain without seeming to be irritable that I was actually describing the things I could see around me with my own eyes. Once, nervous that we might be in the way of a Taliban counter-attack, we dodged into a decayed vineyard which had largely been taken over by wasps. They buzzed angrily round my head as I answered the questions, and during one interview one of them landed on my face. I had to brush it away on camera without letting it sting me. Not at all easy.

Afterwards we were moving cautiously forwards down a lane with the characteristic high mud walls of vineyards on either side of us. Ahead lay what seemed to be the foremost point the Northern Alliance had reached; a couple of armoured vehicles had come to a stop there. As we got nearer, some of the soldiers came running back towards us.

'A tank is breaking out! A Taliban tank! It's coming this way!'

That, at least, is what I assume they were saying, since these were the facts of the situation; but I couldn't really understand their nervous, excited babble. They ran into one of the vineyards, and it wasn't clear to me whether they were trying to escape from the tank, or looking for a position from which they could ambush it. Maybe they weren't sure either.

The group of seven or eight of us felt distinctly vulnerable. If the tank came down this narrow lane, as it seemed it might, its crew would certainly take us for American special forces and fire on us. We had to be under cover, but able to get shots of the tank at the same time. We jogged back down the lane with our gear, looking for somewhere to hide, and at last found an entrance to a vineyard where the walls had been broken down.

Peter Jouvenal, looking back at the Northern Alliance lines, thought he saw some men on the rooftop of a nearby farmhouse, looking in our general direction. Anthony Loyd peered through his binoculars, and said he was sure they were American forward spotters.

'As far as I can see, they've got fair hair and light skins.'

We didn't want them to see us, any more than we wanted the Taliban tank to. In war, soldiers have an understandable tendency to attack first and identify the bodies later. There were so many American planes circling in the sky and coming down into the attack on call, that it would have been very easy for the spotters to have summoned an air strike to get rid of us. Every few minutes another column of dirty smoke would go up in the air, and another explosion would assault our ears.

Then the Taliban tank made its run. I thought it was an act of great courage, to attack an army which was so far superior in weapons and air-power. As it turned out, the tank was a little way away from us as it broke through and made its way across no man's land, and we weren't in any danger from it. Peter Jouvenal got an excellent shot of the forward spotters on the rooftop pointing at it and shouting into their walkie-talkies, and a few minutes later an American plane came screaming down above us, quite low, and dropped a bomb on it. The tank exploded in a sheet of flame. It was the last act of serious resistance by the Taliban.

We made the long walk back through no man's land to find our vehicles. It was 12.15. It seemed clear that the Taliban resistance had crumbled here in the Shomali Valley, and that the Northern Alliance would soon start the big advance on Kabul. But for the moment the pounding still went on. On the edges of the valley, American planes were bombing the Taliban positions in the deserted villages which protected the flanks of the main Taliban force. Joe and I were in one vehicle, Peter in the other.

It was here that we had one of those arguments which sometimes erupt in the tense atmosphere of battle. Peter is by nature and experience a loner. He knows how to get the best pictures, and doesn't want anyone to stop him. I, on the other hand, had to do my next report on the videophone for London, and this was the best position to do it from. It didn't feel very safe, being out here in the open with so many explosions going on around us, but the bombing was clearly visible in the background to the shot. These things cannot be hurried, unfortunately.

I also wanted to make sure that the two cameramen I was working with stayed together. We had bought some walkie-talkies from – no surprise – Hajji Bari, but they didn't seem to work very well, and certainly weren't trustworthy. I didn't want us to split up in the heat of battle, because we might never have found each other again, and I would need both Peter's and Joe's pictures for my report in five or six hours' time.

At the same time, I knew we needed more pictures to link our sequences together and explain to the viewer what was happening. By now we had reached the main Charikar–Kabul road, from which we had branched off earlier that morning, and stopped at the point where it crossed into no man's land. There were good pictures to be had all round us, as the American planes raced across the sky for the kill, and the Taliban positions exploded in flame and smoke. And I needed to do a piece to camera: that linking device which gives you the authority to tell the viewer what is happening, because it shows you are there at the critical moment.

All this was too much for Peter. He didn't want to be hanging round on the road, he wanted to be in there with the first column to break through to Kabul. So he drove off. I was, I confess, pretty angry. But it was a classic example of the difference between the instincts of a freelance cameraman, hungry for the best pictures, and a correspondent who knows what material he needs to build up a good narrative account of what is going on.

So now it was just Joe and Khalil and me. We had to force our unwilling driver to head off the road on a small track which led across no man's land to a position which seemed to be in Northern Alliance hands now, but which had until a few minutes ago been a key part of the Taliban front line. We could see the soldiers standing on the roof, waving with joy.

In the time it took us to get there, the victorious troops received orders to head on to the next position. I looked at my watch: the 10 a.m. news bulletins would require something from me in fifteen minutes, and up here, on the Taliban front line, seemed the best place to do our next set of two-ways. So Joe and I sat on the rooftop and waited, uncomfortably aware that the Northern Alliance army was sweeping forward fast and we were in danger of being left behind. A couple of buses arrived to take the troops further forward, and we still had to wait where we were. Finally the minute hand reached the hour, and we were able to do the two-ways we had been waiting for. At least one of them was less successful than it might have been.

'I know you're not able to see this yourself,' said the interviewer, presumably believing I was in Northern Afghanistan, 'but we're getting reports from the A[gence] F[rance] P[resse] news agency that the Northern Alliance have broken through the Taliban front line. Do you have any confirmation of this in any way?'

I explained politely that the fact that I was talking to her as I sat on the wall of a building which had still been part of the Taliban front line half an hour before meant there was a fairly reasonable chance the report might be true. The poor presenter was thoroughly thrown by this, and ended the interview quite soon afterwards. Maybe she thought I had driven down the motorway from Northern Afghanistan very fast that morning, or maybe her idea of news was that it came in neat paragraphs from news agencies via the screen of a desktop computer, and that the job of journalists was to read it, rather than to experience it. It's easy to mock people who perhaps have only just come on duty, or who haven't had proper briefings about what is going on. And anyway, I'm sure I wouldn't have been nearly as good as she was at presenting the news.

Directly all this was over, Joe packed up the videophone gear and we jumped into the jeep with Khalil. Just at that point a column of jeeps containing Northern Alliance troops came sweeping through the dust and down the track into Taliban-held territory; and we slotted ourselves into the back of the line and followed through, indistinguishable from them. At this stage we were, I suppose, about twenty-five minutes behind the first wave of attack troops, but Peter was with them. And we had the satisfaction of being way ahead of the other journalists.

The dust cleared a little way through the line. We drove fast along the little lanes until we came to a village where the Northern Alliance spearhead had halted. It was twenty minutes to the hour: enough time to do some filming, then set up the videophone and do some more two-ways for the next round of news programmes. There was laughing: a group of soldiers came running towards us, carrying an assortment of things they had looted from the Taliban: rolled-up carpets, a chair, clothes, a cardboard suitcase.

'Taliban!' they shouted into the camera lens, laughing and gambolling around like kids.

Almost immediately afterwards we heard groaning, and saw a large Northern Alliance soldier staggering along under the weight of a man's body, which was draped across his arms like the looted carpet we had just seen. He set his burden down with some care under a tree, and Joe moved in to film the injured man. He had taken a shot, or perhaps a piece of shrapnel, in the chest, and the dark stain was still spreading. He wheezed, and his eyes rolled up. Enthusiasts recklessly tried to hold him up for the camera, but I, standing behind Joe, waved at them to let him lie flat: who knew what damage might have been done to his internal organs?

Not that there was any chance whatever of getting medical care for him; the Northern Alliance might be allied to the Americans, but they got no help from them except for the Russian weapons they carried, and which the Americans had paid for. No field hospitals, no surgeons, no care beyond what the other soldiers could give him: which was nothing at all. And yet such is the magnetic force of television that the man lifted his head to take a look at Joe, then sank back, dying, into the arms of his friends, like Nelson on the *Victory*. I should imagine he was dead within minutes.

We had seen Peter's vehicle abandoned by the side of the road at the entrance to this little village (which was called Singid Darra). He, meanwhile, had followed a group of soldiers who were hunting down the Taliban from the garrison here. They had caught up with them in the fields outside and slaughtered them out of hand. If they had been Afghans, they would certainly have spared their lives. Instead they were Pakistanis, and the Northern Alliance, like a clear majority of Afghans, regarded Pakistan and its people as the source of their country's disasters.

Peter didn't film the deaths; they would of course have been quite unusable in television terms. But he did film the Northern Alliance soldiers going through the pathetic loot they found on the bodies: pens, a few useless Pakistani rupees, letters from home, passports.

'Pakistani! Taliban!' screamed one of the executioners into Peter's lens. He was still almost hysterical with the excitement of having done the passport's poor owner to death.

A little later, Peter came across General Gul Haidar, the overall commander of the attack: the man whose prosthetic leg Peter had paid for. Gul Haidar had just got out of his car to examine a group of prisoners from Singid Darra, including an elderly Turk.

'You old fool!' Gul Haidar shouted at him, partly for the benefit of Peter's camera and partly for his men's. 'What are you doing, coming here to ruin my country like this?'

He grabbed the old man by the beard and shook his head like a cat shakes a bird, while the Northern Alliance soldiers laughed sycophantically. The old man reacted rather well, I thought: he resisted, and shouted something in Turkish. Gul Haidar clipped him round the ear and laughed. He must have thought this was what our viewers wanted to see. The old man was bundled off with the other prisoners onto the back of a truck, and driven away. Once they had been arrested, though, they would all have survived the experience. Afghans can be appallingly brutal in the heat of the moment, but after a while, when the Northern Alliance men cooled down, they will have remembered that there was credit to be obtained for capturing prisoners, and perhaps some reward too. Soldiers must have been like this in the Hundred Years' War, I thought.

Joe, Khalil and I threw the gear into the jeep and raced on. The light was fading fast, and we would have to hurry if we were to do another piece to camera. I felt that it was important, because the one I had done earlier, when Peter had driven off rather than wait for us, wasn't only out of date, it was clearly wrong. Khair Mohammed had told me the day before that the Northern Alliance were planning to capture the front line, then regroup and attack the second Taliban line of defence. But that was all entirely out of date now. The front line had indeed broken like an egg, as I had suggested it would, and the Taliban hadn't stopped to defend their second line of defence in front of Kabul. They were on the run everywhere.

Ten minutes later we reached the second line: a single trench, impressively dug and well defended with sandbags, which stretched east–west right across the southern part of the Shomali Valley. It was entirely empty. No one had done any fighting here at all. We stopped, and I did a piece to camera about the speed with which the Taliban had abandoned it, and the fact that there were no longer any serious defences between the Northern Alliance and Kabul.

The words were right, but the whole atmosphere was completely wrong. The trench was so empty, the absence of fighting so obvious, and I looked so neat and tidy – even my hair was neatly arranged – that it looked as though we had just ambled along, way after the Northern Alliance shock troops, and come across the second line of trenches by surprise. It looked, in other words, very much as though we were just part of the general group of journalists instead of being far ahead of them. I should have done the piece to camera back in Singid Darra, when it was obvious that we were right up with the action and the crowds of looters and the injured would have been all round us. Ah well: *inutiles regrets*. The real problem was having two things to concentrate on at the same time – the live broadcasts via the videophone, and filming for our edited report, to be satellited to London later.

We drove on, in the thickening darkness. The American bombing had stopped soon after the Northern Alliance broke through the Taliban front line, but there was the continuing danger of unexploded bombs all the way along the road, together with the certainty that the Taliban had mined the fields around their positions. Now, though, the landscape changed, as the vineyards and farms gave way to moorland. We had reached the low hills which had obstructed our view of Kabul when we were still in Charikar, and which we had often stared at speculatively through our field glasses. Soon we got to the main Kabul road, down which, from Bin Laden Mansions, we had so often watched the Taliban trucks bringing up reinforcements and supplies, their headlights cutting through the unpolluted darkness of the Afghan night. And now it was all over. Those Taliban who had not surrendered, been captured, or secretly betrayed them to the Northern Alliance had fallen back on Kabul; whether to defend it or to surrender, we had no way of telling.

In the darkness, we found our way down the main road to the village of Qarabagh. Here the thrust towards Kabul had petered out from sheer exhaustion; and here, as a result, we met up with the whole scattered BBC contingent: the radio team, whom we had last seen that morning, well before the Taliban front line was broken, and Peter Jouvenal. Any irritation of mine had long since evaporated. The events we had been through, and Peter's own achievement in terms of the pictures he had obtained, dwarfed our little *contretemps* hours before.

We all wandered round together, looking for pictures in the

darkness. We soon found them. An Afghan Talib lay on the back of the truck with a group of Alliance soldiers gathered round him. He had been injured in the foot. I asked Khalil to whisper to him quietly and find out if he was being badly treated. No, he whispered back. He would be safe now; he just needed treatment for the nasty bullet hole in his foot. By the light of a torch, I asked him what had happened when the attack had taken place.

> We were taken completely by surprise. It never occurred to us that they could attack us so fast. I suppose we were fools, really. We believed what the Taliban told us. They said the enemy would never dare to fight us. We were very shocked, and we scarcely put up any resistance at all.

Afterwards I wandered up and down trying to decide what to do. There was no doubt that we could edit our pictures, as good as anything I had ever seen from a war, and transmit them better if we went back to Bin Laden Mansions, especially now that the dish had arrived and was fully operational. Throughout the day, Peter Greste and the rest of the new reporting and production team which had arrived with it had been doing sterling work, broadcasting almost non-stop. On the other hand, Afghans were capable of anything, whatever arrangements you reached with them; and just because General Gul Haidar assured us now that he would keep his men here all night and attack again at first light, it didn't mean that would necessarily happen. It would be a disaster to miss the next morning's attack on Kabul itself.

Perhaps, I thought, we should make the difficult journey back down the road (during the evening, a bus carrying soldiers hit an unexploded bomb in the roadway, and eight people on board were killed) and then drive back in the early hours of the morning and doss down by the roadside with the soldiers. I looked at Joe Phua: his broken ankle was clearly giving him great pain, and he was exhausted. And the more he protested that he would be happy to drive back, edit our report, and then drive back again, the more I knew I shouldn't really put him through all this.

And then, as so often happened when we really needed him, we came across Hajji Bari. His eyes were red again, but with exhaustion now rather than anger. If we stayed with him, we couldn't go wrong, since he was to lead the attack on Kabul tomorrow.

'I shall go back to Charikar,' he said slowly, as though even the words were too heavy to say. 'And I shall take you to Kabul with me in the morning. I promise it.'

Our decision was made. We loaded up the gear and headed back down the road to Bin Laden Mansions.

The last shot we took that night in Qarabagh before we left was a timeless scene by the roadside, as a group of seven or eight soldiers sat round a fire, happy and exhausted at the victory they had obtained, the red-gold light flickering on their beards and fierce, hawk-like faces. The AK-47s and the camouflage uniforms aside, they could have been Alexander the Great's Macedonians.

§

Twelve hours later, shortly before eight in the morning, we were in Kabul. And that evening, Tuesday 13 November, Joe Phua and I were sitting in our edit suite (which doubled as his bedroom) in the Hotel Inter-Continental, starting to compile our report on the events of that extraordinary day. At six minutes, it was to be the longest piece I have ever done for television news, it contained the best pictures I have ever been fortunate enough to use, and it was seen by more than 400 million people around the world. ABC News in America, NTV in Russia, and NHK in Japan were among the television organizations that broadcast it in its entirety.

I say this merely to marvel at the strange universality of television. The efforts of three very tired men, one of whom was suffering the pain of having walked for two miles with a broken bone in his foot, were seen within a few hours by a substantial proportion of the entire human race. For us, of course, it was no different from any of the other reports we had compiled in our careers; apart from the length, and the extraordinary satisfaction we felt at the job we had done. It happens quite often, of course, that people who are thinking and acting in the most restricted terms – politicians, say, or criminals, or rock stars, or sports heroes – find to their amazement that their names and what they have done are being broadcast around the world, and have become known in the farthest recesses of the globe. It's not the action itself that counts, so much as the medium of communication which makes this universality possible.

Joe and I had no opportunity for such philosophical considerations. We had three hours available for a task which, by the usual rule of thumb for television news, required twice as long. Fortunately, Joe played on the keys of an edit machine like a pianist playing Rachmaninov – I'd often marvelled at it over the previous weeks – and he always kept his nerve. He sat there now with his painful foot propped up, an electric fire to keep us warm in the dank atmosphere of the Inter-Continental, and a regular flow of drinks and snacks which Nick Springate, knowing as a good producer does how important these small things are, kept bringing in like room service; and we revelled in the pictures which Joe and Peter Jouvenal had shot that extraordinary day. And as Joe sped through the pictures, looking for the best sequence to open up with, I knew I scarcely needed to look at them myself; Joe was, if anything, better at matching pictures to words than I was.

Reading my words now, they seem pretty dull and uninspired. A Matt Frei, a Fergal Keane, a Brian Hanrahan would each have provided a far more memorable script. Leaving aside the natural poverty of my phrase-making compared with theirs, though, and the tiredness, and the speed with which we had to work, I found myself deliberately under-writing. The pictures were so good that I didn't want anything to distract from them. We left a great many gaps, too, so that the natural sound which the camera had recorded could come through: the background noise, the voices, the guns.

This was the opening sequence.

> It was just before dawn that the wild dash for Kabul developed: thousands of soldiers intent on capturing the capital. It seemed to take no time at all to cover the twelve or so miles. As we drew nearer to Kabul, the grim evidence of battle. These were former supporters of the Northern Alliance who had switched sides and joined the Taliban. No mercy for them. Then we saw they had captured another man. The presence of our camera probably saved his life. He was paralysed with terror. By now there were no Taliban left to resist . . .
>
> Extract from *Six O'Clock News*,
> Tuesday 13 November 2001

That morning, at Bin Laden Mansions, everything was ready to go before five o'clock. Those of us who had been covering the breakthrough of the Taliban front line and the advance to Qarabagh the previous day had only managed to get three or four hours' sleep. But we were buoyed up by the tension and excitement of the day ahead. You could see the signs: loud voices, noisy laughter, the nervous checking of watches.

I spoke to Joe privately: what was the state of his foot now?

'Oh, fine, fine.'

I could see he was worried that I might tell him he mustn't come. Three or four times during the previous week the bone-setter had come in from the town, an old man with a long white beard and a large green turban, and would manipulate the broken bone in Joe's foot. When it was really bad you could hear the gasp of pain from the corridor outside, but Joe always insisted that he felt fine. I knew what he was thinking: if this got back to London, the foreign desk would go into auto-Auntie mode and order him out.

'I feel this is our story,' Joe had said to me once before, when he resisted the desk's demand that he should hand over to another cameraman and go home.

It was even more our story now, after we had covered the battle the day before. I simply couldn't find the words to tell Joe he mustn't come.

'All right, but on one condition. My doctor has sent me some really strong painkillers, just in case. They came with all the stuff the night before last. You must take the proper dose, and I'll feed them to you.'

They were big horse-tablets, and you felt just by looking at them that you could have confidence in them.

Hajji Bari came storming down the corridor, shouting and waving his arms: it was time to get going. Today, as yesterday, we would use his jeep and he would lead the entire assault on the capital in a little red Japanese-made car. The entire road from Charikar to Kabul was paved, after a fashion, so this was possible.

Sitting in the jeep, our flak jackets holding us erect and upright like Victorians in corsets, we drove very fast down the road we had followed yesterday. Now it was completely open. Even the unexploded bomb which had caused us to take a long and tiresome detour on our way back last night had gone: it was this that had killed the eight soldiers on their bus. We simply edged our way round the fatal crater and sped on. Joe was sitting in the front, and got some sensationally beautiful pictures of the scarlet and purple dawn, with the headlights of the convoy piercing what was left of the darkness. Qarabagh was entirely empty as we drove through it: just the ashes of the previous night's camp fires. The army was ahead of us. The driver jammed his foot down on the accelerator.

They had already done the killing by the time we caught up with them, soon after we had passed through Karez-e Mir. The bodies lay by the roadside. These were men of the Northern Alliance who, about a year before, had defected to the Taliban. By and large, Afghans show a reluctance to kill other Afghans in battle; but in this case they had made an exception. It was pretty clear from the way the bodies lay huddled together that they had surrendered, had been herded together, and shot down as a group. If we had been a little earlier, it wouldn't have happened: the Northern Alliance, even the ordinary soldiers, demonstrated a certain savviness when it came to the media. This had been a massacre, carried out in cold blood.

We stopped a little further on, and I could see, up on a spur by the side of the road, that a group of Northern Alliance soldiers had captured another of the group of defectors. I suppose I felt that we had been partly responsible for the other deaths because we weren't there when they happened. I couldn't bear it to happen again. Joe and John Jennings and I ran up the slope to where the group had gathered, and Tony Davis, our Australian friend, came with us. Joe was first: the painkillers seemed to be working well.

The man they had caught was young, bareheaded, and utterly terrified. They were dragging him round by his arm, kicking him and hitting him with their guns. As we ran up, one of them gave him a terrible kick in the back, enough to injure him badly. The next thing would be to start shooting. Joe and I waded in, shouting. They laughed, and left him alone. For a time he just lay there, stupid with fear. Then he crawled away like an injured animal.

It was getting near the top of the hour, and I got onto the mobile phone which Nick Springate had given me: the type called a Thuraya, which connected direct from the handset to the satellite. I did a couple of quick questions-and-answers with different programmes, which both seemed inclined to get rid of me as quickly as possible – the 'We must leave it there' approach. Fortunately, though, I also spoke to the World Service, where the producer and presenter both showed flair and courage, and let our interview go on and on for a remarkably long time. Often, in the heat of the moment, I would forget about the audience altogether, and shout out instructions to Joe and Peter Jouvenal while I still held the phone in my hand. I even tried to persuade a Northern Alliance commander to take us into Kabul, ignoring the World Service altogether and feeling quite surprised when a distant voice reminded me they were still there. I used a lot of bad language, because at times like this you do. It didn't seem to faze the people in the studio. Having been, years before, a radio producer myself, I could see that if you had the guts and the imagination, it could make good broadcasting.

> . . . Then came the critical moment: would the Northern Alliance simply race on and pour into Kabul itself, even though they had undertaken not to? The commander in charge was determined not to let it happen. He ordered the armoured vehicles to block the way; the great advance was stopped in its tracks.
>
> But Kabul lay temptingly close below us now. The small BBC team decided to head on into the city, on our own, and on foot so no one would think we were soldiers. We ploughed on, radio side by side with television . . .
>
> Extract from *Six O'Clock News*,
> Tuesday 13 November 2001

Looking down the road to where Kabul lay below us, it was clear to me that the Northern Alliance wouldn't take us there. If we wanted to go, and we did, we would have to walk. Hajji Bari drove back up the road in his bullet-riddled red car after trying to negotiate the Taliban's surrender. Gul Haidar reluctantly agreed to let us walk in. The others in the BBC team, having endured so much to get there, were in no mood to stop here and look at Kabul. As for me, I was absolutely determined that the BBC would get there ahead of the rest of the world's journalists, and link up with the three BBC people who were already there. It had suddenly become more important than anything else. I knew it was dangerous, but there are times when that ceases to matter so much. This was one of those times. I gave Joe another painkiller, and we started off.

Well, this is it: we're walking into Kabul city. We don't seem to have any problems around us. There are only people who are friendly – and chanting, I'm afraid, 'Kill the Taliban.' As I understand it, though, as we walk in here, there aren't going to be that many Taliban anyway.

Extract from *Six O'Clock News*,
Tuesday 13 November 2001

We were well on our way down the steep hillside before I even thought about doing a piece to camera. In fact I was so wrapped up in the excitement and nervousness of it all that I might never have thought of it. It was Joe, white-faced with the strain of keeping up with me, who called out to me over the noise of the cheering and excited crowd which had gathered round us.

'Maybe we'd better do a piece to camera as we go.'

There was nothing to be said in it, other than to talk about what was going on. No philosophical reflections, no military or political judgements. These things would have sounded foolish. It was enough, at a time like this, to state the obvious. On the words 'As I understand it' an excited kid tried to grab me, and, concentrating on the camera and what I was saying, I elbowed him thuggishly aside. Every time I have seen it since I have winced at the sight, and a little titter goes round the audience I am showing it to. It was a relief to have got the piece to camera done, and fortunately I only needed the one take, unusual for me. But as I walked on I remembered thinking to myself, 'I wonder if I'll live to do another one?'

> . . . It was 7.53 a.m., local time. Kabul was a free city, after five years of perhaps the most extreme religious system anywhere on earth. Under the Taliban, girls could not be educated, men could be whipped for shaving, all music was banned. It was forbidden to play chess, to sing, to possess a picture of any living creature. No wonder they were happy . . .

Extract from *Six O'Clock News*,
Tuesday 13 November 2001

The post in the middle of the road which marked the city boundary of Kabul was directly ahead. I could see Peter Emmerson walking a little ahead of me, and I sped up, my legs aching with the strain, in a childish effort to get there first. The crowds were huge, and the cheering and shouting made it impossible to hear anyone else. It was now that I lost contact with Joe and Peter Jouvenal, without noticing. Joe had to stop to rest his foot, Peter fell over a bicycle in the crush and cracked the lens of his camera. Joe got one last shot of me as I was swallowed up in the huge crowd of joyful, celebrating people.

John Jennings and I stopped a taxi, and explained to the driver why we needed it. With the usual generosity of Afghans, the passengers got out and gave us their seats. They were excited to be handing over their vehicle to the BBC, anyway. The driver edged his way through the crowd in a U-turn, and headed off with us towards the centre of Kabul. I was disturbed about losing contact with the others, but I knew they'd be safe; it was obvious by now that the Taliban wouldn't be shooting at us. We had made an arrangement with the others to head for the Inter-Continental, and they were all resourceful, experienced people.

I fished out my mobile phone again and tried to get through to London. For some reason it didn't work: there was no signal. Maybe, I thought, it was because we were on the move, so every few minutes I asked Jennings to tell the driver I wanted to stop to call the BBC in London. The same thing happened each time: the phone refused to work, and a crowd gathered round us, heard we were from the BBC, and started the noisy business of congratulation all over again.

It wasn't all rejoicing, though. The word was already going round that the Taliban and their Al Qaida allies were finished, and people were hunting down the foreign volunteers who came to Afghanistan to fight with them: chiefly Arabs and Pakistanis. When they found them, they killed them brutally.

> . . . But there was an ugly price to be paid for so much repression. In the streets, in the ditches, foreign volunteers for the Taliban, especially Arabs and Pakistanis, ended up dead – lynched or shot. They were particularly loathed . . .
>
> Extract from *Six O'Clock News*,
> Tuesday 13 November 2001

We drove past one bloody heap lying in the gutter, an arm flung out in useless self-protection, a small crowd of peering, celebrating people standing round it. Then we passed another. In Afghanistan, power had often changed hands with only a little blood being shed. All over this city, it was being shed now.

> ... In the surroundings of the Inter-Continental Hotel, in the centre of Kabul, we caught side of Arab and Pakistani Taliban trying to escape the vengeance of the people of Kabul. A group of soldiers is hunting them down ...
>
> Extract from *Six O'Clock News*,
> Tuesday 13 November 2001

We reached the private road that leads to the Inter-Continental, the only decent hotel in Kabul, which looks out over a wide expanse of parkland towards the snow-covered hills. A group of soldiers was jumping out of a truck by the entrance to the road. They didn't look like Taliban, but I didn't see how they could be from the Northern Alliance either. John asked them who they were; they said they were allies of the Northern Alliance, and had just arrived from somewhere west of Kabul.

Reaching the Intercon was an important part of our plan, since we would need a sizeable number of rooms when the second wave of BBC people arrived from Charikar with the satellite equipment. Getting to Kabul was only the first phase of the operation; we would need to establish a broadcasting centre in the hotel for weeks to come.

We drove up to the main entrance, sixty-four days after I'd left it, and I searched my pockets for money to pay the driver. He was the luckiest man in the city: all I could find was a hundred-dollar bill, so I gave it to him with my thanks. When I asked him for a receipt he looked helpless, and I decided not to waste any more time over it.

The place was silent and empty as John Jennings, the soldier who had been sent with us, and I got out. The vast, ugly 1960s lobby was dark: the power, as ever, seemed to be cut. I was more than a little nervous. The Taliban often operated from the Intercon, and could still be here. Two figures were sitting huddled together in the gloom, but since they weren't wearing turbans I assumed they weren't dangerous. I turned to the man behind the counter.

'I'd like to book some rooms, please.'

'It's already been done.'

The voice was familiar, and I looked round at the two figures.

Peter Emmerson and Ian Pannell were laughing at the success of their trick. I suppose I was faintly annoyed that they had got here first, but mostly I was relieved: they at least were safe.

They had had a more glamorous entry into the city than John Jennings and I. They had got ahead of us in the crowd by hitching a ride on the backs of two bicycles, and then, when they fell off, they abandoned them for a taxi which had brought them here. It must have been a superb moment for them, speeding through the welcoming crowds on their bikes, and they were still elated by the whole episode, laughing and reminding each other of the things they had done.

The entire hotel was empty and the lift, inevitably, was out of operation. The five of us – Emmerson, Pannell, Jennings, the Afghan soldier and I – made our way through the dark, empty kitchen and up the back stairs to the rooms where Rageh Omaar, Fred Scott and William Reeve were staying. But there was no answer when we banged on the doors. An old man I recognized from my previous visits here shuffled up in hotel uniform and produced a key. Were there still Taliban here? The old man shrugged.

We searched the three rooms for a satellite phone – our mobiles still weren't working – because we were anxious to call the BBC: no point in being here if we couldn't broadcast. But the three of them seemed to have left, taking their satellite phone with them. We found out later that they had gone to the BBC office, and had had a dangerous time of it, being fired at and stopped by a Taliban patrol. They were lucky to have escaped with their lives.

It was the third piece of luck they had had. The night before, the Americans had bombed a house close by the BBC office just as William was in the middle of a live two-way with London. The explosion propelled him out of his seat: the image became one of the most celebrated of the entire fall of Kabul. What was more, although he was still on camera he managed not to swear; which is more than I had achieved that morning, during my live with the World Service. The three of them, William, Rageh and Fred, had decided that there could be further bomb attacks, and they must get out. It was dark, and in the streets they found that the Taliban government and the remnants of Al Qaida were escaping from the city, together with any Talib who could get out with them. Curiously, the Taliban leadership seemed previously to have had the same unconcern as their soldiers, refusing to believe that the Northern Alliance could capture the city.

The BBC team were stopped at a roadblock manned by frightened and jittery Taliban, including one unpleasant character with a black turban who, a day or so before, had threatened to kill them. Fortunately he seemed to be so unnerved by the danger that he didn't remember to carry out his threat. With characteristic courage Fred Scott, the quietest, wittiest and most thoughtful of cameramen, switched his camera on and left it running while they were caught at the roadblock, holding it down by his side. The pictures, dark and skewed as they were, gave a vivid sense of the danger and the chaos of the last hours of Taliban rule. If anyone had realized that Fred's camera was running, they would all have been murdered for certain.

As for us, we were still trying to work out how to get in touch with them when we heard voices outside in the corridor. There was an instant of fear, until I recognized Peter Jouvenal's characteristic tones: he and Joe Phua had arrived. It was a good moment, as we shook hands. The team was now reunited except for Kate Clark, who had gone directly to her old office – the one where William and the others had been blown up – in order to start broadcasting from there. And now that Joe was here we had a satellite phone again.

At that moment the soldier who had come with us put his head round the door and spoke urgently to John Jennings.

'He says there's a group of Arab Taliban heading for the hotel.'

The soldier took us to the window at the end of the corridor and pointed. I got a shock: seven men, clearly not Afghans, in uniform and with AK-47s, were edging their way round the wall of the hotel right below us. Since we were only two floors above them, all they had to do to see us was to look up. It was a reasonable assumption that they'd heard we were here and had come to kill us. The Arabs who volunteered for the Taliban and Al Qaida were notorious for their hatred of Westerners.

It seemed safest to go to the top floor of the hotel, in the hope that they would get bored with searching the other floors before they found us. Joe decided, despite his ankle, to film the whole business. This gave us a strange, reassuring feeling, as we ploughed our way up the emergency stairs, carrying all the gear, and gathered breathlessly on the fifth floor. Another ancient in a hotel uniform appeared. I told him what I thought was going on, and he agreed to hide us in the rooms if necessary.

Time passed. I was increasingly anxious to start broadcasting. In the end we went rather sheepishly downstairs again, with Joe still filming so he could catch the moment when we were all blown away. There was another moment of anxiety while I tried to get through to London from the balcony of one of the rooms, and the Arabs passed close to us in the grounds of the hotel. I lay on the floor of the balcony for a while, but finally got bored with waiting and dialled London anyway.

Jouvenal, though, had noticed what I failed to: the body language of these Taliban showed that they weren't hunting, but being hunted. It turned out that the soldiers we had seen near the entrance to the Intercon were making a sweep in the hotel grounds and were searching for them. Peter announced that he was going out to film what happened.

'Just be careful,' I told him feebly. He paid as little attention to that as he could without actually being rude, and borrowed Joe's camera.

> . . . Another soldier is bringing up some grenades to flush them out. They are trapped inside this building. But some local people have caught another one of the Taliban. He's an Arab. They make him call the others to get them to come out and surrender. Eventually, it works: they are brought out as prisoners. This man is a Pakistani. The Arab gets particularly brutal treatment . . .
>
> Extract from *Six O'Clock News*,
> Tuesday 13 November 2001

It's always hard to get really good action footage. Partly, it's a matter of luck: you have to be on hand, with your camera running, at precisely the right moment. But, equally, everyone seems to want to keep the cameras away from what is happening, either because they are worried about your safety or – more likely – because they think something reprehensible might happen. Afghanistan is different. Safety never seems to be a matter of concern, and no one seems to have the slightest awareness of television's needs, or of the results of broadcasting a particular story. There is an innocence about Afghanistan which makes it a cameraman's paradise.

This was to be one of the finest sequences Peter Jouvenal had ever filmed. He headed straight out into the hotel grounds where, in an ancient building, six members of the Taliban group had gone to ground. The Northern Alliance soldiers surrounded it. A couple stood by the entrance and fired their automatic weapons several times through the open door. As Peter was filming this, he heard some excited shouting behind him, and turned to find that some local people had captured the seventh member of the group and were coming to the Northern Alliance soldiers to hand him over.

They roughed him up, and made him stand at the entrance to the building and shout to the others to come out. Slowly, they emerge one by one out of the darkness, their hands in the air. Watching the pictures, you had the sense of being a spectator to the whole thing; so unusual is it to see events unfolding in this way. An elderly Pakistani Talib with a long grey beard emerged first through the open doorway. The Northern Alliance soldiers searched him and stripped him of his few belongings: the perks of war.

One of the soldiers walked up to the Arab who had been captured first, and hit him a terrible blow on the back of the head with a rifle wrapped in cloth. It was an act of completely gratuitous brutality; but Afghans of all kinds felt that, bad as the Taliban were, the volunteers who had come from other countries to fight for them were far worse. Soon the people would be handed over to the United States, who forcibly shaved their heads and beards and flew them across the world to the American base at Guantanamo Bay in Cuba. Scarcely anything was achieved by this, and only a few pieces of really useful information were obtained from the prisoners.

... In the jeep there are other Taliban prisoners. This one is an Arab, perhaps an Egyptian. The other two are Afghans. This is the end of the Taliban in Afghanistan ...

Extract from *Six O'Clock News*,
Tuesday 13 November 2001

Jouvenal followed the soldiers to a vehicle which contained three other Taliban prisoners. One looked like an Egyptian, with a bloody and swollen nose. He tried to keep his face covered, and as one of the soldiers reached in and pulled his arm away from his face the man glared at Peter's camera with a mixture of fear and defiance. Peter had no sympathy for him.

'They came here to someone else's country to kill people,' he said as we watched the pictures on our edit machine. 'They can't complain now.'

True, of course. Yet, stripped of their guns and their organization, these people were just human beings like the rest of us; and, like Peter and me, they had taken a chance in coming here. We happened to be on the winning side, but maybe next time it could be Peter or me sitting there with the broken, bloody nose.

While he was away I settled down with Peter Emmerson's help at the end of the empty second floor corridor in the Intercon. The satellite phone was set up, and I even managed to get one of the ancients to bring us some coffee: the first thing we had had to eat or drink since 4.30 this morning. It tasted good, and after a month of roughing it in our barracks at Charikar the grubby white cloth on the metal tray, the teaspoon and the battered silvered pot almost made it seem as though we had found civilization again. And I was back in touch with London.

That proved to be a mixed blessing, since not long afterwards I made my foolish joke about the BBC having liberated Kabul, which managed to distract attention away from what was going on and what had been achieved. But at the time there were more important things to think about. Peter Jouvenal and I had often talked about what we should do when we got to Kabul. There were three or four places we wanted to get to quickly when we arrived: an Al Qaida base not far from the Inter-Continental, the house where one of Osama bin Laden's wives lived, and which he used to visit quite often, and a training centre we had heard about. Over the next couple of days we went to all these places, and each time we were the first people to get there.

> . . . It's the end, too, of this country's links with international terrorism. We went to a house where a senior Arab member of Osama bin Laden's Al Qaida organization had lived and worked. There were explosives in one room, anti-personnel mines in another. Notices on the wall were all connected with Al Qaida, including a training certificate and an organizational chart.

Upstairs, there's a manual in English, with notes in Arabic, for sabotage and causing explosions. There were all sorts of guides about timing mechanisms and booby traps . . .

Extract from *Six O'Clock News*,
Tuesday 13 November 2001

The morning wore on. Extraordinarily, the next group of people to arrive at the hotel weren't the reporters from newspapers or some other television organization, they were from the BBC too. Our satellite dish, complete with engineers, had made the long and difficult journey down the road from Charikar. They had talked their way past the Northern Alliance position at the entrance to Kabul, and got here through the dangerous streets of the city to the hotel. I shook hands with Nick Springate, the producer who had managed all this, and told him I thought it was the BBC's best achievement yet. I still do. A camera team is quick and mobile; a three-ton truck full of equipment is ponderously slow. And yet here they were, long before anyone else. It was a triumph of planning, but it took a sizeable amount of courage too. Nick had even better news for me: the engineers thought they could be up and running in time for our *One O'Clock News* in London. We would get our pictures of the morning's extraordinary events in satellite quality on the first available news programme. Not bad.

It's been my good fortune to watch the overthrow of all sorts of hated régimes over the years: in Iran, in Berlin, in Czechoslovakia, in Romania, in Russia, in South Africa, in Indonesia, in Serbia, and now in Afghanistan. There is a purity about the joy at such moments, as people give themselves over entirely to the happiness of the moment. It rarely lasts, of course; and sometimes the new system turns out to be every bit as bad as the old one, and occasionally worse. But the moment of revolution itself is always magnificent. There is nothing so brave, nothing so generous, nothing so fierce, nothing so sentimental as a revolutionary crowd. When the cause demands it, people will give their houses, their cars, their money, their lives. Everything is heightened; and the moment is one which lives in the minds of everyone who witnesses it forever.

In the streets of Kabul, people were savouring their new freedom. Friends were out in the streets, shaving off the beards they'd all had to wear if they wanted to escape a savage beating. Women were walking around and showing their faces for the first time in five years. There was a kind of mass ecstasy, as the things people had longed for secretly for so long came suddenly true. No one in the streets seemed to have expected their liberation; only the previous night the continuing American bombing of Kabul had added to the misery of people who felt the entire world had abandoned them to their fate.

In 1989, when the Russians hastily withdrew from the only country which had resisted them militarily over a period of years in any serious way, it seemed to be a liberation. True, Moscow left its puppet ruler behind them: Najibullah, who strove courageously to unite the country behind him and leave behind the irrelevancies of Marxism–Leninism. But the foreign politicians who had made the most noise about the Soviet occupation of Afghanistan started to go quiet. We no longer heard anything about the horrors that were taking place in Afghanistan from Margaret Thatcher or Ronald Reagan or George Bush or Helmut Kohl. Suddenly, because the Russians were no longer there, it didn't matter. It was just a faraway Third World place of which we knew little and cared less.

Najibullah was imprisoned by the combined force of the mujaheddin in 1992, and for the next four years corruption and civil war and covert foreign intervention reigned in Kabul; and still nobody cared. In 1996 the last, worst twist of the downward spiral brought the victory of the Taliban and the cruel lynching of Najibullah. Even now nobody cared. Afghanistan had become the worst and most lunatic state on earth, but no one did anything about it. It was only when America was attacked that the Taliban, Osama bin Laden's reluctant hosts who had done very little to support him, were discovered to be uniquely evil. It was hard, even at a time like this, to feel too much enthusiasm for the responses of the Western world towards this half-destroyed, half-savage, half-civilized country.

There was only one question left. Having discovered that Afghanistan mattered, would the United States forget it once again and withdraw into its shell; or would it, and the other powers that are in a position to help, understand that countries like Afghanistan aren't simply adventure playgrounds for geopoliticians, but places where real people live, and where real suffering needs to be averted?

But for the moment now it was all over. As I wrote the final words of my script, I felt a powerful sympathy for these people whose misery I had observed over the years: brave and loyal people, who hadn't deserved the disasters that had overcome them. It was an unalloyed pleasure to see them free once again.

> . . . If all that is finished now, so is the system which intruded in everyone's lives. Suddenly you don't have to wear a beard any more if you don't want to. Shaving is a way to show your liberation; so is showing your face if you are a woman. And there's one thing more: children can fly kites again. Freedom is in the air here.
>
> John Simpson, BBC News, Kabul.

Epilogue

The BBC has changed utterly and out of all recognition since the day I first went to work there on 1 September 1966. And yet at the same time it remains essentially the same organization, with the same set of basic values that it has always had. I don't believe it has lost its way, or lost its ideals; I think they're still there, just as strong as ever. What has changed is that the BBC has finally got its act together.

Of course it remains a big slow-moving bureaucracy, taking an infuriatingly long time to respond and to pay its bills, and occasionally treating its own with breathtaking cruelty. But its programmes are as excellent for 2002 as they were for 1966, and define our times as they defined those. This excellence has spread into areas which no one could have conceived of in 1966. Some years ago a friend of mine called Mike Smartt told me he was giving up his job as a television correspondent to become the boss of a new online news service which the BBC was planning to start up. I congratulated him, of course, because he had already taken the plunge; but I remember thinking he was making a terrible mistake to give up one of the best jobs in television for some weird, nerdish experiment which would probably be closed down after a year or two.

Now that BBC News Online has become the most successful website in Europe, I have a feeling that it will soon be one of my main employers; the other being BBC World. Neither of these services existed a decade ago. In some way which I find difficult to define precisely, I suspect that news broadcasting will soon be done predominantly on BBC World and News 24, and news narrow-casting will be done almost exclusively on BBC Online, both to unthinkably vast audiences of hundreds of millions of people; and while there is no question that news programmes will continue to exist on domestic television, the present bulletins with their audiences of five or six million and their mainly domestic focus will no longer call the shots as they do at present.

The BBC's ability to reinvent itself and continue leading the field is extraordinary, given that it is such a large, varied and often quite slow-moving organization. Yet at the same time it hasn't lost its hold on the affection of the British public. When, shortly before the epoch-making fireworks display at the pop concert at Buckingham Palace in June 2002 which marked the Queen's jubilee, the Prince of Wales thanked the BBC for arranging and broadcasting the concert, it was noticeable that the applause was loud and sustained; only the applause for his tributes to the Queen herself and to the country were louder.

In other, lesser ways the BBC has remained exactly its old self. When, on the evening of 1 September 1966, I came home after my first day's work and met my then wife and my father for a celebratory meal, they asked me what it was like.

'Everyone there seems amazingly polite,' I remember answering.

It was true. The tweed-jacketed characters who seemed to fill its corridors were always holding doors open for one another and saying 'Please' and 'Thank you' and 'Would you mind . . .?' Now nobody ever seems to wear tweed, and in the summer quite a few people wear T-shirts and shorts; some even pad around on bare feet. But they still all say 'Please' and 'Thank you' and 'Would you mind . . .?', and they are positively obsessive about holding doors open for one another. Recently a politeness initiative was launched, whereby you mustn't bully the people below you, or be insulting, or – a serious challenge to the corporate ethic, this – blame other departments. As a relatively infrequent visitor to Television Centre, I found it hard to see why any of this (except the business of blaming other departments) could conceivably be thought of as necessary.

Its strange, ramshackle approach to broadcasting is prefigured in its buildings. As you arrive at the entrance to Television Centre in Wood Lane, you can see that there have been at least six different building-stages added onto the original round building, four of them in reddish brick. Yet each section has a different shade of reddish brick. It is, when you come to think of it, quite an achievement to find non-matching bricks quite so unerringly. With luck, by the time of my fortieth anniversary with the BBC in 2006, if I haven't died, been sacked, or stormed out in a rage, the News division will be getting ready to move from the East German wastelands of Wood Lane back to Broadcasting House, near Oxford Circus, where my BBC career began.

Nothing in this career of mine has ever required such sustained physical and mental effort as reporting on the impending fall of Kabul at the age of fifty-seven, with all the hard driving, climbing of mountains, dressing up, sleeping on hard floors, taking cover on front lines and general physical effort which it called for. But it was all thoroughly worth it, both in personal terms and in the sense that it helped to set the seal on the BBC's dominance in international news broadcasting. The whole experience was a delight, a joy. Working closely with people you like and admire, enduring hardships with them, and having something to show for it at the end seems to me to be as satisfying an activity as you could imagine.

There are few things as good as having excellent pictures to write to, and enough time to do justice to the business of editing them. I'd go further: the moment when you sit there in the edit suite, watching the pictures for the first time and working out how to enhance them with words, is one of the most enjoyable moments the job has to offer.

Best of all is the pleasure of the news-hunt. There is, I think, nothing better than to work out what your story requires in the way of pictures, then to launch out into the complexity of events and bring those pictures back. It is, I suppose, your way of making sense of things, of setting an understandable mark on great moments and small ones: you become the novelist who brings out the characters, the playwright who reveals the plot, except that the materials you are working with are unalterable facts rather than creatures of the imagination. It's not easy: it wouldn't be worth doing if it were. But if you feel, after you have finished the editing process and you sit back to watch what you and the picture editor and the producer have laboured away at for the past couple of hours, that you have captured something of the essence of the subject, that is an unbeatable sensation.

And the subject doesn't have to be a gloomy or depressing one, by any means. Let me give you one last example. It begins back in 2000, when my old college at Cambridge awarded me an honorary fellowship. It was a charming gesture on the college's part, and on 1 May Dee and I turned up at Magdalene together with the poet and Nobel Prize-winner Seamus Heaney, an infinitely worthier candidate, to receive it. And because there wasn't really any great tradition attached to the awarding of honorary fellowships, they decided to make one up. Everyone wore academic gowns and someone went to the trouble of composing a pleasant rigmarole in Latin, along the lines of 'Inasmuch as it hath pleased . . .' Some of the dons were friends of mine from my days as an undergraduate. My tutor was there, with a beard as superb as Charles Darwin's. The former chaplain, now a bishop, had performed the ceremony at my first marriage. My director of studies had written a letter to the BBC, recommending me for a job.

The British, as the former US ambassador Ray Seitz pointed out affectionately, like dressing up and having ceremonies. I knew Seamus from my Irish past, and every now and then during the occasion I caught his eye and we exchanged schoolboy grins, as though to say, 'What are a couple of outsiders like us doing in a place like this?'

(A couple of years later Dee and I were in Dublin, buying something cheap and nasty from a Grafton Street vendor for our young nephew Sagan, who was staying with us. A familiar, growling voice broke into the transaction.

'Is this any way for an honorary fellow to behave?' Seamus Heaney asked.

And when Dee told Sagan that this was the most famous poet in the world, the most famous poet in the world said, 'Now stop that sort of thing at once.')

Magdalene is a small college, neither wealthy nor particularly famous, and you usually have to tell people its name is pronounced 'Maudlin'. Samuel Pepys studied there in the 1650s, and there were close associations with a wide range of figures: Kipling, Parnell, the Everest climber George Mallory, T. S. Eliot, C. S. Lewis, and in latter years a slew of media people including Bamber Gascoigne, Michael Binyon of *The Times* and Alan Rusbridger, the editor of the *Guardian*. The college has always contained a streak of the unexpected. In the eighteenth century it became one of the main centres of the anti-slavery campaign, thanks to a campaigning Master of the day, Dr Peter Peckard. At the turn of the century another Master, A. C. Benson, turned the college into the intellectual and social powerhouse of the University.

Throughout the nineteenth century and well into the twentieth it turned out colonial administrators who were famous for their liberal attitudes and their sympathy for the people they governed. Somehow, in our own time, it began to have a connection with South Africa, thanks to a couple of leading alumni; and the Master, the geneticist Sir John Gurdon, and the Senior Tutor, Dr Mark Billinge, a particular friend of mine, hatched up a daring proposal: to invite Nelson Mandela to visit Magdalene and receive an honorary fellowship.

When I heard about it, I didn't believe it would happen. Mandela was getting frail, and on a previous visit to Britain the vice-chancellors of half a dozen universities were summoned to London to give him honorary doctorates in a single ceremony, so as not to tire him. The idea that he would go all the way to Cambridge to visit one small college seemed pretty unlikely. A first attempt was aborted in November 2000, because Mandela was ill.

And then I started getting messages from Mark Billinge that it was looking good for the following May. The college offered to let me cover it for the BBC, and I grabbed at the chance. On 1 May, the anniversary of my own honorary fellowship, Dee and I stayed in the fellows' guest room, a medieval monk's chamber furnished with chairs, chests and furnishings belonging to Samuel Pepys, one of the most famous of earlier Magdalene alumni; and after a night spent on two narrow monkish beds we woke up early on the morning of Wednesday 2 May.

I was nervous, and wouldn't have slept well in any bed. This might have seemed like a piece of cake: everything was laid on for us, and there was no question of having to fight anybody or take risks or struggle to get this story. We had it to ourselves, since the college wanted it that way. And yet there were so many problems; not least that it is difficult to broadcast about these things without offending someone – and these people, who had been generous to me, were the last ones on earth I wanted to offend.

Then there were real procedural difficulties. The South African High Commission in London had made it clear they didn't want Mandela to be interviewed; there were political problems in South

Africa, and they were worried that someone might lure Mandela into criticizing his successor, Thabo Mbeki. And yet I knew it wouldn't be sufficient merely to hear and see the formal business of the day: we needed an interview. Dee and I were also determined to turn the whole event into a *Simpson's World*; and that would certainly require me to speak to the great man. I had promised the BBC to get these things, and didn't like to fail. It wasn't going to be easy.

But there were positive aspects as well. I had explained all this to Mark Billinge the night before, and had a pretty clear idea that the college would support me in getting an interview with Mandela: we even arranged precisely where and when it would take place. I also had a good team. Chris Marlow, a friend of mine for twenty years, was the cameraman – a sharp, mordantly witty man, with whom I had always enjoyed working. I knew he would do a first-class job. Then, apart from Dee, there were several other quick-minded, able people who would be helping me: including Dee's sister Gina, who later became my PA, and Julie Hayman, a student at Magdalene who was keen on a career in broadcasting.

But I was still nervous. We sat at a coffee shop across the River Cam from the college and made our plans, and I cursed the weather. The sky was leaden, and we ideally needed some spring sunshine on this day of days. Magdalene is a small gem of a place, built from the warmest and mellowest of medieval brick, and the sun brings out its best qualities. We did a good deal of standing about with the leading dons of the college before the off, all of us nervous and awkward. Then we moved into the fellows' garden at the back, where Mandela's helicopter was to land.

From here, standing on the grass of the beautiful lawn, I could see the windows of the room I had occupied on the night before my entrance exam to the college, thirty-eight years before. Even then, hunched in front of an inadequate gas fire and doing some pointless last-minute revision, I knew this would be one of the turning-points of my life; and now, at the farther end of my life and career, I reflected how comforting it would have been on that cold night if I had only been able to catch a glimpse of my future self, burly, grey-haired, and almost as nervous at fifty-six as I had been as a skinny, ignorant eighteen-year-old. Now the college had become an important part of my life again. I looked around the lovely gardens where I once danced till four in the morning and partied and played croquet, and shivered, cold in spite of my long ceremonial gown.

There was the faint sound of a helicopter in the cloud-bank above us. Two scarlet-robed figures, the Master and the college President, scanned the sky as anxiously as we did; and soon the equally scarlet tulips in the sacred flower beds were blowing around wildly, and the helicopter was sinking into the damp lawn to half the circumference of its wheels. The door opened. Slowly and with dignified care the latest honorary fellow of the college stepped out. The scarlet figures moved forward to shake hands and welcome him. Then there was a pause.

'Isn't anyone else going to say hello to me?' asked the slow, familiar voice.

Dee and Gina stepped out from behind the camera and shook Mandela's hand with great reverence, and he spoke to them in his courtly, fluent Afrikaans. I knew from my own experience how good he was at making *you* feel good; now it was happening to them too.

Helped by his aides, looking distinctly frail, Mandela walked towards the college buildings: two delightful fifteenth-century squares of cherry-coloured red brick, built around beautifully kept lawns and flower beds, as pretty and intimate a place as you can find anywhere on earth. The college staff, the students, and anyone else who could wangle an admission ticket were waiting on the grass to see him. Mandela stopped and talked and joked with them. If it had been anyone else you would have said he was working the crowd. But this was no mere politician: you could see that on the faces of the people he spoke to and smiled at, as he made his way to the college chapel.

The college's Mandela scholars, drawn from all the main population groups in South Africa, were drawn up there to greet him. One was a young man from the poorest part of rural South Africa, who had suffered from polio as a boy. His mother, who was a servant, was determined to get him a good education; and eventually, through the triumph of their combined wills, he came to Magdalene, a world away from the bitter poverty of his childhood home.

Magdalene is a surprising place. When I was an undergraduate there I never thought there was anything particularly remarkable about the college dons; yet when it started to come out in the 1970s that Britain had broken the German Enigma code during the Second World War, it turned out that several Magdalene dons had played an important part in this.

The atmosphere has always been friendly, even though for years Magdalene kept up the old male-only tradition, and was the last college in either Oxford or Cambridge to resist the arrival of women students. Yet the first woman to teach there told me that on her first night at dinner in the college hall, her neighbour was particularly charming and invited her back to coffee afterwards. It was only afterwards that she found out he'd been the leader of the college's anti-women movement.

After the ceremony in the chapel, Mandela was brought into a grand room nearby to meet the originators of the Mandela scholarship scheme. It was here that we were waiting. Mark Billinge had organized it cleverly so that I, as an honorary fellow, introduced them to Mandela – and then, as a BBC correspondent, was able to ask him some questions. His press minder, a tough blonde Afrikaans woman, started to get angry, and urged the High Commissioner, who was also a woman, to move in and stop me. The High Commissioner, embarrassed, tweaked my jacket. I took no notice; after all, I once did an interview with President Mikhail Gorbachev while one KGB man wrestled with the cameraman and another twisted my arm to make me stop. A job is a job, and it wasn't exactly going to do Nelson Mandela any harm if I asked him a couple more questions. Often these officials get too big for their boots.

The interview secured, we all felt a lot more relaxed. Which was good, since the climax of the ceremony was about to take place in the college hall: a charming, intimate, wood-panelled place with ancient portraits looking down at us, and coats of arms glowing in the stained-glass windows. At night the dons and undergraduates dine here by candlelight, and it was here that, in October 1963, I was first inducted into the college and met the people who are still among my closest friends. I acted in plays here, sang, made speeches, and got mildly drunk celebrating my honorary fellowship. And now I was here in the presence of this mythic figure, whose prison sentence in his native country had only just begun when I was a student.

He felt, he said, looking out at his audience, rather nervous about being here.

'This is for three reasons. Firstly, I am an old-age pensioner.'

There was some mild, deprecatory laughter.

'Secondly, I am unemployed.'

The laughter was louder and more confident.

'And thirdly, I have a baaad criminal record.'

A huge wave of laughter and applause followed that.

The finale was nothing short of magical. The college choir, up in the musicians' gallery, began singing a familiar African song, and Mandela was soon on his feet, moving in time to the music, grinning as he did so. And one by one, some enthusiastically, some embarrassed, but all irresistibly, the dignified figures in their scarlet and blue and black gowns stood up too and danced sedately in time with him, while the voices of the choir filled the hall. And, I kept telling myself, I was there to see this moment and broadcast it. I was so choked with the joy and emotion of it, and what it meant to me, that I could scarcely speak.

But I had to. Dee nudged me.

'You've got to do a piece to camera before everyone leaves.'

She was right. I ran up and joined Chris Marlow in the musicians' gallery. There was just one thing I needed to know.

'How long since the college was founded?' I called down to one of the dons, a particular friend of mine. He did a quick calculation, and gave me the answer. I turned to the camera.

'This college has been in existence for 573 years,' I said, 'but we can safely assume it's never seen anything remotely like this.'

When I talk to audiences in Britain and abroad, it's obvious they tend to associate me primarily with wars, death, and pestilence: trouble of all kinds. The questions they ask are often about how I manage to cope with these things, and whether it all makes me cynical about human affairs.

Not a bit of it. How could it, when I have also been on hand for the release of Nelson Mandela in 1990 after twenty-seven years in jail, for his election as President of South Africa in 1994, and for his induction as an honorary fellow of Magdalene College, Cambridge, and have had the opportunity to try to capture the essence of these superbly uplifting moments for television news?

The poet John Masefield isn't much in fashion nowadays; the world has moved on too much from his celebrations of Britain's history and its commercial romance. But he once wrote a little four-line squib which sums up very well what I feel after thirty-six years of this strange existence of mine. It's called, simply, 'Epilogue':

> I have seen flowers come in stony places,
> And kind things done by men with ugly faces,
> And the gold cup won by the worst horse at the races.
> So I trust, too.

Exactly.

Index